Official Guide to
Texas Wildlife Management Areas

Official Guide to

Texas Wildlife Management Areas

By Larry D. Hodge

Foreword by Andrew Sansom

Texas Parks & Wildlife Press, Austin

LIBRARY OF CONGRESS
CATALOGING-IN-PUBLICATION DATA

Hodge, Larry D.
    Official guide to Texas wildlife management areas /
by Larry D. Hodge ; photographs by Larry D. Hodge
and Texas Parks and Wildlife Department. — 1st ed.
            p.   cm.
    Includes bibliographical references.
    ISBN 1-885696-35-3 (pbk. : alk. paper)
    1. Wildlife management areas—Texas—Guidebooks.
2. Wildlife-related recreation—Texas—Guidebooks.
3. Texas—Guidebooks. I. Texas. Parks and Wildlife
Dept. II. Title
    SK451 .H64 2000
    333.78'2'09764—dc21   00-011017

CONTENTS

FOREWORD BY ANDREW SANSOM   ix

PREFACE BY LARRY D. HODGE   xi

INTRODUCTION   xiii

ACKNOWLEDGMENTS   xv

BIG BEND COUNTRY   1

Black Gap WMA   3
Elephant Mountain WMA   10
Las Palomas WMA—Ocotillo Unit   16
Sierra Diablo WMA   20

GULF COAST   25

Atkinson Island WMA   27
Candy Abshier WMA   29
D. R. Wintermann WMA   32
Guadalupe Delta WMA   34
J. D. Murphree WMA   39
Lower Neches WMA   43
Mad Island WMA   46
Matagorda Island WMA/State Park   50
Peach Point WMA   57
Redhead Pond WMA   61
Tony Houseman State Park/WMA   63
Welder Flats WMA   66

HILL COUNTRY 69

Granger WMA 71
Kerr WMA 78
Mason Mountain WMA 83
Old Tunnel WMA 87
Walter Buck WMA 91

PANHANDLE PLAINS 95

Gene Howe WMA 97
Matador WMA 102
Playa Lakes WMA 106

PINEYWOODS 111

Alabama Creek WMA 113
Alazan Bayou WMA 119
Angelina-Neches/Dam B WMA 123
Bannister WMA 128
Caddo Lake State Park/WMA 132
Moore Plantation WMA 137
North Toledo Bend WMA 142
The Nature Center 146
Old Sabine Bottom WMA 150
Sam Houston National Forest WMA 155
White Oak Creek WMA 163

PRAIRIES AND LAKES 169

Aquilla WMA 171
Big Lake Bottom WMA 177
Caddo National Grasslands WMA 181
Cedar Creek Islands WMA 186
Cooper WMA 188
Gus Engeling WMA 194
Keechi Creek WMA 200
M. O. Neasloney WMA 203
Pat Mayse WMA 206
Ray Roberts Public Hunting Area 210
Richland Creek WMA 215
Somerville WMA 221
Tawakoni WMA 227

SOUTH TEXAS PLAINS 231

Chaparral WMA 233
James E. Daughtrey WMA 239
Las Palomas WMA—
      Lower Rio Grande Valley Units 244

BIBLIOGRAPHY 251

INDEX 255

FOREWORD

By Andrew Sansom

It is said that General Colin Powell, while serving as the Chairman of the Joint Chiefs of Staff of the United States, had on his wall a painting showing a troop of African-American cavalrymen—known as the Buffalo Soldiers—chasing the last great Apache Chief, Victorio, up the great Texas canyon later named for him.

Texas Parks and Wildlife's efforts to conserve and maintain wildlife and natural habitat began in 1946 with the purchase of 5,335 acres, including the majestic Victorio Canyon, in the rugged mountains of far West Texas. Faced with the impending disappearance of desert bighorn sheep, the Department established the Sierra Diablo Wildlife Management Area with the goal of restoring these splendid animals to their native range.

From that first step—and desert bighorn sheep do range today not only the Sierra Diablos but other mountains in Texas as well—efforts to save Texas' wild places and wild things have continued and flourished in a spectacular collection of natural treasures little known to most Texans. Texas' wildlife management areas have grown in number to 50, and the lands owned or managed by Texas Parks and Wildlife for the benefit of many species of animals has increased to approximately 1 million acres.

Texas wildlife management areas contain examples of quality habitat in every ecological region of the state. They serve as laboratories where the public may learn about the wonders of nature and conservation scientists can develop and apply principles of wildlife management that private land managers can use on their own property. Research into white-tailed deer genetics on the Kerr Area provided the basic data that underlies every responsible, science-based game management program in the state today. Ten wildlife management areas serve as research and demonstration areas where anyone can go and learn, from the experts, techniques that really work in habitat management and wildlife conservation. These programs benefit a wide range of game and nongame species alike, from the golden-cheeked warbler to the Texas horned lizard.

But wildlife management areas are much more than places where you may find a doctoral candidate in herpetology at a major university scrounging for lizards under rocks, or a graduate student trapping hog-nosed skunks. They are also places where families can go to view wildlife, hike, hunt, fish, or ride bikes or horses. These areas also contain some of the most scenic and secluded campsites in the state, from riverbank niches in the Angelina-Neches/Dam B Wildlife Management Area to sites perched on a canyon wall in Black Gap Wildlife Management Area amid Big Bend's magnificent desolation.

Some of the best opportunities for public hunting and nature appreciation to be found in the country occur on these great public assets. Birders in particular are finding that our Texas wildlife management areas, with their large blocks of undisturbed habitat, are great places to add species after species to their life lists.

But the best news of all about these 50 natural treasures which are revealed by veteran outdoor writer Larry Hodge on these pages is that they are known about and visited by so few people. Offering unparalleled scenery and natural diversity but few amenities, Texas wildlife management areas are ideal places for visitors with a yen for solitude and the willingness to rough it. These truly are 50 secret spots where Texans can confront nature in its purest form and, quite likely, discover parts of themselves they never knew.

Andrew Sansom

PREFACE

Rare is the writer who can pen a treatise on the outdoors without quoting the father of modern conservation, Aldo Leopold. Some of my favorite quotes from his writings are included in this book. Yet one of my motivations for writing this volume was that, in one highly significant area, Leopold was dead wrong. Consider the following impassioned passage from *A Sand County Almanac*.

Knowledge of the whereabouts of good hunting or fishing [one might add birding, hiking and camping] *is a very personal form of property. It is like rod, dog, or gun: a thing to be loaned or given as a personal courtesy. But to hawk it in the marketplace of the sports column as an aid to circulation seems to me another matter. To hand it to all and sundry as free public 'service' seems to me distinctly another matter. Even 'conservation' departments now tell Tom, Dick, and Harry where the fish are biting, and where a flock of ducks has ventured to alight for a meal.*

All of these organized promiscuities tend to depersonalize one of the essentially personal elements in outdoor sports. I do not know where the line lies between legitimate and illegitimate practice; I am convinced, though, that 'where-to-go' service has broken all bounds of reason.

No one, including Aldo Leopold, who died in 1948, could have foreseen the wrenching changes that would take place in American society in just one generation. World War II and its aftermath uprooted Americans and moved them almost en masse from wild countryside to urban jungle. With this migration Americans lost close connection to the land in unprecedented numbers. Extended families became relics of the past and nuclear families became the endangered species of the future. No longer was knowledge of the haunts of deer and turkey and trout part of a family's collective memory to be passed down from one generation to the next.

Leopold decried the rise of the "where-to-go" service because he failed to realize that the way of life he knew was vanishing as surely as the passenger pigeon and the dinosaurs. Leopold railed against game departments that told people where to hunt and fish, but he failed to realize *why* this service was gaining popularity. It was because,

even as he wrote, the traditional chain of knowledge was being broken by events beyond anyone's control.

Leopold would have agreed with me, I think, that in order to conserve our wild places, we must visit and appreciate them. Lacking a grandfather with a secret fishing hole or a neighbor willing to let us tramp his woods in search of game, we must gather information where we can—or lose our outdoor heritage forever. The world has changed, Aldo, and in begging your understanding for having written this "where-to-go" book, I would fling back at you your most widely quoted words: "Only the mountain has lived long enough to listen objectively to the howl of a wolf." The world has changed, and so must, in some degree, our approach to conservation.

LARRY D. HODGE

INTRODUCTION

Traveling to each of the wildlife management areas covered in this book brought home to me a sobering fact: Texas may be a big state, but it has precious few wild places left, and compared to the whole they are tiny and scattered. Highways, shopping malls, and subdivisions gobble up wildlife habitat at a fearsome rate, chopping the leftover parcels into isolated islands where wild things, cut off from other animal populations, are in danger of withering away as castaways.

Texas has already lost almost all of its wilderness. In geologic time this tragedy has taken only seconds, but its consequences will last eons, if not forever. The limited life span of a human prevents us from appreciating the magnitude of change, because what we see in old age is only incrementally different from what we experienced in youth. If our life span was 200 years, how different might our view of changes in the environment of Texas be!

Like all humans, we wear blinders. Consider the words of Black Hawk, chief of the Sauk and Fox, over a century ago: "Our village was healthy and there was no place in the country possessing such advantages, nor hunting grounds better than those we had in possession. If a prophet had come to our village in those days and told us that the things were to take place which have since come to pass, none of our people would have believed him." Aldo Leopold put it even more eloquently: "It is a kind providence that has withheld a sense of history from the thousands of species of plants and animals that have exterminated each other to build the present world. The same kind providence now withholds it from us."

Texas without wild things and wild places would be a sad place. Wild places have a way of helping us understand our own place in the world. This book is an attempt to get more people involved in the outdoors by encouraging them to visit Texas wildlife management areas to camp, hike, bike, bird, hunt, and fish. Why? The best reason again comes from Leopold: "We grieve only for what we know." Those words underlie this book's mission: To help insure that future generations enjoy our outdoors, not grieve for its loss.

Texas' wildlife management areas and other public hunting lands are preserves not only of wildlife but of outdoor tradition and the opportunity to learn, develop, and apply woods skills as well. Here are places one can teach a youngster the art of reading tracks and signs, the skill of stalking, the science of understanding one's quarry and its habitat, and the pleasures of being outdoors under a clear blue sky with the sun-warmed aroma of freeze-dried grass rising to the nose. Here one can still hear the very real calls of the wild—the snort of a doe catching human scent on the breeze, the howl of coyotes at dusk, the thunder of quail rising to the sky, the haunting cry of sandhill cranes seeking sanctuary.

The lack of affordable places for outdoor recreation, particularly to take youngsters hunting, is oft-lamented in Texas. Yet this is a problem only if one thinks strictly of hunting deer and other big game on leased land. When it comes to hunting small game, and places where one can take a youngster to hunt without paying one thin dime for access for him or her, the story is quite different. Every single person in the state of Texas lives within a half-day drive of at least one public hunting area, many of which allow small-game hunt-

ing year-round. And for the two-thirds of Texans who live within the triangle bounded by Houston, San Antonio, and Dallas-Fort Worth, there are multiple choices.

Lack of available, affordable land is simply no excuse for not introducing young people to the outdoors or for not enjoying the outdoors ourselves. Overlooked outdoor recreational opportunities are on all our doorsteps. Texas wildlife management areas provide the opportunity. This book provides the where-to, the when-to and the how-to.

Ironically, one of the biggest benefits of visiting wildlife management areas is meeting the people you find there. Mark Twain once said that America has no native criminal class except Congress. It might be argued that Texas has no native altruistic class except wildlife biologists. While working on this book I was struck over and over by the concern these individuals displayed for the land under their care and all the plants and creatures on it. The value of their assistance in the preparation of this book, and their contribution to preserving our wild places, cannot be overstated.

Jolting down rocky roads in search of whiptail lizards and sitting on the back porch of the Black Gap WMA bunkhouse late into the night talking conservation with college students doing baseline inventories of plant and animal species convinced me there is hope for the future. Our wide-ranging discussions revealed that a generation just beginning to become familiar with Aldo Leopold's writings has already inculcated many of the basic points he raised. The problem with Leopold's teachings, as with most great ideas, is putting them into practice. On this point Leopold was pessimistic, and while I am afraid that once again he was prescient, I remain hopeful that future generations will prove him wrong.

It is for them, and their kind, that this book was written.

ACKNOWLEDGMENTS

I wish to thank the following individuals for their assistance and courtesies during the preparation of this manuscript: Amy Ging, Betty Ackerson, Bill Armstrong, Bob Bujnoch, Bob Carroll, Bob Cook, Bob Rogers, Bonnie McKinney, Brad Simpson, Brent Ortego, Carl Harris, Cathleen Veatch, Charles Foster, Jr., Charles Foster, Sr., Charles Muller, Charlie Steed, Chip Ruthven, Chris Gregory, Clay Brewer, Dale Prochaska, Darrell Fisher, David Dvorak, David Lopries, David Sierra, David Synatzske, Donnie Frels, Eric Tschanz, Gary Calkins, Gary Waggerman, Gene Fuchs, Georg Zappler, Glenn Ging, Hayden Haucke, I. G. Willmann, James Thomas, Jeffrey Gunnels, Jennifer Barrow, Jim Kitchens, Jim Ray, Jim Sutherlin, John Hughes, John Jones, John Jurek, John Thorne, José Cano, Judy Jurek, Kathy Carriker, Kay Fleming, Kris McIntyre, Larry LeBeau, Linda Lewis, Lisa Green, Macy Ledbetter, Micah Poteet, Michael Pittman, Mike Garner, Mike Gonzales, Mike Wheatley, Monroe Buntyn, Murty Sullivan, Penny Bartnicki, Ray C. Telfair, Richard Hines, Richard Pike, Rick Knipe, Ron Bell, Russell Tinsley, Sara Schuster, Scott Lerich, Ski Clark, Steve Benn, Steve Carriker, Steve Lange, Susan Ebert, T. Wayne Schwertner, Terry Turney, Tim Lawyer, Todd Merendino, Tom Hodge, Trey Carpenter, Tyler Hodge, and Violet Lewis.

I give special thanks to Thayne Smith and Jayco.

BIG BEND COUNTRY

BIG BEND COUNTRY

*Barring love and war, few
enterprises are undertaken
with such abandon, or by such
diverse individuals, or with so
paradoxical a mixture of appetite
and altruism, as that group of
avocations known as outdoor
recreation.*
—ALDO LEOPOLD

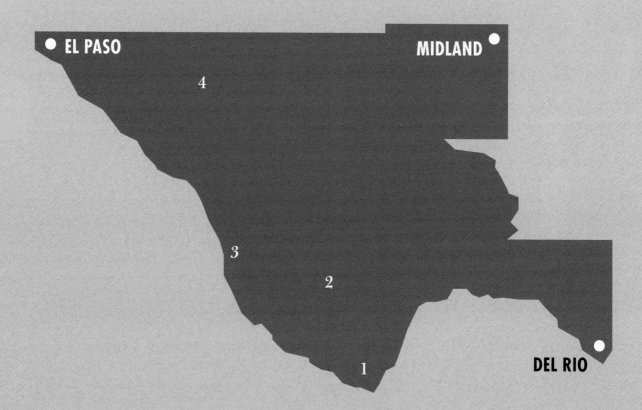

1 BLACK GAP WMA

2 ELEPHANT MOUNTAIN WMA

3 LAS PALOMAS WMA—OCOTILLO UNIT

4 SIERRA DIABLO WMA

107,878 acres
905 W. Avenue B
Alpine, TX 79830
915/837-3251

DRIVING TIMES FROM:
Amarillo: 8.5 hours
Austin: 8 hours
Brownsville: 11 hours
Dallas: 9.5 hours
El Paso: 5.5 hours
Houston: 10.5 hours
San Antonio: 7 hours
DIRECTIONS: From Marathon, take U.S. 385 south 39 miles to its intersection with FM 2627. Take FM 2627 south 16.6 miles to the area entrance.
OPEN: The driving tour route along FM 2627 is open daily. The rest of the area is open March 1 through August 31 and during specified hunting seasons. Except for the driving tour route, the entire area is closed during Special Permit hunts. Do not enter through any closed gate.
ACTIVITIES: Driving tour, camping, wildlife viewing, hiking, bicycling, hunting, fishing.
FACILITIES: Office, bunkhouse, information station, driving tour, equestrian trail, fishing camps, primitive campsites, composting toilet.
SPECIAL REGULATIONS: All users must register on-site. All users except driving tour participants and fishers who enter and exit by boat must possess an Annual Public Hunting Permit, a Limited Public Use Permit or a Texas Conservation Passport. Visitation from March 1 through August 31 is restricted to roads through Horse Canyon and Maravillas Canyon accessing the Rio Grande. Special federal regulations apply to the Rio Grande Wild and Scenic River adjacent to the area. A copy of these rules is posted at the information station.

Black volcanic rock contrasts sharply with creamy limestone; a narrow passage through the former gives Black Gap WMA its name.

ADVISORIES: Be forewarned: This country can kill you. Black Gap WMA is located in isolated, rugged desert country subject to extreme heat and flash floods. Never try to cross running streams. Following flash floods, roads may be impassable by vehicles for up to two weeks; be prepared to walk out if necessary. Cellular phones will not work here due to the isolated location. Poisonous snakes, mountain lions, and black bears are present. Carry first-aid supplies, basic car repair items, food, and water sufficient for at least three days at all times. Potable water is not available on the area. When walking cross-country, wear puncture-proof shin protection.
LODGING IN AREA: Motels are available in Marathon and at Heath Canyon Ranch, at the end of FM 2627.
LOCAL POINTS OF INTEREST: Balmorhea State Park, Davis Mountains State Park, Fort Leaton State Historical Park, Big Bend Ranch State Park, Fort Davis National Historic Site, Big Bend National Park.
DISABILITY ACCESS: One campsite in the headquarters campground and the composting toilet there are wheelchair-accessible.

HISTORY

Although it appears relatively barren to modern peoples, the Big Bend area served up sufficient food and raw materials to support prehistoric peoples who were more willing to eat whatever was at hand. The Rio Grande, numerous springs, and small creeks supplied water; rugged canyons afforded shelter; edible plants and animals were abundant; and the warm climate was ideally suited to peoples living outdoors. About the time Europeans began exploring the area, earlier native peoples were replaced by Apache and Comanche Indians.

Following the removal of Indians from West Texas in the 1870s and the nearly simultaneous arrival of railroads, ranching became the principal land use in Brewster County. The area that is now Black Gap WMA was used for grazing cattle, sheep and goats. Candelilla plants were harvested along the river and their wax rendered in camps there. Limited barite mining also took place on the area. During Prohibition, liquor was smuggled from Mexico into the United States through the area.

The first purchase of lands for Black Gap WMA was made in 1948, and purchase of inholdings continues

to the present. Some 26,500 acres within the WMA boundaries are leased from the Texas General Land Office.

For a time Black Gap played a leading role in the attempt to restore populations of desert bighorn sheep in Texas. These native sheep, never numbering more than perhaps 1,500, were nearly wiped out by food competition with domestic livestock, domestic sheep diseases, restricted movement due to net wire fences and unregulated market hunting (prohibited in 1903).

When it became apparent that the native bighorn sheep were in danger of extinction, efforts to reintroduce wild sheep to former ranges in Texas were begun. A 427-acre brood pasture was constructed on Black Gap WMA and stocked with 16 sheep from Arizona from 1957 through 1959. A painful learning experience followed. Initially, 10 of these sheep did not survive. From the remaining three rams and three ewes, the herd increased to approximately 68 animals. In 1971, 20 sheep were released from the pasture to range free on Black Gap.

These free-ranging sheep experienced good lamb production and survival for two years following their release. But when predator control was cut back and then eliminated, mountain lions and bobcats feasted on bighorn sheep, and the free-ranging sheep disappeared.

In the fall of 1971, the brood herd within the Black Gap enclosure was nearly wiped out by diseases such as blue tongue and pneumonia. These reverses forced the abandonment of propagation efforts at Black Gap, and the focus of bighorn sheep restoration shifted to the Sierra Diablo and, later, Elephant Mountain WMAs. In 1993 restocking efforts began again at Black Gap with the release of 21 sheep from Nevada. An estimated 50 desert bighorn sheep now roam the most rugged parts of the area; these sections are closed to visitation.

The Texas Bighorn Society, a non-profit group dedicated to the restoration of desert bighorn sheep in Texas, annually provides money, labor and materials to build watering facilities on the area to benefit not only the sheep but also all forms of wildlife.

GEOGRAPHY AND NATURAL FEATURES

Black Gap is the largest state-owned wildlife management area in Texas. It lies within the Chihuahuan Desert and includes mountain ridges separated by flat desert basins. The Rio Grande forms its southeastern boundary, and the Sierra Del Carmen Mountains divide it from Big Bend National Park to the west. Rugged canyons slash the area and drain into the Rio Grande. Elevation ranges from 1,700 feet along the Rio Grande to 4,600 feet in the Sierra Del Carmens.

The WMA takes its name from the black volcanic rock prominent around the area headquarters. Entry into the interior of the WMA is via a narrow pass through this rock, the "black gap."

Vegetation includes typical Chihuahuan Desert species such as creosotebush, lechuguilla, sotol, yucca, and various cacti. Drainages contain dense stands of mesquite, chapote, guayacan, granjeno, catclaw, skunk bush, and acacia. In general, Black Gap lives up to the saying about the Big Bend: that everything there sticks, bites, or stings. One federally listed threatened plant species, Lloyd's mariposa cactus, occurs on the area.

Black Gap is similarly rich in wildlife, with nearly 300 species of birds, over 50 species of mammals and nearly 60 species of reptiles and amphibians documented. Desert mule deer, white-tailed deer, Sierra

Wildlife guzzlers store infrequent rains for use by a variety of game and nongame species. Quail hunters often key on areas around water sources.

Del Carmen white-tailed deer, javelinas, desert cottontails, coyotes, mountain lions, bobcats, skunks, gray foxes, and black-tailed jackrabbits are fairly common. Scaled quail may be abundant some years and nearly nonexistent in others; a few Gambel's quail also occur on the area.

Less common mammals include the desert bighorn sheep, beavers and black bears. Inventories of plants and animals on the area are ongoing, as Black Gap is a popular venue for college students doing fieldwork. Federally listed endangered species recorded on the area are the black-capped vireo, peregrine falcon, and southwestern willow flycatcher. The bald eagle, delisted in 1999, has also been seen.

RECREATIONAL ACTIVITIES

DRIVING TOUR

A 10.8-mile self-guided driving tour passes through the western portion of the area along FM 2627. No permit is needed, and the tour is open every day of the year. Tour brochures are available from the box immediately south of the main entry gate to the area. It describes the plants and animals one can expect to see along the highway and at the 10 numbered stops marked by signposts. At each

stop, signs give the names of featured plants such as desert hackberry, notched leadtree, skeletonleaf goldeneye, leatherstem, purple sage, golfball cactus, lechuguilla, and Warnock's neolloydia cactus.

In addition to the paved driving tour, the area has about 220 miles of natural surface roads. About half the roads are normally passable by ordinary passenger vehicles; a high clearance vehicle is recommended for the narrow, rugged secondary roads, which receive minimal maintenance.

PRO'S POINTERS. Javelina, mule deer, and scaled quail are most likely to be spotted in early morning or late evening. Stop 10 overlooks a narrow canyon cut by the Rio Grande, and by walking about a hundred yards, you can stand on a cliff overlooking the river and the remains of mining operations at the Mexican ghost town of La Linda. Less than half a mile beyond, the road dead-ends at the closed bridge to La Linda; Heath Canyon Ranch (lodging) and the Open Sky Cafe are just off the highway to the west. The latter offers a unique dining experience under an ocotillo arbor on the bank of the Rio Grande.

This trip is good preparation for a real adventure: a 15-mile drive, hike, or bicycle ride into the interior of the WMA to one of the prettiest sites in Texas, a plateau above the Rio Grande surrounded on all sides by mountains. Begin by signing in at the information station at area headquarters. Enter your destination as the vicinity of fish camps 7 and 8. Follow the signs pointing the way to the Rio Grande.

Under normal road conditions a two-wheel drive pickup or sport-utility vehicle can navigate this route. The only major drainage crossing comes near the end of the trip, just past fish camps 5 and 6 at the mouth of Maravillas Canyon. If this draw looks too difficult for your vehicle but is dry, it's an easy half-mile walk to the plateau from there.

At 0.7 mile, take the right fork. This section of the road passes through the black gap for which the area is named and is subject to erosion during rainstorms. It may be somewhat rough. At about mile 3 the road passes between an adobe ruin on the left and Dell Tank on the right. Mule deer, roadrunners, and a variety of birds can be seen here in the day, and bats visit at night. At 4.4 miles, a parking lot marks the beginning of the area's equestrian trail, which runs from here to the Rio Grande and then downstream for another 10 miles. About 5 miles into the trip you'll turn south along the west bank of a canyon beneath towering limestone cliffs on either side. Watch for deer and javelina early and late in the day. Scaled quail may skitter across the road.

At 8.2 miles is a turnoff to the left leading about a hundred yards to one of the area's water guzzlers. These guzzlers are an ingenious method of trapping rainwater for use by the area's wildlife. Basically, the guzzler is a metal roof that drains into a storage tank, which then feeds the water via a float valve into a small tank which minimizes evaporation loss. They help make the area habitable by a wide variety of wildlife.

There are interesting adobe ruins just off the main road at fish camps 5 and 6. After 14.5 miles you enter the desert bighorn sheep restoration area; from this point on, visitors are restricted to the strip between the road and the Rio Grande to the right.

Stop at about mile 15. Here you will be surrounded by a level plain covered with creosotebushes, ocotillo, and pale green, straw-like clumps of candelilla. The mountains half a mile south are in Mexico; the Rio Grande flows at their base. To the southeast, a peak in Mexico resembles a rhino horn; just beyond it towers a flat-topped butte. To the north and northwest, limestone bluffs rear abruptly 700 to 800 feet above the desert floor. These mark the beginning of desert bighorn sheep habitat. These magnificent animals prefer the steep canyons and high ledges, bounding up and down them with sure-footed ease. However, it would be highly unusual to see one, since only about 50 inhabit the area, and they are extremely wary of humans. If you can, camp a short hike away at fish camp 7 or 8 and observe the changing palette of nature painting the peaks. In the morning, the desert floor will be closely patrolled by nighthawks swooping low, making a sound like a tiny outboard motor as they look for insects. The sight of early morning light setting the limestone cliffs ablaze is worth the trip.

It is very important to check at the information station for information on road closings and conditions. Late summer is the rainy season here, and there are numerous crossings of canyons that may flash flood. Do not drive into water. Floods will generally recede in a few hours. Deep sand makes four-wheel drive, high-clearance vehicles necessary for travel beyond fish camp 15.

EQUESTRIAN TRAIL

A designated equestrian trail, open from March 1 through August 31, starts at a parking area beside the road 4.4 miles from the information station and follows the road to the river. From the turnoff to fish camps 3 and 4 to the eastern area boundary about 10 miles farther on, horseback riding and all public use are restricted to the area between the river and the road.

PRO'S POINTERS. From the parking area to the river is about 12 miles. Riders must take all water and feed with them. Don't water horses at the wildlife guzzlers along the way, which have a very limited supply. Watering horses from the river is allowed. Horseback riders may camp at any designated campsite along the route. These include numbers 13 and 24 and any of the fish camps numbered 3 through 25. Horses should be tethered to a picket line or enclosed in a portable corral.

Camping

Camping is allowed in 56 designated campsites, including 25 fishing camps on the river, the headquarters campground, and 30 others scattered throughout the area. The headquarters campground has a wheelchair-accessible shelter, a composting toilet that is wheelchair-accessible, and one other shelter. Each fish camp consists of a roofed 10-foot-by-16-foot concrete slab with one wall. Primitive toilets serve each fishing camp. Twenty backcountry campsites have shade shelters and picnic tables, and all have fire rings. A detailed map of the area available at the information station shows the locations of all campsites.

PRO'S POINTERS. Black Gap offers the opportunity for camping in splendid solitude in scenic surroundings, but isolation exacts a price. Campers should be alert to the possibility of flash flooding which may render roads impassable for hours or days. Carry sufficient food and water for at least three days at all times. If roads are impassable or your vehicle breaks down, walking out for help can take up to two days. *Always record the campsite you will be using on the sign-in sheet, even if this means returning to the information station to do so.*

Campsites in certain areas may be closed during research activities; locations will be posted in the information station. Fall, winter and spring offer the best camping weather. Camping is allowed during hunting season unless the area is closed for a Special Permit hunt. See the *Public Hunting Lands Map Booklet* for the current year for closure dates. Hunters and nonhunters alike must wear safety orange when outside campgrounds whenever firearms hunting is permitted on the area.

Camp 5, on the west side of FM 2627, has two shade shelters and several tables and is primarily for research groups, but the public can use it if it is not occupied. Campsites along the highway are easily accessible but offer little in the way of scenery. Some particularly scenic campsites are numbers 8 through 13, 23, and 24. The campsites along the river, especially those past fish camp 15, require four-wheel drive for access due to deep sand.

Wildlife Viewing

Black Gap is rich in birds. Checklists are available in the information station for birds as well as reptiles, amphibians, and mammals. There is no checklist for the more than 400 species of plants, but some of them are identified along the driving tour. Wildlife viewing is allowed anywhere on the area that is not behind a closed gate; there are no designated facilities.

PRO'S POINTERS. Dirt tanks, guzzlers, and the river all attract birds. There are about 37 dirt tanks and 38 guzzlers or other water sources located on the area. Locations of guzzlers are shown on a map available at the information station. Spring and fall are the best birding times, with migration peaks coming from mid-April to mid-May and mid-August to late September.

"Late in the evenings and early in the mornings, the driving tour is a really good area for seeing mule deer, coyotes, and javelinas," says Bonnie McKinney, TPW endangered resources specialist for the Trans-Pecos. "Park at stop 3 and walk a hundred yards west to the guzzler to see red-tailed hawks, black-throated sparrows, roadrunners, cactus wrens, house finches, and Scott's orioles in the summer. In the fall, look around the dirt tanks for shorebirds such as Baird's sandpipers and killdeers. Dell Tank [at about mile 3 on the interior road to the river] is a good place to see mule deer, coyotes, and bobcats

early and late in the day." Roadrunners also favor the tank dam next to the road, near the adobe ruin.

"You can see elf owls along the driving tour, around the information station and at dusk on highline wires," continues McKinney. "There's a nest box on the utility pole at stop 5 on the driving tour. Peregrine falcons and zone-tailed hawks will be along the river. Occasionally, you'll see a gray hawk near camp 5."

The spring and fall migrations provide the best birding, McKinney says. "In spring we get Wilson's, yellow and MacGillivray's warblers and northern parulas. Because we are so close to the big mountains in Mexico, we may get long-billed thrashers, Mexican jays, and acorn woodpeckers. During the fall migration, along the river is good for black-crowned and yellow-crowned night herons, upland sandpipers, and Lucifer hummingbirds." Gambel's quail also occur along the river.

Black Gap also has a resident population of black bears, recent migrants from Mexico, and visitors occasionally spot one. Perhaps the most likely time to see a bear is in June and July, when males are traveling about looking for females to breed.

Hiking

Hiking is allowed on all 220 miles of dirt roads on the area, but there are no designated trails. All supplies must be packed in and all trash packed out. In a desert environment, a minimum of one gallon of water per person per day is recommended.

PRO'S POINTERS. Black Gap is different from other wildlife management areas in Texas in the following important way. On most WMAs, foot access is permitted to areas behind gates blocking vehicle access. *On Black Gap, if a gate is closed, the area behind it is closed to the public and all access is prohibited.*

"We don't require a hiking plan, but we do ask hikers to give us an idea of where they will be in case they don't show up," says area manager Michael Pittman. Cross-country hiking is permitted, but hikers should be aware that the limestone rock is very fractured and does not lend itself to climbing.

For a hike through flat desert country, begin at the camp 2 access road about 5 miles south of Stillwell's on FM 2627 and walk south to the area headquarters along the dirt road parallel to the highway. It's about 5 miles one way.

A loop hike of about 10 miles through more rugged country begins at the headquarters and follows the river road to just past Dell Tank (3 miles), where a road branches south to camp 14. About half a mile past camp 14, turn right and follow the road back to the highway. Go north on the highway about 3 miles to the area entrance.

The most scenic hiking is along the main road to the river through the interior of the area; see the driving tour section for a description.

BICYCLING

Bicycling is permitted on all 220 miles of dirt roads within the area, but there are no designated trails. See the sections on driving tours and hiking for cautions and recommended routes.

PRO'S POINTERS. Riders with touring bikes will enjoy the driving tour route along FM 2627 the most. The route has gentle hills and is about 11 miles one way. The Open Sky Cafe at the La Linda bridge offers a place to rest and refuel for the return trip. There's also a pay phone at the bridge. A trip of about equal distance is from Stillwell's Store to the area headquarters and back. This stretch of the highway is more level.

An offroad bike is recommended for riding interior roads on the area.

These roads are rocky and rough. Crossings at drainages range from loose sand and gravel to washboarded bedrock. There are long, steep hills with loose rocks. Expect punctures and spills: Wear protective gear and carry first-aid supplies.

HUNTING

Hunting is allowed for quail, mourning doves, rabbits and hares, mule deer, white-tailed deer, coyotes, and javelinas. Youth hunts may be available for quail, deer and javelinas. See the *Public Hunting Lands Map Booklet,* and the *Applications for Drawings on Public Hunting Lands* for species, seasons, and bag limits.

PRO'S POINTERS. "The area is usually open the whole month of September for dove hunting by Annual Public Hunting Permit," says

The Rio Grande separates Black Gap WMA from Mexico.

Michael Pittman. "We have mostly mourning doves, but there are some white-wings. Hunt doves on the dirt tanks, if they have water. You will probably find doves in the canyons as well, unless they get blown out by a cold front. When the tanks have water and we have not had a cold front, the dove hunting can be excellent. Call ahead and ask about conditions."

Quail hunting can be superb on Black Gap, or it can be dismal. In years when adequate rain falls at the right times, scaled quail seem to be under every creosotebush. In dry years, you can hunt for days and not see a bird. Always call ahead and ask about conditions. Quail hunting is allowed by Annual Public Hunting Permit only on specified dates. Scaled quail are the most common, but there are some Gambel's quail on the flats along the river. Both are legal species unless noted otherwise in the *Public Hunting Lands Map Booklet.* Also check the regulations to see if an ongoing research project on quail is still in progress; if it is, hunters are required to turn in one wing from each quail killed.

Scaled or blue quail richly deserve their reputation as desert speedsters. They prefer to streak through the brush on foot rather than fly, and hunting them can be frustrating to someone accustomed to hunting bobwhites. It bothers some people to shoot a quail on the ground, but the rule with blues is, shoot them any time you get a chance, because they will often run out of range without flushing.

Quail hunting is generally better from early January through February. At that time the birds gather into large coveys for the "shuffle," a mingling of birds from different coveys for breeding purposes. A single covey may contain 100 birds. One good way to hunt them is to drive the roads, watching for a covey to flush, then get out and hunt. If a covey crosses the road in front of you, speed up, honk your horn and try to make them fly off in different directions. Birds separated from the covey tend to hold tight rather than run, and you have a better chance of flushing them with a dog or walking them up.

Coveys tend to be found along drainages and near water sources. The guzzlers in particular can be good hunting venues, as they are always located on the edge of a draw or on a hillside. If you flush a covey and the birds fly up onto a steep hillside, they will not run. Walk the hillside out carefully; the birds often will not fly unless you almost step on them. In this situation an open choke and 7½ shot works best, whereas for running birds you need a tight choke and bigger shot, such as 6s.

All deer hunting is by Special Permit. Due to low numbers, archery hunts and youth gun hunts are for bucks only. "Basically, all deer hunting is for mule deer, although we do have a few Sierra Del Carmen whitetails in the mountains," says Pittman. "Some people hunt the water; others spot and stalk, particularly the gun hunters. The deer aren't very active when we hunt, as it is usually not during the rut, so those who cover the most country have the best chance of success. Mule deer are not as spooky as white-tails, so it is actually possible to walk them up and get one."

All Special Permit hunters are required to arrive by 9 A.M. for sign-in and orientation. Each hunter or group of hunters is assigned a hunt compartment of from 2,000 to 6,000 acres. Hunters are provided with a topographic map of their hunt compartment, and they are restricted to that compartment for the entire hunt. Switching compartments or camping in another compartment is not allowed. At least one designated campsite is in each hunt compartment.

"We will advise hunters on how they might want to hunt their compartment based on current conditions," says Pittman. "Hunters are allowed to drive roads within their compartment. Area personnel will assist in tracking wounded deer when necessary; we have dogs trained for the purpose. Deer should be dressed in the field, then brought to the headquarters check station for collection of biological samples. We have no cold storage on the area; the closest is in Alpine. Bring plenty of ice chests; Stillwell's Store has ice."

Javelina hunts are conducted in the same way as deer hunts. "Cover the country," advises Pittman. "Javelinas usually hang out in the thick, nasty stuff in the draws; people walk them up as a rule."

Whatever type of hunting you do, wear clothes that will protect you in thorny, rocky country. Hard-soled boots and lower leg protection are necessary.

FISHING

All fishing is in the Rio Grande, which forms about 20 miles of the southeastern boundary of the area. Fishing is primarily for blue and flathead catfish. Fishers who enter and exit the area by boat are not required to possess an access permit. Fishers who cross the WMA to fish only, but not hunt, may do so if they possess a Limited Public Use Permit, Annual Hunting Permit or a Texas Conservation Passport. See federal rules regarding use of the Rio Grande posted in the information station.

PRO'S POINTERS. "Most people use trotlines, throwlines, and jugs to fish for catfish," says Pittman. "Serious fishers use boats; jetboats are the only ones that are normally usable, as the river is often two feet or less in depth."

INSIDER'S CORNER

RETURN OF THE BLACK BEAR

"Black Gap is the only WMA that has a breeding population of black bears," says Bonnie McKinney, who is trapping and fitting bears with radio collars. In the summer of 1999, she was tracking seven bears known to be living on Black Gap WMA. "What's really unique about that is that Black Gap is a lower desert system, whereas bears are thought of as being woodland creatures."

Still rare, black bears create a stir when sighted in Big Bend today, but they are merely repopulating their historic range. "There were actually annual bear hunts in this country at one time," says McKinney. "Early settlers depended on bears for meat, lard, and hides. By the 1940s they were extirpated in Big Bend. However, landowners in Mexico protected them, and in 1986 Mexico placed them on the endangered list. Texas did the same in 1987. There is now a tremendous population in Mexico, and they are moving back into Texas and reclaiming territory they once used."

McKinney's research project is studying the black bears' home range, diet, mortality, survival rate of young, ingress and egress routes, and preferred habitat types. Tracking studies show their activity slows from late November until April, but they do not hibernate. Scat analysis reveals what the bears eat on a month-by-month basis. "Bears are governed by their stomachs," McKinney says. "Spanish daggers are a staple in their diet. The bears pull the heart out and eat only about the bottom inch or so, which is very sugary. They lay it beside the plant and then move on to the next. It's very easy to see where they've been and is a good way to document bear use of an area."

McKinney's research will provide biological data that can be used by managers of public and private lands in the Chihuahuan Desert to develop management techniques for desert black bears. "They are bringing themselves back, and is up to us to make sure they can coexist with traditional land uses like farming and ranching. So far it's working very well," McKinney says. "The bears have pretty well stayed out of trouble. Bears will occasionally kill livestock, but not all bears are livestock killers. If there is a problem bear somewhere, we help the landowner trap and remove it. As long as natural foods are available, bears keep their noses clean. It's only when natural food is scarce that they may take a sheep."

McKinney points out that bears are beneficial to the environment.

"They scatter lots of seeds—algerita, persimmons, prickly pear, acorns—that are used by other animals. Quail and bears eat a lot of the same foods. The bear is a barometer: You know the country is in good shape if it can support a bear."

Black Gap is popular with bears because of the water guzzlers, which may be the key to their ability to survive on the area. "They love to drink and play in the water," she says. "We had to bearproof our troughs by putting heavy mesh wire over the floats. Otherwise, they will play with the float and let the water run until it drains the tank."

"A fed bear is a dead bear—it will keep coming back and become a problem," McKinney says. She offers these tips to landowners to help them coexist peacefully with black bears.

1. Burn dead sheep or cattle so bears won't learn to feed on them.

2. Keep garbage burned.

3. Don't give them free groceries. Keep grain and livestock food where bears can't get to it.

23,147 acres
HC 65, Box 80
Alpine, TX 79830
915/364-2228

DRIVING TIMES FROM:
Amarillo: 7.5 hours
Austin: 7.5 hours
Brownsville: 10.5 hours
Dallas: 8.5 hours
El Paso: 4 hours
Houston: 10 hours
San Antonio: 6.5 hours
DIRECTIONS: From Alpine, take Texas 118 south for 26 miles.
OPEN: Daily except on designated dates; only designated portions of the area as posted at the information station are open. Driving tour is open May 1 to August 31. Elephant Mountain's top is closed at all times. Slopes are open portions of the year.
ACTIVITIES: Driving tour, camping, wildlife viewing, hiking, hunting.
FACILITIES: Office, education center, bunkhouse, campground with composting toilet, nature trail, wildlife-viewing station.
SPECIAL REGULATIONS: All users must register on-site. All users except driving tour participants must possess an Annual Public Hunting Permit, a Limited Public Use Permit, or a Texas Conservation Passport. Camping is permitted within the designated camping area only. Visitors are restricted to the camping area from two hours after sunset until two hours before sunrise. Trapping, bicycles, and horses are not allowed. All vehicles must remain on designated roads.
ADVISORIES: Rattlesnakes are present on the area. The nearest public telephone is in Alpine. Be alert for illegal aliens crossing the area; avoid any suspicious-looking strangers. Carry your own supply of potable water.
LODGING IN AREA: Motels are available in Alpine.
LOCAL POINTS OF INTEREST: Balmorhea State Park, Davis Mountains State Park, Fort Leaton State Historical Park, Big Bend Ranch State Park, Fort Davis National Historic Site, Big Bend National Park.
DISABILITY ACCESS: The wildlife viewing station is wheelchair-accessible.

HISTORY

Elephant Mountain lies in a natural travel corridor between the Rio Grande and mountain ranges to its north, and it likely saw seasonal movements of Jumano and Cibolo Indians as they hunted bison and pronghorns. The Trans-Pecos region of Texas was one of the last strongholds of First Americans resisting the spread of European settlement. Archaeological sites on the area consist mainly of campsites.

The area comprising Elephant Mountain WMA remained state land until 1882, when it was homesteaded by Robert Neville, who came to own one of the largest ranches in West Texas. Part of the Neville ranch was acquired by C. G. Johnson of Houston and later donated to Texas Parks and Wildlife in 1985. Conditions of the gift included that the property be used for the conservation and development of desert bighorn sheep and other large game animals, wildlife-oriented research, and compatible recreational uses, including public hunting.

At present Elephant Mountain WMA is the primary source of broodstock for the Texas bighorn sheep restoration program. Sheep being reintroduced on other areas come from here. Twenty sheep were stocked on the area in 1987; since that time, the number has increased to over 100. Bighorn sheep hunts, part of the Texas Grand Slam package, are conducted on the area.

GEOGRAPHY AND NATURAL FEATURES

Elephant Mountain WMA lies within a transition zone from Chihuahuan Desert scrub to high desert grassland. The mountain itself rises to 6,225 feet above sea level and stretches about 8 miles from north to

Wild turkeys come as a surprise in West Texas, but a small flock inhabits the Calamity Creek area.

south. Texas Highway 118 serves as the area's western boundary. Between it and Elephant Mountain is Calamity Creek, an intermittent stream. To its east, Chalk Valley separates the flat-topped mountain from the rugged Del Norte Mountain range; the area boundary runs along their crest.

Standing in majestic isolation in a broad valley, Elephant Mountain is a prominent feature visible from many miles away. The mountain's base covers about 6,000 acres and its top some 2,200. Elephant Mountain itself is igneous, while the Del Nortes are sedimentary limestone.

Elephant Mountain was formed by the intrusion of igneous rock some 35 million years ago and subsequent erosion of overlying volcanic lavas and tuffs. As the rock cooled, it fractured along vertical lines, producing column-like forms prominent on the mountain's north and east faces. The rough terrain forming an apron around the base of the mountain resulted from rock breaking off from the vertical faces and tumbling down.

"The area is very diverse because of the geology and natural features," says area manager Clay Brewer. "We have a number of springs, although most of them dry up in the summer. There are big differences in habitat types between the north-facing and south-facing slopes and between the desert floor and the top of the mountain, which due to elevation is about six degrees cooler. Most of the hardwood areas are restricted to the drainages and shaded canyons, where there is more water. Chisos red oak and pinyon pine occur in the Del Norte Mountains, which are also a travel corridor for black bears and other wildlife species. Elk and pronghorns range up and down the Chalk Valley at certain times of the year."

Desert scrub dominates the valleys, with creosotebush, mesquite, ocotillo, cholla, lechuguilla, sotol, and yucca commonly occurring. Narrow strips of woodlands follow the drainages, where hackberry, mesquite, western walnut, and Arizona ash are sprinkled with occasional desert willow and cottonwood trees. In canyons on mountainsides grow ashe juniper, pinyon pine, agarito, sumac, Texas madrone, and mountain laurel. Grasses include gramas, threeawns, and muhly.

RECREATIONAL OPPORTUNITIES

Elephant Mountain WMA offers a driving tour, a nature trail, primitive camping, wildlife viewing, hiking, and hunting.

DRIVING TOUR

No permit is required for the 6-mile driving tour, but visitors must register at the information station at the entrance, where maps of the route are available. The tour road opens May 1, after the desert bighorn sheep lambing season, and closes August 31, just before the beginning of hunting season. "This is a desert bighorn driving tour," says Brewer. "Its primary purpose is to put people into a position where they will have a chance to see sheep. The route gives good views of the western and southern slopes of the mountain, which have all the primary elements of good sheep habitat: good views, easy access to escape cover, and natural water. As you travel, you leave the transition zone on the north side and enter the true desert scrub on the south end. You may see white-tailed and mule deer, pronghorns and bighorn sheep, as well as javelinas and various birds. Morning is the best time to see the sheep as well as other wildlife."

PRO'S POINTERS. Begin the driving tour at the information station parking lot. Just past, turn left and cross the cattle guard. Leave all gates as you find them, open or closed. At mile 0.2 the road curves sharply to the right at the parking lot for the Calamity Creek nature trail. Cross the creek; at mile 0.3 a road leads left to the campground. Follow the right fork at mile 0.4. In early morning or late evening this is a good place from which to look for bighorn sheep atop the mountain. With binoculars of eight power and above you can see sheep clearly from here if they are present. From the fork in the road, look at the rim of the mountain at its highest point, between the two utility poles in front of you. The sheep will probably be near the point where the mountaintop drops off slightly to the right.

For the next three miles or so you will be in the Calamity Creek valley, one of the richest wildlife areas on Elephant Mountain WMA. In early morning, keep an eye out for mule deer and javelinas. In the evenings, mourning and white-winged doves feed and gravel along the road. At mile 0.8, the watering trough on the right attracts a variety of birds and other wildlife. The plank across it was placed there to make it easier for birds to water. You may see sheep atop the mountain from here by looking directly over the top of the small house to the left of the large building, the education center, atop the hill to your left. This area is closed to driving tour visitors. Continue straight ahead. The solitary mountain in the distance is Santiago Peak. It's about 15 miles away. Watch for mule deer in the brush for the next 2 miles.

At mile 4.2, the road dips into the channel of Calamity Creek. Never drive into running water; flash flooding can be deadly. At mile 4.5 the road turns left and runs along the southern fenceline of the WMA. Watch for mule deer and pronghorns in the flat across the fence. At mile 6 you reach the bighorn sheep viewing area. The sheep use the south-facing slopes below the rimrock for lambing, and a spring partway up the mountain is an important water source. The shelter inside the fence has benches and an armrest to help you steady your binoculars. Interpretive panels give information about the sheep and restoration efforts. The three-wire fence around the shelter is wildlife-friendly, allowing deer, sheep, and antelopes access to the water collected from the shelter roof, stored in the tank, and dispensed by the drinker.

The driving tour ends here. Return to the headquarters area by the same route.

NATURE TRAIL

Nature trail users must register at the information station. There is no trail guide, but a map of the trail is posted, and wildlife checklists are available.

PRO'S POINTERS. You may walk from the information station or drive to the nature trail parking lot on the bank of Calamity Creek, 0.2 mile past the cattleguard. The trail runs along the bank of Calamity Creek to the primitive campground, about 1.5 miles one way. Walking is restricted to the marked trail. You must wear safety orange when walking the trail during dates when firearms hunting is permitted on the area.

"The trail offers consistently good birding year-round," says Brewer. "The trees around the headquarters attract birds, as does a seep spring along the creek near the campground. The spring is just a big, muddy puddle, but it stays there year-round and is heavily used by wildlife. Spring is a fairly good time for walking the trail, but most years the best time is late summer and early fall. Rainy season is July and August, so animals are more visible then."

CAMPING

Camping is allowed except when the area is closed for Special Permit hunts, when the campground is reserved for the use of hunters. See the current *Public Hunting Lands Map Booklet* for dates the area is closed. The campground has 15 individual campsites and one group campsite. Each has a shade shelter, fire ring, and picnic table. A composting toilet serves the area. Potable water is not available. A few campsites have small trees or screening brush while others are open.

PRO'S POINTERS. Hunting is not allowed in or immediately around the camping area. Camping is limited to 14 consecutive days; a Limited Public Use permit is required. To reach the camping area, turn left across the cattleguard immediately past the information station (leave the gate the way you find it, open or closed) and follow the road 0.3 mile. Turn left onto the campground road and follow it 0.8 mile to the campground.

WILDLIFE VIEWING

From May 1 through August 31, wildlife viewing is permitted along the driving tour trail and the nature trail and in the campground, all discussed above. The area is also open for wildlife viewing during the hunting season, from September 1 through the end of February. You must wear safety orange when outside the camping area during dates when firearms hunting is permitted on the area.

PRO'S POINTERS. "The area along the nature trail is the best on the WMA for wildlife viewing," says Brewer. "The birds most likely to be seen are white-crowned sparrows, black-throated sparrows, turkey vultures, brown towhees, roadrunners, mockingbirds, vermilion flycatchers, pyrrhuloxias, blue grosbeaks, scaled quail, Montezuma or Mearns' quail, mourning doves, white-winged doves, and curved-bill thrashers. Wild turkeys may sometimes be seen along the creek and around the headquarters complex."

The scarcity of water in the desert means that the numerous watering troughs on the area draw wildlife. The water tanks are easily spotted, and roads go to most of them. Desert cottontail and black-tailed jackrabbits are numerous along the roads. White-tailed and mule deer may also be seen along Calamity Creek. Pronghorns frequent Chalk Draw, but due to brush may be hard to spot unless you find an elevation to watch from. Javelinas travel the draws, especially early and late in the day.

For information on viewing desert bighorn sheep, see the driving tour section, above.

HIKING

The nature trail (see above) is the only designated hiking trail on the area. However, from September 1 through the end of February, hiking is allowed on roads and across country except in areas that are closed. *If a gate is closed and locked, all entry into the area is prohibited.* This is necessary to prevent disturbance of the desert bighorn sheep during the lambing season. Hikers must wear safety orange on dates when firearms hunting is permitted.

PRO'S POINTERS. A good starting point for a 6.6-mile (one way) hike around the north side of Elephant Mountain is at mile 0.4 of the driving tour. The road is rocky and rough; wear hiking shoes with good ankle support and hard soles.

Instead of following the driving tour road to the right, go left. Elephant Mountain is to your right. The highest part of the mountain is a good place to see desert bighorn sheep early and late in the day. Look for them against the skyline or feeding just below the rim. Good binoculars are required; they are a mile and a half away.

Ahead of you lies a high desert habitat. You are likely to see scaled quail and possibly pronghorns. The black plastic pipe running along the road is part of an extensive system that provides water for wildlife and cattle, which are used as a management tool and to demonstrate proper grazing.

At mile 0.3, turn right at the fork and ascend the slope toward Elephant Mountain. To the west as you make the turn are Cienega Mountain (on the left), which looks like an unmade bed, and Cathedral Mountain, which looks somewhat like a headless Sphinx.

In summer, when the narrow flat between the road and the low hill just beyond at mile 0.8 is covered in croton, or doveweed, this area is a favored feeding ground for white-winged and mourning doves.

At mile 1.3, follow the road to the right as it is joined by another from the left. You are now traveling parallel to the northern boundary fence of the WMA. Do not cross the fence. At mile 1.8, a service road for communications equipment located on top of the mountain turns right. This road is closed to the public at the gate in the distance. You are free to walk in the area between the road and the foot of the mountain, but climbing the mountain is strictly prohibited in order to protect the bighorn sheep from disturbance.

As you descend into the draw at mile 2.8, notice the earthen embankment on your right. This is a spreader dam, designed to hold runoff temporarily and enable more rainfall to sink into the ground. There are 160 of these on the WMA. The added water supply increases plant growth and makes the area more attractive to wildlife. You may spot a white-tailed deer in the area.

At mile 3.3, the piles of stone on either side of the road mark the site of a quarry where material was obtained for buildings on the area. The original ranch house on the area, built from this native stone, lies another 0.7 mile down the road. Access to the house is prohibited. The area around the house and the brushy draw just beyond are excellent birding areas due to the presence of water and ample cover. Scott's orioles have been spotted here in the summer. Sheep may be present on the north end of the mountain near the road; do not disturb them in any way.

Entering Chalk Valley at mile 4.3 gives a spectacular view of the east face of Elephant Mountain and the vertical fracturing of the rock.

Straight ahead are the Del Norte Mountains, which mark the eastern boundary of the WMA. Between is mile-wide Chalk Draw. This drainage extends a considerable distance north and south and is a known travel corridor for smugglers carrying drugs out of Mexico. These smugglers often wear camouflage clothing and carry backpacks and have been known to assault people. Avoid strangers.

At mile 5.5, take a right at the water trough. If desired, you can take the left road to the foot of the Del Norte Mountains and loop back to this road. Keep a sharp lookout for pronghorns in this area. They are usually best spotted by climbing up the slope a short way and looking back down into the valley. At mile 6.6

Covering some 2,200 acres, the top of Elephant Mountain serves as an ideal refuge for desert bighorn sheep, which are protected by the mountain's nearly vertical slopes.

HUNTING

is a set of cattle pens and the end of this hike.

Hunting is allowed for white-tailed and mule deer, javelinas, scaled quail, doves, rabbits, and hares. Elephant Mountain also hosts the bighorned sheep hunting segment of the Texas Grand Slam (see Insider's Corner, below). For information on species, seasons and bag limits, see the *Public Hunting Lands Map Booklet, Applications for Drawings on Public Hunting Lands* and *Outdoors Annual* for the current year.

PRO'S POINTERS. "The Calamity Creek area where the road starts up the hill to the education center and other buildings can be a hotspot for doves," says Brewer. Vegetation in the area is low and offers insufficient

The southern end of Elephant Mountain (left) is used as a nursery area by desert bighorn sheep during the spring lambing season.

cover for a standing person, so bring a five-gallon bucket, ice chest, or other seat. Park along the driving tour road, walk a hundred yards or so from your vehicle, and sit down amid the low brush. "Infrequently, we have cold fronts that move the doves out. Call before you come," advises Brewer.

For scaled quail, the Calamity Creek and Chalk Valley drainages are the best areas. Blue quail are notorious for their ability to sprint through the brush ahead of hunters. Dogs trained on bobwhite quail sometimes become frustrated by these quail, which won't hold for a point. Hunters have two choices. One is to chase the quail through the brush, trying to get close enough for a shot. The other is ground-swatting, acceptable behavior when dealing with blues. Wear protective clothing on arms and legs to protect yourself from thorny brush. When chasing quail, a modified choke and #6 shot may be needed.

Another method for hunting the little speedsters is to rush the covey and make it flush, hoping the birds will divide into more than one group. If they do, watch where the groups come down. Birds isolated from the rest of the covey are more likely to hold tight and can be walked up or hunted with dogs. Hunting this way allows the use of an improved cylinder or skeet choke and loads of #7½ or #9 shot.

Montezuma quail, which are also present on the area, are not a legal game species. "They have a mask, or clown face, while scaled quail have a little topknot on their head," explains Brewer. "Montezumas are sometimes mistaken for bobwhites; don't shoot anything that looks like a bobwhite. Look at the pictures of quail in the information station before you hunt." Quail populations tends to be very weather-dependent, so it's best to call for information before going.

14

Rabbits and hares are everywhere on the area and may be hunted concurrently with doves and quail; there is no bag limit.

Both white-tailed and mule deer are present on the area in limited numbers. Hunting is generally archery only, but gun hunts may be offered some years, depending on deer numbers. "For Special Permit deer hunts, groups are assigned a compartment ranging from 700 to 3,000 acres," says Brewer. "There are no trees to hang a stand in, nor is there enough cover to use a tripod stand. Most of the successful hunters find a vantage point from which they can view the area, spot a deer and then stalk it. It's quite a trick to sneak up on a deer. Baiting is not allowed. Hunts take place before the rut, so rattling is not effective. During dry years, hunt water sources." Deer archery hunters are also allowed to take one javelina.

On javelina Special Permit hunts, archery equipment and any legal firearm is allowed except rimfires. Crossbows are not allowed. Baiting is not allowed. Hunting is done by assigned compartments. "Walk and cover the country," Brewer advises. "Use vantage points to spot and stalk. Look for them along drainages." Javelina tend to move most early and late and bed down in heavy cover along drainages. One good method for hunting them is to work in pairs and move quietly along either side of a drainage, flushing them from cover.

Feral hogs and coyotes are also legal on Special Permit hunts; there is no bag limit on either.

INSIDER'S CORNER

BIG TIME TEXAS HUNTS

For a $10 fee, hunters may enter the Texas Grand Slam, a lottery in which the grand prize is four hunts—white-tailed deer, mule deer, pronghorn and desert bighorn sheep. Food, lodging, taxidermy, and guide fees are included. The estimated value of the package is over $100,000. The Grand Slam is one of five Big Time Texas Hunts offered to raise money for conservation and to create more hunting opportunities. "Most people enter hoping to win the bighorn sheep hunt, which is held on Elephant Mountain WMA," says area manager Clay Brewer. Income from the drawing funds the entire bighorn sheep restoration program in Texas. Chances may be purchased wherever hunting licenses are sold.

"The winning hunter is allowed to bring a nonhunting companion," Brewer explains. "They lodge in the bunkhouse. We hire a real cowboy cook, who prepares all meals over an open campfire in dutch ovens."

Brewer personally guides the sheep hunter on what may be the most physically demanding hunt in Texas. "We go up the mountain on mules—otherwise I'd kill [the hunter] before we got to the top," Brewer says. "Then we hike to get into a shooting position. There's a lot of climbing and crossing rockslides on very steep slopes. Sometimes I have to tell the hunter where to place hands and feet. It's also at an elevation of 6,000 feet, which makes a difference. I call the winner of the hunt months in advance and advise starting an exercise program."

Hunts begin on the east side of the mountain. Rams are located by glassing the slopes. Getting within shooting range is extremely difficult. Bighorn sheep eyesight is approximately equivalent to eight-power binoculars; they can see a human a mile and a half away. They also have good noses and are very skittish. Even so, as of 1999 none of the five-day hunts had taken longer than two. "If I can ever get someone to be patient enough, there are several record-book rams up there," Brewer says. "But it's hard to get a hunter willing to wait and able to stand up to the physical demands."

Brewer enjoys the hunts as much or more than the hunters. "For me, there is nothing like looking at the sheep when you are close enough to see scars from battles they've fought for breeding rights," he marvels. "They stand with such pride—they are a very regal animal. You can see forever you are so high. You see the sheep and the mountains behind it, and it makes you feel like you are the only person in the world—a very small person."

2,082 acres
905 W. Avenue B
Alpine, TX 79830
915/837-3251

DRIVING TIMES FROM:
Amarillo: 9.5 hours
Austin: 9.5 hours
Brownsville: 13 hours
Dallas: 11 hours
El Paso: 5 hours
Houston: 12 hours
San Antonio: 8.5 hours
DIRECTIONS: From Presidio, follow FM 170 north for 36 miles to Ruidosa. The WMA begins at the cattleguard just past town; the headquarters and sign-in station are 1.6 miles past the store at Ruidosa.
OPEN: Daily.
ACTIVITIES: Camping, wildlife-viewing, hunting.
FACILITIES: Headquarters building, primitive campground.
SPECIAL REGULATIONS: No trapping is allowed. Horses are prohibited. All users must register on-site. Parking is permitted at entrances to designated roads and along the shoulder of FM 170 provided the vehicle is pulled completely off the road. Do not enter areas behind locked gates.
ADVISORIES: Rattlesnakes are present on the area. Mosquitoes are abundant in the riparian area. Illegal border crossing and drug smuggling are problems in the area; avoid strangers. Carry your own supply of potable water.
LODGING IN AREA: Motels are available in Presidio. Cabins are available at Chinati Hot Springs.
LOCAL POINTS OF INTEREST: Big Bend Ranch State Park, Fort Leaton State Historical Park, Davis Mountains State Park, Balmorhea State Park, Big Bend National Park.
DISABILITY ACCESS: Not wheelchair-accessible.

HISTORY

This area of Texas was inhabited by Mescalero Apaches, who raided a local farm as late as 1879. European occupation began in 1824, when the Mexican government established a penal colony at Ruidosa. Convicts known as the Condemned Regiment were sent to guard northern Chihuahua against Comanche and Apache raids.

Farming in the Rio Grande Valley began about 1872; in the early 1900s cotton farming expanded, and cotton gins were built at Ruidosa and Candelaria. Judging by the number of graves in Hispanic cemeteries along FM 170, one of which occurs on the WMA, there was a substantial population. In 1911 there were a reported 287 students and 1,722 total persons in the Ruidosa area and about 550 residents at Candelaria.

The area was heavily impacted by the activities of border bandits during the teens. An army post at Candelaria was supplied from Fort Russell in Marfa, and troops moved through the area regularly until the post was closed in 1919. Population fell during the Depression years and never recovered to previous levels.

Farming underwent a brief revival beginning in the mid-1950s, when Otto Walker bought the land now comprising most of the WMA. Walker's granddaughter, Linda Walker of Lajitas, reports that her parents lived in the house that now serves as the area headquarters building. They used river water to irrigate cantaloupe and cotton fields along the river and ran goats in the upland areas and canyons.

After two or three years, Walker says, her grandfather sold the land to the Pelton family. The Peltons ranched the land, raising grain and hay, and had as many as three center-pivot irrigation systems. The grain fields attracted many doves, and the Peltons also ran an active dove-hunting operation.

Texas Parks and Wildlife bought the area in two parcels in 1985 and 1986 as part of the Las Palomas WMA; the other tracts in this WMA are in the Lower Rio Grande Valley near Brownsville. Until 1992 Texas Parks and Wildlife continued to plant sunflowers, sorghum, and wheat on the area to attract doves. After farming ceased, salt cedar (tamarisk) began to invade the riparian area and now covers it almost completely.

GEOGRAPHY AND NATURAL FEATURES

About 585 acres consist of bottomland in the Rio Grande floodplain; the balance is rocky desert upland cut by numerous canyons. FM 170 runs lengthwise through the area from north to south. Most of the bottomland area lies west of the highway.

Flat and mostly level, the bottomland is covered in an extremely dense growth of trees. Salt cedars dominate, but there are also huisache, mesquite, and willow trees. The rugged canyons and uplands support ocotillo, creosotebush, and leatherstem. The latter is a preferred food source for white-winged doves, which feed on its large seeds. These seeds, about the size of garbanzo peas, are too large for mourning doves to eat.

The Ocotillo Unit's physical setting is spectacular. From the upland areas there are sweeping views of the Rio Grande, farms along the Mexican side of the river, mountains in Mexico, and the Chinati Mountains to the east. From the sea of salt cedars along the river in summer comes the continuous cooing of nesting doves. The area brings to mind an astronaut's description of the moon as "magnificent desolation"; to that one can add isolation, for this is one of the most remote spots in Texas. The paved highway to Presidio was not completed until 1985.

RECREATIONAL OPPORTUNITIES

Camping, wildlife viewing, hunting, and fishing are allowed on the Ocotillo Unit. Hunters must possess an Annual Public Hunting Permit; nonconsumptive users and fishers must possess a Limited Public Use Permit, Annual Hunting Permit or Texas Conservation Passport.

CAMPING

Camping is allowed at the primitive camping area adjacent to the area headquarters. Shade shelters and fire rings are provided, but there is no water or other facilities.

PRO'S POINTERS. Fall, winter, and spring are the best months to visit, as summers here are usually brutally hot. The camping area is a cleared space of about two acres that apparently was once used to store farm equipment.

WILDLIFE VIEWING

Due to the juxtaposition of river floodplain and upland desert habitats, birding here is excellent. Approximately 150 birds have been identified on the area, including painted buntings, buffleheads, yellow-billed cuckoos, mourning doves, white-winged doves, prairie falcons, vermilion flycatchers, blue grosbeaks, sharp-shinned hawks, green-backed herons, western kingbirds, various orioles and sparrows, Gambel's quail, summer tanagers, Nashville warblers, and lesser yellowlegs.

PRO'S POINTERS. For a sampling of both the riverine and upland habitats, enter gate 1, which is 0.8 mile on the left past the area headquarters. (Due to lack of maintenance on this road, it's best to park at the highway or just inside the gate.) The road runs about half a mile along the base of the upland area. Salt cedars and mesquites border the road on the river side; desert species on the upland side.

Dove hunting is perhaps the principal use of the Ocotillo Unit, which is lightly used due to its remote location.

HIKING

Hiking is allowed on designated roads or any part of the area that is not behind a locked gate.

PRO'S POINTERS. For a spectacular view of the area, enter at gate 9. To reach this gate, take Hot Springs Road north from FM 170 at the southern boundary of the WMA and go 1.8 miles to a faint road to the left off the county road. About 100 yards down this road, turn left and continue 0.4 mile to the gate. Once on the area, paths lead to points overlooking several draws. Views in all directions are superb.

Entering gate 2, a mile past the headquarters on the left, takes you to a point of land with a historic cemetery overlooking the river bottom. Gate 7, across FM 170 from the headquarters, leads into a box canyon about half a mile long with interesting rock formations at its upper end.

HUNTING

For information on species, bag limits and seasons for the current year, see the *Public Hunting Lands Map Booklet* for the current year. Hunting is generally allowed for doves, quail, rabbits, and hares. A youth-adult quail hunt may be available in some years.

PRO'S POINTERS. The salt cedars along the river are ideal dove nesting

17

and roosting habitat. The birds here are migratory; often most of the population pulls out around the first of September, especially if there is an early cold spell. Contact the area office before driving a long distance to hunt. Traditionally, opening weekend is a busy one, with groups traveling from as far as Dallas and Houston to hunt.

The most popular dove food in the area is leatherstem, which grows along the bluffs just above the river. Doves roost along the river and fly out to the uplands to feed before returning to the river to water. Doves also use the shoulders of FM 170 extensively to get gravel. Therefore, the best hunting spots in the early morning will be on high points between the river and the highway.

At other times of the day, game warden James Kitchens of Marfa advises hunters to base their choice of hunting locations on how the birds use the area. "In the morning, the flight pattern is generally scattered across the top. Coming off the roost, there is no flyway—the birds go everywhere. Most times on top, the birds fly too high for good shooting. Hunting is best when the birds are going back to the river in late morning and afternoon. Hunt in the draws, because the birds funnel through them to go to the river. When they get to a draw, the birds will just fold up and drop down into it." Mouths of draws where they empty into the river bottom are hotspots in late morning and evening.

There are a few Gambel's and scaled quail on the area, but numbers are too low to make a trip just for quail worthwhile.

TOP:
Canyons on the upland portion of the Ocotillo Unit feature walls arranged in layers like a giant cake.
ABOVE:
The slopes and bottoms of canyons and draws are good places to look for wildflowers following infrequent rains.

INSIDER'S CORNER

SALT CEDAR: FRIEND OR FOE?

Dr. Dale Rollins, wildlife extension specialist for the Texas Agricultural Extension Service in San Angelo, is famous for his reply to questions about whether some aspect of nature is good or bad: "It depends."

Dr. Rollins's statement is similar to the old saw, "It's an ill wind that blows no one good." Those statements might well have been developed with salt cedar (also called tamarisk) in mind.

Salt cedar is an exotic (nonnative) shrub or small tree commonly found in floodplains, riparian areas, wetlands, and lake margins in the western United States. It is an aggressive invader with a number of undesirable traits. It can replace or displace native woody species such as cottonwood, willow, and mesquite. It consumes large quantities of water. It can draw water from underground sources, but once it is established, it can survive without access to ground water. Tamarisk can tolerate saline soils, and it concentrates salts in its leaves. As fallen leaves accumulate, the soil can become highly saline and prevent growth of many native plant species.

Salt cedar is of concern to wildlife managers, because research has shown that species density and diversity generally are lower in salt cedar communities than in native riparian vegetation. Few insects are present in salt cedar thickets, and no native birds feed on the seeds. Is salt cedar then a foe of wildlife?

It depends.

Other studies have shown that some birds prefer to nest in the denser salt cedar than in more open stands of cottonwoods or mesquites. In riparian areas with few large native trees, salt cedar may actually increase the number of birds using the area. White-winged doves nest quite well in salt cedars, as do mourning doves. Since doves tend to fly out to agricultural areas or native seed-producing areas to feed, salt cedar appears to have an overall positive benefit on doves by providing an abundance of nesting habitat. In fact, researchers state that reduction of salt cedar would likely result in decreased numbers of white-winged doves. On the other hand, invading salt cedar can cause the extinction of narrowly distributed endangered species if it destroys their habitat.

Regardless of whether salt cedar is friend or foe, it is probably here to stay. Eradication by chemical or mechanical means is difficult and expensive. Salt cedar readily resprouts from underground buds when cut, burned, or sprayed with herbicides. It also produces abundant small seeds easily blown by the wind. Due to the fact that there are no members of the same family native to the Americas, biological control, such as the importation of an insect that preys on the tree, would seem to offer the most hope. So far this has not been done.

Salt cedar is a good illustration of the fact that there are few if any easy answers to environmental problems—and that most such problems are the result of human activities.

11,624 acres in four
noncontiguous tracts
HC 65, Box 80
Alpine, TX 79830
915/364-2228

DRIVING TIMES FROM:
Amarillo: 7 hours
Austin: 8 hours
Brownsville: 12.5 hours
Dallas: 9 hours
El Paso: 2 hours
Houston: 11 hours
San Antonio: 8 hours
DIRECTIONS: The WMA is located
in the Sierra Diablo Mountains
northwest of Van Horn.
OPEN: Restricted access.
ACTIVITIES: Hunting.
FACILITIES: Office complex, resi-
dence, bunkhouse, brood pens.
SPECIAL REGULATIONS: Visitors
must be accompanied by Texas
Parks and Wildlife personnel.
ADVISORIES: Topography is ex-
tremely rugged, and considerable
walking is required at altitudes up to
6,300 feet. Land access through
surrounding private property may
not be available. Carry your own
supply of potable water.
LODGING IN AREA: Motels are
available in Van Horn.
LOCAL POINTS OF INTEREST:
Balmorhea State Park, Davis Moun-
tains State Park, Magoffin Home
State Historical Park, Franklin
Mountains State Park, Hueco Tanks
State Park, Fort Davis National
Historic Site, Guadalupe Mountains
National Park.
DISABILITY ACCESS: Not wheel-
chair-accessible.

HISTORY

Sierra Diablo WMA holds the distinction of being the first wildlife
management area established in
Texas. The first land acquisitions
took place in 1945 (before then, most
of the area was public school land).
Additional parcels were acquired by
purchase and donation as late as the
1980s. Ironically, despite its long
history, Sierra Diablo remains one of
the least-known and least-visited of all
Texas WMAs.

Remote and rugged, this part of
West Texas was one of the last to be
made safe from Indian raids. Driven
from more hospitable territory,
Apaches under Chief Victorio ranged
from the Guadalupe Mountains into
Mexico for 10 years, using the Sierra
Diablo and other mountain ranges in
the area for refuge. Victorio was killed
in Mexico in 1880; surviving remnants of the tribe fought Texas Rangers in the last significant battle with
Indians in Texas in Bass Canyon in
the Sierra Diablo Mountains the
following year.

European settlement was delayed
until after a transcontinental railroad
was completed through the area in
the early 1880s. Even then growth
was slow, and ranching remained the
chief activity, with hunting for mule
deer and desert bighorn sheep a
sideline.

The story of desert bighorn sheep
in Texas is both a sorry statement on
attitudes toward native wildlife a
century ago and a shining example of
how far these attitudes have advanced
since. Members of the sheep and goat
family, desert bighorn sheep are
descended from the wild sheep of
central Asia; ancestors of the North
American sheep are believed to have
crossed the Bering Strait when low
Ice Age sea levels created a land
bridge. Pictographs indicate that the
sheep were harvested by Native
Americans for thousands of years.

By the 1880s an estimated 1,500
sheep remained in Texas. This
population was hunted for food by
railroad builders, miners, and ranchers. Market hunting was banned in
1903, but by then the sheep were
already in serious trouble. The
introduction of domestic sheep into
desert bighorn range brought competition for food, disease, and net wire
fences that prevented migration to
sources of food and water. Bighorn
sheep numbers declined rapidly.
Some of the few remaining small
bands were ruthlessly slaughtered by
those who chanced upon them. On
one particularly infamous day, a
single individual killed most of the
sheep in a herd and left the carcasses
to rot.

Such abuses finally led the Texas
Legislature to establish the Sierra
Diablo Wildlife Management Area as
a sanctuary for the few sheep left in
1945. Without any attempt at management, however, the population
continued to decline, and by 1960
the last native Texas bighorn sheep
was gone.

Efforts at propagating desert
bighorn sheep for restocking began at
Black Gap WMA in the late 1950s
using sheep transplanted from other
states. In 1970, an eight-acre pen was
built on Sierra Diablo WMA and
stocked with sheep from Black Gap.
By 1979, 14 sheep had been released
from the pen into the Sierra Diablo
Mountains. In June 1983 the Texas
Bighorn Society, a private group
dedicated to the return of bighorn
sheep to Texas, built a brood facility
on Sierra Diablo WMA and donated
it to Texas Parks and Wildlife. Sierra
Diablo became for a time the chief
brood facility. By 1992, 48 rams and
16 ewes had been released into the
surrounding mountains. However,
persistent disease problems and low
production of female lambs due to
stress led to the program being shut
down in 1997. The remaining 46
sheep were released from the pens. In
1999 an estimated 300 sheep roamed
the Sierra Diablo, Beach, and Baylor
Mountains.

Extremely limited hunting has been permitted on Sierra Diablo WMA. Mule deer hunting was permitted from 1983 to 1989. Desert bighorn sheep hunts began in 1987. The first ram was taken in 1990. At present a limited number of permits are issued each year for hunts on private land surrounding the WMA, and future plans include drawings for guided sheep hunts on the area.

GEOGRAPHY AND NATURAL FEATURES

The Sierra Diablo Mountains lie west of Texas 54 north of Van Horn. TPW owns a strip of land along the tops of the mountains but does not own the lower slopes nor any deeded access to the WMA. The topography is extremely rugged; as area manager Clay Brewer puts it, "Everything is straight up." He estimates that Texas Parks and Wildlife owns about 90 percent of the best sheep habitat.

The WMA lies within the Chihuahuan Desert. Elevation in the mountains reaches a maximum of about 6,300 feet, some 2,000 feet higher than the surrounding desert. Much of the acreage is located above the rimrock level, which consists of vertical bluffs some 200 feet high. Natural water consists only of potholes in the limestone rock, which catch infrequent rainfall. Artificial water sources have been constructed on the area.

Vegetation at lower levels is the sotol-lechuguilla association common to the Chihuahuan Desert. Yuccas and junipers dominate at mid-level elevations, with pinyon pines, junipers, and oaks on higher ridges. Grasses include gramas, bluestems, and a variety of others.

Other than bighorn sheep, wildlife on the area includes mule deer, javelinas, bobcats, coyotes, mountain lions, rabbits, gophers, scaled quail, and white-winged doves. Golden eagles and red-tailed hawks are present in winter.

RECREATIONAL OPPORTUNITIES

One of the characteristics of bighorn sheep is extreme sensitivity to human disturbance; they will leave an area if pressured. Since Sierra Diablo is set aside first and foremost for the sheep, human intrusion is kept to a minimum. Therefore, only a fortunate few will get to visit this WMA. For the foreseeable future, limited hunting

Because desert bighorn sheep will leave an area at the first hint of human pressure, Sierra Diablo has restricted access. Visitors must be accompanied by TPW personnel.

and special events will be the only activities allowed.

HUNTING

However, a huntable population of surplus rams exists on the area, and some form of Special Permit hunt will be instituted on the area when conditions permit. The information on hunting below will be of interest to those lucky enough to be chosen to hunt and to hunters on private land as well as anyone interested in desert bighorn sheep. For the current status of the area, call the area manager at the number above.

While desert bighorn sheep are thought of primarily as mountain dwellers, this is more a reaction to human pressure than a natural preference. The 200 or so sheep in the Van Horn area migrate across the desert floor and move among the Beach, Baylor, and Sierra Diablo Mountains.

Once each year Texas Parks and Wildlife biologists fly over the area and issue hunting permits based on the number of harvestable rams they see, but never for more than 10

percent of the total ram population in the Baylor, Beach and Diablo mountains. "On Sierra Diablo, I plan to issue as many permits as I can," says Brewer. "That may be anywhere from zero on up. It's important that we not harvest all the mature rams, because they educate the younger animals. There are historic travel routes they use, and the older rams teach these to the younger ones."

Ranchers on whose land harvestable rams are spotted during the aerial survey may also receive hunting permits. A harvestable ram is defined as a class IV ram that is at the upper end of the category or is an older, mature ram that will never achieve trophy status. "Chances are using these criteria will increase the number of permits we will issue and provide more hunting opportunities," says Brewer.

A class IV ram has horns that form a three-quarter curl or better, with heavy mass at the bases that carries out all the way to the end. "Often horns will be broomed off from rubbing them on the ground,"

says Brewer. "It may be necessary for maintaining unobstructed vision or for foraging purposes. Others have horns that flare out. They cannot swim, because their heads are so heavy they would sink like a rock."

Hunters on Sierra Diablo may be rewarded with more than a trophy ram. They will walk in the footsteps of Burch Carson, a taxidermist who was hired in the 1940s by Texas Parks and Wildlife's predecessor to observe sheep in the Sierra Diablos. "He sat and watched sheep for hours, and while he was waiting, he carved his initials into the rock," says Brewer. "You'll find them all over the mountains."

Brewer advises anyone chosen to hunt sheep on Sierra Diablo to start a conditioning program well in advance of hunting season. It takes half a day just to hike into good sheep country from the headquarters, and once in sheep habitat most of the terrain is nearly vertical. After the day's hunt, there's the hike back out in the dark. Anyone who takes a desert bighorn sheep earns it.

DESERT BIGHORNS:
SO HARDY, YET SO FRAGILE

There are four kinds of wild sheep in North America: Dall's, Stone's, Rocky Mountain and desert bighorn. Now confined to only 4 percent of their historic range, desert bighorns in North America now number about 25,000, with Arizona having the largest population. The historic range of desert bighorn sheep in Texas was in the mountains west of the Pecos River. They arrived there perhaps 10,000 years ago.

Adult males weigh between 160 and 200 pounds, with the skull and horns alone weighing as much as 45 pounds. Adult females weigh from 75 to 130 pounds. Bighorns are gray or amber-colored with a white muzzle, eye rings, back, rump patch, and rear legs. Their tail is black.

The horn sheaths originate in the skin and grow over bony cores. The horns are not shed. Each year an annual ring is formed during the rut, with the largest ring forming during the fourth year, when rams achieve breeding age. Brooming, or wearing and breakage of the tips of the horns, occurs during fights or while feeding. The size of the horns determines social dominance. Life expectancy is 12 to 14 years.

A number of adaptations suit bighorns for living in rugged, arid habitat. The outer edges of their feet are hard and sharp, while the inner, protruding portions are spongy to provide traction on slick rocks. Bighorns can go up to six months without drinking. However, they normally water every two to three days, and when doing so drink quite rapidly, downing about two and a half gallons a minute.

Bighorn sheep have sweat glands but sweat very little. They can withstand loss of up to 30 percent of their body weight through dehydration, more than a camel can endure, and their body temperature can reach 107 degrees. Their eyesight is approximately eight times as good as that of humans; they can see a person from a mile and a half away. They can run at 30 miles per hour over terrain people cannot walk on.

It would seem that such rugged animals would be able to survive anywhere, but bighorns have very little resistance to disease and parasites. They are very susceptible to diseases carried by exotics, domestic sheep, and goats. Any bighorn herd that has ever come in contact with significant numbers of either has suffered heavy mortality.

Ironically, these animals that were nearly wiped out by people and contact with domestic livestock now cannot survive without human assistance. The leader in this preservation effort is the Texas Bighorn Society, in partnership with Texas Parks and Wildlife.

In the early 1980s the Texas Legislature reduced funding for desert bighorn sheep restoration, leading a group of concerned Texans to become involved in securing funding for projects. The ultimate result was the Texas Bighorn Society. The society succeeded in getting renewed funding for sheep restoration, raised $250,000 to build the brood pens at Sierra Diablo, and turned the completed facility over to Texas Parks and Wildlife to operate. C. G. Johnson, a member of the Texas Bighorn Society, donated Elephant Mountain WMA to the department to be used primarily for desert bighorn sheep restoration.

In addition to its work at Sierra Diablo, the Texas Bighorn Society has raised funds and obtained donated materials and services to build watering facilities at Elephant Mountain, Black Gap, Sierra Diablo and on private ranches in sheep range. It also paid for the transplanting of numerous sheep from other states to Texas. Each year the society donates money to the bighorn sheep program. It has also donated endowments to each of the three WMAs with desert bighorn sheep.

Members of the society receive no privileges for their efforts. They have to compete for permits with everyone else. To learn more about the Texas Bighorn Society and its work, contact Ace High, Secretary, at 203 Post Oak Way, Cuero, TX 77954. Or visit Wildgoose Manufacturing at 402 Highway 27 East, Ingram, TX 78025, 830/367-5553. Wildgoose is the unofficial headquarters of the society and has displays related to desert bighorn sheep.

GULF COAST

GULF COAST

*We abuse land because we regard
it as a commodity belonging to us.
When we see land as a community
to which we belong, we may begin
to use it with love and respect.*
—ALDO LEOPOLD

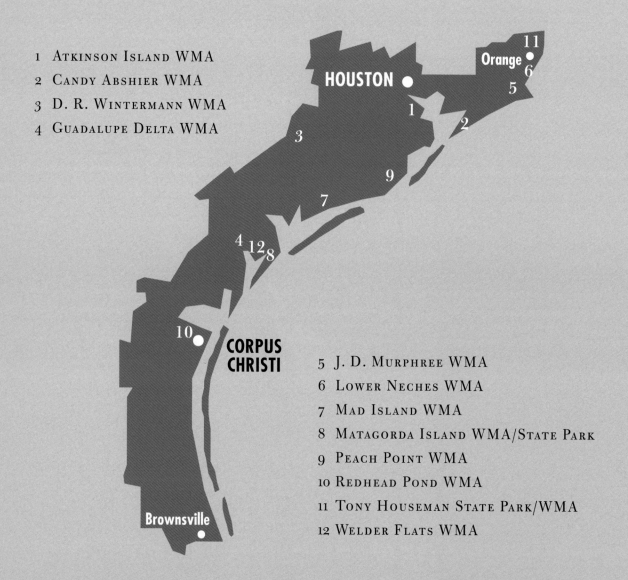

1 ATKINSON ISLAND WMA
2 CANDY ABSHIER WMA
3 D. R. WINTERMANN WMA
4 GUADALUPE DELTA WMA

5 J. D. MURPHREE WMA
6 LOWER NECHES WMA
7 MAD ISLAND WMA
8 MATAGORDA ISLAND WMA/STATE PARK
9 PEACH POINT WMA
10 REDHEAD POND WMA
11 TONY HOUSEMAN STATE PARK/WMA
12 WELDER FLATS WMA

ATKINSON ISLAND WMA

152 acres
10 Parks and Wildlife Dr.
Port Arthur, TX 77640
409/736-2551

DRIVING TIMES FROM:
Amarillo: 11 hours
Austin: 3 hours
Brownsville: 6.5 hours
Dallas: 4.5 hours
El Paso: 13 hours
Houston: 0.5 hours
San Antonio: 3.5 hours
DIRECTIONS: Accessible by boat
only. Launch at the public boat
ramp at Bayland Park in Baytown,
on Texas 146, and run southeast
past Hogg Island about 3 miles to a
dock on the east side of Atkinson
Island.
OPEN: Daily. For use of the area,
contact the area manager at the
number above.
ACTIVITIES: Wildlife viewing.
FACILITIES: Boat dock.
ADVISORIES: Mosquitoes can be
present any time of year. Heat and
humidity can make visiting the area
unpleasant from April through
October. A boat is necessary for
access.
LODGING IN AREA: Motels are
available in the Houston area.
LOCAL POINTS OF INTEREST: Lake
Houston State Park, San Jacinto
Battleground and Monument State
Historical Park, Battleship *Texas*
State Historical Park, Brazos Bend
State Park, Galveston Island State
Park, Varner-Hogg Plantation State
Historical Park, Stephen F. Austin
State Historical Park, Anahuac
National Wildlife Refuge, Big
Thicket National Preserve, Brazoria
National Wildlife Refuge, Sam
Houston National Forest.
DISABILITY ACCESS: Not
wheelchair-accessible.

Atkinson Island (background) is accessible only by boat. The Houston Ship Channel separates it from the mainland.

HISTORY

One of the most persistent myths of Texas history is associated with this unlikely spot, a narrow island running alongside the Houston Ship Channel east of La Porte. Just to the west, on Morgan's Point, lived Emily West (often erroneously called Emily Morgan), a black woman whose capture by Mexican troops just prior to the Battle of San Jacinto gave rise to the legend of the Yellow Rose of Texas. Concocted by 20th-century journalists, this story attributed Santa Anna's defeat at San Jacinto to his being preoccupied with a pretty captive at the time of Houston's attack.

At the time of these events, the land we know as Atkinson Island was attached to the mainland and was part of the acreage owned by the New Washington Association. The island was created in 1876, when the first serious effort to create a ship channel linking Houston to Galveston Bay sliced off the tip of Morgan's Point.

In years since, the ship channel has been deepened and widened to the point that some 400 meters now separate the island from the mainland.

The southern portion of the island that forms Atkinson Island WMA was donated to Texas Parks and Wildlife in 1990 by Conoco. Only the 152 acres of the island in Harris County are owned by Parks and Wildlife.

GEOGRAPHY AND NATURAL FEATURES

The island today contains a 20-acre, compartmentalized spoil area where dredged material from the ship channel was dumped. The spoil impoundment is just west of the Texas Parks and Wildlife boat dock, which is on the east side of the island about midway down its length. An approximately 40-acre woodlot composed mainly of hackberry and yaupon is on the southwest end of the island. About 90 acres are brackish marsh. A sandy beach is on the west side of the island.

The setting could hardly be less inviting. The busy Houston Ship Channel handles approximately 5,000 ships annually, and wave-wash erosion is a major problem. The surrounding area is heavily industrialized.

RECREATIONAL OPPORTUNITIES

Incidental use by waterskiiers and jetski users of the sandy beach on the west side is about the only activity on the island. Fishers sometimes wade the flats on the east side seeking redfish and speckled trout. However, such disturbance may have caused waterbirds that once nested on the island to move elsewhere.

WILDLIFE VIEWING

There are no facilities on the island other than a small Texas Parks and Wildlife boat dock on the east side. The spoil site holds some rainfall, and the fresh water attracts some birds, making this a possible birding site. The marsh area is used by a variety of waterbirds, waterfowl, and rails. In spring and fall, migrating raptors and neotropical passerines use the island, and September brings large numbers of hummingbirds.

PRO'S POINTERS. Boat ramps are located on Morgan's Point and at Bayland Park, on Texas 146 in Baytown.

THE LEGEND OF THE YELLOW ROSE

Most myths contain at least a grain of truth, and this one is no exception. Emily West came to the area in 1835 under contract with James Morgan to work as a housekeeper at the New Washington Association's hotel at Morgan's Point. The point of land lay where the San Jacinto River emptied into Galveston Bay and was named for James Morgan, founder of New Washington and agent for a company formed to promote Texas real estate. Morgan bought land for the company and ran a store at New Washington.

During the Texas Revolution in 1836, ad interim president of the Republic of Texas David G. Burnet fled to New Washington ahead of the Mexican army, which was advancing across Texas after the fall of the Alamo. As Mexican cavalry troops swept into New Washington on April 16, 1836, Burnet escaped by boat. Santa Anna arrived the next day with the remainder of the army and spent the next three days resting and looting Morgan's warehouses. Then, taking Emily West with him, Santa Anna departed in pursuit of Sam Houston's army camped 10 miles away at Lynch's Ferry, a site known today as the San Jacinto Battleground and Monument State Historical Park.

According to *The New Handbook of Texas,* no reliable documentary evidence exists for the story that West knew of Houston's plan for a surprise attack on the afternoon of April 21 and arranged to keep Santa Anna distracted. The story appears to fall into the category of those too good not to be true.

208.77 acres
10 Parks and Wildlife Dr.
Port Arthur, TX 77640
409/736-2551

DRIVING TIMES FROM:
Amarillo: 11.5 hours
Austin: 4.5 hours
Brownsville: 8 hours
Dallas: 5 hours
El Paso: 14.5 hours
Houston: 1.5 hours
San Antonio: 5 hours

DIRECTIONS: From Houston, take I-10 east to Hankamer, then take Texas 61 south 4 miles to its intersection with FM 562. Follow FM 562 south 22 miles to the village of Smith Point, where state maintenance ends. Continue another 0.8 miles to a set of oil tanks on your left. Turn left onto Abshier Road and park near the observation tower.

OPEN: Daily.

ACTIVITIES: Wildlife viewing.

FACILITIES: Wildlife-viewing tower. A public restroom is located 1.5 miles west at a public boat ramp at the end of Hawkins Camp Rd.

ADVISORIES: Mosquitoes can be present any time of year; bring plenty of insect repellent. Heat and humidity can make visiting the area unpleasant from April through October. Carry your own supply of potable water.

LODGING IN AREA: Motels are available in Anahuac.

LOCAL POINTS OF INTEREST: Sabine Pass Battleground State Historical Park, Sea Rim State Park, Village Creek State Park, Texas Point National Wildlife Refuge, McFaddin National Wildlife Refuge, Anahuac National Wildlife Refuge, Big Thicket National Preserve.

DISABILITY ACCESS: The wildlife-viewing platform is wheelchair-accessible. However, it is a long, steep climb to the top.

A mixture of beach, prairie, woodland and wetland habitats supports a variety of plants and animals at Candy Abshier WMA.

HISTORY

Ironically, one of the smallest of Texas' WMAs has one of the most fascinating histories. Events connected with it resulted in the election of David G. Burnet as the ad interim president of the Republic of Texas.

Somewhere on the area is believed to be the homesite of John Moses Smith, for whom the point of land and small settlement nearby are named. Smith's plantation, established in the 1830s, was the site of a murder in October 1835. Smith's son killed his brother-in-law, and John Smith was tried as an accessory and convicted along with his son. Smith's wife hired attorney David G. Burnet to appeal the convictions, and the following spring the two rode to Washington-on-the-Brazos, where the Convention of 1836—the Texas Revolution being then in progress—was meeting. Burnet obtained a 30-day stay of execution for his clients and a surprise for himself. Reluctant to elect one of their own number, the delegates to the convention chose Burnet as temporary president of the new republic.

Using his new powers of clemency and pardon, Burnet had the Smiths transferred to Harrisburg. As Mexican armies advanced into Texas and residents fled in the Runaway Scrape, John Smith escaped in the confusion and went to Louisiana, never to return. His son joined the Texas Army, served at the Battle of San Jacinto, and was pardoned by the new president, Sam Houston.

In the 20th century the land was used for grazing, oil production, and real-estate development. In 1989 the Abshier WMA became the first land to be acquired by Texas Parks and Wildlife using the Nongame Special 506 Fund. It was named for Catherine ("Candy") Cain Abshier, a deceased Texas Parks and Wildlife employee who advocated wetland preservation, recycling, and preservation of historic sites.

GEOGRAPHY AND NATURAL FEATURES

Smith Point, while not unique, is one of the few publicly owned places of its type along the Texas coast, and this makes it a highly significant site for birders. The funnel-shaped point tapers from approximately 20 miles wide to a few hundred yards as it approaches Trinity and Galveston

Bays, which it divides. East Bay borders the area on the south. Birds migrating south in the fall concentrate as they approach the water. Thermals generated over the land are utilized by a variety of hawks, which pass over the area in numbers that can exceed 2,500 per day in peak periods. In spring, Smith Point is a fallout area for birds ending a long flight across the Gulf of Mexico.

Combined with its location, the WMA's vegetation makes it particularly important for migrating birds. While the bulk of the area is coastal prairie dotted with small ponds, about 60 acres are covered in live oak mottes, which are heavily used by migrating birds. In addition, the area fronts on a bay, offering opportunities to see coastal species.

RECREATIONAL OPPORTUNITIES

The Abshier WMA is one of the premier birding spots in Texas. It is a jumping-off point for birds migrating south across the Gulf of Mexico and a first landfall for birds heading north.

WILDLIFE VIEWING

Through the efforts of Texas Parks and Wildlife and the Gulf Coast Bird Observatory, with funding by the National Fish and Wildlife Foundation, Entergy/GSU, and The Ornithology Group, a hawk watch tower provides an elevated platform overlooking the WMA and the bay. The project is supported by Exxon Baytown, Hawkwatch International, the Ornithology Group of the Houston Outdoor Nature Club, and Gulf Coast Bird Observatory Friends. A parking lot is at the foot of the tower.

An annual hawk watch begins each August 15 and continues until

The hawk-watch tower (background) is used to conduct hawk counts during the fall migration; as many as 400 hawks an hour may pass over.

November 15. During that period of time, someone representing one of the supporting organizations will be present during daytime most days. Observers report seeing an average of over 400 raptors per hour. The count here is one of four recognized by the Hawk Migration Association of North America.

Species sighted on the area include Mississippi kites, sharp-shinned hawks, swallow-tailed kites, American and peregrine falcons, brown pelicans, terns, frigatebirds, anhingas, and wood storks.

Other birds migrate through the area as well during spring and fall.

Mowed paths through the live oak mottes and across the prairie allow closeup views of warblers, many kinds of sparrows, buntings, hummingbirds, blue-gray gnatcatchers, and other species. Walking the paths through the majestic live oaks is like entering a cathedral. Sturdy trunks seem to support not only the overarching branches but also the sky itself, like the mighty ribs of some ancient church. Sprinkled among the branches one may see neotropical birds as colorful as the finest stained-glass window.

PRO'S POINTERS. If planning travel to the area, key on cold fronts. The passage of a cold front in fall can bring large numbers of kettles of hawks over the area. Sharp-shinned hawks tend to be sighted early in the day, but large kettles of broad-winged hawks generally form after midmorning, when thermals begin to rise over the land. In spring, birds returning north may "fall out" in the trees after fighting a headwind across the Gulf of Mexico. Birding is generally slow in the afternoon.

INSIDER'S CORNER

NEOTROPICALS IN TROUBLE

One of the most fascinating sagas of birding involves the story of how the quality of birding in Texas came to be recognized. Connie Hagar, an amateur birder living in Rockport, began reporting sightings of birds the "experts" said did not exist in Texas. Hagar invited them to come see for themselves, and millions of birders have followed in their footsteps, binoculars at the ready.

Points of land such as the one where Candy Abshier WMA is located hold a special place in the birding world, because they tend to concentrate birds heading south in the fall and north in the spring. Many of these birds are called neotropicals because they migrate between their breeding grounds in North America and the tropics of the New World—the "neotropics."

There is nothing new about this migration—it has been going on for thousands of years. Whether it will continue for another thousand years is in question. Bird populations in the United States have been declining since at least the 1960s. Bird counts and examinations of radar records of migration flights indicate that the number of birds today may be half what it was just 40 years ago.

Declining numbers of neotropicals—which includes both songbirds and birds of prey—seem to be linked primarily to loss of habitat on both ends of the migration route. These migratory birds tend to return to nest in the area where they were brooded. Increasingly, birds returning in the spring find their natal sites occupied not by trees but by buildings or farm fields or reservoirs. What habitat is left is often in small, fragmented blocks, which makes nesting birds more vulnerable to predators and to nest parisitism by brown-headed cowbirds. The news is even worse when birds go south for the winter. Tropical forests are being cut at a rate that will lead to their total disappearance in the first half of the 21st century. Pesticides banned in the United States continue to kill birds in countries to the south.

No one knows if neotropicals can be saved, averting the silent spring prophesied by Rachel Carson, but an effort is being made through an international program called Partners in Flight. This program involves national and state governments, private organizations and the public. In Texas, where 97 percent of the land is privately owned, involvement of private landowners is vital if the program is to succeed. Texas Partners in Flight, the local link to the program, sponsors workshops and publishes a newsletter, *Flyway*. You can get involved by calling 512/389-4403. Information on the program is available on the Texas Parks and Wildlife website at www.tpwd.state.tx.us/nature/birding/pif/txpif.htm. The site includes guidelines for carrying out your own backyard habitat conservation projects, which can involve steps as simple as keeping your cat indoors or as intensive as growing native plants used by migrating birds for food or cover.

246 acres
1120 Hodges Lane, Room 105
Wharton, TX 77488
409/532-2170

DRIVING TIMES FROM:
Amarillo: 11 hours
Austin: 2.5 hours
Brownsville: 5.5 hours
Dallas: 5 hours
El Paso: 12.5 hours
Houston: 1 hour
San Antonio: 3 hours
DIRECTIONS: The area is located
about 15 miles northwest of
Wharton. Access is restricted.
Contact the area manager.
OPEN: Only to organized groups on
specified dates when Texas Parks
and Wildlife personnel are present.
ACTIVITIES: Wildlife viewing and
outdoor education.
FACILITIES: None.
ADVISORIES: Mosquitoes and
poisonous snakes can be present any
time of year. Heat and humidity can
make visiting the area unpleasant
from April through October. Carry
your own supply of potable water.
LODGING IN AREA: Motels are
available in Wharton.
LOCAL POINTS OF INTEREST:
Brazos Bend State Park, Varner-Hogg
Plantation State Historical Park,
Stephen F. Austin State Park, Lake
Texana State Park, Attwater Prairie
Chicken National Wildlife Refuge.
DISABILITY ACCESS: Not
wheelchair-accessible.

HISTORY

The vicinity of the Wintermann
WMA was within the historic range
of the Karankawa Indians. Numerous
European explorers passed through
the region, and 31 of Stephen F.
Austin's Old Three Hundred received
land grants in Wharton County. The
community of Egypt, about 5 miles
southwest of the area, was an important settlement during the Republic
of Texas.

The rich soil allowed the development of the plantation system of
agriculture, with sugarcane and cotton
being the principal crops. Farming
declined after the Civil War, and cattle
raising became the main industry.
Shortly after 1900, Japanese farmers
were brought to Texas to advise local
farmers on rice farming, which was
being practiced on a small scale.
Improvements in irrigation and higher
yields from seed imported from Japan
made rice production boom, and
Wharton County became a state
leader in rice yields.

The Wintermann family came into
possession of the land in 1922, and
they used it for rice farming and cattle
raising. An experiment in soybean
farming failed. Because of drainage
problems, the field was allowed to lie
fallow after 1991. In 1995 David R.
Wintermann, through Ducks Unlimited and the Wetlands America Trust,
conveyed the land to Texas Parks and
Wildlife.

GEOGRAPHY AND NATURAL FEATURES

The area is part of the flat coastal
prairie, which stretches for miles in all
directions. It is unusual in that it
contains a number of small natural
depressions, eight of which have been
deepened and connected by ditches.
Water purchased from the Lower
Colorado River Authority courses
through a series of water-control
structures, allowing seasonal flooding
and drawdown. Water is delivered to
the area from an LCRA canal at the
northeast corner of the property and
exits into a ditch along the southern
boundary.

Wetlands cover about 37 acres of
the total, with most of the balance
being fallow rice fields. Vegetation in
the wetlands includes smartweed,
spike rush, paspalum, and duck
potato. Sedges and marsh elder cover
the higher ground, and wet prairie
areas support bluestem, switchgrass,
and Indian grass.

Abundant food and water within
and around the area attract large
numbers of waterfowl in winter. Bald
eagles, sandhill cranes, curlews, white

LEFT:
*Managed flooding and deflooding of wetlands
produce waterfowl food such as duck potato,
whose roots are a favored food of many ducks.*
ABOVE:
*Levees and channels direct water flow through
the D.R. Wintermann WMA, providing food and
shelter for large numbers of waterfowl in winter.*

ibis, white-faced ibis, glossy ibis, pied-billed grebes, pintails, blue-winged teal, green-winged teal, shovelers, snow geese, Ross' geese, Canada geese, and white-fronted geese all use the area, as do neotropical migrants. Nesting species include mottled ducks, fulvous, and black-bellied whistling ducks.

RECREATIONAL ACTIVITIES

Use of the area is limited by deed restrictions and lack of access. Reaching the area requires traveling several miles of private road across private property; therefore, all visitors must be guided to the site by Texas Parks and Wildlife personnel.

The Wintermann WMA serves primarily as an outdoor laboratory for school groups. Students can take part in preparing checklists of plant and animal species, monitoring water quality, carrying out habitat improvement projects and learning about wetlands management.

The Wintermann area is also used as a demonstration area for private landowners. "A lot of my responsibility is working with private landowners to do private lands development," says area manager David Lobpries. "I use the Wintermann WMA as a demonstration area to show people how to manage wetlands, working either one-on-one or holding field days for groups."

PRO'S POINTERS. Teachers or other individuals or groups interested in using the area should contact David Lobpries at the number above.

HUNTING

Youth-only hunts are held during the teal season and on the special youth-only hunt day in October. Blinds and guides are provided.

PRO'S POINTERS. Check the *Public Hunting Lands Map Booklet* for the current year. Reservations for the hunt must be made by calling the number given during the specified time period.

INSIDER'S CORNER

RICE IS NICE—FOR NOW

The importance of rice farming to Texas waterfowl hunters can scarcely be overstated. Waste grain in harvested fields forms a major food source for the millions of geese that winter along the Texas coast. Goose hunting usually centers around these fields. Leasing land for hunting and guiding hunters are important sources of income for Texas rice farmers.

Texas rice farming began as a subsistence activity during the early 1880s. Farmers plowed small fields with oxen, planted seed by hand, and—if there was sufficient rainfall—harvested the crop with sickles for threshing by hand and milling with mortar and pestle.

Rice farming remained on a small scale until the 1890s, when Joseph Broussard of Beaumont built a canal system for irrigating rice and converted a gristmill to a rice mill. Cheap coastal land and a flood of immigrants helped fuel an explosion in rice growing, and by 1903 Texas farmers worked 234,000 acres of rice fields.

That same year the Houston Chamber of Commerce and the Southern Pacific Railroad invited Seito Saibara, a Japanese agriculturalist, to come to Texas to teach rice production to local farmers. Saibara brought his family and 30 others to Texas and founded a Japanese colony at Webster, where they farmed 1,000 acres of rice. The first crop sprang from seed sent as a gift by the emperor of Japan. This crop was distributed as seed in Texas and Louisiana, and farmers using the improved variety saw average yields jump from 20 barrels an acre to 34 barrels.

The peak year for acreage planted to rice was 1954, when 654,000 acres in Texas produced rice. Since that time the acreage planted to rice has fallen almost one-half as farmers have taken land out of production in response to federal programs paying them not to farm, sold water rights to cities, and sold farmland to developers.

"The big impact of those programs initially was east of Houston," says David Lobpries. "However, the decline in rice production has slowly been moving west. If we lose much more rice production, we will lose a lot of the infrastructure—seed companies, equipment companies, the water-delivery system. If we lose the water-delivery system, we will lose the waterfowl."

The long-range implications for Texas waterfowl and waterfowl hunters are serious. Arkansas now farms more rice than Texas does, and geese have been expanding into that area. Even though snow goose numbers have increased dramatically over the last few decades, the population wintering in Texas has remained fairly constant. More and more geese are wintering in Arkansas. "If we want to maintain the good waterfowl hunting in Texas, we must do a better job of planning for the future," Lobpries warns.

Waterfowl are recognized as a valuable resource, but their presence thus far has been principally a gratuitous benefit of rice farming. Whether Texans will value waterfowl enough to provide the needed habitat should the rice industry no longer do so remains a hard question.

6,594 acres in three tracts
County Courthouse, Room 101
Bay City, TX 77414
409/244-7697

DRIVING TIMES FROM:
Amarillo: 11 hours
Austin: 3 hours
Brownsville: 3.5 hours
Dallas: 6 hours
El Paso: 14 hours
Houston: 2.5 hours
San Antonio: 2.5 hours

DIRECTIONS: Mission Lake Unit— From Victoria, take Texas 185 south 22 miles to Texas 35; take Texas 35 south 1.3 miles to the area headquarters. Guadalupe River Unit— From the area headquarters, take Texas 35 south 4 miles to River Rd.; turn left and go 1.4 miles to the entrance. Hynes Bay Unit—From the area headquarters, take Texas 35 south 7 miles (through Tivoli) to Barber Rd., turn left, and go 1.8 miles to a sharp right curve; at the beginning of the curve, drive straight ahead to the entrance.

OPEN: Mission Lake Unit—Open only to hunters on designated days. Open to organized groups for tours on a special request basis. Open every day for bank fishing at sites on bayous and rivers accessible by boat. An observation platform on the Texas 35 right-of-way a mile south of area headquarters overlooking Buffalo Lake is open daily. Guadalupe River and Hynes Bay Units—Entire area closed every day from midnight to 4 A.M. Portions open only to hunters on designated days. Open every day for fishing and nonconsumptive use in zone C of the Guadalupe River Unit (see below). Open to organized groups for tours on a special request basis.

ACTIVITIES: Wildlife viewing, hiking, bicycling, hunting, fishing.

FACILITIES: Hunter check station, numbered hunting sites, observation platform.

SPECIAL REGULATIONS: All hunters must check in and out. Permits for waterfowl hunts are issued at the check station beginning two hours before legal shooting time and continuing until 30 minutes before shooting time. Bank fishers must have an Annual Public Hunting Permit. Nonconsumptive users in zone C of the Guadalupe River Unit (the area between River Road and the Guadalupe River) are not required to have a permit. Hunting is not allowed in zone C of the Guadalupe River Unit. Waterfowl hunters on the Guadalupe River and Hynes Bay Units must park in the designated numbered parking space for the numbered hunting site used.

ADVISORIES: Waterfowl hunters should bring waders, insect repellent, and a good flashlight. The area is unpleasantly hot and humid in the summer. Carry your own supply of potable water.

LODGING IN AREA: Motels are available in Victoria and Port Lavaca.

LOCAL POINTS OF INTEREST: Lake Texana State Park, Fannin Battleground State Historical Park, Goliad State Historical Park, Copano Bay State Fishing Pier, Port Lavaca Fishing Pier, Fulton Mansion State Park, Goose Island State Park, Matagorda Island State Park, Aransas National Wildlife Refuge.

DISABILITY ACCESS: A Texas Department of Transportation viewing platform on Texas 35 adjacent to the area is wheelchair-accessible.

HISTORY

Karankawa Indians were the first known inhabitants of this area; evidence of campsites remains. Due to periodic flooding of the area, farming was limited to upland areas. Most historic land use seems to have been for livestock grazing and waterfowl hunting.

In 1977 the U.S. Fish and Wildlife Service and Texas Parks and Wildlife identified wetlands in the Guadalupe delta as being of high priority for acquisition to preserve wildlife habitat. State waterfowl stamp funds were used to purchase land beginning in 1985 and continuing until 1994.

GEOGRAPHY AND NATURAL FEATURES

The delta of the Guadalupe River dominates this WMA. Fifteen miles long, 7 miles wide, and growing seaward at the rate of 40 feet per year, the delta is a richly diverse environment of freshwater lakes, brackish lakes, saline marshes, and riparian woodlands. Elevation is generally four feet or less above sea level, and what land is above water is subject to Gulf storm surges as well as flooding from the river. The flood of October 1998 did considerable damage to roadways on the area and left water standing in normally dry areas for months afterward, creating a bonanza of food and water for wintering waterfowl. Ducks far outnumber geese, as the area is a bit too far from rice-growing areas to lure many geese.

Narrow strips of riparian habitat along the river and numerous bayous attract many neotropical birds. Pecan, black willow, cedar, elm, hackberry, mesquite, and huisache are common. A surprise is large cypress trees along the Guadalupe—a sight more often associated with the Texas Hill Country.

Human activities have considerably altered drainage patterns on the WMA. The Victoria Barge Canal forms the eastern boundary of the

The narrow strip of riparian habitat along the Guadalupe River forms a shaded bower for fishers and birders.

Mission Lake Unit; saltwater intrusion barriers on Hog Bayou and Goff Bayou and the volume of flow from the Guadalupe River help keep salinity levels in the marshes and bays among the lowest on the Texas coast. A siphon system carries Goff Bayou's waters under the Victoria Barge Canal to supply Port Lavaca and area industries. Two large industrial plants just across the canal from the Mission Lake Unit are the most visible features on the landscape; their lights and flares brightly illuminate the night sky.

On the Guadalupe River Unit, levees protected the land for farming in the past, but these levees have now been breached in numerous places. River Road, the county road into the area, runs parallel to the river and just

yards from it, making it subject to flooding. A narrow band of old farm fields slowly growing up in brush borders the road. Virtually the entire area away from the river in the Guadalupe River Unit consists of marshes and small lakes. The Hynes Bay Unit enjoys the most variety in topography. It rises from marshes to a bluff perhaps 20 feet high and then levels off into an upland historically used for farming but now being invaded by huisache. The change in vegetation from trees and brush to grassy marshes when one drops off the bluff is striking.

Recreational Opportunities
Mission Lake Unit

Wildlife Viewing

The Mission Lake Unit offers guided tours to organized groups on request. Conservation scientist Brent Ortego guides the tours and will tailor them

to the group's interest, whether it be birds, wildflowers, or plants. Birding tours start at daybreak in the marsh area, where Ortego calls to rails. A variety of waterfowl can be observed flying inland from roosts on the marsh. Hog Bayou has a scenic woodland good for songbirds. Buffalo Marsh offers views of water birds and grassland birds. After lunch, the tour continues at the Hynes Bay Unit, where the attraction is birds of the tidal marsh. Some species not normally found farther north may be seen in the thorny scrub along the bluff—groove-billed anis, olive sparrows, and paraques. Expect to see about 100 species in a day's time.

Not part of the area is a Texas Department of Transportation viewing platform on the Texas 35 right-of-way overlooking Buffalo Lake, a little over a mile south of the headquarters. You should be able to see considerable numbers of shorebirds and waterfowl.

PRO'S POINTERS. Buffalo Lake stretches from very near the highway to half a mile away. Good binoculars are a must for viewing waterfowl.

HUNTING

Check the *Public Hunting Lands Map Booklet* and the *Applications for Drawings on Public Hunting Lands* for information on hunting opportunities for the current year. Regular Permit hunts for waterfowl are generally offered. Youth-only waterfowl hunts will be offered on dates authorized by the U.S. Fish and Wildlife Service.

This unit is a duck hunter's dream come true. Several bayous twist through the area, and water-control structures maintain numerous ponds and small lakes. Considerable cover around the edges of ponds makes concealment easy. Each hunter is furnished a map upon arrival. Signed roads guide you to parking areas for numbered hunting sites. Mowed paths and reflective stakes lead you to hunting areas and show you where to set up. A sign at the check-in station lists the best and worst sites based on the last hunt, but you are free to request any unoccupied stand.

PRO'S POINTERS. When I last

hunted the area, much of the land normally above water was still flooded from the October 1998 flood on the Guadalupe River. The area was literally a paradise for ducks. There was almost no place shallow-feeding ducks could not land and find food. Ducks swarmed from every direction, seeming to pay no attention to decoys. There were so many ducks one could choose to shoot only males and only species such as pintails and teal and still limit out by 9 A.M.

First-time hunters are encouraged to ask as many questions as they want before choosing an area. Every part of the unit will offer excellent hunting at one time or another during the season, and area personnel are eager to help you pick a spot where you will have a good hunt, since they are very competitive with other areas along the coast and want hunters to bag as many birds as possible.

Most of the hunters are repeat visitors who have their favorite spots. If you want to be assured of hunting one of the current hotspots, be prepared to be in line at the check station by 4:30 A.M. Permits are issued from two hours before shooting to 30 minutes before shooting time. You will improve your chances of success by hunting as many spots as possible in order to learn how to find them in the dark. Should your first choice be taken, you can go to a backup spot.

Alligator hunts are available through public drawings. Hunts are early in September, so the application deadline is early August. Applications are available by request from Texas Parks and Wildlife headquarters in Austin during July. Hunts take place in a narrow time frame between the time baby alligators hatch and the

arrival of cool weather which slows alligator activity.

An alligator hunting license is required. Alligators inhabit the freshwater marshes. If you have never hunted alligators before, check with an experienced hunter or area personnel regarding hunting methods before attempting it.

Feral hog hunts are offered through public drawings. The hunts are usually in late January and early February. Tripod stands are furnished, and each hunting area is prebaited before the hunt. Bring corn to continue baiting the area after the hunt begins. Most success has been with rifles.

A youth deer hunt is held in October. Permits are obtained through the public drawing. An adult must accompany the youth, but only the youth can hunt. Blinds are provided. The deadline for this hunt is early September. No application fee or permit fee is required for this hunt. Baiting is allowed.

FISHING

Access is by boat only via San Antonio Bay and the Victoria Barge Canal from public boat ramps at Austwell or Seadrift, or from the public boat

LEFT:
Duck hunting on Guadalupe Delta WMA can be excellent, as this hunter's limit of ducks shows.
RIGHT:
Birders find a variety of woodland, water and grassland birds. Edges where different habitat types meet are prime birding spots.

ramp on Texas 35 at Goff Bayou. The best spot is the circular basin just below the saltwater intrusion dam at the junction of Goff Bayou and the Victoria Barge Canal. It is popular in spring, when high water flow and open gates on the dam concentrate baitfish below the structure, which attracts a lot of catfish.

PRO'S POINTERS. High water flow and open gates on the saltwater dam mean good fishing. Contact the Guadalupe River Authority office in Port Lavaca to see if the gates are open before planning a trip.

RECREATIONAL OPPORTUNITIES GUADALUPE RIVER UNIT

HIKING

Hiking is allowed along River Road, the county road that accesses the area and runs parallel to the river. Approximately 2 miles of the road are on the area, which extends another mile through private land after exiting the WMA. Hiking is also allowed in the narrow strip between the road and the river (zone C), although thick undergrowth in most places makes walking difficult.

PRO'S POINTERS. This low-lying road is unsurfaced natural clay and can be quite sticky and slippery when wet.

BICYCLING

Bicycling locations and regulations are the same as for hiking.

HUNTING

No check-in is required for hunting on this unit. You must have a hunting license and an Annual Public Hunting Permit. Hunting is allowed every day of the South Zone dove season, the early teal season, the South Zone duck season, and the Eastern Zone goose season. Snipe, rails, and gallinules may be taken with steel shot only during seasons concurrent with early teal, duck, and goose seasons. Regulations are posted at an information board a mile inside the entrance.

Maps are in the mailbox beside the sign.

Dove hunting is allowed in the wooded area to the right of River Road from the entrance gate to the southern boundary. A thin scattering of huisache covers old fields; the hunting area boundary extends to an old fence line and is not marked. Dove hunters may park along the road.

PRO'S POINTERS. Dove hunting is not permitted between River Road and the river. Dove hunters must exit the area by one-half hour after sunset. Area manager Todd Meredino said the Hynes Bay Unit generally has more doves but is more wooded and therefore harder to hunt.

The unit is divided into two zones, A and B, for waterfowl hunting. Ease of access determines the zones. Zone A is nearest River Road and features numbered hunting areas with corresponding numbered parking spaces at the information signboard. Zone B requires a much longer walk in and has no designated hunting areas or parking spaces.

The marked sites get the heaviest use. Both zone A and zone B have numerous small ponds scattered about, and hardy hunters who wish to hunt the east shore of Goose Roost Lake may do so if they are willing to pay the price of a long walk in and out burdened with decoys and harvested game. The area is closed until 4 A.M. to prevent hunters from "camping" on choice hunting spots.

Youth-only waterfowl hunts will be offered on dates authorized by the U.S. Fish and Wildlife Service. See the current issue of the *Public Hunting Lands Map Booklet* for information.

FISHING

You may access the Guadalupe River for fishing either by car from River Road or up the river by boat. Anglers must have an Annual Public Hunting Permit. The chief species caught are redfish and catfish.

PRO'S POINTERS. "The catfishing is really good when the Guadalupe River is out of its banks," said area manager Todd Merendino. "The fish come up into the flooded areas to feed." Tangled undergrowth makes bank fishing difficult in many places. One good area is about three-fourths of a mile inside the entrance, just before the information board, a large live oak shades a brush-free bank. Another good spot is about a hundred yards north of the point where River Road exits the area at its southeastern corner. Park off the road just before the cattleguard and hike up the river to an area shaded by large cypress trees.

RECREATIONAL OPPORTUNITIES HYNES BAY UNIT

HUNTING

No check-in is required for hunting on this unit. You must have a hunting license and an Annual Public Hunting Permit. Hunting is allowed every day of the South Zone dove season, the early teal season, the South Zone duck season and the Eastern Zone goose season. Snipe, rails, and gallinules may be taken with steel shot only during seasons concurrent with early teal, duck, and goose seasons. Regulations are posted at an information board a mile inside the entrance. Maps are in the mailbox beside the sign.

Dove hunting is allowed on the entire upland area above the bluff. The greater part of the dove hunting area is north of the information board and consists of old farm fields being reclaimed by brush.

PRO'S POINTERS. Since roosting trees are at a premium in the area, your best dove hunting success will likely come late in the day when birds are returning from feeding.

The waterfowl hunting area is divided into zones A and B. Ease of access determines the zones. Zone A is nearest the road and features numbered hunting areas with corresponding numbered parking spaces at various locations along the road. Zone B requires a much longer walk in and has no designated hunting areas or parking spaces. You may hike in up to a half-mile to hunt around Goose Roost Lake or Hynes Bay. Marked sites get the heaviest use. The area is closed until 4 A.M. to prevent hunters from "camping" on favorite sites.

Youth-only waterfowl hunts will be offered on dates authorized by the U.S. Fish and Wildlife Service. See the current issue of the *Public Hunting Lands Map Booklet* for information.

FISHING

Access is by boat only from San Antonio Bay from public boat ramps in Austwell and Seadrift. Redfish and flounder are the most common fish. At the lower end of Hynes Bay, you can wadefish oyster reefs for redfish and trout.

PRO'S POINTERS. An Annual Public Hunting Permit is not required for fishing from a boat but is required for bank fishing. In fall, fishing can be really good at the mouth of Townsend Bayou when a cold front pushes water and baitfish out of the marshes, attracting redfish and flounder. Due to the shallowness of the marsh, fishing is slow in summer.

INSIDER'S CORNER

A SURFEIT OF SNOWS

The low numbers of geese on Guadalupe Delta WMA as compared to coastal refuges farther east is striking. Surprisingly, however, the reason has little to do with natural factors. The concentration of geese (especially snow geese) along the upper Texas coast is mainly due to human activities, principally rice farming.

For thousands of years, a limited amount of food in coastal salt marshes reduced overwinter survival and kept snow goose numbers in check. Then came rice farming on the Texas coast. Abundant supplies of waste grains on the wintering grounds enabled more birds to survive and make the trip north to breed and reproduce. During this same time, Arctic winters became milder, and numerous state and national wildlife refuges were established, also increasing survival rates. Principally because of human activities, living suddenly became easy for snow geese, and their numbers rose sharply.

The mid-continent population of lesser snow geese now greatly exceeds the carrying capacity of its Canadian nesting grounds. Perhaps six million birds—four times as many as biologists think desirable—are systematically destroying the habitat where they live six months of the year. Unless something is done soon, millions of snow geese will die slowly from starvation and disease.

After much study and debate, an international team of wildlife professionals settled on increased hunting effort as the most effective and least controversial way to reduce the snow goose population. Relaxed hunting regulations now allow hunters to take more snow geese, but it is unlikely this will solve the problem.

Wildlife managers historically have been oriented toward increasing the numbers of managed species, and they admit to being somewhat at a loss in trying to deal with the surplus of snow geese. New skills will be required to deal with the task now before them. Property owners stand at a fork in the road as well. Managing habitat for wildlife without the well-being of the species as the guiding principle seems a hollow endeavor indeed. Perhaps it's time for wildlife managers and property owners to move to the next level, that of learning how to work together to maintain an international population of free-roaming animals in balance with the habitat and with human needs. As complex as the task of bringing back species from the brink of extinction has been, it pales in comparison with what lies ahead.

24,498 acres in three units
10 Parks and Wildlife Dr.
Port Arthur, TX 77640
409/736-2551

DRIVING TIMES FROM:
Amarillo: 12 hours
Austin: 5 hours
Brownsville: 8.5 hours
Dallas: 5.5 hours
El Paso: 15 hours
Houston: 2 hours
San Antonio: 5.5 hours

DIRECTIONS: Big Hill Unit—From Port Arthur, take Texas 73 west 3 miles. At the first crossover past Jade Street, turn back and go to the entrance. Hillebrandt Unit—From the area headquarters on Texas 73, go east about 200 yards to Jade Street. Turn left and follow Jade Street 1.7 miles to FM 385. Turn left onto FM 385 and go 2.5 miles to an entrance gate on the left side of the road. Salt Bayou Unit—From the area headquarters on Texas 73, go east 2.5 miles to Texas 82. Go south on Texas 82 for 2.5 miles to Texas 87. Follow Texas 87 south another 4.7 miles to the Lost Lake check station.

OPEN: Big Hill Unit—Open to hunters only on designated days and to fishers during daylight hours only March 1 through August 31. Big Hill Bayou is open to fishers from the Monday following the close of the South Zone duck season until October 31. Open for wildlife viewing any day a hunt is not in progress. Hillebrandt Unit—Open to hunters only on designated days. Open for wildlife viewing any day a hunt is not in progress. Salt Bayou Unit—Open to hunters only on designated days and to fishers during daylight hours only during the period March 1 through August 31. Keith Lake, Johnson Lake, and Salt Bayou are open to fishing 24 hours a day year-round. Open for wildlife viewing any day a hunt is not in progress.

ACTIVITIES: Wildlife viewing, hunting, fishing.

FACILITIES: Hunter check stations, boat ramp, wildlife-viewing platform.

SPECIAL REGULATIONS: All hunters must check in and out. Permits for waterfowl hunts are issued at the check station beginning two hours before legal shooting time and continuing until 30 minutes before shooting time. Shooting hours end at noon. Fishers must possess an Annual Public Hunting Permit unless all activity is confined to a boat within navigable waters. No commercial fishing or crabbing are allowed except in Keith Lake. Fishing is permitted during daylight hours only except as noted above. The use of airboats is prohibited except on Keith Lake, Big Hill Bayou, and Blind Bayou. Airboats of less than 10 horsepower may be used by waterfowl hunters south of the Gulf Intracoastal Waterway. Water sports are prohibited on the area.

ADVISORIES: Waterfowl hunters should bring waders and a good flashlight. Mosquitoes can be present any time of year; bring plenty of insect repellent. Heat and humidity can make visiting the area unpleasant from April through October. Travel within the WMA is by boat only. A shallow-draft, flat-bottom boat with a 10- to 25-horse-power outboard motor is necessary. Carry your own supply of potable water.

LODGING IN AREA: Motels are available in Port Arthur.

LOCAL POINTS OF INTEREST: Sabine Pass Battleground State Historical Park, Sea Rim State Park, Village Creek State Park, Texas Point National Wildlife Refuge, McFaddin National Wildlife Refuge, Anahuac National Wildlife Refuge, Big Thicket National Preserve.

DISABILITY ACCESS: The wildlife-viewing platform in compartment 1 of the Big Hill Unit is wheelchair-accessible.

HISTORY

The bulk of the area now comprising the Murphree WMA was once part of the extensive landholdings of the McFaddin family, pioneer settlers in the Beaumont area. William M. McFaddin and his son William Perry Herring McFaddin ranched about 120,000 acres in Jefferson County. William M. McFaddin received his first land in Jefferson County as a reward for his service in the Texas Army during the Texas Revolution.

Father and son were involved in companies that bought and sold land, raised cattle and rice, milled rice, dug irrigation ditches, and drilled for oil. The Lucas Gusher, the discovery well of the Spindletop Oilfield, was drilled on land leased from the McFaddins some 6 miles north of the present WMA headquarters. William Perry McFaddin also farmed muskrats, producing as many as 200,000 pelts a year. The area was also well known for waterfowling; a world-famous hunting club operated on what is now the Salt Bayou Unit.

The discovery of oil and the building of the Gulf Intracoastal Waterway brought tremendous changes to Southeast Texas in general and the Murphree WMA in particular. Canals were built across freshwater marshes, opening them to saltwater intrusion and increased tidal energy. A burgeoning population created problems with poaching, trespassing, and illegal whiskey making along Big Hill Bayou.

In the three decades following 1950, the McFaddin holdings were sold off piecemeal. The Big Hill Unit of the J. D. Murphree WMA was purchased by Texas Parks and Wildlife in 1958 and the area was named shortly thereafter for a game warden killed by poachers in Orange County. Major additions to the area were made in 1983, when 4,074 acres were purchased, and in 1997, when 11,231 acres formerly part of Sea Rim State Park were acquired and the two

combined to form the Salt Bayou Unit. The 591 acres of the Hillebrandt Unit were purchased in 1989.

GEOGRAPHY AND NATURAL FEATURES

The Murphree WMA is located on the Texas portion of the Chenier Plain, the westernmost geologic delta of the Mississippi River. Its outstanding feature is extensive coastal prairie, receiving in excess of 55 inches of rainfall a year, making for extensive wetlands. Taylor and Big Hill bayous join half a mile south of area headquarters and meander southward toward the Gulf Intracoastal Waterway, which slices across the middle of the area and divides it into two distinctly different parts. North of the intracoastal canal, the wetlands are principally fresh; south of it they grade from intermediate to brackish to saline.

Much of the Big Hill Unit has been divided into compartments by levees. The compartments are numbered and signed and may be accessed by foot via boardwalks or by boat using boat rollers.

ABOVE:
Alligator eggs hatch in late summer, flooding the leveed compartments of the J.D. Murphree WMA with baby alligators.
FACING PAGE:
Boats, airboats, and tracked vehicles such as this "swamp buggy" used by area personnel are the only way to access most of the interior of the J.D. Murphree WMA.

RECREATIONAL OPPORTUNITIES

For persons with a small boat and a spirit of adventure, the Murphree WMA offers almost unlimited opportunities for birding. However, facilities are very limited.

WILDLIFE VIEWING

A wildlife observation platform is located on the south side of Texas 73 about 1.5 miles west of the area headquarters. Enter at the gate marked by the wildlife viewing area sign and follow the dirt road about 300 yards to a parking area beside the old metal silos. Go through the walk gate, climb atop the levee, and follow the mowed path to your left 0.7 mile to the platform, which overlooks an area that is flooded seasonally. Brush along the levee holds a variety of passerine birds, and depending on water levels and time of year, you can expect to see rails, moorhens, wading birds, ducks, geese, marsh wrens and yellow-throated sparrows. Be aware that private land borders the levee on the left until you reach the observation platform. The ponds to the right of the levee are on the WMA.

If you have a small boat with an outboard motor, you can launch from the public boat ramp beneath the Texas 73 bridge over Taylor Bayou, about a mile west of area headquarters. Follow Taylor Bayou east to its confluence with Big Hill Bayou and turn right into Big Hill Bayou at the

sign marking the entrance to the WMA. You'll see a wide variety of wildlife in the compartments on the Big Hill Unit. Drag your boat over the levees using the boat rollers provided and motor along the ditch encircling each compartment. Watch for alligators, otters, bobcats, coyotes, minks, muskrats, nutrias, raccoons, swamp rabbits, and cottontails, as well as a variety of birds and waterfowl. Feral hogs also inhabit the area, and several mountain lion sightings have been reported.

PRO'S POINTERS. Area manager Jim Sutherlin highly recommends wildlife watching using a boat. "Wildlife watching on the Murphree WMA using just the observation platform is like looking at a flower from the bottom side," he says. "You need a boat to see this area from the inside." Big Hill Bayou and Salt Bayou are navigable waterways; no Annual Public Hunting or Limited Public Use Permit is required as long as you remain in your boat on these waters. Spring, winter, and fall are the best times because of wintering birds.

HUNTING

Duck hunting and alligator hunting are the main activities here. Check the *Public Hunting Lands Map Booklet* and the *Applications for Drawings on Public Hunting Lands* for information on hunting opportunities for the current year. Youth-only alligator and waterfowl hunts are available. Except for Special Permit hunts, all hunts are by Regular Permit or Annual Public Hunting Permit.

PRO'S POINTERS. With an alligator population estimated at one per acre, the Murphree area is the number-one alligator-hunting WMA in Texas, hosting from 200 to 250 hunters each September. Alligator hunts are available through public drawings only. Hunts are early in September, so the application deadline is early August. Applications are available by request from Texas Parks and Wildlife headquarters in Austin during July. An alligator-hunting license is required.

Alligator hunts take place during the brief period between the time baby alligators hatch and the arrival of cool weather, which slows alligator activity. Alligators inhabit the ditches along the levees. If you have never hunted alligators before, check with an experienced hunter or area personnel regarding hunting methods before attempting it. Hunters receive a pre-hunt orientation which includes a video depicting hunting methods. During hunts, locals experienced in skinning and processing alligators are available for hire. Cost is about $5 per foot of alligator length including scraping and salting the hide, a bargain if you've never done it before.

The Murphree WMA is known for the quality of its puddle duck hunting. Green-winged and blue-winged teal, shovellers, gadwalls, mallards, mottled ducks, pintails, widgeons, lesser scaup, ring-necked ducks, wood ducks, and ruddy ducks are all common. Hunting is allowed every day during the early teal season. During the regular duck season, hunting is allowed on alternate days on the Big Hill and Salt Bayou Units, making it possible to hunt every day of the week except Monday. Rails, gallinules, and snipe may be taken in season during waterfowl hunts.

Waterfowl hunters are required to check in at the area headquarters for hunts on the Big Hill Unit and at the Lost Lake check station 9.7 miles south of area headquarters on Texas 87 for hunts on the Salt Bayou Unit. Check-in begins at 4:30 A.M. On opening days and weekends, some hunters arrive the day before and spend the night in their vehicles to be sure of getting the compartment of their choice. Hunters are assigned to the compartment of their choice whenever possible, but there are no designated hunting stations within compartments. Hunters are asked to keep 200 yards between groups. Hunting is done from available cover, but hunters are encouraged to cut

marsh cane from the levees and use it to build temporary blinds.

For hunts on the Big Hill Unit, hunters must launch from the ramp at headquarters. The Salt Bayou Unit has no ramp; after registering at the Lost Lake check-in station, most hunters proceed another 2.8 miles south on Texas 87 to a private launch site, Junior's Landing, which is located on Keith Lake.

The Murphree WMA is divided into 18 compartments, which are signed at entry points. Compartments range in size from 200 acres to over 1,000 acres. The Big Hill Unit comprises compartments 1 through 11; the Salt Bayou Unit numbers 12 through 18. Compartments 10 and 14 are sanctuaries and are closed to hunting. Hunters travel by boat to their compartment and use boat rollers to access ditches inside the compartments for travel. Some compartments have boardwalks across the ditches to allow hunters to walk in if they do not want to pull their boats over the levees. Compartment 1 and the Hillebrandt Unit allow hunters to walk in from the highway.

Finding your way in the dark through miles of water across thousands of acres of featureless marsh can be difficult. "We suggest that new hunters come in after the gate opens—about 5 or 5:15—so they will have time to look at maps, choose a

hunt site, and talk to staff after the rush is over," advises Jim Sutherlin. "Since the area is open for daytime use to holders of an Annual Public Hunting Permit anytime a hunt is not in progress, I recommend that hunters come ahead of time and scout before they attempt to make their first trip in the dark."

One of the best ways to scout is during fishing trips in the off season, when you can locate ponds with submerged vegetation that ducks will use for food. Entry to these areas of open water can often be gained from the ditches running around the perimeters of the compartments in the Big Hill area. Most begin as small bayous opening off the ditch; knowing where they are is critical to being able to find them. The best way is to visit with area personnel at headquarters, where you can study aerial photographs of the compartments, then conduct on-the-water scouting.

The most popular compartments on the Big Hill Unit are numbers 2 through 8. They are the most accessible and provide many good places to hunt ducks. Compartment 1 is especially good for blue-winged teal during the early teal season. Compartment 5 is historically good for mallard hunting and, late in the season, pintails, but it attracts a lot of hunters and may be hard to get into. In the Salt Bayou Unit, compartments 13, 16, 17, and 18 are the most popular. Wildlife

technician Danny Summerlin especially recommends compartment 16. "It's a big, wide area of marsh, so there's no problem getting 300 to 400 yards from other people," he says. "You have to learn to pick an area where you can get away from other people. Use four or five dozen decoys. Make sure your boat is hidden well 100 yards or so away. Be sure you are well hidden in marsh grass, or bring cane with you to hide yourself."

The visibility that comes with the low, flat country has an added benefit for hunters. If you are not doing well at your hunting location, watch for areas attracting a lot of ducks. After hunters in those areas leave, you can often move in and fill out a limit in a short time.

Remember that this is shallow marsh country. You need a shallow-draft, flat-bottom boat and all Coast Guard safety equipment for operating in the dark in coastal waters. South of the Gulf Intracoastal Waterway low tides can strand a boater. Be aware of tides and wind events that may leave you perched on a mud flat. Take a cellular phone and the area headquarters phone number with you. If you use a retriever for waterfowl hunting, keep it close by you: Alligators love to eat dogs.

FISHING

The fresh waters of the Big Hill Unit provide fishing for bass, crappie, bream, and catfish. The Salt Bayou Unit is good for redfish, speckled trout, and flounder. Blue crabs are abundant and may be taken with no more sophisticated equipment than a chicken neck tied to a string.

PRO'S POINTERS. Shallow waters in Big Hill Bayou offer the best bass fishing. Keith Lake and Johnson lake have excellent fishing for redfish, speckled trout and flounder. An Annual Public Hunting Permit is required unless you stay in your boat in navigable waters.

INSIDER'S CORNER

CHANGING WETLANDS

"This country has really been changed by channelization," says area manager Jim Sutherlin. "Beginning about 1898, ship channels were dug from Sabine Pass and continued to be enlarged over time. In the 1930s the Gulf Intracoastal Waterway was built. The ship channel and the intra-coastal canal allowed seawater to come into marshes not accustomed to tidal energy and that volume of water. This country used to sheet flood, but construction of the intracoastal canal changed the hydrology, because its spoil banks prevent that."

Most of the Big Hill Unit has been leveed in order to make possible control of water levels and prevent dewatering of the marsh by a drainage project intended to lower water levels by about 18 inches over a wide area. It is principally a freshwater marsh divided into compartments by the levees.

South of the Gulf Intracoastal Waterway, the Salt Bayou Unit is aptly named. Mostly unleveed, it is subject to tidal activity and has degraded from intermediate to brackish marsh.

"Through controlling water flow, we try to mimic historical water conditions seasonally in the Big Hill Unit," explains Sutherlin. "South of the intracoastal canal, we have very little control over water flow. A lot of what is happening here is similar to what happened in the Dust Bowl, but instead of losing topsoil to wind, we are losing it to water. Increased water flow through the area creates more open water space by washing away the topsoils. This damage has occurred since the 1930s. In geologic time, the speed with which we've lost this marsh country is shocking. Coastal wetlands are our nurseries for organisms in the Gulf Of Mexico that support our commercial and sport fisheries, as well as providing a wintering area for wading birds, shorebirds, and migratory waterfowl. Coastal wetlands are also important as a barrier for absorbing energy from hurricanes as they come ashore. Once the waves cross the beach and hit grass, they really slow down. If we lose these plant communities, then the coastal towns are more exposed to energies from the Gulf of Mexico, and the potential damage from hurricanes is greater."

Despite the challenges facing him, Sutherlin remains optimistic about long-term plans for restoring coastal wetlands to health. "Aldo Leopold pointed out that land can be restored with the same tools that destroyed it, namely, the axe, the plow, the cow, fire and the gun," he says. "These wetlands were destroyed with the barge, the dredge, the dragline, steel, and concrete. We can restore them using the same tools."

6,550 acres in three units
10 Parks and Wildlife Dr.
Port Arthur, TX 77640
409/736-2551

DRIVING TIMES FROM:
Amarillo: 12 hours
Austin: 5 hours
Brownsville: 8.5 hours
Dallas: 5.5 hours
El Paso: 15 hours
Houston: 2 hours
San Antonio: 5.5 hours
DIRECTIONS: Old River Unit—
From Texas 73/87 in Bridge City,
take Lake Street south 1.5 miles to a
parking area on the left. Nelda Stark
Unit—From I-10 east of Vidor, take
FM 1442 south about 6 miles to
Bessie Heights Road. Turn right and
go 0.9 mile to a gate on the left; enter
and follow the road a quarter of a
mile to the parking area. Adams
Bayou Unit—Accessible only by boat
from the Sabine River or Adams
Bayou below West Orange.
OPEN: Daily.
ACTIVITIES: Wildlife viewing,
hiking, hunting, fishing.
FACILITIES: Wildlife-viewing platform, hiking trail.
SPECIAL REGULATIONS: Only the
Old River Unit is open for hunting.
No commercial crabbing or bait
fishing are allowed. Trapping,
airboats, and use of horses are
prohibited. Bank anglers must
possess an Annual Public Hunting
Permit except when fishing from the
right-of-way of Texas 73/87.
ADVISORIES: Mosquitoes can be
present any time of year; bring
plenty of insect repellent. Heat and
humidity can make visiting the area
unpleasant from April through
October. A shallow-draft boat is
necessary for access to most of the
area. Carry your own supply of
potable water.
LODGING IN AREA: Motels are

*Fishers casting for bait in the marsh on the
Lower Neches WMA ignore a couch dumped
into the water by one of many thoughtless
people who foul this area.*

available in Port Arthur, Groves, and
Bridge City.
LOCAL POINTS OF INTEREST:
Sabine Pass Battleground State
Historical Park, Sea Rim State Park,
Village Creek State Park, Texas
Point National Wildlife Refuge,
McFaddin National Wildlife Refuge,
Anahuac National Wildlife Refuge,
Big Thicket National Preserve.
DISABILITY ACCESS: The wildlife-
viewing platform in the Old River
Unit is wheelchair-accessible.

HISTORY

Most of the Lower Neches WMA was
donated to Texas Parks and Wildlife
by Mrs. Nelda Childers Stark between 1987 and 1993. Mrs. Stark was
the third wife and widow of entrepre-
neur Henry Jacob Lutcher Stark, a
leader in Southeast Texas lumber,
banking, insurance, manufacturing,
real-estate, and petroleum industries.
The charitable foundation they
organized has made numerous donations to art and education in Texas.

GEOGRAPHY AND
NATURAL FEATURES

Channelization associated with
petroleum exploration, subsidence,
and saltwater intrusion have
significantly altered the native fresh-

water marshes of the Lower Neches
WMA. The area is now predominantly composed of intermediate and
brackish marsh. The Sabine River and
Gulf Intracoastal Waterway run along
the southeastern boundary of the
Adams Bayou Unit, a 338-acre freshwater wetland. The Adams Bayou
Unit is a remnant of the Sabine River
bottom; a large part is a spoil area
from dredging in the Sabine River
channel.

Old River Cove, a former mouth
of the Neches River, bounds the Old
River Unit on the south, and its
wetlands form a rough U around the
town of Bridge City. The Old River
Unit is about two-thirds intermediate
marsh, with marshhay cordgrass the
dominant vegetation. Shallow ponds,
canals, and ditches lace the area. A
busy highway, Texas 73/87, cuts
across the area en route to the high
bridges over the Neches River just
south. The view of these bridges
dominates the southeast horizon.

The Nelda Stark Unit is a classic
example of the impact channelization
and canal dredging can have on fragile
coastal marshes. Seen from the shore,
the area looks like a large lake. Seen
from the air, a network of now-sub-
merged canals dug for oil exploration
and production becomes visible,
resembling the street pattern in a
suburban subdivision. Increased water
flow eroded topsoil, and subsidence
caused by mineral extraction completed the conversion of a marsh into
shallow, barren waters. Four small
islands on the northeastern part of the
tract remain above water. The largest,
Gum Island, is named for the sweet
gum trees found there.

RECREATIONAL ACTIVITIES

The wetlands of the Lower Neches
WMA harbor a considerable wildlife
and fish population. Because of its
accessibility and location in a populated area, the area is heavily visited by
locals. Some of their activities, such as
using parts of the area for a dumping

ground in a county that has no public landfill, detract considerably from the area's appeal.

WILDLIFE VIEWING

A designated wildlife-viewing area is located on the Old River Unit, on Lake Drive 1.5 miles south of its intersection with Texas 73/87. Open expanses of marsh offer opportunities to see migratory waterfowl, shorebirds, and ducks. Tall grasses along the road attract perching birds, which feed on the seedheads. Monarch butterflies migrate through the area in October. A wildlife viewing platform perches on the edge of the marsh, which harbors large populations of muskrats, mink, river otters, raccoons, and alligators.

The Nelda Stark Unit has a walking trail about three-quarters of a mile long that takes you to two islands surrounded by marsh. This unit is maintained as a wildlife sanctuary; no hunting is allowed. As a result, it supports large numbers of migratory waterfowl, colonial waterbirds, shorebirds, hawks, muskrats, mink, river otters, raccoons and alligators.

PRO'S POINTERS. The Adams Bayou Unit hosts a variety of wildlife comparable to the preceding two, but it suffers from lack of accessibility. While it is open for wildlife viewing, it can be reached only by boat, and heavy vegetation along its banks thwarts landing in most places. Only the hardy should consider visiting here.

HIKING

Hiking is limited to two trails. One is the walking trail in the Nelda Stark Unit described in the section above. The other is adjacent to the wildlife viewing platform on the Old River Unit. A boardwalk leads from the parking area to a levee that runs east about a quarter of a mile into the marsh. An unimproved trail leads through cane, grass, and small shrubs. Perching birds, including

red-winged blackbirds, use the shrubs, while wading birds such as egrets and small blue herons probe for minnows along the margins. Ducks paddle the ponds.

PRO'S POINTERS. Waterproof footwear is advised for walking this trail, as it has several low spots that can be quite muddy. The trail winds through tall grass and brush and is more suited for wildlife viewing than for brisk walking. Cover is so thick along the trail that you should be able to approach waterfowl closely if you move slowly and quietly.

HUNTING

All hunting on the area is by Annual Public Hunting Permit. Check the *Public Hunting Lands Map Booklet* for information on hunting opportunities for the current year. Hunters are not allowed on the area before 4 A.M.

Hunting is allowed only on the Old River and Nelda Stark Units. Check-in is not required, but waterfowl hunting is generally allowed on alternate days east and west of Texas 73/87.

PRO'S POINTERS. Assistant area manager James Thomas says that while duck hunting on the area can be good, it doesn't live up to the days before degradation of the marsh. "Opening up canals for oil exploration and production increased the

rate of water flow through the marsh and eroded it away," he explained. "The freshwater marsh used to be great for ducks. People have told me that in those days, when the first shots were fired, the sky would turn black with ducks." Thomas added that the key to duck-hunting success is to find a pond with widgeon grass, a submerged plant that is a favorite food.

Hunters can walk into the Old River Unit on the hiking trail mentioned above and hunt the marsh on either side of the levee. A stile over the fence on the east side of Texas 73/87 about half a mile north of the Neches River bridge also gives land access to the marsh. The best hunting will be found farther from the highway; a shallow-draft boat will allow you to reach these areas. It's possible to launch from the bank along Texas 73/87 or Lake Drive in numerous places. Taking Lake Drive to the end brings you to Old River Cove and Bailey's Fishing Camp, which has a private ramp and campground. From there you can run into Sabine Lake and under the bridges over the Neches River to the Gulf States Canal, which runs along the western edge of the area.

On the Nelda Stark Unit, numbered parking spaces in the parking

A wildlife viewing platform overlooks the marsh on the Old River Unit of the Lower Neches WMA.

lot correspond to marked, numbered hunting locations in the marsh. You are free to hunt any unoccupied site, but in consideration of other hunters, stay within 25 yards of the marker.

FISHING

Fishing is allowed on both the Old River and Nelda Stark Units, but only during daylight hours. Flounder, redfish, and black drum are the most common types of fish caught. A canal running along Lake Street is commonly used by bank fishers. The Gulf States Canal runs from Old River Cove under Texas 73/87, and where it crosses under the highway is a favored fishing spot. You can also launch a shallow-draft boat here, although there is no boat landing. North of the canal about a quarter of a mile, on the west side of the highway, a salt-water plug (a low concrete dam built to impede the flow of salt water into the marsh) forms a diversion where migrating flounder stack up. A boat roller allows you to pull your boat across the plug. On the Nelda Stark Unit, the submerged system of canals offers good fishing, especially for flounder.

PRO'S POINTERS. Spring and fall are the best times for flounder fishing. Thomas advises, "If you see lots of cars around the salt plug and people fishing, you know the flounder are running." Thomas also shared this tip for easy scaling of flounder: Use a power washer. Bank fishing for redfish and flounder can be really good in the fall off the levee trail in the Old River Unit or from the nature trail in the Nelda Stark Unit. Or, you can use either trail for access for wade fishing.

A visit to Bailey's Fishing Camp at the end of Lake Drive on the Old River Unit can get your fishing trip off to a good start. Bailey provides a map of Sabine Lake showing fishing hotspots and bank fishing locations, including some on the WMA. He also sells bait, snacks, and tackle and has a campground and boat ramps.

INSIDER'S CORNER

GETTING DUMPED ON

WMAs offer the opportunity to enjoy the sounds, smells, and sights of nature—the agitated barking of squirrels contesting for a prime cluster of acorns, the sweet aroma of a field of wildflowers, a ballet of geese wheeling in unison around a roost pond.

Unfortunately, some WMAs offer a different set of sensory stimuli: the clatter of aluminum cans blowing down a road, the stench of rotting garbage, the visual cancer of a discarded sofa sitting cushion-deep in a pond. Nowhere is the problem worse than in Orange County, which has no public landfill, but not one single WMA in Texas is completely free of litter.

WMAs make ideal dumping grounds for the uncaring. Usually unstaffed, accessible by road yet often isolated and infrequently visited, WMAs offer a place where furtive dumpers can unload and make their getaway unseen. They leave behind a lingering plague of litter that despoils the landscape and discourages visitation.

Litter lingers long after the culprit has departed to begin amassing another heap of refuse. How long does litter last? A simple cigarette butt or a fast-food container of plastic-coated paper may still mar the landscape five years later. A plastic film can may lurk in the grass for up to 30 years. A tin can takes 50 years to rust away, while an aluminum one endures 500. Glass bottles can easily last a millenium; fired ceramics such as dishes stay around at least 7,000 years, far longer than Egypt's pyramids have sat on the plains of Giza. Styrofoam, the ubiquitous component of everything from ice chests to flotation devices, may stick around more than 10,000 years.

As WMAs are opened to more visitation, the problem of litter will increase. However, there are things that can be done.

First, face the fact that dumpers will dump. The amount of trash along Texas highways clearly shows that public education will not eliminate litter. Some people just don't give a damn.

Second, the only thing that gets litter off the ground is someone picking it up.

Third, you are the only solution to the problem. As long as all of us wait for someone else to get rid of the garbage, it will stay right where it is. Only when each of us takes an active role will it go away.

Here's what you can do to help:

- Never litter yourself.
- Visit your WMA often. Nothing discourages illicit activity like the presence of witnesses.
- When you see litter, pick it up. On walks or drives through a WMA, carry a small trash bag. You don't have to pick up every piece of litter you see. Just fill one small bag—and encourage others to do the same.
- Express your concern about litter on WMAs to local health and sanitation officials. Request they look into cleaning it up. If they try to get off the hook by saying their resources or jurisdiction are limited, suggest they coordinate with local criminal justice officials, who are often looking for projects for offenders sentenced to community service.
- Form a friends' group for your local WMA. Coordinate with the area manager to organize clean-up days.
- Don't wait for Earth Day. Do it now.

Mad Island WMA

7,200 acres
County Courthouse, Room 101
Bay City, TX 77414
409/244-7697

DRIVING TIMES FROM:
Amarillo: 12 hours
Austin: 3.5 hours
Brownsville: 5.5 hours
Dallas: 6 hours
El Paso: 14.5 hours
Houston: 2 hours
San Antonio: 3 hours
DIRECTIONS: From Bay City, take Texas 35 west 15 miles to FM 1095. Turn left (south) onto FM 1095 and go about 13 miles to Brazos Tower Road. Turn left onto Brazos Tower Road and go 2 miles to A. P. Ranch Road. Turn left again and proceed to the entrance gate.
OPEN: Saturday and Sunday during teal and regular duck season (hunters only). Open by reservation only to holders of a Texas Conservation Passport for birding tours in spring and fall.
ACTIVITIES: Hunting, wildlife viewing.
FACILITIES: Hunter check station, numbered hunting sites.
SPECIAL REGULATIONS: All hunters must check in and out. Permits for waterfowl hunts are issued at the check station beginning two hours before legal shooting time and continuing until 30 minutes before shooting time. Shooting hours end at noon, and hunters must be checked out by then. Boat use is restricted to compartments 9 and 10, and only electric motors may be used.
ADVISORIES: While most roads on the area are gravel-surfaced, all-weather roads, users must travel across land owned by the Texas Nature Conservancy to enter the WMA, and this road can require a high-clearance vehicle when wet. Waterfowl hunters should bring

Mad Island WMA boasts what is surely the most unusual sign identifying a Texas WMA.

waders, decoys, insect repellent, and a good flashlight. Carry your own supply of potable water.
LODGING IN AREA: Motels are available in Bay City.
LOCAL POINTS OF INTEREST: Lake Texana State Park, Big Boggy National Wildlife Refuge, San Bernard National Wildlife Refuge, Port Lavaca State Fishing Pier.
DISABILITY ACCESS: Not wheelchair-accessible.

HISTORY

Karankawa Indians inhabited the area when Europeans arrived, and a number of shell middens associated with these Native Americans have been recorded on the WMA. The Cabeza de Vaca expedition was shipwrecked on the Texas coast in 1528, and survivors trekked across the area searching for Mexico. The French explorer La Salle established a short-lived fort on Matagorda Bay in 1685. Later settlers farmed, ranched, and fished. However, the land that is the Mad Island WMA remained relatively untouched, says area manager Todd Merendino. "This area has never been farmed, as far as we can determine," he says. "It probably looks pretty much as it did in Karankawa Indian days."

The land was acquired by purchase in 1987 and 1992.

GEOGRAPHY AND NATURAL FEATURES

About half the area's 7,200 acres is upland, a short- to midgrass prairie dominated by little bluestem and gulf cordgrass. The other half is composed of marshes, lakes, and ponds. The entire area is mostly level. In fact, the overwhelming impression one gets is of unrelenting flatness. The wetlands are all less than 5 feet above sea level, and the salty prairies rise no higher than 10 feet.

Robbins Slough, Crab Bayou, and Rattlesnake Island Bayou bring fresh water onto the WMA, which then mixes with brackish and saline waters. The marshy area is treeless and covered with oystergrass and other salt-tolerant grasses. It is flooded much of the time, with small ponds scattered about. Weathered logs in the grass testify to storm surges that bring Gulf waters inland. Walking through the waist-high grass is difficult unless you follow a feral hog trail, as wind lays the grass over and mats it together.

The land rises slightly away from the coast but never attains significant elevation. Still, it is enough for some small brush to survive in the area between Brant Lake and Big Muddy Lake. A significant plant in the fresh-water lakes is sago pondweed, a favorite food of many species of ducks.

The Gulf Intracoastal Waterway

borders the WMA on the south, while to the northeast the view across the flat coastal prairie is dominated by the twin reactor domes of the South Texas Nuclear Project.

The area's low elevation makes it prone to tidal flooding and storm surges and enabled it to resist human attempts at alteration until well into the 20th century. However, since 1934 the hydrology of the WMA has been considerably altered by several projects. First, the Colorado River was cleared of logjams and a channel was cut from Matagorda to the Gulf of Mexico to improve the rate of flow. Second, the Gulf Intracoastal Waterway was built in the 1940s. This project connected what had been inland wetlands directly to the bays. Third, a diversion canal built in 1986 diverted fresh water from Robbins Slough into the Colorado River. These projects allowed fresh water to flow through the area faster and significantly increased the salinity of many of the wetlands on the WMA. (Freshwater Lake no longer lives up to its name and is now brackish.) In 1992 the river flow was redirected into West Matagorda Bay, which should reduce its salinity and lower saltwater intrusion into the WMA.

Recreational Opportunities

Wildlife Viewing

Texas Conservation Passport tours are offered to organized groups in the spring and fall and are led by a Texas Parks and Wildlife conservation scientist. Tours start near the entrance gate, next to Skeeter Marsh, where the tour leader will call to rails. Geese, ducks, and herons can be spotted as they fly off the marsh. Using information gained by the conservation scientist on a scouting trip the day before, the group will then go to where the birds are, taking roads around the marshes and through the salt prairies. The group will walk the levee at Brant Lake, where shrubs harbor songbirds. Rails and gallinules may be in the marshes around the lake. Later in the day, the tour continues on adjacent Texas Nature Conservancy land along the Gulf Intracoastal Waterway, looking for woodland species. Usually 120 to 125 species will be spotted in a day's time.

A checklist of birds recorded on the area or nearby is available at the check station. Some 300 species in all have been sighted. The more commonly seen birds include the pied-billed grebe, American white pelican, cormorants, herons, egrets, ibis, ducks, geese, sandhill cranes, sandpipers, wrens, starlings, sparrows, red-winged blackbirds, and grackles. Some species are quite seasonal in their presence, but bobwhite quail, rails, moorhens, avocets, willets, gulls, terns, mourning doves, yellow-throated warblers, and seaside sparrows are common year-round. The number of species recorded here during the annual National Audubon Society Christmas Bird Count is among the highest in the nation.

PRO'S POINTERS. Knee boots or other waterproof shoes are a good idea. Walks don't get into really marshy areas, but the grass can be wet. If you don't like to do a lot of walking, this is a good tour, because you can drive to within 50 yards or so of most of the marshes and best viewing areas.

Hunting

Alligators, waterfowl, and feral hogs may be hunted here. Check the *Public Hunting Lands Map Booklet,* the *Outdoor Annual,* and the *Applications for Drawings on Public Hunting Lands* for information on species, seasons, and bag limits for the current year.

Waterfowl hunting, especially duck hunting, is a passion with many visitors to this WMA. So determined are some hunters to get their preferred hunting area that they arrive the day before scheduled hunts and sleep in their cars in order to be near the head of the line when the gate opens about 4:30 A.M. Waterfowl hunting is by Regular Permit or Annual Public Hunting Permit.

Approximately 40 numbered hunting locations are scattered across the WMA. Sites are assigned on a first-come, first-served basis, and hunters are allowed to choose any unoccupied site. Hunters drive to designated parking areas and then walk in from 50 yards to a quarter of a mile to hunting sites. No blinds are provided; hunters use vegetation for cover. Expect very wet, muddy conditions.

Some geese—mostly snow, Canada, and white-fronted varieties—roost on the area. They are legal during the South Zone duck season. The main ducks on the area are teal, gadwall, widgeon and pintail.

Feral hog hunts are offered in spring through public drawings. Tripod stands are provided for hunters, and beginning about a week prior to the hunt, each stand is baited with corn. Rifles, shotguns, primitive weapons and archery are allowed.

Alligator hunts are also available through public drawings. Hunts are usually the first full weekend in September, so the application deadline is early August. Applications are available from Texas Parks and Wildlife headquarters in Austin during July. Hunts take place in a narrow time frame between the time baby alligators hatch and the arrival of cool weather, which slows alligator activity.

PRO'S POINTERS. Area manager Todd Merendino says to ask a lot of questions if you are not familiar with the area. "We're all duck hunters, and we like to have a good hunt, and we like for people who come here to have a good hunt," he says. "We try to put people in places where we'd like to hunt ourselves." Texas Parks and Wildlife staff on the WMAs along this stretch of coast are quite competitive with each other, and they strive to put hunters in locations that will result in the highest average harvest per hunter.

That often results in hunters taking home limits of ducks.

One regular duck hunter at Mad Island is Glenn Ging of Bay City. The following tips are a summary of what he's learned over several years of hunting there. "I like hunting in compartments 5 and 8, along the Intracoastal Canal. You get a lot of birds moving up and down the canal. Boats passing along the canal often scare up birds that may fly over or decoy to you," he advises. "Later in the season, a lot of geese roost in section 8, and that gives you some bonus birds." His favorite spots are 5b, 5c, 7a, 7c, 7f, 8a, 8b, 10c, 10d, and 10e, although he advises hunting different locations so you'll know how to find them in case one of your choice spots is taken.

Wildlife technician Kevin Kriegel often hunts the area where he works. He keys on food. "Figure out where the widgeon grass and sago pond-

Waterfowl hunters on Mad Island WMA find that traffic on the Gulf Intracoastal Waterway (far background) tends to keep birds stirred up and moving.

weed is, and that's where the ducks will be," he says. Later in the season, the ducks will have eaten the grass out and will go elsewhere, so be sure to ask before you choose a location.

Ging uses 5 to 6 dozen pintail, teal, widgeon, and gadwall decoys. Although he feels most hunters call too much, when he does call, he uses pintail whistle calls and sometimes a diver duck call on bluebills and redheads. "Keep low and don't look at the birds, because your face shines so badly," he says. "Using a full facemask helps. And don't hold your gun vertical trying to keep it clean—the ducks will spot it. Hunt with a gun you don't mind getting dirty."

Ging says mosquitoes can be bothersome even in December unless you use insect repellent. "Also, take a good flashlight along to help you spot the reflectors that mark the hunting locations," he says. "You can spot the reflectors from several hundred yards away."

As for other equipment, Ging advises wearing an upland bird-hunting vest. "It gives you something to carry your shells in and to put

empty hulls in," he explains. "Plus, you can still get a bag of decoys on over it." His favorite load for ducks is 3-inch 12-gauge shells with number 3 shot. He takes along a few BBs in case geese come in.

Waders are essential. Don't count on having a dry surface on which to place clothing, cameras, guns, or other gear. Take along a plastic ground sheet or heavy-duty garbage bags to hold items you want to keep dry and free of mud.

Hog hunters should bring their own corn to continue baiting after the hunt starts. If possible, hunt with a buddy so you can help each other retrieve game; some of the hogs taken on the area have dressed as much as 180 pounds. Get to your stand early and stay late; hogs are often nocturnal and appear only at dusk and dawn.

Alligator hunting requires a special license. The best places are Brant Lake—a big freshwater lake—and the Savage Marsh. If you have never hunted alligators before, check with an experienced hunter or area personnel regarding hunting methods before attempting it.

INSIDER'S CORNER

BIRDS, CATS, AND YOU

The National Audubon Society's Christmas Bird Count has been called the oldest and largest wildlife survey in the world. Each year over 40,000 birders take part. On a given day within two weeks of December 25, groups count all the birds they can find within a 15-mile diameter circle. There are some 1,500 circles spread across North, Central, and South America, with most being in North America. This is the biggest single event in the birding year.

The Christmas Bird Count was begun in 1900. It cannot be considered a reliable scientific survey, since it uses volunteers of varying ability and the circles used for counts are not randomly distributed. However, it does provide valuable information that can be analyzed for long-term trends.

Birds serve as a "barometer" of habitat health. Degraded habitat attracts fewer birds. In the United States, habitat destruction is the number-one problem facing wildlife, and this is reflected in the declining number of species and individuals recorded in the annual bird counts.

In the case of many environmental problems, there seems to be little an individual can do. However, cat owners in particular can have a positive impact on the numbers of birds surviving in their area. Studies indicate that the approximately 100 million cats in the United States kill hundreds of millions of birds and more than 1 billion small mammals each year. Cats kill not only backyard birds but also threatened or endangered species such as the snowy plover, wood thrush, least tern, and piping plover.

Domestic cats are not native to North America. Their importation by European colonists introduced a prolific new predator into the ecosystem. Today almost half the cats in North America are feral and must hunt to survive. Even lap kitties can lead secret lives as killers, however. According to the American Bird Conservancy, cats worldwide may have been involved in the extinction of more bird species than any other cause except habitat destruction.

Cats can actually have a greater impact than wild predators. People protect cats from disease, predation, and competition—factors that can control numbers of wild predators. People feed cats, so their numbers remain high when prey species decline, enabling cats to hunt even rare species. Cats fed regularly still retain a strong desire to hunt.

If you are a cat owner and wish to limit the number of wild animals your cat kills, here are some things you can do.

- If possible, keep your cat indoors. Indoor cats live three to four times longer on average than outdoor cats.
- Keep only as many pet cats as you can feed and care for.
- On farms, keep only as many free-ranging cats as needed to control rodents.
- Neuter your cats or prevent them from breeding.
- Locate bird feeders in sites that do not provide cover for cats to wait in ambush for birds.
- Put animal guards around any trees in your yard that may have nesting birds.
- Eliminate sources of food that attract stray cats, and don't feed strays. This will help reduce their numbers.

The American Bird Conservancy provides educational materials on the impact of cats on birds and practical advice on how to convert an outdoor cat into a contented indoor pet. For information, contact Cats Indoors!, American Bird Conservancy, 1250 24th Street NW, Suite 400, Washington, DC 20037; 202/778-9666; email: abc@abcbirds.org.

43,900 acres
P.O. Box 117
Port O'Connor, TX 77982
361/983-2215

DRIVING TIMES FROM:
Amarillo: 11 hours
Austin: 3 hours
Brownsville: 3.5 hours
Dallas: 6 hours
El Paso: 14 hours
Houston: 2.5 hours
San Antonio: 2.5 hours

DIRECTIONS: Access is by boat only from Port O'Connor. A Texas Parks and Wildlife ferry operates Thursday through Sunday.

OPEN: Daily.

ACTIVITIES: Camping, wildlife viewing, hiking, bicycling, hunting, fishing.

FACILITIES: Ferry service, visitor center, bunkhouse, primitive campground, picnic area, cold water shower, wildlife observation platform, hunting stands, game-processing area.

The Matagorda Lighthouse

The Matagorda Lighthouse was first lit on December 31, 1852.
During the Civil War, Confederate Forces partially destroyed the lighthouse. In 1873, the Lighthouse was rebuilt two miles to the southwest at its present location to a height of 92 feet.
It was the oldest operating lighthouse on the Texas Coast when the light was dismantled in 1995.
The Matagorda Island Lighthouse is listed on the National Register of Historic Places.

SPECIAL REGULATIONS: Shotgun-only area except during Special Permit hunts. Waterfowl shooting hours are on Saturday and Sunday only until noon except in the designated marsh unit. No Annual Public Hunting Permit is required for fishers or for waterfowl hunters in the designated marsh unit. Trapping is not allowed.

ADVISORIES: Access is by boat only; call 361/983-2215 to reserve a spot on the ferry. Once you are on the island, you must remain until the ferry's return trip. Beware of stingrays, Portuguese men-of-war, rattlesnakes, and water moccasins. Do not walk in seaweed along the beach, which may contain medical waste washed from Mexico. Electricity, telephone, drinking water, and food are not available. Emergency assistance and medical attention are not readily available. Hunters should be aware that endangered whooping cranes may be found on part of the area. Carry your own supply of potable water.

LODGING IN AREA: Motels are available in Port O'Connor.

LOCAL POINTS OF INTEREST: Lake Texana State Park, Fannin Battleground State Historical Park, Goliad State Historical Park, Copano Bay State Fishing Pier, Port Lavaca State Fishing Pier, Fulton Mansion State Historical Park, Goose Island State Park, Matagorda Island State Park, Aransas National Wildlife Refuge.

DISABILITY ACCESS: Not wheelchair-accessible.

LEFT:
Although not on the WMA portion of Matagorda Island, the Matagorda Lighthouse serves as a landmark for all visitors to the island.

FACING PAGE:
Park personnel guide school groups on learning expeditions to Matagorda Island and introduce them to many aquatic species by seining.

HISTORY

One of five barrier islands on the Texas coast, Matagorda Island has remained an anomaly throughout its 5,000-year life span. Centrally located and visited regularly by myriad peoples, it has largely been bypassed by development.

Cabeza de Vaca and companions were shipwrecked here in 1528 and spent several years among the Karankawa Indians who occupied the coast and its barrier islands. In 1685 La Salle landed on the southern end of the island at Cedar Bayou but lost his supply ship, *L'Aimable,* on the bar at Cavallo Pass, on the island's northern end.

Despite the treacherous sandbar at its entrance, Cavallo Pass remained vital to early Texans, as it provided passage to Indianola, which for a time vied with Galveston to be the primary port of the Republic of Texas. Its importance may be inferred from the fact that the first operational lighthouse on the Texas coast—which still stands—was erected in 1852 to guide ships seeking the pass.

There were attempts at settlement on the island early on, but the towns of Calhoun and Saluria, dating from the 1830s and 1840s, failed to survive. More tenacious were ranchers such as the Hawes and Hills families, who began to buy land and run cattle as early as the 1850s and continued uninterrupted for nearly a century. Although suffering greatly from destructive hurricanes in 1875 and 1886, the families were able to hold onto their possessions until an even greater storm broke in the mid-20th century: World War II.

Matagorda Island proved to be ideal for use as a bombing and gunnery range for training military pilots. It was isolated, inaccessible except by water and therefore easy to secure, and had water all around to receive stray bombs or projectiles. Condemnation proceedings were carried out beginning in 1940 for the northern two-thirds of the island; some 11,500 acres on the southern end remained in private hands. The Matagorda Bombing and Gunnery Range became operational in July 1943 and continued to be used intermittently through the Vietnam War. Federally owned lands were designated as the Matagorda Island Unit of the Aransas National Wildlife Refuge in 1971.

By 1977 all military activity ceased. Ordnance was cleared from the area, and some 19,000 acres of federally owned land were transferred to the United States Fish and Wildlife Service. This created much ill will toward the government among the early ranching families, who believed they had been promised the opportunity to buy back their former holdings.

Additional lands were added by purchase in the 1980s, including the southern end of the island. Today the entire island is under state and federal protection. The U.S. Fish and Wildlife Service owns 30,502 acres; the Texas General Land Office, 26,166. Some 43,900 acres of the total are part of the WMA and state park. The state park is about 7,000 acres and the WMA about 36,000, but for all practical purposes the two are one. The wildlife management area officially begins about a mile south of the visitor center, but both park and WMA are operated by the same staff.

In an arrangement that may be unique in Texas, the U.S. Fish and Wildlife Service, Texas Parks and Wildlife, and the General Land Office agreed to share responsibilities for managing the land. All state lands were made part of the national refuge system, and all federal lands were made part of Matagorda Island WMA and State Park. Texas Parks and Wildlife has lead responsibility for public use, and the Fish and Wildlife Service has lead responsibility for wildlife and habitat management. All holdings were combined under one Memorandum of Agreement signed in 1990.

GEOGRAPHY AND NATURAL FEATURES

Much evidence remains of the military use of the island. The embarkation point for the Texas Parks and Wildlife ferry serving the island served the same purpose for the military, as did the docks on the island. The present visitor center on the island was an air force warehouse, and some other nearby buildings also date from the military era. The 8,000-foot main runway and taxiways remain, although they are now closed. The Army Hole, a popular fishing spot, is a depression in the bay where fill material was obtained to level the landing strip. Darlington Road, a one-lane strip of pavement running from the dock area to the island's southern tip, was also built by the military.

Significant as they are, these structures have little impact on the island as a whole, which stretches for

Trees of any size are scarce on Matagorda Island, which is swept by constant winds and occasionally devastated by hurricanes.

38 miles north to south and varies in width from 0.75 to 4.5 miles. Maximum elevation is 22 feet. At the southern end is Cedar Bayou, a narrow channel that periodically fills in as prevailing Gulf currents eat away at the north end of the island and deposit material on the southern end. At the northern end is Cavallo Pass, which migrates south as the land recedes. This progress is relatively rapid at times; the Matagorda Lighthouse, built in 1852, had to be moved 2 miles south less than 20 years later because it was in danger of being washed away.

Beginning on the Gulf side and proceeding bayward, the island includes a swash zone washed by Gulf waters, a dune complex, barrier flats that constitute the interior, salt marshes, and wind-tidal flats along the bay. While the Gulf shore is a smooth arc of sand typical of barrier islands, the bay side and both ends of the island display hundreds of coves and inlets where bay and marsh meet. This area is a prime nursery for fishes and crustaceans and, therefore, also a feeding ground for wading and shorebirds. Endangered whooping cranes wintering along the Texas coast often use the south end of the WMA on the bay side.

Vegetation on the island is typically short but dense. Vast areas of the barrier flats are covered in a thick organic blanket of marshhay cordgrass and dewberry vines pimpled with clumps of Macartney rose. This thigh-high protective cover provides shade and humidified air and moderates temperatures for the creatures living within it, which include white-tailed deer, coyotes, badgers, ornate box turtles, horned lizards, rabbits, feral hogs, and raccoons. Wild turkeys, stocked on the southern end of the island by the U.S. Fish and Wildlife Service, are expanding their range northward.

Wildflowers such as Indian blanket, white daisies, sensitive briar, yellow primroses, plains wild indigo, and prickly pear make the barrier flats a riot of color in spring. Trees are scarce. Some honey mesquite and Mexican persimmon occur along bayside shell ridges and between the air base and the J-Hook on the north end of the island. Huisache can be found along the main road and around the J-Hook. Salt cedar is scattered across the interior, but one notable stand favored by birders is near the lighthouse. The air base area contains introduced exotics such as cottonwoods, retama, oleander, Chinese tallow, and Russian olive.

RECREATIONAL OPPORTUNITIES

Unlike most WMAs, which are managed for research, demonstration, and habitat improvement purposes, with limited hunting being the main human activity, Matagorda Island is a popular tourist destination. It offers a degree of isolation and unspoiled natural beauty not found elsewhere in Texas—except perhaps in Big Bend. The northern end of the island comprises the state park and is the most heavily visited.

A Texas Parks and Wildlife ferry makes regularly scheduled trips Thursday through Sunday. The number of visitors is limited to space available on the ferry. Reservations are required, and there is a charge for the service. Ice chests, camping gear, and bicycles are carried for the basic fee, but there is an additional charge for kayaks. Racks are available for up to eight kayaks; visitors bringing one are advised to reserve a space.

Visitors are allowed to go to the island in their own boat, but this is not encouraged because of the distance from aid in case of an emergency. All visitors are encouraged to take a cell phone with them to the island and carry the number for the park office (361/983-2215) and the Calhoun County sheriff's department (361/553-4646).

Free events include a beach clean-up each April in conjunction with the Texas Trash-off. Ferry fare and lunch are provided by Texas Parks and Wildlife. Each May 1 features an open house and free ferry service to the island; reservations are required for the ferry.

CAMPING

Army Hole campground surrounds the dock area. Primitive campsites (fee) offer shade shelters, barbecue pits, and fire rings. Pit toilets and a cold-water shower with sidewalls but no roof serve the area. When Texas Parks and Wildlife staff are on the island, which is generally Thursday through Sunday, campers are allowed to use the restrooms and showers in the visitor center.

PRO'S POINTERS. Beach camping is allowed in two areas served by an on-island shuttle provided by Texas Parks and Wildlife; the cost is included in the ferry fee. Most campers choose to use one of these areas, but persons with special needs may request to be dropped elsewhere. One beach camping area is about 2.5 miles east of the dock area, in what is called the J-Hook area. A peninsula projects into Cavallo Pass and provides the opportunity to camp either on the Gulf side or on the cove on the lee side. There are no facilities here. The other beach camping area is on the Gulf of Mexico southeast of the dock about 2 miles. Shade shelters and picnic tables are provided at this area.

According to the management agreement governing operation of the island, the Gulf beach is maintained in a natural condition, meaning no heavy equipment can be used to clean it. Although volunteers periodically pick up trash, the beach is heavily littered with lumber, driftwood, and sargassum.

For those not equipped to camp, a spartan bunkhouse is available near the visitor center for a fee. Reservations must be made by calling 512/389-8900. Some linens and cooking utensils are provided, but it is recommended that you bring your own.

"A lot of people use Army Hole campground because it gives some protection from the prevailing winds," says park manager Erik Tschanz. "The cove side of the J-Hook area will have more people, because the water tends to be a little calmer there for swimming. People who come in their own boats like it because the surf is not as rough, and they can keep their boats in the water." Beachcombers and shellers prefer the Gulf beaches because the hunting is better. (Live shells may not be kept, nor can native plants or whale and dolphin bones. Park staff should be notified of the remains of or bands from any endangered species.)

Campers should bring all the water they will need, plus food, sunscreen, insect repellent, first-aid items, and a raincoat. Gathering firewood on the beach is allowed, but fires are not permitted in the dunes area. Longer than normal tent stakes are recommended, because the strong wind will pull out short ones and blow the tent over. The best weather for camping is March through May.

Beach campers should use extreme caution around the masses of sargassum washed up on the beach. Never walk in it. It can conceal tentacles from the Portuguese man-of-war, which can inflict painful stings. A recurring problem is the presence of used hypodermic syringes which are believed to drift from a hospital on the Mexican coast. Never handle any such items.

WILDLIFE VIEWING

Matagorda Island offers a never-ending feast for wildlife watchers, especially birders. Both guided tours and do-it-yourself watching are available. The area's abundant deer can be seen just about anywhere on the island, but park ranger Mike Gonzales says the best time and place to see the better bucks on the WMA is during January and February in the dock area.

Endangered and threatened species documented on the island are the whooping crane, peregrine falcon, brown pelican, piping plover, Southern bald eagle, Eskimo curlew, least tern, American alligator, Kemp's Ridley sea turtle, Atlantic hawksbill turtle, leatherback turtle, loggerhead turtle, green turtle, reddish egret, white-faced ibis, white-tailed hawk, American swallow-tailed kite, wood stork, sooty tern, and horned lizard.

Matagorda Island is the jumping-off place for birds migrating south in August and September and the first landfall for birds completing their 700-mile journey from the Yucatan Peninsula in spring. Shorebirds and wading birds throng the beaches, tidal flats, and freshwater ponds from November through February. Great blue, little blue and tricolored herons; black-crowned and yellow-crowned night herons; great, snowy, cattle, and reddish egrets; white and white-faced ibises; roseate spoonbills; and wood storks are the most common. Whooping cranes and sandhill cranes also visit.

Other commonly seen birds include snowy and Wilson's plovers, killdeer, black-necked stilts, American avocets, and willets. Spring and fall migrants include black-bellied, semi-palmated, snowy, and piping plovers; long and short-billed dowitchers; dunlins; western sandpipers; greater and lesser yellowlegs, and ruddy turnstones. Eight species of tern may be seen on beaches and bayside marshes: royal, caspian, black, sandwich, Foster's, gull-billed, sooty, and least. Black skimmers appear on both Gulf and bay sides of the island; there is a nesting colony on the J-Hook.

Spring migratory bird tours take place on the north end of the island during March, April, and May. Beachcombing and shelling tours run from February through June. Whooping crane tours are offered in winter.

A black-headed gull sits atop a piling near popular fishing spot Army Hole.

Tours of the marine environment, which include the use of a trawl net behind the ferry and a hand-pulled seine in the bay, are offered in May and June. A history tour visits the lighthouse area, Civil War trenches, and cemeteries. Tour fees are charged for non-Texas Conservation Passport holders.

PRO'S POINTERS. Visitors striking out on their own often request the shuttle drop them off at the lighthouse, where a stand of salt cedars gets heavy use by perching birds, especially during spring fallouts.

Lighthouse Cove and Pringle Lake are prime places for viewing shorebirds and wading birds. Lighthouse Cove is an easy walk of about a mile northeast of the dock area via Darlington Road. Pringle Lake, about 3 miles south of the dock, is well protected and has lots of cuts frequented by birds feeding on baitfish moving in and out. Numerous freshwater ponds hold ducks in winter.

Whooping cranes use the bay-side marshes in the Cedar and Panther Point areas, from 10 to 15 miles down the island. The best way to see them is on one of the guided tours offered by the park in November, January, February, and March. Both bus tours on the island and boat tours of the Welder Flats WMA shoreline (across San Antonio Bay from the Aransas NWR) are available. A transportation fee is charged in addition to the tour fee.

Linda Lewis, whose husband, Violet, captains the ferry, is a park volunteer and leads birding tours. "April is the best month for migratory warblers; winter is best for ducks," she says. Linda says the main species visitors can expect to see include scarlet and summer tanagers, painted buntings, yellow- and white-billed cuckoos, yellow-headed blackbirds, white-tailed hawks, white-tailed kites and "lots of warblers—black-and-

white, yellow, prothonotary." Aplomado falcons have been released by U.S. Fish and Wildlife Service on the southern end of the island and sometimes make appearances on the WMA. Watch for them swooping low over the runway or barrier flats looking for prey.

Assistant park manager Cathleen Veatch leads beachcombing, shelling, and history tours. "On the beachcombing and shelling tours, we take people 10 miles or so down the beach, where few people ever go," she says. "The best time is in February or March after a cold front. We usually find lightning whelks, pear whelks, Scotch bonnets, eastern murex, purple sea snails, and very rarely, a Michelin's window trap."

To fully appreciate the history tour, prepare ahead of time by reading *A Naturalist's Guide: Matagorda Island,* by Wayne and Martha McAlister (1993: The University of Texas Press).

HIKING

Matagorda Island offers about 80 miles of roads, beaches and mowed pathways. Visitors are free to hike or bike anywhere. In fact, except for the shuttle service, those are the only modes of transportation on the island.

PRO'S POINTERS. The shuttle driver will drop hikers off at access points to any of the island's attractions and give directions from there. The flat terrain and narrow width of the island make navigating easy. "We recommend hikers stay on the roads, because there are a lot of freshwater ponds on the area that hold snakes and alligators," says Tschanz.

BICYCLING

A bike is one of the best ways to see the island. Texas Parks and Wildlife takes bikes across on the ferry for free.

PRO'S POINTERS. Darlington Road is paved the entire length of the island and is in fair condition suitable for any kind of bike. To the lighthouse is about a 4-mile round trip, and the road is signed. Pringle Lake, a prime birding area, is about 2 miles southwest down the road, then another mile north across the island. "Bikers will find the beach heavy going, because it is covered with debris," says Tschanz. "Most people bike and bird along the main road or ride to the lighthouse."

HUNTING

Waterfowl hunting is by Annual Public Hunting Permit and Regular Permit. Special Permit hunts may be offered for white-tailed deer and feral hogs. See the *Public Hunting Lands Map Booklet, Applications for Drawings on Public Hunting Lands,* and the *Outdoor Annual* for the current year for seasons, species, and bag limits. Hunters find it convenient to stay in the bunkhouse, which has a game-processing area but no cold storage; make reservations by calling 512/389-8900.

PRO'S POINTERS. Duck hunters are advised to call during July or August to book space in the bunkhouse, and hunters on Special Permit hunts should book as soon as they receive notice they have been selected. "With the lack of protection from the wind and the high humidity, when it is cold here, conditions can be extremely rigorous," says Veatch. Deer and hog hunters, who must sit on 12-foot tripod stands, should come prepared to dress for extreme exposure.

Freshwater ponds scattered down the middle of the island attract a lot of ducks. Hunters are allowed to use dogs, but they must be kept leashed except when hunting. Hunters draw for ponds each day. Blinds are provided at some of the ponds, but there is usually plenty of natural cover. Hunters are dropped off and picked up at prearranged times by Texas Parks and Wildlife personnel.

While waterfowl hunting is allowed only on weekends until noon on ponds on the island, there are no such restrictions for hunting in the Marsh Unit. This is the bay side of the island southwest of the docks; signs mark the boundaries. Access is by boat only. No Annual Public Hunting Permit or Regular Permit is required. Pringle Lake and Contee Lake, as well as other coves and inlets, are principal entry points. Cuts called "twisties" by locals run back from the beach into potholes where pintails, widgeons, redheads, scaup, teal, mottled ducks, and buffleheads feed. Pintail and redhead decoys work well. Use natural cover along the edges of the water. There are blinds built in the marsh unit by hunters, and it is legal for anyone to use them, but this is not advised due to the possibility of a conflict.

Shallow water requires using a boat that can operate in less than a foot of water. Pringle and Contee Lakes have very soft, muddy bottoms that make wading difficult.

Deer and feral hog hunts are similar except for success rates: high for deer, low for hogs. Hunters draw for numbered tripod stands (some of which are double) scattered down the middle of the island. Hunters are taken to stands and picked up by Texas Parks and Wildlife personnel. Baiting is allowed on both deer and hog hunts. Persistence seems to be the key to success on these hunts. Visibility is excellent due to lack of tall cover, so being there when the animals move is about the only thing one can do to influence the outcome. While Texas Parks and Wildlife personnel offer midday pickup and return service, the most successful hunters are usually those who stay on stand all day.

FISHING

Matagorda Island offers a variety of fishing opportunities that is almost unmatched. Army Hole, just south of the dock area, is about 16 feet deep. The bay side of the island offers shallow flats ideal for wadefishing and is popular with kayakers. The Gulf side has surf fishing either from the beach or, when the sea is calm, from a boat.

PRO'S POINTERS. Ferry captain Violet Lewis is a good source of fishing tips and is happy to share information during the 45-minute ride to the island. "The Army Hole is excellent fishing for redfish in winter and trout in summer," he says, adding that it offers some of the best summer fishing on the entire Texas coast. However, on days with no wind, biting flies can be troublesome unless you use plenty of insect repellent. The water tends to be clear because the Army Hole is protected from wind, and artificial lures seem to work well there as well as live bait such as mud minnows and shrimp. Ponds on the island hold finger mullet and shad, and fishers are allowed to use cast nets to gather bait. Live bait is sometimes scarce in Port O'Connor; get yours early.

The Gulf side surf is good for trout in summer, but a variety of species can be caught there, including pompano, Spanish mackerel, and tarpon. Fishers may have to wade out some distance to be able to reach the second and third gut where the fish usually congregate; be alert for stingrays.

Surf fishing for bull redfish is excellent from mid-September through the end of December, with 35- to 45-pound fish not uncommon. Bring heavy gear and extra terminal tackle; you're going to be broken off a lot.

The lakes on the bay side produce good numbers of redfish and trout in spring and fall. Fish the middle of the lakes for trout and the edges for redfish. Sightcasting to redfish with topwater lures is an exciting way to fish these shallower waters. Another technique is to use a Bass Assassin beneath a Mansfield Mauler for drift fishing in the deeper water. (The Mansfield Mauler is a trade name for a kind of popping cork.)

INSIDER'S CORNER

THE MATAGORDA LIGHT

Although it is on the state park portion of the island, the Matagorda lighthouse is a magnet for visitors to the WMA as well. Standing 79 feet tall, it towers above the island and is visible for miles, even though its last light, a solar-powered unit, was turned off about 1994, ending a remarkable 142 years of service.

Over the years the lighthouse endured both natural and human-caused injuries. Put into operation on December 21, 1852, it met its first test in 1862, when Confederate troops attempted to blow it up to prevent it from falling into Union hands. However, the only damage from a keg of powder exploded inside was a few split cast-iron plates. Fewer than 20 years after construction, the lighthouse was in danger of being washed away by southward-moving Cavallo Pass. Its construction of cast-iron plates bolted to an interior metal framework allowed it to be dismantled and moved by ox team to its present site in 1870. At that time it was decided to increase its height from the original 55 feet by having new plates cast and added, and it was 1873 before the work was completed.

An 1875 hurricane destroyed all the towns on the island and nearby mainland, but the lighthouse stood firm. During the 1886 hurricane that destroyed Indianola, water stood four feet deep inside the tower, and winds rocked the tower so badly a bull's-eye prism in the lens was shaken loose and broken. Other than that, humans, nature, and time have been able to do little damage to the structure.

In 1952 the Matagorda lighthouse became the last functioning on the Texas coast when the Port Aransas lighthouse was closed. In 1977 the light was extinguished and the lens placed in the Calhoun County Museum in Port Lavaca. In 1986 a solar-powered light was activated, but it, too, was turned off in 1994.

By road the lighthouse is about 3 miles from the visitor center. Head east across the runway, then take the beach road. A sign at a shade shelter marks the turnoff to the lighthouse. As you approach the lighthouse, a viewing platform provides enough elevation for you to make out the faint outlines of Civil War–era trenches. Which side dug them is uncertain, but since the lighthouse was not moved here until after the war, their purpose was not to guard it. At the lighthouse, a boardwalk across a wetland area provides a view of numerous blue crabs before leading to a nature trail. Foundations remain of the lighthouse keeper's dwelling, but there are few other reminders of the historic importance of this place.

You can read more about this and other lighthouses on the Texas coast in *Lighthouses of Texas*, by T. Lindsay Baker (Texas A&M University Press, 1991).

11,190 acres in two units
County Courthouse, Room 101
Bay City, TX 77414
409/244-7697

DRIVING TIMES FROM:
Amarillo: 12 hours
Austin: 4 hours
Brownsville: 6 hours
Dallas: 5.5 hours
El Paso: 15 hours
Houston: 1.5 hours
San Antonio: 4 hours
Add one-half hour to all times for travel to the Bryan Beach Unit.
DIRECTIONS: Main Unit—From Freeport, take Texas 36 west 5 miles. Turn left into the WMA on the southern edge of the town of Jones Creek, then proceed about 2 miles to the headquarters. Bryan Beach Unit—From Freeport, take Texas 36/Texas 288 south to FM 1495. Turn right on FM 1495, cross the swing bridge over the Gulf Intracoastal Waterway, and continue to a stop sign where state maintenance ends and County Road 750 begins. Follow the county road to the beach, turn right, and drive along the water's edge about 3 miles.
OPEN: Main Unit—The public use area adjacent to Texas 36 is open from sunrise to sunset, 7 days a week. The remainder of the area is open only to hunters on designated days and to organized groups for guided tours by special request. Bryan Beach Unit—Open 24 hours a day, 7 days a week.
ACTIVITIES: Main Unit—Interpretive nature trail, picnicking, wildlife viewing, hiking, bicycling, hunting. Bryan Beach Unit—Camping, fishing, hunting.
FACILITIES: Nature trail, hiking and biking trail, picnic area, hunter check station, numbered hunting sites.
SPECIAL REGULATIONS: Main Unit—All hunters must check in and

Peach Point WMA provides blinds for the use of deer and feral hog hunters.

out. Permits for waterfowl hunts are issued at the check station beginning two hours before legal shooting time and continuing until 30 minutes before shooting time. Bryan Beach Unit—Hunting is allowed every day of the dove, early teal, duck, and goose seasons. Hunters are not required to check in and out.
ADVISORIES: Waterfowl hunters should bring waders, insect repellent, and a good flashlight. Users of the Bryan Beach Unit should be aware there are no facilities and that travel to and from the area at high tide can be difficult due to deep sand and debris. Carry your own supply of potable water.
LODGING IN AREA: Motels are available in Freeport.
LOCAL POINTS OF INTEREST: Varner-Hogg Plantation State Historical Park, Brazos Bend State Park, Christmas Bay State Park, Big Boggy National Wildlife Refuge, San Bernard National Wildlife Refuge, Brazoria National Wildlife Refuge.
DISABILITY ACCESS: The Live Oak Loop nature trail is wheelchair-accessible.

HISTORY

Peach Point lies within the bounds of lands granted to Stephen F. Austin in 1821 by Mexico for the purpose of settling 300 families. Austin himself was deeded land between Jones Creek and the Brazos River in 1830, and a portion of the Peach Point WMA lies within that grant. Austin sold the land in 1832 to his sister, Emily, and her husband, James F. Perry. They operated Peach Point Plantation, growing chiefly cotton and sugar cane, and prospered until the Civil War and Reconstruction brought hard times. Much of the land was sold to satisfy debts.

After passing through various owners, the land that is now the WMA was sold to the Seadock Corporation, which intended to build an offshore terminal for oil tankers. The oil bust of the 1980s ended those plans, and the Texas Nature Conservancy bought the property and in turn sold it to Texas Parks and Wildlife in 1987. Ironically, in the late 1990s the area was touted as the prime location for a spaceport.

The Bryan Beach Unit was once slated to be a state park but was made part of the WMA in 1993. Purchased from private owners in 1973, the area was named for James Perry Bryan, who built a home there in 1881 and operated a store nearby. Bryan Beach was physically separated from the rest of the WMA by the construction of the Gulf Intracoastal Waterway in the 1940s.

GEOGRAPHY AND NATURAL FEATURES

Peach Point WMA deceives the visitor. Upon entering and until traveling some distance past the area headquarters, one passes through a dense growth of trees—live oaks, water oaks, pecans, hackberries, elms, and Chinese tallow. Abruptly, however, the scenery changes to flat, poorly drained coastal marshes and

prairies that march away to the horizon. Elevations are generally less than 5 feet above sea level, occasionally rising to near 10 feet.

Peach Point lies between the San Bernard and Brazos Rivers. The mouth of the latter has been diverted 8 miles west of its natural location, near Quintana, and now enters the Gulf of Mexico about 4 miles east of the WMA. The Gulf Intracoastal Waterway forms the southern boundary of the area and meets Jones Creek at the area's eastern boundary and the San Bernard River at its western limit. Diversion of the Brazos and construction of the Gulf Intracoastal Waterway brought increased saltwater intrusion into the marshes on Peach Point WMA.

Most of the main unit consists of coastal prairie or coastal marsh. Most of the marsh area is inundated from October through May. Brackish and saline marshes are dominated by cordgrasses, saltgrass and bulrushes. Widgeongrass, a preferred duck food,

occurs in less saline areas that are shielded from tidal action. Numerous freshwater ponds and sloughs occur on the area as well, and these support sedges, millet, senna bean, cattail, and other plants. Upland prairies grow gulf cordgrass, seacoast bluestem, little bluestem, switchgrass, tallow trees, and pepper vines. A variety of trees grow on two ridges running north to south through the area.

Because of its rich and varied habitats, Peach Point WMA hosts a wide variety of resident and migratory water birds. The Christmas Bird Count location on the area often reports the nation's highest number of species, 300-plus in a single day. Snow geese, white-fronted geese, Canada geese, teal, shovelers, widgeons, gadwalls, pintails, and mottled ducks make up the principal game species.

The Live Oak Loop Nature Trail passes by a number of large trees spectacularly decorated with ferns and fungi.

RECREATIONAL OPPORTUNITIES
MAIN UNIT

NATURE TRAIL

Two nature trails begin at the picnic area just inside the WMA entrance on Texas 36. These trails are open daily during daylight hours.

PRO'S POINTERS. Live Oak Loop is a half-mile paved trail that winds through a low, almost swampy area with large live oak trees heavily overgrown with ferns. Palmettos fan through the thickly tangled undergrowth. Deer, feral hog, and raccoon tracks are plentiful, and a regular user of the trail reports seeing all three during early morning walks. This trail is level and wheelchair-accessible.

Jones Creek Trail is a 2.5-mile, natural-surfaced path that loops through a small, flooded bottomland where you are likely to see wood ducks and other waterfowl. The trail can be quite wet and muddy—waterproof footwear is recommended.

PICNICKING

Four picnic tables with barbecue grills are provided immediately adjacent to Texas 36. The picnic area is shaded by large trees.

PRO'S POINTERS. The picnic area is open daily from dawn to dusk. Be prepared to remove your own trash from the area.

HIKING

There are no designated hiking trails other than the two nature trails described above.

BICYCLING

There is no designated bicycling trail. See the nature trail section, above.

PRO'S POINTERS. Bicycles are permitted on the Live Oak Loop and Jones Creek Trail nature trails as well as the entrance road. Street bikes should be able to negotiate all three paths with no problem, but there may be muddy places along the Jones Creek Trail.

WILDLIFE VIEWING

A wildlife observation platform overlooks the creek bottom on the Jones Creek Trail (see above). During high water you will see ducks and herons; at low water, shorebirds frequent the area. Walk the Live Oak Loop to spot upland species. A bird checklist is available at area headquarters.

PRO'S POINTERS. As many as 35,000 snow geese winter on the area. A ryegrass field furnishes food for them and for sandhill cranes. The wooded ridges and the live oak woodlands are important fallout sites for neotropical migrants in spring.

Guided wildlife viewing tours of the area are offered to organized groups on an as-requested basis. Birds flying off the marsh inland will include egrets, ibises, and waterfowl. Then the tour will move along Big Ridge to salty prairie habitat to locate grassland-type birds. As the tour moves along the road back toward the headquarters, it passes through successional stages of vegetation, moving from prairie to brush to taller trees and finally blocks of woods.

The dam at Redfish Lake offers a vantage point from which to look at freshwater marsh birds, which may include black-necked stilts, coots, and blue-winged teal. Bald eagles and caracaras work the area looking for sick or crippled birds. Very near the headquarters area, the Barn Slough, a freshwater wetland, may offer sighting of a vermilion flycatcher. Later in the day, activity shifts to the 36 Pasture, a block of woodland along Texas 36 where woodland species may be seen. Expect to see between 100 and 110 species of birds in a day's time.

March, April, September, and October are peak months for seeing birds due to migratory activity. October is rutting time for white-tailed deer on the area, so you are more likely to see them that month because of increased daytime activity. Feral hogs and raccoons will be most active at dawn and dusk. Live Oak Loop and the Jones Creek Trail offer good viewing opportunities for neotropical species during spring fallouts.

HUNTING

Waterfowl, white-tailed deer, and feral hogs are the main game species. Youth-only deer hunts are offered. Check the *Public Hunting Lands Map Booklet* and the *Applications for Drawings on Public Hunting Lands* for information on hunting opportunities for the current year.

PRO'S POINTERS. Waterfowl hunting, particularly for ducks, is the main activity. Waterfowl hunting is by Regular Permit or Annual Public Hunting Permit. Hunters are allowed to take geese during that portion of the Eastern Zone goose season that falls within the duck season. Snipe, rails, and gallinules are legal during waterfowl hunts. Hunters must register at the check station; permits for marked hunting locations are issued beginning two hours before shooting time and continuing until 30 minutes before shooting time. Hunting locations are assigned on a first-come, first-served basis. Some hunters arrive the day before a hunt to be assured of getting a favorite spot, but there are no camping facilities.

Peach Point has five hunting compartments that can accommodate a total of 46 duck-hunting parties and an additional two goose-hunting parties. Most of the hunting sites are along Redfish Bayou, which runs through the southern half of the area. The main road from the check station leads directly to these sites. Numbered signs show where to park for each hunt site, each of which is marked with a reflective numbered sign. Most hunt sites are within a quarter of a mile of parking. Hunters are required to stay within 25 yards of the marker for their site.

Area manager Todd Merendino advises, "Hunt waterfowl early in the season down in the marsh along Jones Creek, in the 1200-Acre Pasture. Look for areas with lots of widgeon grass. Later in the season, hunt freshwater impoundments. Ducks will tend to use those areas more after the widgeon grass gets depleted." Goose hunters will probably have best success in the Lower Little Ridge Marsh area around McNeal Lake.

Feral hog hunts are offered through public drawings. The hunts are usually two weekends in February. Box blinds or tripod stands are furnished, and each hunting area is prebaited before the hunt. Hog hunters may bring aflatoxin-free corn to continue baiting the area after the hunt begins. Most success has been with rifles, although shotguns and archery equipment are allowed.

A youth deer hunt is held in October. Permits are obtained through a public drawing. Blinds are provided.

RECREATIONAL OPPORTUNITIES
BRYAN BEACH UNIT

CAMPING

Camping on the beach or in the dunes is permitted, but there are no facilities provided.

PRO'S POINTERS. Camp on the beach when possible so the sea breeze will protect you from mosquitoes. Access to this unit requires driving about 3 miles down the beach. The strip of hard-packed, wet sand near the water's edge may not be accessible during high tide. Debris on the beach and loose sand make driving away from the water's edge difficult or impossible. Unless you are prepared to deal with these conditions, visiting this area is not recommended.

HUNTING

A hunting license and an Annual Public Hunting Permit entitle you to hunt ducks and geese. A pond at the southern end of the beach can be a good place to hunt ducks. Geese can be hunted as they visit the beach to get grit.

PRO'S POINTERS. Due to the small size of the area, your best chance to have a good hunt is if you are the only person there.

FISHING

The Brazos River enters the Gulf of Mexico through a cut along the southern end of the area, offering the opportunity for surf fishing and river fishing within a small area.

PRO'S POINTERS. Visiting this area will be much easier if you have a boat. You can access it via the Gulf Intracoastal Waterway.

INSIDER'S CORNER

FERAL HOGS: SWINE DIVINE OR PORCINE PLAGUE?

The flat Texas coast may not look like good habitat for hogs, but there are few if any places in the state where feral hogs have failed to thrive. European explorers brought pigs to Texas with them for food, and escapees from La Salle's Fort St. Louis on the Texas coast were probably among the first to go wild.

American colonists brought hogs with them and allowed them to range in the wild for acorns and other mast. When meat was needed, the hogs could be rounded up or hunted down and shot. Salt pork, along with cornbread, was the basis of the common peoples' diet; travelers remarked on the monotonous meals of "pone and fry." By the early 1900s, wild hogs were prevalent throughout the eastern half of the state.

During the 20th century, people continued to release hogs into the wild to increase hunting opportunity. Changing land use practices, eradication of diseases, and elimination of the screwworm led to a population explosion of feral pigs after 1950. The feral hog population in Texas is now estimated at over 1 million, making hogs the second most numerous big game animal in the state, after white-tailed deer.

While many people like to hunt feral hogs and find them a worthy trophy and tasty table fare, wildlife biologists almost universally regard them as a scourge they would like to eliminate. Feral hogs compete with native wildlife species for food, water, and space. Since they are omnivorous and voracious, they can have severe negative impacts on animals that depend on limited foods. Hogs are known to prey upon the young of both wildlife and domestic livestock. Hogs may, through their rooting, have a positive impact by stimulating the production of early succession plants such as croton, partridge pea, sedges, and rushes, but their overall impact is generally regarded as negative.

While hunters, land managers, and wildlife biologists often come up with different answers when adding up the pluses and minuses of feral hogs, they all agree on one thing. Feral hogs are here to stay, and we have to learn how to live with them.

37 acres
County Courthouse, Room 101
Bay City, TX 77414
409/244-7697

DRIVING TIMES FROM:
Amarillo: 11.5 hours
Austin: 3.5 hours
Brownsville: 3 hours
Dallas: 7 hours
El Paso: 12.5 hours
Houston: 4 hours
San Antonio: 2.5 hours
DIRECTIONS: From Texas 358
(South Padre Island Drive, or SPID)
in Corpus Christi, exit at Waldron
Road. Continue on the frontage road
to Laguna Shores Road. Turn right
and go 1.9 miles.
OPEN: For guided group tours on an
as-requested basis. However, viewing is possible from a public street,
as noted below.

*Redhead Pond's wildlife viewing platform
overlooks this small WMA wedged between the
Laguna Madre and suburbs of Corpus Christi.
The only fresh water for miles, the pond
attracts thousands of ducks.*

ACTIVITIES: Wildlife viewing.
FACILITIES: Observation platform.
ADVISORIES: Carry your own
supply of potable water.
LODGING IN AREA: Motels are
available in Corpus Christi.
LOCAL POINTS OF INTEREST: Lake
Corpus Christi State Park,
Lipantitlan State Historical Park,
Copano Bay State Fishing Pier,
Fulton Mansion State Historical
Park, Goose Island State Park,
Mustang Island State Park, Aransas
National Wildlife Refuge, Padre
Island National Seashore.
DISABILITY ACCESS: Wheelchair-
accessible.

HISTORY

The 7.8-acre pond on this wetland
site appears to have been excavated to
furnish fill material for the construction of the Corpus Christi Naval Air
Station in the 1940s. The land was
perhaps used for livestock grazing
before being sold to the Texas Nature
Conservancy in 1990. While title has

since been transferred to Texas Parks
and Wildlife, the Texas Nature Conservancy retains a conservation
easement on the site, allowing them
to participate in decisions about site
management.

GEOGRAPHY AND NATURAL FEATURES

Only a city street and a strip of beach
separate this site from the Laguna
Madre, the saline body of water
between the mainland and Padre
Island. While the entire site is
classified as a wetland, the excavated
pond is the only permanent water on
the site. Water depth in the pond is
about two feet maximum, and it is
continually replenished by some
unknown freshwater source so that
salinity remains quite low, generally
five to six parts per thousand. This
makes the pond an important source
of fresh water for wildlife in the area,
particularly waterfowl.

Much of the shoreline of the pond
is screened from view by vegetation,

chiefly escaped ornamentals from the surrounding subdivision. A chain of narrow islands runs down the center of the elongated pond, providing added shoreline. A scattering of mesquite and salt cedar trees provides roosting and perching sites.

RECREATIONAL OPPORTUNITIES

WILDLIFE VIEWING

As the only permanent body of fresh water for miles, Redhead Pond is a magnet for waterfowl wintering in the area. As many as 5,000 ducks at a time may be on the pond. Redheads are the most numerous, but other species are common, among them scaup, ring-necked ducks, northern pintails, gadwalls, widgeons, shovelers, blue- and green-winged teal, buffleheads, ruddy ducks, canvasbacks, mergansers, mottled ducks, and black-bellied whistling ducks. The latter two are present year-round and use the pond area for nesting.

Wading and shorebird species that use the pond include blacknecked stilts, avocets, sandpipers, great blue herons, great egrets, coots, white pelicans, roseate spoonbills, ibis, and snowy egrets.

A wheelchair-accessible wooden viewing platform is located near the center of the pond's east side. A parking area and access gate are planned to allow daily access to the platform.

PRO'S POINTERS. From November through March, Redhead Pond can have one of the highest numbers of ducks per acre in the world. The key is the lack of other fresh water in the surrounding area. The pond gets its heaviest use in drought years. When the area is not open, birds may be viewed from Glenoak Road, a public street that runs along the southern end of the area. Offstreet parking is possible on the public right-of-way.

INSIDER'S CORNER

THE TEXAS NATURE CONSERVANCY

The Nature Conservancy (TNC) is an international, private, nonprofit conservation organization that uses its resources to preserve unique and significant natural areas and the flora and fauna dependent on them. Conservancy preserves comprise the largest system of private sanctuaries in the world.

The Texas Chapter of The Nature Conservancy was initiated in the 1960s by a handful of volunteers. The chapter's first purchase was the Attwater Prairie Chicken National Wildlife Refuge in Colorado County. Since then The Nature Conservancy of Texas has conserved over 365,000 acres of ecologically unique lands through acquisition, including Redhead Pond.

The Nature Conservancy of Texas has three main programs. (1) Through the Texas Land Stewards' Society, it works with private landowners who are voluntarily protecting the unique elements of our natural heritage that occur on their land. (2) It acquires through gift or purchase lands for transfer to other private and public groups that have expertise in natural areas management, such as Texas Parks and Wildlife. (3) Working only with willing sellers and donors, it acquires land and legal interest in land through gift or purchase and manages these nature preserves with the most sophisticated ecological techniques available.

As of 1999, The Nature Conservancy of Texas had acquired or helped to acquire unique natural areas all over Texas. TNC owned or managed 36 of these tracts as private nature preserves. Over 200,000 acres acquired by the Nature Conservancy are now managed as state or national parks or wildlife refuges, and 142 sites are protected by private landowners who belong to the Texas Land Stewards' Society.

The Nature Conservancy's mission is to preserve the plants, animals, and natural communities that represent the diversity of life on earth by protecting the lands and waters they need to survive. To assist in this effort, contact The Nature Conservancy of Texas at P.O. Box 1440, San Antonio, TX 78295-1440; 210/224-8774; www.tnc.org.

3,313 acres
10 Parks and Wildlife Dr.
Port Arthur, TX 77640
409/736-2551

DRIVING TIMES FROM:
Amarillo: 12 hours
Austin: 5 hours
Brownsville: 8.5 hours
Dallas: 5.5 hours
El Paso: 15 hours
Houston: 2 hours
San Antonio: 5.5 hours
DIRECTIONS: The WMA is located just east of Orange, where I-10 crosses the Sabine River.
OPEN: Daily.
ACTIVITIES: Nature trail, camping, wildlife viewing, hiking, hunting, fishing.
FACILITIES: Boat ramp, swamp boardwalk, interpretive displays, primitive campsites.
SPECIAL REGULATIONS: Hunting is not allowed in that portion of the WMA within the city limits of Orange. This includes all the area south of I-10 and the approximately 1,000-foot-wide strip north of I-10 between the highway and a canal running parallel to it. No unattended fishing lines or crawfish traps are allowed. Use of ATVs, airboats, and horses is not allowed. Use of buckshot while hunting is not allowed.
ADVISORIES: Mosquitoes can be present any time of year; bring plenty of insect repellent. Heat and humidity can make visiting the area unpleasant from April through October. Travel within the WMA is primarily by boat or canoe. High water may restrict land access to parts of the area at times. Carry your own supply of potable water.
LODGING IN AREA: Motels are available in Orange.
LOCAL POINTS OF INTEREST: Sabine Pass Battleground State Historical Park, Sea Rim State Park, Village Creek State Park, Texas Point National Wildlife Refuge, McFaddin National Wildlife Refuge, Anahuac National Wildlife Refuge, Big Thicket National Preserve.
DISABILITY ACCESS: The interpretive displays and swamp boardwalk at the Texas Travel Information Center are wheelchair-accessible.

Tony Houseman State Park/WMA offers access to the Sabine River from a public boat ramp beneath the I-10 bridge.

HISTORY

The area was known historically as the Blue Elbow Swamp, so named for a very deep, sharp bend in the Sabine River in the northeastern part of the area. The swamp was logged by the Lutcher-Moore Lumber Company around the turn of the century. Later it was acquired by developer Tony Houseman, who sold off most of the higher ground. The Texas Department of Transportation purchased the land in the mid-1990s as mitigation for wetland losses due to construction of a new travel information center on I-10, and then transferred ownership to Texas Parks and Wildlife. The area is known as Tony Houseman State Park/WMA. This is a misnomer, however, as there are no plans to develop traditional state park facilities on the area.

GEOGRAPHY AND NATURAL FEATURES

The Sabine River forms the eastern boundary of the WMA, and Little Cypress Bayou cuts diagonally across it. About 80 percent of the area is covered with bald cypress-water tupelo swamp. Small areas of uplands occur as islands in the northwestern portion of the area. Other small areas of land dry at normal water levels occur throughout the area, primarily as spoil banks from old logging canals or sandbanks deposited by the river. The sandbanks support pines and water oaks in narrow strips beyond which lies the swamp.

Blue Elbow, the bend in the Sabine River which gave the traditional name to the area, is about a mile north of I-10. The river here is about 60 feet deep—about twice the depth of the rest of the channel. Little Cypress Bayou enters the river from the northwest right at the bend; a large industrial plant is visible just up the bayou. Once you pass the plant, private land is on the left and the WMA is on the right.

Running off the river are numerous canals left from logging operations. The loggers dug T-shaped ditches some 50 yards off the river channel and anchored winch barges there. The winch dragged logs to the river, creating a spoke-like pattern of canals running for considerable distances back into the swamp. These narrow canals, only 8 to 10 feet wide, make very good canoe routes as there is virtually no current in them.

Historically, water coming down the Sabine River in floods would go straight south at the bend at Blue Elbow and sheet flow across the swamp until rejoining the river south of present-day I-10. This deposited soil in the swamp and flushed it, keeping the swamp healthy. Spoil banks associated with logging canals and the barrier created by I-10 stopped this flow, causing the swamp to deteriorate. Under way now are projects to help the swamp regenerate. The projects will cut channels across the logging canals and allow water to flow more freely, making for a better water exchange and improving the health of the swamp.

RECREATIONAL OPPORTUNITIES

The Tony Houseman area offers a unique mix of recreational activities and facilities due to its location, geography and creative collaboration between Texas Parks and Wildlife and the Texas Department of Transportation.

WILDLIFE VIEWING

The most accessible facility for wildlife viewing is the 600-foot boardwalk extending into the swamp from the rear of the Texas Travel Information Center on I-10. Interpretive displays inside the center orient visitors, who can then follow the boardwalk into the swamp for a closeup look at the plants and animals inhabiting it. Species most likely to be spotted are wood ducks, mallards, raccoons, squirrels, rabbits, mink,

The great egret is just one of many wading bird species found in the swamps of the Tony Houseman WMA.

wading birds, raptors, and neotropical songbirds. White-tailed deer and feral hogs also live on the area but are mostly confined to upland areas.

Some of the best wildlife viewing will be from boat or canoe within the swamp area. A public boat ramp is located beneath the I-10 bridge, or you can launch at a county ramp adjacent to the Bluebird Fishing Camp half a mile south of I-10 on Business U.S. 90. There is also a private ramp (fee charged) in the community of Pine Bluff, on the Sabine River in the northeastern corner of the area. From I-10, go north on Texas 87 for 1.8 miles to FM 3247. Go east on FM 3247 for 1.25 miles to Holiman Road (where the divided road begins—street sign may be missing). Turn left and go to Pine Bluff Road, then right on Pine Bluff Road to the river.

PRO'S POINTERS. Spring and fall are the best times to visit. More birds will be present, and temperatures will be more bearable. If you plan to travel on the Sabine River by boat, be aware that a 1903 railroad bridge across the river between Blue Elbow and Pine Bluff may block passage of boats when the river is high.

CAMPING

At three places along the Sabine River where enough high ground exists, Texas Parks and Wildlife has cleared underbrush and installed picnic tables and fire rings. Camping is permitted only in these areas. The areas are located where old logging ditches were cut through the river bank. Approximate locations for these sites are shown on the WMA map.

PRO'S POINTERS. These campsites have no potable water, and you must carry out your trash.

HIKING

There is no designated hiking trail. Hiking is limited to Sand Ridge, an island that can be accessed by foot from Pine Bluff Road. Walk-in gates are located at a pipeline crossing about 0.8 mile east of the intersection of Holiman Road and Pine Bluff Road. From I-10, go north on Texas 87 for 1.8 miles to FM 3247. Go east on 3247 for 1.25 miles to Holiman Road (where the divided road begins), turn left, and go to Pine Bluff Road.

PRO'S POINTERS. From the walk-in gates, walk south about a quarter of a mile to Sand Ridge, an area of high ground about three-quarters of a mile long by a quarter of a mile wide vegetated with loblolly pine, sweet gums, and water oaks. Waterproof footwear and leg coverings are suggested due to the possibility of damp vegetation.

HUNTING

Hunting is permitted on the Tony Houseman WMA for rabbits, hares, feral hogs, waterfowl, squirrels, predators, and frogs for holders of an Annual Public Hunting Permit. Check the *Public Hunting Lands Map Booklet* for information on species, seasons, and bag limits for the current year.

Tony Houseman is the only WMA

on the Texas coast open all day for duck hunting. This makes it possible for you to hunt wood ducks returning to roost just before sunset, a favorite local tactic.

PRO'S POINTERS. Hunting is allowed only in that portion of the area north of an old logging canal that runs parallel to and about 300 yards north of I-10. Note that hunting with buckshot is prohibited on the area. Rifles and shotguns with slugs are permitted for hog hunting. Hunters are not required to check in or out. Hunt hogs by accessing islands by boat, then walking them up and jump-shooting them. Or you can find an area with fresh sign and hide in a temporary blind. Permanent blinds and baiting are not permitted.

The sand ridges with oak trees provide good squirrel hunting. The squirrels feed on the acorns and build nests from bark stripped from cypress trees. You'll see the squirrel nests in the treetops. A favorite local hunting tactic is "vine-pulling" or "vining." Spot a nest in a tree and pull on vines in the tree to disturb the squirrels and chase them out of their nests into view.

FISHING

Although you need a boat to access them, the spoil banks created when the logging canals were dug furnish good spots for bank fishing. Fishing is good where the logging canals enter the river channel. Catfish are the primary quarry.

PRO'S POINTERS: When running the Sabine River, you may not always be sure where the main river channel is—large bayous branch off at intervals. To stay in the main channel, watch for white bands painted around trees on the Louisiana side. They mark the boundary of a Louisiana WMA. The Texas side is marked with yellow signs.

INSIDER'S CORNER

SWAMPED BY MISUNDERSTANDING

Swamps are like bats in that people who do not understand them sometimes develop unfounded fears of them. Contrary to what you might see in Grade B movies, bats do not get caught in hairdos, and swamps do not harbor mysterious, blood-thirsty monsters. Swamps were once thought to be the breeding ground of disease and pests, and in an era when mosquito-borne diseases took many human lives, swamps were regarded as public enemies to be subdued.

The truth is much more benign. Swamps are simply a form of wetland. Wetlands are areas that contain water or saturated soils for at least part of the year, plants that have adapted to life in wet environments, and special soils that develop under depleted oxygen conditions. Wetlands can be swamps, bottomland hardwoods, marshes, bogs, springs, resacas, playa lakes and saline (alkaline) lakes. Wetlands are found along rivers, streams, lakes, and ponds; in upland depressions where surface water collects; and at points of groundwater discharge such as springs or seeps.

Wetlands are some of the most important wildlife habitat in Texas. By their very nature they produce significant quantities of the food, cover, and water animals need to survive and are vital spawning grounds for a number of aquatic species. Among the other benefits of wetlands are flood and erosion control, removal of sediment and toxicants, groundwater recharge, outdoor recreation, and commercial uses such as timber production.

Unfortunately, humans have not always respected wetlands, and especially swamps, for their benefits. Texas has lost over 50 percent of its presettlement wetlands, primarily due to human activities. Wetlands held to the same standard of economic use as drylands, whether it be for agriculture or as building sites, were often seen as worthless unless drained or filled.

Ironically, many wetlands in Texas have been destroyed by submergence under lakes built to supply water, flood control, and recreation. Only in recent years has the role of wetlands in reducing water pollution come to be appreciated. Wetlands absorb and filter a variety of sediments, nutrients, and other natural and artificial pollutants that would otherwise degrade rivers, streams, and lakes. Water flowing from uplands into water bodies often passes through wetlands, which maintain and improve water quality by filtering out nutrients and sediments before they reach the river or stream. Wetlands lessen the effects of nonpoint pollution by reducing flow velocities and by acting as a sediment, nutrient, and heavy metals trap.

In addition, wetlands are beautiful places. Few people can view a swamp forested with majestic, moss-draped cypress trees and not be impressed. Playa lakes and coastal marshes thronged with thousands of colorful ducks delight both birders and hunters. Legends of swamp monsters notwithstanding, wetlands are a precious resource now recognized as worth saving.

1,480 acres
County Courthouse, Room 101
Bay City, TX 77414
409/244-7697

DRIVING TIMES FROM:
Amarillo: 11 hours
Austin: 3 hours
Brownsville: 3.5 hours
Dallas: 6 hours
El Paso: 14 hours
Houston: 2.5 hours
San Antonio: 2.5 hours
DIRECTIONS: Access is by boat only.
From Seadrift, take the Victoria
Barge Canal south to its intersection
with the Gulf Intracoastal Waterway.
The WMA is submerged land east
and north of those two waterways.
OPEN: Daily.
ACTIVITIES: Wildlife viewing,
fishing.
FACILITIES: None.
SPECIAL REGULATIONS: No Annual
Public Hunting Permit is required
for fishers.
ADVISORIES: Only submerged lands
and wetlands are public; dry land is
private property. Boundaries are not
clearly marked. Boaters should be
aware of shallow water and oyster
reefs in San Antonio Bay. Carry your
own supply of potable water.
LODGING IN AREA: Motels are
available in Seadrift.
LOCAL POINTS OF INTEREST: Lake
Texana State Park, Fannin Battle-
ground State Historical Park, Goliad
State Historical Park, Copano Bay
State Fishing Pier, Port Lavaca State
Fishing Pier, Fulton Mansion State
Historical Park, Goose Island State
Park, Matagorda Island State Park,
Aransas National Wildlife Refuge.
DISABILITY ACCESS: Not
wheelchair-accessible.

*Welder Flats WMA is typical of many areas
along the Texas Coast but unique among Texas
WMAs in that it consists of submerged land. It
was established to help protect the habitat of
the whooping cranes that winter here.*

HISTORY

Welder Flats WMA might be compared to an iceberg: The visible
portion is but a hint of what lies
hidden. This bit of submerged land is
part of 2.4 million acres of coastal
land that was the object of a struggle
between Texas and the federal government lasting nearly 120 years. See
the Insider's Corner, below, for a
more detailed treatment of the Tidelands Controversy.

From the establishment of the
Republic of Texas in 1836, Texas
claimed ownership of submerged
lands for three leagues (10.35 miles)
offshore. Therefore, the underwater
land now comprising Welder Flats
has been considered to be state-
owned since that time. Historical uses
of the area included waterfowl hunting, fishing, and crabbing. Dry lands
abutting the wetlands have been
grazed as part of the Cliburn Ranch
since the 1940s.

The Welder Flats area has been used as a wintering ground by endangered whooping cranes since the 1930s and was designated critical habitat by the U.S. Fish and Wildlife Service. In 1988 the Texas General Land Office, which administers state-owned lands, signed a lease agreement giving Texas Parks and Wildlife the right to manage the property for recreational purposes and to protect its ecological resources.

GEOGRAPHY AND NATURAL FEATURES

Welder Flats is on the east side of San Antonio Bay and consists of submerged land between the Victoria Barge Canal and the Gulf Intracoastal Waterway and the low-tide mark. The WMA extends approximately 1.5 miles along the Victoria Barge Canal and 4.5 miles along the Gulf Intracoastal Waterway, but because of complex interdigitation with private land consists of only about 1,480 acres.

The area is a highly productive marine nursery. Shoalgrass and widgeongrass on the submerged land serve as shelter and food for a variety of marine animals. The shoreline has long been used by Texas Parks and Wildlife as a stocking area for red drum and spotted sea trout because of its high nursery value.

Exact boundaries of the area are difficult to determine because of the highly reticulated nature of the shoreline. Narrow necks and pockets of public land occur within and around private land. Navigation by boat is extremely difficult due to shallow water.

A diversity of wildlife uses the area—pelicans, shorebirds, waterfowl, and some whooping cranes in winter. Bobcats, deer, and feral hogs use the sand ridges jutting into the bay.

RECREATIONAL OPPORTUNITIES

WILDLIFE VIEWING

Whooping cranes are the chief attraction, although you may also see roseate spoonbills and a variety of ducks and geese. "Welder Flats is near the Aransas National Wildlife Refuge, so you have a good chance of seeing whoopers there, mostly along the shore, from October through February," says area manager Brent Ortego.

PRO'S POINTERS. Ortego advises keeping at least 200 yards away from whooping cranes to avoid disturbing them. Whoopers are most likely to be present on the area from late December into early January. Visitors may boat to the area from Seadrift, Port O'Connor or Charlie's Bait Camp on the Gulf Intracoastal Waterway. To reach the latter, go east from Seadrift on Texas 185 for about 10 miles to Lane Road. Follow Lane Road about 4 miles to the boat ramp. From Charlie's it is about 7 miles south via the Gulf Intracoastal Waterway to its junction with the Victoria Barge Canal.

Matagorda Island State Park also offers birding tours to the area during the whooping crane season. Visitors pay the ferry transportation fee plus a tour fee. For information contact the park at 361/983-2215.

FISHING

Red drum (redfish), black drum, spotted sea trout, and flounder are the main fish caught here. Only a fishing license and saltwater stamp are required of fishers.

PRO'S POINTERS. Since the area is used for stocking redfish and trout, there are a lot of undersized fish at times. Shallow water makes access difficult unless you know the area well.

The best fishing will probably be in the spring and fall. Fish for black drum in potholes, grassy depressions. Use artificial baits such as shrimp tails or natural baits such as cut mullet or fresh dead or live shrimp. For redfish and trout, topwater baits and spoons work well because there is less than two feet of water over grass.

From late spring into summer as the water heats up, action shifts to the edge of the Gulf Intracoastal Waterway. Shell clumps along the edge offer shallow feeding areas for trout and redfish, which can then go to deeper water in the canal when the water heats up. Fish the shallow water early and the deeper water later in the day. Artificial baits and live croakers will both produce.

THE TIDELANDS CONTROVERSY

Who owns submerged lands—the state or the federal government? This question is almost as old as the republic. But as with many disagreements, not until large sums of money became involved did the argument come to a head.

The Texas tidelands are 2,440,650 acres of seabottom in the Gulf of Mexico between the low tide mark and the state's territorial boundary three leagues (10.35 miles) offshore. The three-league boundary was proposed by General Sam Houston while still on the battlefield at San Jacinto in 1836 and adopted by the Congress of the Republic of Texas later that year. While the three-league limit was not specifically written into the act annexing Texas to the United States in 1845, language was included that seemed to recognize state ownership of the submerged lands as well as all vacant and unappropriated lands within its boundaries. Income from these lands was dedicated to public education.

Discovery of oil under submerged lands in the 20th century led directly to the Tidelands Controversy. Oil operators could lease federally owned lands for 25 cents per acre under federal law. Typically, Texas and other states charged more than a hundred times this amount for leases. It would be greatly to oil companies' benefit to have the submerged lands that were claimed by Texas and other states declared federal lands. In 1946 the United States sued California, claiming ownership of its tidelands, and in 1947 the Supreme Court ruled in favor of the federal government.

The reasoning cited by Justice Hugo Black in the opinion created a firestorm of criticism and fear. He stated that because of its responsibility for national defense and international affairs, the federal government had rights that transcended legal title and property ownership. In effect, the ruling held that the United States could take the oil without compensation, arousing fears the rule might someday be applied to private property. This was not a popular idea in Texas, where 97 percent of the land is privately owned.

In 1948 newly elected president Harry Truman directed the attorney general to file suit against Texas. In a summary judgment made without hearing evidence, the Supreme Court ruled 4 to 3 in favor of the federal government. In 1952 Congress passed a bill restoring title to the states of all submerged lands within their boundaries, but Truman vetoed it.

General Dwight D. Eisenhower made restoration of the states' rights to submerged lands a campaign issue in the 1952 presidential election, stating he would sign a bill if Congress passed it. So vital was the issue to Texas that it voted for a Republican candidate for president for the first time since Reconstruction. The State Democratic Convention passed a resolution calling on all Texas Democrats to vote for Eisenhower. President Eisenhower signed a bill into law on May 22, 1953, restoring submerged lands to the states. Later, Texas successfully turned back an attempt to set the boundary of the state 3 miles offshore rather than three leagues.

HILL COUNTRY

*There is, as yet, no sense of pride
in the husbandry of wild plants
and animals, no sense of shame
in the proprietorship of a sick
landscape. We tilt windmills in
behalf of conservation in convention halls and editorial offices,
but on the back forty we disclaim
even owning a lance.*
—ALDO LEOPOLD

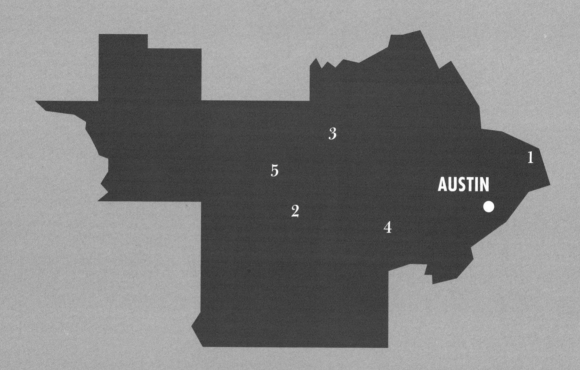

1 GRANGER WMA

2 KERR WMA

3 MASON MOUNTAIN WMA

4 OLD TUNNEL WMA

5 WALTER BUCK WMA

11,116 acres
213 Thomas Ridge Rd.
Burnet, TX 78611
512/859-2668

DRIVING TIMES FROM:
Amarillo: 8 hours
Austin: 1 hour
Brownsville: 7 hours
Dallas: 3 hours
El Paso: 11 hours
Houston: 3.5 hours
San Antonio: 2.5 hours
DIRECTIONS: From Taylor, take Texas 95 north 5 miles to Circleville. To access the south side of Granger Lake, take FM 1331 east. To access the west side of the lake, continue on Texas 95 across the bridge over the San Gabriel River, then turn right onto County Road 347. This road, and roads 378, 390, 391, and 348, will take you to all access points on the west end of the lake. To access the north side, continue from Circleville to Granger on Texas 95, then go east on FM 971.
OPEN: Daily. The park is closed to all but hunters during Special Permit hunts.
ACTIVITIES: Camping, wildlife viewing, hiking, bicycling, hunting, fishing.
FACILITIES: Boat ramps and restrooms at Corps of Engineers parks, primitive campground, small craft launch.
SPECIAL REGULATIONS: Driving on the area is not permitted, except for some limited access during Special Permit hunts. Shotguns are the only firearms permitted. Only hunters are required to possess an Annual Public Hunting Permit. Hunting is not permitted within the Corps of Engineers parks.
ADVISORIES: Due to the thick cover, long pants and sleeves are recommended for hunters at all times. Carry your own supply of potable water.
LODGING IN AREA: Motels are available in Taylor. Camping is available at four Corps of Engineers parks adjoining the WMA.
LOCAL POINTS OF INTEREST: Bastrop State Park, Buescher State Park, Lake Somerville State Park, Mother Neff State Park, McKinney Falls State Park, Pedernales Falls State Park, Inks Lake State Park, Longhorn Cavern State Park.
DISABILITY ACCESS: Restrooms at Corps of Engineers parks are wheelchair-accessible.

HISTORY

Prior to Anglo settlement, the Blackland Prairie was buffalo range. The fertile prairie was plowed for farming as settlers moved in, and before the beginning of the 20th century, cotton farming became the principal land use. Grain sorghums, wheat and corn were other principal crops on small farms typical of the area. Most of the bottomlands were cleared for farming or for the creation of pecan bottoms along the river.

Flooding was a problem on the San Gabriel River, and the flood of September 1921 was of historic proportions. In the early 1970s the U.S. Army Corps of Engineers purchased the land within the Granger WMA. In 1977 Texas Parks and Wildlife signed an agreement to manage the wildlife areas around the lake. Beginning at the dam and moving clockwise, these are known as the Pecan Grove, San Gabriel, Willis Creek, and Sore Finger wildlife areas.

Ring-necked pheasants and Rio Grande turkeys were stocked on the area after Texas Parks and Wildlife took over management of the wildlife, but only the latter is present today.

Trotliners regularly take large flathead catfish in the San Gabriel River channel between the Texas 95 bridge and the Fox Bottom primitive camping area.

GEOGRAPHY AND NATURAL FEATURES

The Granger WMA lies totally within the Blackland Prairies Ecological Region. The broad river valley of the San Gabriel is only slightly lower than the surrounding flat prairie except on the south side of the lake at the dam, but even here relief is limited. On the north side of the lake, the land is flat and the lake shallow.

Willis Creek joins the San Gabriel River west of the dam, and other minor drainages enter from surrounding farmlands. The result is a V-shaped lake with a large peninsula jutting into its center, with numerous smaller peninsulas and protected coves along the entire shoreline.

Vegetation on the Blackland Prairie before human intervention consisted largely of grasses such as little bluestem, big bluestem, Indiangrass, switchgrass, Illinois bundleflower, Engelmann daisy, and Maximillian sunflower with wooded areas along drainages. Most of these original plant communities have been destroyed. A Blackland Prairie

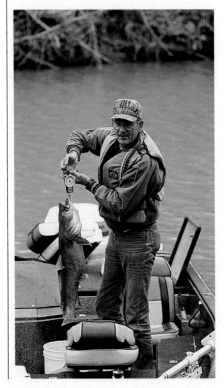

Replication Site and Gene Bank have been established below the dam between the Corps of Engineers office and the stilling basin in an attempt to return a small portion of the area to its pre-development state.

Today much of the area has been invaded by nonnative species such as chinaberry, Japanese honeysuckle, Johnsongrass and Kleingrass. Old fields are dominated by grasslands, while cedar elm, cottonwood, black willow, and hackberry have grown into thickets in many bottomland areas. Old pecan orchards contain many grafted varieties as well as native nuts.

The result of all these changes is three wildlife areas that are heavily wooded for the most part but contain some open fields away from drainages. These are the Pecan Grove, San Gabriel, and Willis Creek areas. The Sore Finger wildlife area consists of mostly open grassland with very little woody cover sloping gently to the lakeshore.

Recreational Opportunities

Camping

The Granger WMA offers one of the finest campgrounds in the entire WMA system from the standpoints of beauty and convenience to hunting areas. That's the good news. The bad news, if it can be considered that, is that the campground is accessible only by foot or by boat.

The Fox Bottom campground sits in a bend of the San Gabriel River east of the Texas 95 bridge. To hike or bike to the campground, park at the Comanche Bluff trailhead at the end of County Road 496. This trailhead is about three-quarters of a mile north of FM 1331. The entry gate to the trail is at the west end of the parking lot, opposite the restroom building. The trail closely follows the lakeshore and then the riverbank. Waterproof footwear is highly recommended, as the trail crosses a number of small drainages that may be wet

and muddy. Larger drainages are spanned by footbridges.

To boat to the campground, you must either run up the river from the lake or, if you have a small flat-bottom boat or canoe, you can put in at entry point 7 and go downstream about a quarter of a mile. To reach entry point 7, take County Road 347 east from Texas 95 for 1.7 miles and turn right at the 90-degree bend in the road. The parking lot three-tenths of a mile down the graveled road permits parking within 10 yards of the riverbank and a small-craft launch.

The Fox Bottom campground is an area of a little more than an acre that is completely shaded by large cedar elm and pecan trees. Campsites have fire rings and tent pads, and there is a composting toilet at the site. The site was used for entertaining by the people who owned the land before the lake was built, and local lore holds that the late president Lyndon B. Johnson was a guest at a barbecue held here.

PRO'S POINTERS. There is no charge for use of the campground. Stays are limited to 14 days, and users must inform the Corps of Engineers office of their presence by calling 512/859-2668. Upstream and downstream from the campground for approximately 3 miles are some of the prime feral hog areas in the WMA, and fishing for catfish, crappie, and white bass can be productive.

Wildlife Viewing

An isolated setting offering plentiful food and cover—an island of diversity in a sea of agricultural monoculture—Granger WMA attracts a variety of birds. The remnant prairie habitat below the dam is home to sparrow species not common elsewhere, while woodland birds find ample habitat ringing the entire lake. Hawks are commonly seen working the grasslands on the north side of the lake. The lake itself attracts white pelicans, great blue herons, and ducks.

PRO'S POINTERS. Walking slowly

and quietly along the Comanche Bluff hiking trail or along any of the mowed paths crisscrossing the area—especially at dawn or dusk—increases your chances of seeing deer, feral hogs, coyotes, wild turkeys, rabbits, squirrels, or birds. However, the best place to have a chance to see one of the area's trophy bucks is also one of the most open and most visited parts of the area—the parking lot at the stilling basin below the dam. Deer emerge from the surrounding woods at dusk and make their way onto the dam to feed. Feral hogs travel the river banks from the Texas 95 bridge to the lake and are often seen by fishers and boaters. Indeed, the wildlife viewing from a boat can be the most productive of all, because you can slip into small coves using a trolling motor and get close to wildlife without spooking it.

Hiking

In addition to the Comanche Bluff hiking and biking trail along the south shore of the lake, there are approximately 35 miles of mowed paths on the Granger WMA. These paths provide hunter and fisher access but may also be used for hiking any time the area is not closed for a Special Permit hunt. Dates the area is closed are listed in the *Public Hunting Lands Map Booklet* and posted at all entry points to the area prior to and during hunts, or you can call the Corps of Engineers office at 512/859-2668.

The nature of the land traversed by the mowed paths varies considerably depending on location. In general, those paths on the north side of the lake, accessed at entry points 1, 2, and 3, pass over flat grasslands with few trees. Except for views of the lake in the distance, scenery is minimal, and there is no shade. Entry point 4, on the west side of the lake, is in the thickly wooded bottomland of Willis Creek and offers limited hiking and biking. Better is entry point 5, from which a gravel road leads about a mile between fencelines about 50 yards apart. The road is lined with small trees in places, and in spring the ground may be covered with bluebonnets and Indian paintbrushes. This is an ideal path to walk with small children or a dog. An added benefit of this road is that it is always clear of vegetation, whereas the mowed paths can be choked with plants after not having been mowed for a time.

The mowed paths from entry points 6 and 7 lead into the extremely thick bottomland of the San Gabriel River. In places there are huge pecan trees, but in general hackberry trees that have invaded old agricultural fields dominate. The trail downstream from entry point 7 closely follows the riverbank and gives good views of the river as well as furnishing access for fishers.

Entry point 9, at the Texas 95 bridge, is a jumping-off point for the trail that runs along the south side of the San Gabriel River to the primitive campground about 3 miles distant and then on to the trailhead off County Road 496 (about another 3 miles). From there, it's another mile and a half to the Taylor Park Corps of Engineers campground. This narrow trail is twisting and shaded throughout its entire length. It crosses several small drainages that may be wet and muddy; waterproof footwear is advised. About midway between the County Road 496 trailhead and Taylor Park is a 1921 iron truss bridge formerly used over Willis Creek on the north side of the lake and moved here by the Corps of Engineers in 1982. The trail skirts the lake but never goes to the shore. Wildflowers, especially bluebonnets, are abundant on well-drained slopes. When I last walked this trail, six turkey hens greeted me when I returned to the parking lot.

All but scattered bits of the original Blackland Prairie were plowed under long ago; a restoration site on the Granger WMA serves as a demonstration area and gene bank.

BICYCLING

Bike riding is allowed anywhere on the area. In general, the better hiking paths are also the ones best suited for bike riding, with the exception of the trail running downstream from entry point 7. The most pleasant route begins at entry point 9 and parallels the river all the way to the Taylor Park campground, a ride of about 7.5 miles one way.

PRO'S POINTERS. Access gates are built in a narrow V to permit humans to pass but prevent cattle on the area from escaping. A bike can be passed through these gates by standing it on the rear wheel and guiding it through.

HUNTING

Check the *Public Hunting Lands Map Booklet* and the *Applications for Drawings on Public Hunting Lands* for information on hunting opportunities for the current year. Deer, feral hogs, waterfowl, and turkeys are the main game species. Note that hunter orientations for Special Permit hunts are held at the Corps of Engineers office where FM 971 meets the dam. The check station for Special Permit hunts is at the entrance to Willis Creek Park on County Road 346.

The Granger WMA is famous for the size and quality of the bucks in its white-tailed deer herd. Bucks in the 150 to 160 class are sometimes passed up by bowhunters here, because they know there are much better bucks on the area. The secret to the size of the deer is also the thorn in the side of those who hunt them. The Granger WMA has such good cover and food for deer that seeing one in daylight hours, much less having the chance to shoot one, is a rare event. Yet for the bowhunter, this represents the ultimate challenge. Hunting here is an excellent way to develop and hone scouting and hunting skills, and taking a deer from this WMA could well be the achievement of a lifetime.

Despite the size of its bucks, the Granger WMA is best known for its hog hunting. Feral hogs run the bottomlands of the San Gabriel and infest the thick cover in every part of the WMA except the very open Sore Finger area. At night, hogs leave the area to feed in surrounding farm fields. Archery and crossbow hunting of hogs is allowed every day except when the area is closed for Special Permit hunts, when shotguns and muzzleloaders may also be used. Hogs may be hunted only during daylight hours. Baiting is allowed, but the use of dogs is not. There is no bag limit on feral hogs.

PRO'S POINTERS. Deer hunting is archery only and by Special Permit only. The best chance of seeing a buck is during the rut, which peaks here in mid-November. Hunters are assigned compartments based on where area manager Trey Carpenter knows the deer live. "I put people where I think they will have the opportunity to kill a good deer," he says. "Most people want to hunt below the dam, but there are deer all over the area except in the Sore Finger area. I would hunt by sitting on a scrape and waiting."

Hunters are allowed to use tree stands and temporary blinds, but where to place them can be puzzling. Much of the area is grown up in small hackberry trees that reduce visibility and make finding shooting lanes difficult. However, based on my experiences, the following tips may be helpful.

Scout the area as much as you can before the hunt. You are not looking for deer so much as you are places where deer are likely to be. When the land for the lake and surrounding wildlife management area was purchased, there were many homesites on it. Look for old foundations or other evidence of buildings. In such areas you will often find chinaberry trees. Bucks love to rub on smooth-barked trees, and I've found many, many rubs on chinaberry trees on the area. Where there are rubs there will many times be a scrape. If the sign is fresh, find a suitable tree nearby and put your stand there.

Also look for trails. Deer feed on the dam at night and use the wooded area just below the dam as a staging area where they gather while waiting for dusk. Find the trail they are using and hunt there. Another travel corridor for deer is the finger of woods that runs north from the river below the dam, following the eastern edge of the Blackland Prairie Replication Site. Bucks cross the river at a riffle about 300 yards below the dam where this narrow strip of woods runs to the bank between cleared areas on either side. Deer trails can also be found a few yards inside the woods surrounding old fields. Food plots on the south side of the river below the dam also attract deer. In years when the native pecan trees bear, hunting over this favored food source can be productive. The bottomlands along the San Gabriel River hold some very large pecan trees suitable for ladder stands.

Don't be intimidated by the very thick cover. Remember that deer are creatures of the edge. Hunt the edges of fields, concentrating on game trails

This 1921 iron truss bridge was moved from Willis Creek on the north side of the WMA to a hiking trail near the Corps of Engineers Taylor Park on the south side of Granger Lake.

that enter them. Bucks sometimes use the tall grass in the open fields for bedding areas during the day; try to intercept them on their way there. You'll find this situation when hunting the compartments accessed by entry points 5 and 6.

Note that while the official entry point for the Pecan Grove wildlife area below the dam, point 8, is on FM 1331 at the extreme southern edge of the area, this is the worst possible place to enter. Access is much easier from the parking lot at the stilling basin below the dam.

Recently, farmers around the area have begun growing less cotton and more corn and milo. While the habitat on the WMA is so good that deer have not been dependent on these food sources in the past, the potential effect of having these bonus groceries available may be significant. Granger bucks may become even bigger and more legendary in the future. Hunting trails leading to croplands may be the ticket to a Big Game Awards dinner.

Hunting pressure has made the hogs on the Granger WMA become very nocturnal. "The west end of the lake is still probably the best, and hog hunting seems to really pick up right after deer season," says Trey Carpenter. "However, during deer season is a good time to hunt, because you will probably pretty much have the area to yourself."

At one time baiting worked well for hunting hogs, but this is no longer the case. "People who kill them on a consistent basis sit, listen for hogs, get the wind on them and go to them," says Carpenter. To find an area hogs are using, look for fresh tracks in trails, fresh rooting, and recently used wallows. In hot weather, hogs will spend part of the day in muddy drainages. Areas accessed from entry points 5 and 6, and the finger of woods running north from the parking area below the dam, may have wallows. Hunting trails at dawn and dusk can also pay off.

The Granger WMA offers bowhunters an unusual opportunity: the chance to hunt using a boat or canoe. While hunting from a boat is not permitted, using one can get you into an area easier and more quietly than walking, and bringing a hog out by boat is much easier than dragging it. Hunters may use the primitive campground on the area or one of the Corps of Engineers parks and launch from there, or they can use the small-craft launch at entry point 7 off County Road 347.

Waterfowl hunting is mainly limited to ducks, as geese do not winter on the lake. Species seen on the area include teal, mallards, pintails, widgeons, gadwalls and wood ducks.

Granger Lake is primarily managed for maintaining a flood control pool, so drawdowns are generally not timed for the production of food for waterfowl. Corps of Engineers operating procedures call for maintaining the level of the lake as nearly constant as possible. Ideal conditions for duck hunting would call for the lake to be drawn down in summer to allow vegetation to grow on exposed flats, then refilled in winter to create shallow, grassy flats. Texas Parks and Wildlife is working on developing ponds whose water level can be controlled for the benefit of ducks. One such pond is on the south side of the lake near the Fox Bottom primitive campground; others are on the north side of the lake around entry point 3.

The best duck hunting is in the coves on the north side of the lake. Hunters can boat in or use entry points 1, 2, and 3. Natural cover is very limited, so some type of artificial blind will be required. The best launching site is at Friendship Park just off FM 971; the gate is not staffed except during the summer, so launching is free during hunting season. If you wish to launch from the south side of the lake, the gate at Taylor Park is unstaffed from October through February, so launching is free

there as well during most of the duck season.

Rio Grande turkeys are present on the area and may be hunted in the spring by Special Permit only. Shotgun, archery, and crossbow hunters may take one gobbler; archery and crossbow hunters are also allowed to take unlimited feral hogs during these hunts.

Turkeys tend to roost in large trees along drainages. Consequently, the most likely places to find turkeys will be along the San Gabriel River west of the lake, the south shore of the lake, and the river channel below the dam. Pre-hunt scouting at dawn to listen for gobbling is the best way to locate roosts. Hunters will be assigned to compartments known to be frequented by turkeys. However, hunting will likely be difficult due to the heavy cover on most of the area. Turkeys tend to fly down into open areas at dawn, and gobblers prefer to strut where there is good visibility. Corps of Engineers parks and surrounding farmlands, both off limits to hunters, tend to attract turkeys.

Given these factors, and based on personal experience, the Pecan Grove wildlife area below the dam may offer the best chance for success. Food plots provide cleared areas for strutting activities, and the wooded areas provide shade and cover where turkeys may spend the midday hours. A good strategy under these conditions will likely be to hunt the edges of cleared areas from mid-morning until early afternoon, when gobblers without hens may respond to calling.

Rabbits and hares can be found mainly in the upland areas around the fringes of the lake. Open grasslands occur mainly in the Sore Finger and San Gabriel wildlife areas. Squirrels occur in wooded areas all over the WMA but are most numerous in the pecan bottoms below the dam, along the San Gabriel River and in the vicinity of Willis Creek. May and June are the best months to take tender young squirrels for eating.

There is no closed season or bag limit, making rabbit and squirrel hunting an ideal way to introduce youngsters to hunting. Youths below the age of 17 may hunt free on WMAs when accompanied by a permitted adult.

Furbearing animals—primarily raccoons, grey foxes, opossums and coyotes—may be hunted during daylight hours from September 1 until March 31. Dogs, mouth-blown calls or electronic calls may be used to hunt furbearers. Archery equipment or shotguns with nontoxic shot or lead shot no larger than #4 may be used.

Pelts will be in best condition during the colder winter months. Calling predators is one of the most exciting ways to hunt. Days with little or no wind are best. Wear complete camouflage, including gloves and face mask, and get well hidden before you begin calling. Rabbit distress calls work for all types of predators. Be prepared to shoot quickly; foxes and coyotes will generally rush in. Allow at least 15 minutes for animals to show themselves before moving to a new location.

Quail hunting is allowed on the area, but numbers are low. Mourning doves are attracted to the general vicinity by the grain fields all around. As more fields are planted to grain instead of cotton, dove hunting can be expected to improve.

The greatest numbers of doves can be expected in the Pecan Grove area below the dam, in the open fields around entry points 2 and 3, and along the road leading into the center of the San Gabriel wildlife area from entry point 5. This latter area may offer the best dove hunting. Doves are fond of perching on the barbed-wire fences lining the road, which is also a source of gravel the birds need. Waste grain from cattle feed in the adjacent pasture, when present, also attracts birds.

FISHING

Fishing is the main use of the Granger WMA, especially during the spring white bass and crappie runs in the river. The lake offers fair large-mouth bass fishing, but the water tends to stay turbid, decreasing its appeal to bass fishers. Flathead and channel catfishing are good in the river channel.

PRO'S POINTERS. The San Gabriel River and Willis Creek offer the best fishing. Both maintain good flows throughout the year. Access by boat is excellent from Corps of Engineers boat ramps at Friendship, Fox, Taylor and Willis Creek Parks. Boat launching is free at Friendship Park and Taylor Park during the winter months when gates are not staffed; otherwise, there is a $2 launch fee.

Locals have placed many brush piles in the lake to attract and hold crappie; use your depth finder to locate them. Fish straight down with curly-tail jigs slowly lifted about four inches and dropped.

Bank fishing along the San Gabriel takes place in two main locations. The first is 0.7 mile east of Texas 95 on County Road 347. A parking lot lies just across the road from a bend in the river where the WMA property line meets the right-of-way. Steps lead down the bank to a footpath that runs along the river. You can fish from the bank or from gravel bars at water's edge. Use minnows or small jigs floated downstream under a cork for white bass and crappie. You'll know the white bass are running when the parking lot is full of cars.

A second bankfishing area with easy access is at entry point 7. Take County Road 347 east from Texas 95 for 1.7 miles. At the 90-degree bend to the left, turn right onto the gravel road and follow it 0.3 mile to the river. There is a bankfishing area and small-craft launch here, and trails lead along the riverbank to other fishing spots. This is a good spot to put in a canoe or hand-launch a small flat-bottom boat and go downstream about a quarter of a mile to the Fox Bottom primitive campground to set up a fishing camp.

Trotlining with live bait for flathead catfish can pay off with fish in the 15- to 40-pound range or even larger. The best area for trotlining is from the Texas 95 bridge downstream to the Fox Bottom primitive camping area. Large yellow cats are taken from this stretch of water.

For exciting rod and reel action for white bass, channel cats, and yellow cats, try the stilling basin below the dam, especially when water is being released. Local fisher Jerry Lalla likes to catch small perch on rod and reel, then use them to fish for yellow cats on the bottom. When fishing for channel cats, he uses stinkbait or worms under a cork set to suspend the bait just off the bottom, which is 7 to 8 feet deep. "I don't try to fish between the stilling basin walls—I throw straight out," he says. "Most fish I've caught have been during the daytime, between 4 and 6 P.M. but as early as 1 P.M." Lalla and his son have taken flatheads weighing up to 30 pounds on rod and reel in this way. When fishing off the rocks, be careful not to snag your line on the backswing; a broken rod is the sure result.

INSIDER'S CORNER

THE BLACKLAND PRAIRIE

Running in a narrow band from Sherman to San Antonio, parallel to and east of I-35, the Blackland Prairie contains some of the most productive land in Texas as well as several of its largest cities. Cotton, corn and milo fields spread almost unbroken across the rural landscape. The rich, black, waxy soil once supported a sea of grass. Most of this native prairie has been lost to the plow and the subdivision plat.

The Granger WMA, located in the lower half of the Blackland Prairie, provides an ideal location for a prairie restoration site. About 150 acres between the U.S. Army Corps of Engineers office and the dam serve as a demonstration site and gene bank. "We're trying to restore the area to its original condition," says Trey Carpenter. Indiangrass and bluestem have been planted, and the site is monitored and burned in a manner that replicates historic conditions,

when buffalo and pronghorns roamed a prairie periodically swept by wildfires.

The Native Prairies Association of Texas is a partner in the effort with the Corps of Engineers and Texas Parks and Wildlife. Cooperating is the Texas Department of Transportation. "When the Department of Transportation is putting in a highway and finds an interesting species, they plant it here and enter the information into a computer database," explains Carpenter. "If DNA is ever needed from that species, a sample can be obtained here. It's kind of a storage facility for genes." White rods in the prairie replication site mark the locations of the various species.

The prairie restoration site is open to visits from school and other groups. "We try to help them understand that all the plowed ground they see around here was not always that way," says Carpenter. "Prairies were not just tall grass. They included trees, forbs, wildflowers, and many other

kinds of plants. Most people think of a prairie as a monoculture, but nature creates more diversity."

Preserving that diversity is the purpose of the prairie restoration site and the goal of several organizations that assist private landowners in similar efforts. Persons interested in preserving or restoring native prairies should contact one of the following:

Texas Section,
Society for Range Management
33 East Twohig, Room 108
San Angelo, TX 76903

Private Lands Enhancement Program
Texas Parks and Wildlife Department
4200 Smith School Road
Austin, TX 78744

Native Prairies Association of Texas
301 Nature Center Drive
Austin, TX 78746

Texas Nature Conservancy
P.O. Box 1440
San Antonio, TX 78295

6,493 acres
Route 1, Box 180
Hunt, TX 78024
830/238-4483

DRIVING TIMES FROM:
Amarillo: 7 hours
Austin: 2.5 hours
Brownsville: 7 hours
Dallas: 5 hours
El Paso: 8 hours
Houston: 5.5 hours
San Antonio: 2 hours
DIRECTIONS: From Kerrville, take Texas 27 west 7 miles to Ingram. There take Texas 39 west 7 miles to Hunt. At Hunt go west on FM 1340; continue 13 miles to the area entrance.
OPEN: Daily.
ACTIVITIES: Driving tour, nature trail, wildlife viewing, hiking, bicycling, hunting, fishing.
FACILITIES: Office, indoor classroom, restrooms, deer research pens, hunter check station, driving tour, nature trail.
SPECIAL REGULATIONS: All users must perform on-site registration. Trapping and use of horses and ATVs are prohibited.
ADVISORIES: Trails are rocky and steep in places. Sturdy walking shoes or hiking boots are recommended. Rattlesnakes are present on the area. Carry your own supply of potable water.
LODGING IN AREA: Motels are available in Kerrville and Ingram.
LOCAL POINTS OF INTEREST: South Llano River State Park, Fort McKavett State Historical Park, Kerrville-Schreiner State Park, Admiral Nimitz Museum and Historical Center, Lost Maples State Park, Garner State Park, Enchanted Rock State Natural Area.
DISABILITY ACCESS: Office, classroom, and restroom buildings are wheelchair-accessible.

HISTORY

The land that is now Kerr County lay within the range of Lipan Apache, Comanche, and Kiowa Indians. Anglo settlement began in the 1850s as shingle makers began to exploit cypress trees along the streams. Indian attacks continued to plague settlers until the late 1870s.

Cattle and sheep ranching dominated the area economy in early times; goats gained prominence in the early 20th century. Overgrazing followed Anglo settlement. At the same time, suppression of range fires led to the invasion of brush, and like the rest of the Hill Country, a native grassland was transformed into a brush land. White-tailed deer increased in number until, like domestic livestock, they became severely overpopulated. Deer and goats eradicated the better-quality browse, and by 1940 ashe juniper remained as the principal brush species. Deer die-offs due to starvation became such a regular feature of the landscape that people who had known nothing else began to accept this human-caused anomaly as natural.

In the mid-20th century tourism based on the area's scenic resources grew rapidly. About this same time, many ranchers turned to exotic wildlife for additional income, and hunting became one of the county's primary economic activities.

The tract that is now the Kerr WMA was assembled from small parcels in the early 1900s by Robert Real, who wanted to establish a refuge for deer. The land later passed through other owners until it was purchased in 1935 by Houstonite Dan Moran, former president of the Continental Oil Company. After Moran's death in 1948, the Presbyterian Synod of Texas purchased the Mo-Ranch, as it was then known, for use as a conference facility. In 1950 Texas Parks and Wildlife purchased the unimproved rangeland of the Mo-Ranch, and it became the Kerr WMA.

In the mid-1970s the Kerr WMA began a series of studies on white-tailed deer that established the relative importance of age, nutrition, and genetics in the development of quality bucks. The area also served as a laboratory where many of the principles of holistic resource management, or ecosystem management, were worked out and applied. The Kerr conducts frequent seminars and field days to share knowledge learned with landowners and all interested persons.

GEOGRAPHY AND NATURAL FEATURES

The Kerr WMA is typical of the Edwards Plateau—gently rolling, rocky hills cut by small draws, with limestone bedrock barely concealed beneath shallow soil. Average elevation is about 2,000 feet. The North Fork of the Guadalupe River forms part of the area's southern boundary, and in fact, the most upstream springs on the Guadalupe pour forth just south of the area headquarters, across FM 1340.

Other than the ashe juniper, which is ubiquitous in the Hill Country, the main trees on the area are live oaks, white shinoaks, and Texas oaks. Grasses include Texas wintergrass, little bluestem, curly mesquite and sideoats grama.

As a research and demonstration site, the Kerr WMA maintains a mixture of habitat types and research programs. Game-proof fencing around a number of pastures allows controlled experiments on deer genetics. Some exclosures exclude all animals to allow scientists to monitor the effects of "hands-off" management. High-impact, low-frequency livestock grazing; prescribed burns; brush removal and hunting are used as habitat management tools. As a result, visitors can see the effects of various management techniques. Once severely overgrazed, the Kerr area now exemplifies good wildlife habitat in the Edwards Plateau.

Wildlife on the Kerr is diverse, ranging from native species such as white-tailed deer, wild turkeys, and javelina to exotics such as axis deer, aoudad sheep, sika deer, and feral hogs. Also common are cottontail rabbits, jackrabbits, raccoons, skunks, and opossums. Coyotes and bobcats are rare, as they are generally in the Hill Country, having been the objects of extermination attempts by sheep and goat ranchers. Game birds found on the area include mourning doves and bobwhite quail, although neither are numerous.

Two federally listed endangered species of birds nest on the area—the black-capped vireo and the golden-cheeked warbler. The opportunity to add these neotropical migrants to their life list attracts many birders to the Kerr in spring.

The North Fork of the Guadalupe River forms the southern boundary of the Kerr WMA and is easily accessible from parking areas along FM 1340.

RECREATIONAL OPPORTUNITIES

Kerr WMA is open every day except during public hunts.

DRIVING TOUR

A 4-mile (one-way) self-guided driving tour travels from the headquarters building approximately 5 miles into the area. Information kiosks along the paved road present information about the area, management practices used, and native plants.

PRO'S POINTERS. "What we're trying to do is demonstrate to the public the tools of wildlife management," says area manager Donnie Frels. "These tools are the ones enumerated by the father of conservation, Aldo Leopold: the axe, the cow, the plow, fire, and the gun. We don't use much plow, but we use a lot of fire, axe, and cow. When used properly, these tools can be beneficial to wildlife habitat and populations. In the Hill Country, livestock grazing has degraded many acres of wildlife habitat. But with a proper grazing regime, cattle can be used to improve wildlife habitat, along with prescribed burning, cedar control, and hunting of native and exotic game species. The tour explains how we are using these tools at this site."

Wildlife field days—open and free to all—are held from March through October, usually on the first Friday of each month. Tours are also available for organized groups. Wildlife biologist Bill Armstrong, who began work at the area in the mid-1970s, begins each session with a profound two-word statement: "Deer eat." During two hours in the classroom followed by two hours on the driving tour route, participants learn that such a simple statement can have many and complicated ramifications.

The Kerr WMA is popular with birders, because they have a very good chance of spotting both golden-cheeked warblers and black-capped vireos on the area. Non-hunting dogs must be leashed on all WMAs.

It is mostly level except for a stretch of about 100 yards near the end of the loop. To reach the trail, drive east of the main entrance 0.7 mile on FM 1340 to the Spring Trap gate on your left (just past Stowers Road). Park on the right-of-way and enter the gate, which looks like it is locked but is not. Follow the pasture road straight ahead for about 50 yards to a weathered wooden arrow pointing to the right; from that point the path is hemmed by trees.

"This is what the entire area looked like when it was acquired in 1950," says Frels. "It was left like this because staff members knew the area was occupied by golden-cheeked warblers. Through the tools mentioned earlier, we've provided more diversity of habitat, which is benefical to many different wildlife species. The cedar provides mostly cover, but it is a monoculture. That's not the way this land was prior to Anglo settlement. This was a grassland. The cedar is the product of human intervention. Once people visit here and see what can be done with proper management, we can steer them toward regulatory biologists who can help them achieve the same results on their own property."

WILDLIFE VIEWING

Kerr WMA is very popular with birders hoping to see golden-cheeked warblers and black-capped vireos. Both arrive on the area to nest in late March. Area personnel monitor the activities of both and will suggest the best places to see them.

PRO'S POINTERS. To see golden-cheeked warblers, visit the Spring Trap detailed in the nature trail section above. However, these birds are scattered throughout the WMA. If area personnel know of the locations of singing males, they will direct visitors there.

Black-capped vireos are also widely distributed over the area. One of the prime areas lies along the driving tour road 1.7 miles from the

NATURE TRAIL

An approximately 1-mile-long birding trail winds through the Spring Trap, the first pasture east of the headquarters along FM 1340. This pasture, with its stand of mature cedar (ashe juniper), is prime golden-cheeked warbler habitat.

PRO'S POINTERS. Wear sturdy walking shoes with good ankle support; the trail is very rough and rocky.

cattleguard at the headquarters building. Black-capped vireo habitat—scattered low brush—extends on either side of the road. Look fast—these diminutive darters rarely sit still for more than a few seconds. Knowledge of their call will help in knowing where to look. If you wish to leave your car and walk a short distance from the road while birding, check with area personnel at the headquarters for permission.

Wildlife such as white-tailed deer, wild turkeys, and various exotics may sometimes be seen along the driving tour road, especially in early morning and late afternoon. However, don't expect to see an abundance of game animals, since populations are kept within the carrying capacity of the range.

Bird and mammal checklists for the area are available at the office.

HIKING

There is no designated hiking trail other than the nature trail in the Spring Trap, described earlier. Hiking is also allowed along the driving tour road.

PRO'S POINTERS. Hiking is *not* allowed on any roads branching off from the driving tour road. However, you are allowed to walk along the Guadalupe River, which runs along FM 1340. In fact, hiking along the river offers what is perhaps the biggest reward for the shortest hike of any Texas WMA. A walk of about 30 yards takes you to the site of the origin of the Guadalupe River, springs that issue from limestone fissures almost beneath FM 1340.

To reach the spring area, angle slightly to the left as you exit the WMA main entrance and cross the highway, passing to the left of three mailboxes and going between two large junipers. The gravel road, almost invisible even when you know it's there, opens immediately into a small riverbank parking area. To view the springs, follow the footpath southwest through a gap in the

junipers, then turn left along the boundary fence. A few steps put you atop the ledge beneath which the springs flow. Upstream from the springs is private property. State property extends downstream only to the midpoint of the river.

BICYCLING

Bicycling is allowed only along the driving tour road.

PRO'S POINTERS. From the headquarters area to the turnaround at the end of the road is 4 miles. The entire route is paved and generally level, free of bumps and potholes. Many people staying at church camps along FM 1340 come here to bicycle. Information kiosks along the route explain the mission and methods of the WMA. See the sections on the driving tour and wildlife viewing, above, for more information.

HUNTING

Most hunting on the Kerr WMA is by Special Permit. The exception is a mourning-dove hunt the first week of the season. See the *Public Hunting Lands Map Booklet* and the *Applications for Drawings on Public Hunting Lands* for information on these hunts.

PRO'S POINTERS. Archery and gun Special Permit hunts are held for white-tailed deer, feral hogs, exotics, and spring turkeys as populations permit. Exotic, deer, and hog hunters are allowed to take unlimited hogs and exotics. Youth-only deer hunts may be available.

Hunters on the Kerr have the opportunity to learn more about the role hunting plays in wildlife management during an orientation session. "We're taking the research from the deer pens and applying it to the rest of the management area—we're practicing what we preach," says Frels. "The Kerr WMA is known for providing the opportunity to harvest quality white-tailed deer. Hunters take some very large-bodied, large-antlered bucks scoring in the 140 to 160 class."

After orientation, each hunting party receives a map of its hunting compartment, which is a pasture or a portion of a pasture with well-defined boundaries such as roads and fences. Roads and blinds in each compartment are marked on the map. Then hunters are taken out by a staff member, who shows them their hunting compartment.

Skinning racks, cold storage, and coffee are provided.

Some stands are suited for archery hunters, but archers are allowed to bring their own stands. Lean-on or ladder-type stands will work best, as there are few straight trees on the area.

Hunters should field dress their game before taking it to the check station at the headquarters, where biologists will age and weigh each deer and may collect tissue or blood samples for research purposes. Bucks are scored and photographed.

Exotic hunts for feral hogs, sika and axis deer, and aoudads have no bag limits and are the most popular hunts on the Kerr. In a recent year over 5,000 people applied for 14 permits. There are generally no standby positions offered on the exotic-only hunts.

All hunters would do well to key on food sources such as Texas oak and live oak acorns when possible.

Buck hunts on the Kerr are generally timed to cover the peak rutting period, but antler point and spread restrictions may prevent the taking of larger bucks during some hunts. Check the dates listed in the *Applications for Drawings on Public Hunting Lands* and consult with area biologists by calling 830/238-4483 before applying if your goal is to harvest a mature buck.

FISHING

Fishing in the Guadalupe River is allowed year-round except during public hunts. Mailboxes at access points contain registration materials. The river within the area is shallow but does contain some perch and largemouth bass.

PRO'S POINTERS. Serious fishers will want to fish elsewhere. For persons just wanting to wet a line, two access points are provided, both on the south side of FM 1340. The first is directly across the highway from the main entrance to the area. The other is 0.8 mile east of the entrance, at the west end of the highway embankment. Fishing is allowed during daylight hours only. Upstream from the spring is private property. State property extends downstream only to the midpoint of the river.

DONNIE HARMEL'S LEGACY

Almost anyone with an interest in white-tailed deer, and particularly the production of quality bucks, knows the name Donnie Harmel. Harmel, now deceased, was manager of the Kerr WMA from 1975 to 1997. It was under his direction that studies were carried out proving that antler traits are heritable, that nutrition and age play major roles in buck development and that culling spike bucks from a well-managed herd improves the chances of producing trophy deer. But most people overlook what may well prove to be his most enduring legacy: proving that holistic resource management—caring for the entire ecosystem rather than just the individual pieces—is the key to producing and sustaining wildlife populations. Bill Armstrong, a conservation scientist who worked beside Harmel the entire time he was on the Kerr, recalls the traits that made Harmel one of the leading figures in the field of ecosystem management. "He was always trying something new. Sometimes it worked and sometimes it didn't, but he was always trying to make it better. The whole Kerr area was really a reflection of his personality."

One of Harmel's strongest traits was his willingness to listen to and learn from others. "Several people originated the idea of the deer pens [where the first long-term genetic studies of deer were carried out]. A lot of the ideas took shape around the campfire at the Ringtail Cabin, an old hunter's cabin on the area. Biologists from all around the state would build a campfire in the evening and sit and talk," Armstrong recalls.

"He was the control, a project manager who allowed all those things to happen. He was willing to listen to other people and try new things, and he wasn't afraid to fail on some things. What resulted was the development of ecosystem or holistic resource type management. We began to manage all the things out here, not just the deer or the birds."

In the relatively short time of 22 years, Harmel and his coworkers dispelled many myths about wildlife management and provided a solid foundation of science that still guides the work of wildlife biologists all over the nation.

Only Donnie Harmel's body left this place. His spirit is still present.

5,301 acres
Box 1583, Mason, TX 76856
915/347-5037

DRIVING TIMES FROM:
Amarillo: 8 hours
Austin: 2 hours
Brownsville: 7 hours
Dallas: 5 hours
El Paso: 9 hours
Houston: 4.5 hours
San Antonio: 2 hours
DIRECTIONS: From Fredericksburg, take U.S. 87 north for 42 miles to Mason and the intersection with FM 386 on the town square. Take FM 386 north 2 miles to Old Mason Road. Follow Old Mason Road northwest for 2 miles to the entrance.
OPEN: Restricted access. Open to hunters holding Special Permits on designated dates and to groups by appointment.
ACTIVITIES: Hunting.
FACILITIES: Office, check station, bunkhouse, lodge, cold storage, hunting blinds.
SPECIAL REGULATIONS: All hunters must sign in and out at the check station when entering or leaving the area. Camping is not allowed on the area.

ADVISORIES: Archery hunters should bring their own stands, preferably tripods. High-clearance, four-wheel-drive vehicles are recommended. Lodging for hunters is available on the area for a fee; make reservations by calling the area office at the number above. Carry your own supply of potable water.
LODGING IN AREA: Motels are available in Mason, Llano, Fredericksburg, and Brady.
LOCAL POINTS OF INTEREST: Admiral Nimitz Museum and Historical Center, Lyndon B. Johnson State Historical Park, Lyndon B. Johnson National Historical Park, Blanco State Park, Enchanted Rock State Park, Kerrville-Schreiner State Park, Government Canyon State Park, Guadalupe River State Park, Pedernales Falls State Park, San Angelo State Park, South Llano River State Park.
DISABILITY ACCESS: Not wheelchair-accessible.

Mason Mountain WMA offers guided hunts for both exotic and native wildlife species in spectacular granite-studded surroundings.

HISTORY

The area in and around Mason Mountain WMA was used by Lipan Apache and, later, Comanche Indians for summer hunting grounds for hundreds of years. In the 1840s German immigrants expanding north from New Braunfels and Fredericksburg began settling along the Llano River, 15 miles to the south. Settlers at Fredericksburg met with Comanche chiefs near Mason and negotiated a peace treaty, but troubles with Indians continued into the 1870s. Fort Mason was established at the site of the present town of Mason to guard the frontier.

Rugged hills and rocky soils kept farms small and scattered, and ranching became the chief economic activity. In the cattle drive era following the Civil War, the Mason area was a hub for both ranchers and cattle drovers. An interesting sidelight is that one of the most popular books for young people ever written, *Old Yeller*, was set in Mason County during this time period and penned by Mason native Fred Gipson.

The land now contained within Mason Mountain WMA was part of one of the large area ranches, the Thaxton ranch. C. G. Johnson donated the land to Texas Parks and Wildlife in 1997; the property was a working exotic game ranch specializing in large African plains species. These animals, numbering approximately 1,000 individuals of 11 different species, were donated to Texas Parks and Wildlife with the land.

The Texas Parks and Wildlife Commission accepted the donation on condition that the area pay its own way. The commission decided to sell off some of the exotics as brood stock and conduct an aggressive public hunting program to remove the rest over time, using the income to build an endowment large enough to generate interest sufficient to sustain operations. In the meantime, the exotics on the area will be subjects in

north, south, east, and west blend. Roy Welch, Texas Parks and Wildlife Region 2 wildlife director, says Mason Mountain has "a variety we don't have in any other management area." Live oaks and Texas oaks dominate Mason Mountain's slopes, which overlook rolling pink granite hills studded with large boulder outcrops and flats stubbled with blackjack oaks, post oaks, and mesquites. Grasses found on the area include little and big bluestem, indiangrass, sideoats grama, vine mesquite, silver bluestem, plains bristlegrass, buffalograss, curly mesquite, Texas wintergrass, Canada wild rye, and Texas bluegrass.

Mason Mountain is the only WMA in Texas having eight-foot game-proof fences around the entire perimeter and all interior pastures. It also has a number of structures dating from the time of private ownership. These improvements provide housing and boundaries for researchers, hunters, and other individuals engaged in activities taking place on the area. An early-intervention program for at-risk teenagers is operated by the Brown Schools of Central Texas here. Groups of students and counselors use various pastures for 28-day highly structured campouts. More traditional uses include serving as the location for college and high school students' research projects and wildlife conservation groups' field days.

RECREATIONAL ACTIVITIES

The main focus of Mason Mountain WMA is research and demonstration. However, the availability of a large population of exotic wildlife as well as native wildlife makes possible a public hunting program. All hunts

research studies to determine the extent to which they compete with native wildlife.

GEOGRAPHY AND NATURAL FEATURES

Mason Mountain is located in the Central Mineral Region, a part of the Texas Hill Country known for its geologic diversity. The northern one-third of the area, Mason Mountain itself, is underlain by limestone. The limestone in turn sits atop a massive granite batholith which rises to the surface on most of the remaining two-thirds of the area. Elevations range from about 1,500 to near 2,000 feet, and the rocky nature of the ground and the relief between the southern and northern portions creates a rugged landscape covered in places with jumbles of granite boulders.

Vegetation on the area is also varied, as the WMA sits at a meeting point of the Edwards Plateau and the Llano Uplift and is a transition zone in which plant communities from

Two sizeable reservoirs on Mason Mountain WMA furnish water for exotic mammals and birds introduced to the area by its former owner.

are by Special Permit; some are by special drawings separate from the usual ones. Unlike other WMAs, Mason Mountain retains all income generated from application fees; this money—plus that from the sale of exotic brood stock—is intended to fund an endowment that will generate interest enough to continue operations after all the exotics are removed.

HUNTING

During its first two years in operation, Mason Mountain operated a massive public hunting program in an attempt to reduce the number of exotics on the area. The number of hunts was scaled back as the number of animals decreased. "Our goal is to remove all the exotics," says area manager T. Wayne Schwertner. "Hunting is done specifically for conservation purposes, so hunting depends on what the resource tells us we can hunt." See the *Applications for Drawings on Public Hunting Lands* for the current year for information on species and hunts available.

PRO'S POINTERS. White-tailed deer hunts are offered by Special Permit during both archery and rifle season. Antlerless and either-sex hunts may be available depending on numbers. As part of the continuing effort to remove exotics, hunters may be allowed to take unlimited numbers of doe blackbuck antelope, feral goats, and feral hogs on these hunts. Exotic-only hunts will be phased out as numbers decline to the point where insufficient numbers exist to provide a quality hunt.

Hunts are conducted by compartments assigned on the basis of party size. Archers may bring their own stands; tripods are recommended because of the lack of large trees in some areas. Rifle hunters are assigned ground blinds and must hunt from that blind for safety reasons. Hunting locations are prebaited; hunters are not allowed to bring their own bait. Lodging with kitchen facilities is available on the area for a fee; cold storage and ice are available at no charge.

"The white-tailed rut peaks the last week of November. It will shift somewhat, but if you have to pick a time to hunt in the Hill Country, hunt Thanksgiving weekend," says Schwertner.

Spring turkey hunts are also available by Special Permit drawing. Hunts are by assigned compartment, and shotguns and archery equipment only may be used. The area does not have a notably large population of turkeys.

Mason Mountain is one of the locations for the Big Time Texas Hunts, which are guided hunt packages including food, lodging, on-site transportation, and taxidermy services for large game animals. These hunts are available through special drawings separate from other drawings for Special Permit hunts; these special drawings carry a higher application fee (typically $10), but no permit fee is required of drawn hunters. As many chances may be purchased as desired for each type of hunt. See the *Applications for Drawings on Public Hunting Lands* for information on hunts available for the current year.

The Texas Exotic Safari is exclusive to Mason Mountain WMA and allows two hunters per year (one using primitive arms, the other modern arms) the opportunity to harvest two super exotics such as waterbuck, gemsbok, scimitar-horned oryx, greater kudu, sable antelope, or impala. This hunt is expected to continue through approximately 2012.

Drawn hunters for the Texas Exotic Safari may bring a companion, who may hunt antlerless axis deer and hybrid ibex goats. Hunters arrive the evening before the hunt, meet with guides, and have time to check weapon accuracy before dinner. Hunters are housed at a lodge overlooking a small lake in a particularly scenic area. Hunts last three full days and are typically spot and stalk for rifle hunters; archers may choose to hunt from a stand. "Most hunters will not have seen these species before and don't know how to judge which ones are mature, trophy-quality animals, so guides will advise the hunter on which animals are the most desirable," says Schwertner. Experienced exotics guides who are members of the Texas Outfitters and Guides Association donate their services for this hunt. Shoulder mounts for two animals are provided at the taxidermist of Texas Parks and Wildlife's choice.

In 1999 Mason Mountain WMA added guided hunts for white-tailed deer, axis deer, Rio Grande turkey, and varmints to its mix of hunting opportunities. These hunts are also exclusive to Mason Mountain and include meals, lodging, on-site transportation, and taxidermy.

Two groups of up to two hunters each will win a four-day white-tailed deer hunt. Each hunter will have the potential to take a 130-class buck as well as unlimited feral goats and hogs. The hunt is timed to coincide with the rut and is conducted in a pasture managed for trophy white-tails. One shoulder mount per hunter is provided.

Two permits are also available for buck axis deer hunts; up to two hunters on each hunt will be allowed to take an axis buck and unlimited feral goats and hogs. Axis hunts are timed for peak antler development and may take place in either June or September. One shoulder mount per hunter is provided.

The spring turkey hunt and varmint hunt packages also are for two groups of up to two hunters each. Turkey hunters may take one gobbler; varmint hunters may take up to four furbearers each. On each of these hunts, one full body mount per hunter is provided. Varmint hunts are conducted mainly at night to take advantage of predator movement.

INSIDER'S CORNER

RESEARCHING FOR A MISSION

Texas wildlife management areas really are one of the best-kept secrets in the state. Many hunters either do not know they exist or know very little about them, and the general public is even less well-informed. Yet in addition to providing most of the public hunting opportunity in a state that is 97 percent privately owned, wildlife management areas serve as theaters for research projects that have direct impacts on birders, hunters, wildlife managers, and landowners statewide.

Out of about 50 wildlife management areas, fewer than a dozen are designated as research and demonstration sites, although some research is carried out on all areas. The primary function of the research and demonstration areas is to develop greater understanding of the ecology of the regions in which they are located and make information available to private landowners that will assist them in making better management decisions on their property.

"What we do here on Mason Mountain WMA can effect recommendations for private landowners statewide," says area manager T. Wayne Schwertner. "Our real impact is not on the 5,300 acres here but on the private lands throughout the state through Texas Parks and Wildlife's technical assistance programs. We can have a profound impact by making information available to private landowners."

One example of such information is the data on factors influencing antler development in white-tailed deer gathered on the Kerr WMA. The Kerr and Mason Mountain WMAs took this subject a step further in a study designed to determine if age and antler size affect a white-tailed buck's breeding opportunities. In other words, do big bucks do most of the breeding or not? Results of the study, which should be available about 2002, could have major implications for managers of deer herds.

It's the potential Mason Mountain offers for this type of study that excites Schwertner. "While public access is important, we feel like we do more good for the wildlife resources statewide through research than by allowing public hunts. Because all our pastures have high fences, we can do research here that no one else can. We can do the same study at the same time in multiple pastures, cutting down on the time needed to obtain results."

Besides the "who breeds who" study, proposed research projects at Mason Mountain WMA would deal with the effects of land-use practices such as prescribed burning on the ecosystem, the utilization of granite outcrops by cave-roosting bats, and preferred habitats for a number of small nongame mammals. Researchers also hope to study limiting factors for quail in the Hill Country, food habits of exotic mammals to determine if they compete with native wildlife, and the effects of brush control on rainfall runoff and recharge.

Exotic animals will be removed from Mason Mountain WMA by hunting and trapping.

10.5 acres
P.O. Box 1167
Comfort, TX 78013
830/995-4154
For information on tours and bat emergence times, call Lyndon B. Johnson State Historical Park at 830/644-2478.

DRIVING TIMES FROM:
Amarillo: 8 hours
Austin: 1.5 hours
Brownsville: 6 hours
Dallas: 4.5 hours
El Paso: 9 hours
Houston: 4 hours
San Antonio: 1 hour
DIRECTIONS: From Fredericksburg, take U.S. 290 east to Old San Antonio Road. Go south on Old San Antonio Road 10.5 miles to the parking area. From I-10 near Comfort, take the Texas 27 exit. At the first flashing light on 27, veer right onto Highway 87 north. Turn right at the next flashing light onto FM 473 and go about 5 miles. At the point where FM 473 takes a sharp right turn, go straight ahead on Old Highway 9, and follow it 8 miles to the area.
OPEN: Daily from dawn to 10 P.M. Bats are present from May through October.
ACTIVITIES: Nature trail, wildlife viewing, hiking.

FACILITIES: Information station, picnic area, nature trail, wildlife-viewing platforms, composting toilet.
SPECIAL REGULATIONS: Fires, firearms, alcohol, and bicycles are prohibited. Artificial lights may not be used during the bat emergence. Visitors must remain on trails. No pets are permitted in the evening during bat emergence tours.
ADVISORIES: Pregnant women should use caution when walking the nature trail because of the risk of contracting histoplasmosis. Do not drink, touch, or wade in the water from the creek that crosses the trail, as it is contaminated with bat feces. Do not handle any bat found on the ground because of the risk of rabies. Rattlesnakes are present on the area. The walk to the lower viewing area and the nature trail require climbing a very steep hill coming back. Summer temperatures can be very hot. Bring plenty of water to drink.
LODGING IN AREA: Motels are available in Fredericksburg, Stonewall, Kerrville, Blanco, Boerne, and Comfort.
LOCAL POINTS OF INTEREST: Admiral Nimitz Museum and Historical Center, Lyndon B. Johnson State Historical Park, Lyndon B. Johnson National Historical Park, Blanco State Park, Enchanted Rock

State Park, Kerrville-Schreiner State Park, Government Canyon State Park, Guadalupe River State Park, Pedernales Falls State Park, South Llano River State Park.
DISABILITY ACCESS: One picnic table, the upper viewing deck, the composting toilet, and a special viewing area are wheelchair-accessible.

HISTORY

The Old Tunnel WMA is located on land once roamed by Lipan Apaches, Kiowas, and Comanches. These tribes still held sway over the area when German settlers began arriving in the 1840s. Although the Germans made a peace treaty with the Comanches, raids on farms in the area remained frequent until the 1870s.

George Wilkins Kendall, a frontier journalist and rancher, played a large role in introducing sheep to the Texas Hill Country and is generally regarded as the father of the sheep business in Texas. Sheep and goat ranching are still major occupations in the area, and the land now comprising the Old Tunnel WMA was used for this purpose.

The history of Old Tunnel WMA is closely connected with that of the nearby town of Fredericksburg. Germans settled the town in 1846, and the town's industrious farmers and craftspeople needed a market for their products. San Antonio was only 75 miles away, but traveling through the rugged Hill Country on primitive roads made for a five- to six-day trip. As railroads began to build across Texas after the Civil War, the people of Fredericksburg worked to get one to come their way.

Unfortunately, the "Big Hill" that is now the site of Old Tunnel WMA was in the way. This big hill marks the divide between the Guadalupe and Pedernales Rivers and reaches an

Visitors to the Old Tunnel WMA may attend lectures on the biology and life history of bats prior to the emergence at dusk.

elevation of 2,300 feet. It posed a formidable obstacle to early track layers. As a result, numerous attempts to attract a railroad to Fredericksburg failed.

By 1912 the patience of the Fredericksburg people was wearing thin. They decided that the only way to get a railroad to town was to raise the money to pay for the construction, and by the following year work had begun on the San Antonio, Fredericksburg and Northern Railroad. The railroad would run from Fredericksburg to Comfort, where it would join the existing San Antonio and Aransas Pass Railroad line to Kerrville.

Work started on the pièce de résistance, the tunnel through the big hill, in March 1913. The 920-foot tunnel was complemented by a large trestle just south. Long cuts were necessary at both ends in order to reduce the grade to the level of the tunnel floor. Work proceeded from both ends using explosives, picks, shovels, scrapers, and narrow-gauge dump cars. On July 15 workers joined the two bores, and the first train passed through the tunnel little more than a month later, although the tracks did not reach Fredericksburg until late October. Cost of the tunnel was $134,000.

A large pleasure resort called Mount Alamo was proposed for the big hill site, complete with electricity, water and wastewater systems, a 75-room hotel, and an 18-hole golf course, but the Depression ended those plans.

Train service left much to be desired. Average speed for the trip was 12 miles per hour, and the engineers would sometimes stop the train to go hunting if they saw a nice white-tailed buck. Sometimes the train would run out of water or coal. Nevertheless, the railroad continued to operate until 1942, when the tracks were torn up and sold for scrap. Reportedly rails and timber from the line were used in constructing the Alcan Highway, rail spurs to army camps, and rail lines in Australia. Like the cultural heritage left by the early German settlers, the legacy of the Fredericksburg and Northern long outlived its genesis.

Texas Parks and Wildlife acquired the property in 1991. A local ranching family donated half the site, and Texas Parks and Wildlife purchased the rest. Interestingly, the department owns only the southern 90 feet of the tunnel; the rest lies under the county road and private property to the north. While the bats do not roost in the part of the tunnel owned by Texas Parks and Wildlife, most of them choose to exit through this southern port, although as bat numbers increase in the tunnel, many go out the other end and fly over the upper viewing deck to join the ones coming out the south end.

LEFT:
Bats roost in the 920-foot-long abandoned railroad tunnel; most emerge from this southern end directly in front of a viewing area.
ABOVE, RIGHT:
Thousands of bats fill the sky nightly as they depart the tunnel to search for food. The bats range tens of miles in all directions, feeding mainly on moths whose larval stage is the cornborer.

GEOGRAPHY AND NATURAL FEATURES

Topography of the Old Tunnel WMA is extremely varied considering it is the smallest wildlife management area in Texas. From the flat hilltop on the north side of the area, the land drops away steeply to the south, with slopes reaching 30 percent. Elevation increases from about 1,750 feet on the south to about 1,900 feet on the north. The hillside is typical of the Texas Hill Country—fractured, rugged limestone exhibiting thick horizontal bedding. County roads form the western and northern boundaries of the area, and private property joins the other two sides.

The site falls away into the railroad cut and then a natural canyon to the south, providing a sweeping view of hills dominated by live oak trees. The tunnel floor and railroad cut are permanently wet from seepage from the tunnel walls and ceiling. The heavy vegetation and reliable water supply attract white-tailed deer, rabbits, armadillos, foxes, squirrels, wild turkeys, mourning doves, ruby-throated hummingbirds, cliff swallows, scrub jays, mockingbirds, robins, and other birds as well as a number of reptiles and amphibians.

RECREATIONAL ACTIVITIES

NATURE TRAIL

A half-mile nature trail begins at the iron ranger at the lower viewing area and passes through a dense stand of live oaks before crossing the drainage below the southern entrance to the tunnel. It then climbs atop the old railroad roadbed and follows it to the southern property boundary. Obtain a trail guide at the iron ranger; keyed to numbered posts along the way, it identifies many of the plants along the trail.

PRO'S POINTERS. Old Tunnel WMA is staffed only in the evenings, but the nature trail is open from dawn until one hour before sunset. Arriving

an hour or two before the bat emergence gives plenty of time to walk the short trail. One of the benefits of doing so becomes apparent at the first stop along the trail. At the footbridge, look north. You'll be able to see all the way through the tunnel and observe the swarming bats inside.

The trail is level once it climbs atop the old roadbed, but the return climb from the drainage bottom to the parking lot is very steep. The trail is not wheelchair-accessible.

WILDLIFE VIEWING

"This area is primarily about bats, but we do get quite a few birders on the nature trail," says area manager Tim Lawyer. "Nearly 100 species of birds have been documented on the area. We have stream, hardwood bottomland, and upland habitats. Visitors should see several species of flycatchers, white-eyed vireos and many common birds of the Hill Country." A bird checklist for the area was in preparation at the time of writing.

PRO'S POINTERS. Two species of bats live in the tunnel. The Mexican free-tailed is the primary species and comprises about 99.9 percent of the colony. The second species is the cave myotis; there may be only 300 to 500 of them. "The population goes

up and down, but we estimate the peak population is about 1 to 2 million bats in late summer through early fall," Lawyer says.

The bats emerge in the evening, taking from 15 minutes to an hour and a half to do so. The emergence time varies; call Lyndon B. Johnson State Historical Park (830/644-2252) for the current time. To get the most from your visit, plan to arrive about an hour and a half before emergence time. Texas Parks and Wildlife's Wildlife Division personnel and volunteers give informative talks on bats around the world, on the history of this site, and on the life cycle of the Mexican free-tailed bat.

There are three options for viewing. Nightly, informal viewing open to the general public is conducted at the upper viewing deck, which has bleacher-style seating and is located about 60 yards from the south tunnel opening. A Texas Parks and Wildlife seasonal employee or volunteer member of Friends of Old Tunnel presents information about bats and the site. Viewing from the upper deck is free of charge, and no Annual Public Hunting Permit, Limited Public Use Permit, or Texas Conservation Passport is required.

Texas Conservation Passport tours are held at the lower viewing area every Thursday and Saturday night from June through October. These tours are first-come, first-served—no reservations are accepted. Up to 60 people can be accommodated on these tours. Holders of a Texas Conservation Passport, Annual Public Hunting Permit, or Limited Public Use Permit and members of their immediate family are admitted free. Persons without one of these permits pay a fee. Those who take this tour get a 45-minute to 1-hour lecture dealing with the site, railroad history, and bats worldwide. They also view the bats from 25 to 30 feet as they emerge. Bats usually do not fly over the benches in the seating area, but they circle right in front of it as they gain altitude.

A wheelchair-accessible viewing area is located between the upper and lower viewing areas; a driveway allows parking a few feet away. Contact Texas Parks and Wildlife personnel on duty for access to this area.

Special group tours are available for organized groups. Reservations must be made through Lyndon B. Johnson State Historical Park at the number above. These tours take place on nights other than Thursday or Saturday and are conducted the same as the Texas Conservation Pass tours. When the reservation is made, a fact sheet is mailed or faxed giving fees and directions to the site.

To avoid crowds, plan to visit Monday through Wednesday. Weekend nights attract up to 300 people, and there is inadequate parking for crowds this size—requiring you to park along the county road and walk to the site.

HIKING

All hiking is on the nature trail. See the description above.

PRO'S POINTERS. Hikers must stay on the designated nature trail.

INSIDER'S CORNER

MEXICAN MIGRANTS ON THE MOVE

Mexican free-tail bats spend their winters in Mexico and breed there, but they birth and rear their young in Texas, among other places. The bats are quick to take advantage of new housing. Soon after the railroad stopped operation in 1942, the bats moved in. "One area rancher remembers seeing significant numbers of bats in the tunnel in 1946," says seasonal employee Richard Parsons.

The Old Tunnel colony is unusual in that its composition changes several times during the period when the bats are present. "When the bats start arriving in March and April, the colony is mainly comprised of pregnant females and males," says Lawyer. "During early to mid-June, the population drops off significantly as the pregnant freetails leave for other cave sites that serve as maternal roosting sites. Numbers at the Old Tunnel will remain relatively low until mid-July to mid-August, when populations swell as females and their newly flying juveniles return to the tunnel. In the early fall months, as cold fronts arrive, we see further increases in bat populations as northern bats begin their migrations south. Typically, the Old Tunnel bats make their fall migration to Mexico in late October through mid-November."

What's behind this roller-coaster in bat numbers? The key is the tunnel itself. "Females leave this site to have pups, then come back to this colony," Lawyer explains. "The reason is that the tunnel is open at both ends, unlike a cave, and there is constant airflow through it. The temperature and humidity vary too much for the young to survive, so the females go to select other caves in the Hill Country to have their young and nurse them until they are ready to fly at approximately five to six weeks of age. Then the juveniles join their mothers here."

Where do the bats go? Research now underway is providing some answers. Females banded at Old Tunnel have turned up at the Eckert James River Bat Preserve in Mason County, a U.S. 290 bridge near Fredericksburg, the McNeil bridge near Round Rock, the Congress Avenue Bridge in Austin, and Bracken Cave near San Antonio. One showed up at a bank in Seguin. These well-traveled migrants from Mexico live, literally, on the fly.

2,123 acres
P.O. Box 392
Junction, TX 76849
915/446-3994

DRIVING TIMES FROM:
Amarillo: 7 hours
Austin: 2.5 hours
Brownsville: 7 hours
Dallas: 5 hours
El Paso: 8 hours
Houston: 5.5 hours
San Antonio: 2 hours
DIRECTIONS: From Junction, follow U.S. 377 south for 5 miles, then follow the road to South Llano River State Park. The wildlife management area may be accessed by foot or bicycle from park headquarters.
OPEN: Year-round for day use. The area is closed to all except hunters during Special Permit hunts.
ACTIVITIES: Wildlife viewing, hiking, bicycling, hunting, fishing.
FACILITIES: Shop building, check station, box blinds, tripod stands.
SPECIAL REGULATIONS: All public users must obtain a day use permit from park headquarters before entering the WMA. Access to the area is by foot or bicycle only except during Special Permit hunts.
ADVISORIES: Trails are rocky and steep in places. Sturdy walking shoes or hiking boots are recommended. Rattlesnakes are present on the area. Carry your own supply of potable water.
LODGING IN AREA: Motels are available in Junction.
LOCAL POINTS OF INTEREST: South Llano River State Park, Fort McKavett State Historical Park, Kerrville-Schreiner State Park, Admiral Nimitz Museum and Historical Center, Lost Maples State Natural Area, Garner State Park, Enchanted Rock State Natural Area.
DISABILITY ACCESS: Not wheelchair-accessible.

Prairie verbena, as its name suggests, can be found throughout the Hill Country in open grassy areas.

HISTORY

The area that now makes up the Walter Buck WMA and the adjacent South Llano River State Park was purchased by Walter Buck, Sr., in 1910. He and his son, Walter Buck, Jr., ranched the land. The son donated it to Texas Parks and Wildlife in 1977. Part of Buck's motivation for the donation was his desire to protect the wild turkey roosts along the South Llano River. Several hundred turkeys roost on the area during the winter.

GEOGRAPHY AND NATURAL FEATURES

The Walter Buck WMA is more rugged than many. While the floodplain of the South Llano River is flat, the state park occupies almost all this section. The WMA itself contains deep canyons and steep hills, with elevation ranging from about 1,700 to over 2,100 feet. Two major drainages run north to south through the area. Highest elevations occur around the east, west, and south boundaries.

Bottomlands along the drainages are narrow, but they contain the best wildlife habitat. Vegetation includes mesquite and live oak trees and grasses such as little bluestem, Indiangrass, sideoats grama, and Texas wintergrass. Some of these same grasses appear on hillsides and are joined by ashe juniper, Texas persimmon, and shin oak. Uplands are hilly and are dominated by live oaks and ashe juniper except where brush control has removed the latter.

Although Tobusch fishhook cactus is listed as an endangered species by the U.S. Fish and Wildlife Service, it occurs fairly commonly on the Walter Buck WMA. This small cactus, generally only an inch to three inches tall, is endemic to the Edwards Plateau. An ongoing research project on the Walter Buck WMA aims to gather more information on factors impacting this rare plant's survival. You are urged not to approach or disturb any plants you may find.

RECREATIONAL OPPORTUNITIES

Situated as it is adjacent to a popular state park with excellent swimming, tubing, fishing, and a beautiful campground, the Walter Buck WMA attracts many people. It offers solitude and great natural beauty within easy walking distance of campsites. Special Permit hunts are held for white-tailed deer, exotics, and turkeys.

WILDLIFE VIEWING

Perhaps the best time to visit the area is March through May. In mid-February to mid-March, the Tobusch fishhook cactus will likely be in bloom. Yucca blooming continues into April, and birds nest from May through August. Rio Grande turkeys will be engrossed in their mating rituals in March and April. The turkeys roost along the river and spend a good part of the morning working their way toward the management area, strutting in campground roads and campsites, putting on a marvelous show. Deer feed undisturbed between the entrance on U.S. 377 and park headquarters. During spring and fall a number of migrant neotropical songbirds frequent the area; some are particularly desired by birders.

PRO'S POINTERS. The 18 box blinds provided for hunters are ideal for wildlife viewing and photography. Get a map of the state park and WMA at park headquarters; locations of the blinds are shown quite accurately on this map, with walking distances noted. Beware of wasps and snakes when using these blinds. Wildlife such as white-tailed deer and axis deer are found on the area. In the past occasional sightings of feral hogs, javelina, coyotes, ringtails and porcupines as well as exotics such as sika deer and fallow deer have also been documented. Morning and evening are the times they tend to be most active. Your best bet for seeing an axis deer is probably in the area just east of the campground in the state park.

Near blind 9, a spring comes out of the wall of the bluff just east. Sitting quietly near the spring can reward you with sightings of a variety of birds and animals coming to bathe and drink. Among the birds you may see are endangered black-capped vireos, which nest on the area on the flats and hillsides adjacent to the state park. The MacGillivray's warbler, a western bird, can sometimes be found along the drainages. Zone-tailed hawks, scarlet tanagers, and common and Chihuahuan ravens have also been spotted, says Terry Turney, former wildlife biologist for the area.

Rio Grande turkeys are the most noticeable residents, especially in the state park river bottom and campground areas, but they move onto other areas such as the WMA as the breeding season ends in late spring. The turkeys on the WMA tend to travel along the drainages and associated roads. However, for close-up viewing of these magnificent birds, perhaps the best place in Texas is the state park campground. "Most of the pictures of strutting gobblers you see in wildlife magazines are taken here," says Turney. It's possible to approach within 15 to 20 yards of gobblers intent on wooing females.

HIKING

The Walter Buck WMA has about 16 miles of unpaved roads available for hiking. These roads are fairly well maintained, as they are used by hunters and Texas Parks and Wildlife personnel. However, there are some steep hills with loose rock—marked on the map you can get at park headquarters—and some draws that will flood in wet weather. Ask at the park headquarters about road conditions.

PRO'S POINTERS. Most hikers favor the Fawn Trail, a signed 2.8-mile walk that loops from the walk-in camping area back to the headquarters building a short distance west. There are two steep hills on this route; in walking the loop, you'll go up one and down the other.

Starting from the walk-in camping area, you walk into the WMA through a gate, turn left onto a paved road, and in a few yards take another left down a gravel road. Shortly after crossing a creek bottom, you can take a side trip to a scenic overlook that gives a panoramic view of the South Llano River bottom. Although it is only about half a mile from Fawn Trail to this lookout, it is almost all uphill, and the trail is very steep and strewn with loose rocks, making it a strenuous hike. Only persons in good physical condition and wearing good hiking footwear should attempt this climb.

After the turnoff to the scenic overlook, Fawn Trail leads first through bottomland thickly covered in brush; visibility is limited. As you approach hunting blind 2, the bottom widens and opens up. This is an area favored by turkeys. Just past blind 3, a trap designed to capture herptiles sits across the creek to the right of the road. The metal flashing wings on the trap guide crawling critters into plastic 5-gallon buckets buried in the ground; biologists collect these specimens for study. When not in use, the buckets are covered to prevent creatures from falling in.

A short way past blind 3 the road passes along the base of a 30-foot

LEFT:
Hunters may participate in hunts for white-tailed deer, turkeys and exotic mammals on the Walter Buck WMA. The turkeys roost in the adjacent South Llano River State Park and may be easily viewed there during the spring mating season.
FACING PAGE:
A steep, rocky side trail leads from Fawn Trail to a scenic overlook offering a panoramic view of the South Llano River bottom.

limestone bluff, then climbs a steep hill. Just past blind 9, take a right where your road joins another at a fence. In about three-quarters of a mile, a sign directs you to the right again.

You'll pass a windmill on your left just before this turn. The headquarters building is another 0.7 mile along.

BICYCLING

Mountain bikers may choose from any of the trails that twist and climb over almost the entire area. Access begins from either end of Fawn Trail. Refer to the map available at park headquarters to plan your route and estimate distance; the length of each segment of road on the entire area is noted, and hills are marked.

PRO'S POINTERS. For a sample of all the topography and scenery the area has to offer, begin at the walk-in tent campground and continue on to the left where Fawn Trail turns back to the right. At the next junction, take

a right. You'll have to climb a hill, but expansive views to the north and west make the climb worth it. Most of the ashe juniper in this part of the WMA has been cut, opening up the vista.

Follow the road of your choice through the center of the area on to the western boundary of the WMA and then back south along the west fenceline. The road falls away sharply (be sure your brakes are good), giving you a grand view of the canyon on your right. This canyon is especially beautiful in fall when the Spanish oaks blaze red and gold.

HUNTING

Hunting on the Walter Buck WMA is by Special Permit only. For information on the hunts available, see the *Applications for Drawings on Public Hunting Lands* for the current year. Hunts generally offered include either-sex gun hunts for whitetail deer, antlerless and spike hunts, archery deer hunts, and spring turkey hunts. On all hunts, hunters can take

unlimited exotics—sika, axis and fallow deer, feral hogs, and Spanish goats. Hunters are assigned blinds for deer hunts and compartments for spring turkey hunts.

PRO'S POINTERS. "We have good deer for the Hill Country," says Turney. "Hunters have harvested deer in the 140 to 155 class." Deer numbers are lower than on private property surrounding, and the habitat is in good shape and improving due to prescribed burning and cedar eradication.

If you are interested in harvesting an axis deer, hunting area 2 may be your best bet. The axis tend to feed in the mesquite flat east of the park campground and cross over into hunt area 2 to bed. Feral hogs have been seen in the bottomland between blinds 9 and 10, and there is a turkey roost in this same area. All species tend to travel along the drainages, and turkeys are prone to use the roads. Gobblers prefer open areas for strutting; find a park-like area near a drainage or road and try hunting there.

When applying for spring turkey hunts, consider applying for a hunt later in the season rather than for the first hunt or two. With large numbers of hens to choose from and the river bottom to range, gobblers are more likely to enter the WMA in search of hens late in the season. Even then, gobblers will dawdle in the river bottom and campground area early in the morning and not come into the WMA until midmorning. Hunters drawn for the spring turkey hunts on Walter Buck WMA can sleep late and not miss out on the action. Beginning your turkey hunt at 8:30 or so in the morning is usually early enough.

INSIDER'S CORNER

THE TOBUSCH FISHHOOK CACTUS

The Tobusch fishhook cactus (*Ancistrocactus tobuschii*), a federal and state endangered species, is known to occur on the Walter Buck WMA. This tiny cactus, often only an inch or two tall, was not discovered until 1951 by Henri Tobusch. The plant has been found in fewer than 50 locations. It propagates by tiny seeds spread primarily by ants feeding on its fruits.

Part of the reason for the plant's low profile is its low profile. It is very difficult to spot—even when you know where it is—because of its small size and its tendency to grow within grass, moss or rock fractures. It is easiest to find in February and March when it blooms and its bright yellow flowers give away its presence.

The Tobusch fishhook cactus prefers the very shallow soil over fractured limestone that is a hallmark of the Edwards Plateau. Studies indicate that its secretive nature, and the fact that most of its habitat lies on private land, may have misled researchers into thinking that it is more rare than it actually is.

PANHANDLE PLAINS

The practices we now call conser-
vation are, to a large extent, local
alleviations of biotic pain. They
are necessary, but they must not
be confused with cures. The art of
land doctoring is being practiced
with vigor, but the science of land
health is yet to be born.
—ALDO LEOPOLD

1 GENE HOWE WMA
2 MATADOR WMA
3 PLAYA LAKES WMA

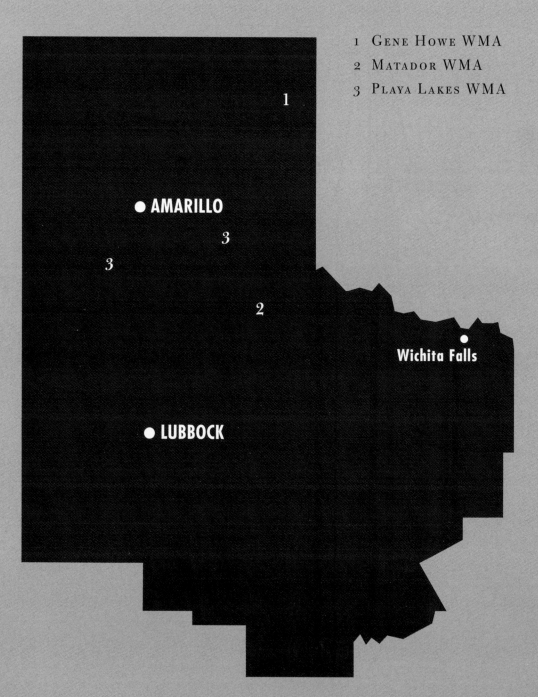

6,713 acres in two tracts
Route 3, Box 19
Canadian, TX 79014
806/323-8642

DRIVING TIMES FROM:
Amarillo: 2 hours
Austin: 9.5 hours
Brownsville: 16.5 hours
Dallas: 7.5 hours
El Paso: 11 hours
Houston: 12 hours
San Antonio: 10.5 hours
Add one-half hour to all times for
travel to the Murphy Unit.
DIRECTIONS: Main Unit—From
Canadian, take U.S. 60/83 north 2
miles to FM 2266. Go east 6 miles
on FM 2266. Murphy Unit—From
Canadian, take U.S. 60 north 8
miles to Glazier, then Texas 305
north 11.5 miles. An entrance with
sign-in station is on Texas 305 half a
mile north of its intersection with
Texas 213.
OPEN: Year-round for day use and
camping in designated areas, except
during Special Permit hunts.
ACTIVITIES: Main Unit—Nature
trail, camping, wildlife viewing,
hiking, horseback riding, bicycling,
hunting, fishing. Murphy Unit—
Wildlife viewing, hiking, hunting.
FACILITIES: Main Unit—Office,
nature trail, wildlife-viewing blind,
primitive campsites, composting
toilet, nonpotable water. Murphy
Unit—none.
SPECIAL REGULATIONS: All users
must register. Driving is permitted
only on roads appearing on the area
map. Camping is permitted only in
designated areas.
ADVISORIES: A high-clearance,
four-wheel-drive vehicle may be
required for some roads. Carry your
own supply of potable water.
LODGING IN AREA: Motels are
available in Canadian.
LOCAL POINTS OF INTEREST:
Black Kettle National Grasslands.
DISABILITY ACCESS: Not
wheelchair-accessible.

HISTORY

The Gene Howe WMA main unit
was one of the first properties purchased by the state for the purpose of
conducting wildlife research. Before
its purchase in 1950, the land was
used for cattle ranching.

In the 1880s railroads penetrated
the area, and an early settlement
called Hogtown flourished in what is
now the Upper Meadow pasture, just
south of present FM 2266. The town
of Canadian is descended from this
temporary hamlet catering to the
needs of track layers.

In 1918 J. C. Studer, from whom
the bulk of the land comprising the
WMA was purchased, donated a site
for a professional rodeo arena, Anvil
Park, in what is now the Upper
Meadow pasture. The old red barn
there dates from the time of Studer's
ranch. The rodeo arena was a few
hundred yards southeast of the
barn. A Texas historical marker on
FM 2266 tells the story.

The Murphy Unit of the Gene
Howe WMA was donated to Texas
Parks and Wildlife in 1991 by W. A.
Murphy. Before that time the land
was used for dry-land wheat farming
and cattle grazing.

GEOGRAPHY AND NATURAL FEATURES

The Gene Howe main unit is a
wonderful mix of habitat types.
Situated along the north bank of the
Canadian River, the area contains
riparian habitat with meadows and
large trees. On the south side of FM
2266, swamps support waterfowl and
beavers. Along FM 2266, which runs
parallel to the river and just above the
flood plain, a narrow transition zone
joins the bottomlands to the south
and the sandhills to the north. Immediately north of the highway, the land
rises quickly into rolling sandhills
with large dunes. This combination
of diverse habitat types in such close
proximity supports a rich and varied
wildlife population.

The Murphy Unit suffers in
comparison to the main unit. Of the
889 acres in the unit, about 800
consist of old farm fields and native
short-grass prairie that offer little
cover for wildlife. However, hidden
within a ravine bisecting the area
from south to north flows Plum
Creek, a perennial stream. Plum
thickets and huge, gnarled old cottonwood trees compete for attention
with abandoned farm buildings and
equipment, all in a state of ruin.

RECREATIONAL OPPORTUNITIES MAIN UNIT

The main unit of the Gene Howe
WMA offers a variety of activities. It
is open year-round except during
public gun deer and turkey hunts,
when the entire area is closed to
anyone not holding a Special Permit.

NATURE TRAIL

Enter the West Bull Pasture on the
south side of FM 2266 1 mile past
the area headquarters. Follow the
paved road 200 yards to an oil well
pad, bear right, and turn into the
parking area just before the cattle
guard. Follow the trail (not wheel-
chair accessible) across the footbridge about 100 yards to a viewing
blind situated on the edge of a marsh.
At the blind begins a nature trail that
winds for a quarter of a mile through
the riparian bottomland.

PRO'S POINTERS. Assistant area
manager John Hughes says, "Beaver,
waterfowl, and songbirds use the
area. You'll see great blue herons on
the pond, as well as widgeons, gadwalls, mallards, and teal during the
spring and fall migratory seasons.
Mississippi kites nest nearby. Springtime is the best time of year for
birding. The water level is high, and
the birds are coming through on
migration."

A wildlife viewing blind in the West Bull Pasture of the Gene Howe WMA overlooks a wetland frequented by waterfowl and feral hogs.

Camping

A primitive campground with fire rings and composting toilet is located on the north side of FM 2266 half a mile east of the area headquarters. Camping is free, but a permit is required. Camping is allowed any time the area is not closed for a Special Permit hunt.

PRO'S POINTERS. Two of the sites, the ones nearest the highway, are sized to accommodate RVs. The others are scattered among trees that offer some shade.

Wildlife Viewing

Gene Howe offers the opportunity to see an abundance of wildlife. On my first visit there, feral hogs darted down a road ahead of me only moments after my arrival. Coots, Canada geese, white-tailed deer, turkeys, lesser prairie chickens, numerous songbirds, prairie dogs, burrowing owls, and ornate box turtles have all come within range of my binoculars.

The area offers two wildlife-viewing blinds. One sits on the edge of a marsh in the West Bull Pasture. Enter the West Bull Pasture on the south side of FM 2266 1 mile past the area headquarters. Follow the paved road 200 yards to an oil well pad, bear right, and turn into the parking area just before the cattle guard. Follow the trail (not wheelchair-accessible) across the footbridge about 100 yards to the blind. Ducks, geese, and beavers populate the pond.

The other blind overlooks the prairie dog town in the Middle Pasture. To reach it, enter the DeArment Pasture half a mile east of the area headquarters, on the east side of the hunter campground. Follow the road straight ahead for 0.6 mile to a fork just inside the North Pasture. Bear right and continue 0.4 mile to a fork; again bear right and go another 1.1 miles. Just past a windmill with a green fiberglass water tank, bear left to two oil tanks. Park at the tanks and walk 100 yards to the observation blind on the east side of the prairie dog town.

Driving the roads on the area and glassing will also let you see many animals. On one visit, I spotted a white-tailed buck with one antler missing perched prettily atop a hill beside the campground. Wild turkeys can often be spotted along FM 2266 between the area headquarters and Canadian, especially in the vicinity of the Anvil Park historical marker. Prairie chickens and pronghorns are most likely to be found in the Middle and Persimmon pastures. Beavers are present in the pond in the West Bull Pasture and at the low water crossing on the road through the Williams Meadow Pasture.

PRO'S POINTERS. Prairie dogs will dash into their burrows at your approach, but if you remain quiet, they will reemerge after a few minutes. Sit very still and be very quiet, as they can probably pick up vibrations through the ground. The little creatures graze on the grass around their numerous mounds, and you may get to see a family with young on an outing. Watch for burrowing owls perching on mounds. Ornate box turtles also live in the mounds and graze on the grass among the prairie dogs. They will also dart—in turtle terms, of course—into a burrow if disturbed.

HIKING

The entire area is open to hiking, even across country. However, the 25 or so miles of roads—some caliche-surfaced to support heavy oilfield trucks and some barely improved—should satisfy most walkers. The best walking is north of FM 2266.

PRO'S POINTERS. Hughes suggests two routes. "Leave your vehicle at the windmill on the north side of North Pasture and walk east into the Middle Pasture and the prairie dog town."

Another good hike takes you through the Persimmon Pasture, a sandhill area with a creek running through it. Avoid the very sandy road on the north side of the pasture; a four-wheel drive is required year-round. The best entry is along the south road. From the turnoff into the DeArment Pasture at the campground, go 1.9 miles to the fork just past the windmill with the green fiberglass water tank. Take the right fork and continue another 2 miles to Persimmon Creek. Immediately after turning off, a sandy stretch of road may be difficult to negotiate in dry weather unless you have four-wheel drive. Park at the top of the hill overlooking the creek and walk from there. "Persimmon, cottonwood, and soapberry trees line the creek," says Hughes. "White-tail deer inhabit the creek bottom, along with bobwhite quail, western meadowlarks, Mississippi kites, Swainson's hawks, red-tailed hawks, bull snakes, and prairie rattlesnakes. Very rarely, antelope will show up on the area. They have been spotted in the west end of Persimmon and the east end of the Middle Pasture." On my last visit, I was fortunate enough to flush four lesser prairie chickens in the Middle Pasture at the point where the road branches to go to the Persimmon Pasture.

BICYCLING

Bikes must remain on roads. However, some roads are very sandy and should be avoided, particularly the one along the north side of North Pasture and Middle Pasture.

PRO'S POINTERS. For the best rides, stay on the caliche roads north of FM 2266 or on the highway itself. FM 2266 between Canadian, 7 miles west of the area headquarters, and Lake Marvin on the Black Kettle National Grasslands, 4 miles to the east, is a winding, fairly level route, parts of which are overhung by a canopy of trees. A good loop ride begins at either the area headquarters or the campground and follows FM 2266 before turning north into the DeArment Pasture and the southern portion of the North Pasture. This route offers excellent views of the Canadian river bottom from atop the sandhills.

EQUESTRIAN TRAIL

A designated horse trail begins at the campground half a mile east of the area headquarters and goes north through the DeArment, Middle and Persimmon Pastures, passing several windmills along the way. The first part of the trail follows a caliche road, but the route through the Persimmon Pasture is over barely improved, sandy roads. Except for climbs out of the Canadian River and Persimmon Creek bottoms, the route is fairly level; it covers about 6 miles.

PRO'S POINTERS. Horses are allowed only on this one trail, and only from March 15 to August 31.

HUNTING

Check the *Public Hunting Lands Map Booklet*, the *Outdoor Annual,* and the *Applications for Drawings on Public Hunting Lands* for information on hunting opportunities for the current year.

The Gene Howe WMA offers holders of an Annual Public Hunting Permit archery hunting for white-tailed deer and feral hogs, as well as shotgun hunting for quail, mourning doves, rabbits and hares, ducks, and geese. Pheasant hunting—a rarity on Texas WMAs—is available in December. Spring turkey hunts are available by drawing.

PRO'S POINTERS. Hughes offers these suggestions on where to seek the various kinds of game. "The best places for turkeys are the bottomland pastures on the southern portion of the area—the East and West Bull, Bunkhouse, Hay Meadow, Upper Meadow, and South Williams Pastures. Deer are found in these same pastures, while hogs stay mainly along the very southern boundary of the area in wet meadow habitat. Geese and ducks frequent mostly the West Bull slough area and the South Williams Pasture. Quail are found throughout the area but are most common in the Persimmon, North Williams, South Williams, and DeArment Pastures. Rabbits and hares are everywhere. Dove hunting will be best near the windmills in the sandhills pastures on the northern part of the area. Pheasants are pretty scarce but will be in the Hay Meadow, Bunkhouse, and South Williams Pastures."

FISHING

Fish for bass and catfish in the slough in the West Bull Pasture. The Canadian River is generally too shallow to support good fishing.

"Pronghorns are fairly common on the area in the summertime," says Hughes. "If the neighbors have wheat, pronghorns will hang out on the Murphy and feed on the wheat fields." Hughes has documented two lesser prairie chicken leks on the area, but viewing opportunities at present are limited.

Hiking

You are free to hike anywhere on the area. A network of interior farm roads gives easy access to any part of the area and good hiking possibilities. The Plum Creek bottomland, lined sporadically with large cottonwood trees, offers the only visual interest aside from abandoned farm buildings and junked equipment. While these are an eyesore and are slated for removal when possible, they do cause one to reflect on the hardships endured by dryland wheat farmers.

PRO'S POINTERS. The road from the entrance signboard descends a steep caliche hill, and deep ruts indicate that wet weather passage by automobile might be difficult.

Plum Creek forms a small pond immediately south of the old farmstead. The pond is overshadowed by one of the larger cottonwoods, and the clear stream, though less than two feet wide in most places, beckons as a pleasant place to spend a few hours on a summer day.

Hunting

Mourning dove hunting is allowed during the north zone season. Quail hunting runs from the end of October through the end of January. Rabbit hunting is allowed concurrently with bird hunting.

PRO'S POINTERS. The only areas that support quail are the bottomlands along Plum Creek and the easternmost pasture, a 256-acre tract that is being reseeded with native grasses.

Windmills and colorful sunrises combine to delight visitors to the Gene Howe WMA.

PRO'S POINTERS. In addition to a fishing license, you must have an Annual Public Hunting Permit to fish.

Recreational Opportunities Murphy Unit

Use of the Murphy Unit has historically been negligible. One reason is its isolation. Area manager Dave Dvorak says it has been totally ignored except for a handful of quail hunters. In recent years, special youth hunts for quail have been offered on the area in an effort to increase use. Besides hunting, wildlife viewing and hiking are approved activities.

Wildlife Viewing

White-tailed and mule deer, bobwhite quail, and northern harriers are the animals you are most likely to see. More infrequent visitors include pronghorns and lesser prairie chickens.

PRO'S POINTERS. The bottomlands along Plum Creek are the most likely to hold deer and quail.

INSIDER'S CORNER

PRAIRIE DOGS

The known range of the black-tailed prairie dog once extended as far east as Montague and Tarrant Counties and as far south as Bexar County. Today these cousins of the ground squirrel are confined to the Panhandle and Trans-Pecos. Gene Howe WMA is the only wildlife management area in Texas with a resident population of prairie dogs.

The prairie dog town on the Gene Howe WMA is minuscule compared with the giant one in the Texas Panhandle that once covered 25,000 square miles and contained an estimated 400 million prairie dogs. Not surprisingly, these social animals regulate their towns through a system of geographic areas. Each town is divided into wards, analogous to counties; within each ward are numerous coteries with a male, several females, and young under the age of two. Members of coteries greet each other with bared-teeth "kisses." Each coterie covers about an acre and may contain 70 burrow entrances.

Prairie dog towns are easily recognized by the raised rings, rather like the cone of a volcano, that surround burrow openings. These rings provide a vantage point for lookouts. Sentries keep watch as others feed, and any disturbance in the town elicits a warning bark, at which all the prairie dogs dart into their burrows, coming out only when the "all-clear" signal is barked. The raised entrances also keep water from running in and screen animals from view as they emerge. Your first view of many prairie dogs will be their nose and eyes peering over the lip of the mound as they check out the area before emerging.

Prairie dogs play an important part in their native short-grass prairie ecosystems. They serve as food for predators such as coyotes, bobcats, badgers, black-footed ferrets, golden eagles, and prairie falcons. Their tunnels house burrowing owls, black-footed ferrets, Texas horned lizards, rabbits, rattlesnakes, and even ornate box turtles.

Farmers and ranchers have virtually exterminated prairie dogs from most of their former range. Only about 1 percent of the presettlement prairie dog population of about 5 billion remains. One reason early settlers gave for eliminating prairie dogs was the hazard their burrows posed to riders on horseback. The burrows have funnel-shaped openings about four inches in diameter that slope steeply downward for about three feet before leveling off. It was said that a horse could step in one of these holes and break a leg. Prairie dogs also compete with livestock for grass, which makes up most of their diet. One researcher calculated that 32 prairie dogs eat as much as one sheep; 256 as much as a cow. Obviously, ranchers would have little use for the little rodents. However, some stockmen have reported that eliminating prairie dogs led to brush invading grassland, reducing the available feed for livestock.

During summer prairie dogs store up fat for the winter. In northern Texas, hibernation begins in November, although it is not complete. Young are born in March or April. Blind and hairless at birth, they open their eyes at 33 to 37 days, at which time they are able to run, eat grass, and bark. Weaning occurs shortly after they emerge from the burrow for the first time, at about six weeks of age. Young males disperse throughout the colony upon reaching sexual maturity at age two, helping to maintain genetic diversity.

The prairie dog's active lifestyle, foraging for food, and scampering about the town causes many people to admire their industriousness. Others appreciate them more as a novelty, a cute little critter. To learn more about prairie dogs, listen to their sounds, and descend into a virtual burrow, visit the website www.nationalgeographic.com/burrow/tl.html.

28,183 acres
Route 1, Box 46
Paducah, TX 79248
806/492-3405

DRIVING TIMES FROM:
Amarillo: 2.5 hours
Austin: 7 hours
Brownsville: 14 hours
Dallas: 5 hours
El Paso: 8.5 hours
Houston: 10 hours
San Antonio: 7.5 hours
DIRECTIONS: From Paducah, go north 7 miles on U.S. 62/83, then west 2 miles on FM 3256.

OPEN: Year-round for day use and camping in designated areas, except during public hunts.

ACTIVITIES: Nature trail, camping, wildlife viewing, hiking, bicycling, hunting, fishing.

FACILITIES: Office, nature trail, equestrian trail, primitive campsites, composting toilet, nonpotable water.

SPECIAL REGULATIONS: All users must register at the information station. Driving is permitted only on roads appearing on the area map. Camping is permitted only in designated areas.

ADVISORIES: A high-clearance, four-wheel-drive vehicle may be required for some roads. Carry your own supply of potable water.

LODGING IN AREA: Motels are available in Paducah and Childress.

LOCAL POINTS OF INTEREST: Copper Breaks State Park, Caprock Canyons State Park.

DISABILITY ACCESS: Not wheelchair-accessible.

HISTORY

The Matador WMA takes its name from the famous Texas ranch of which it was once a part. The ranch was begun by Texas rancher Henry H. Campbell in the late 1870s, when he selected land along the Upper, Middle, and Lower Pease Rivers, an area recently cleared of buffalo and Indians. The ranch was later sold to a group of investors from Dundee, Scotland, and grew to include divisions of leased and owned land in other parts of Texas, the northern United States, and Canada.

In the 1950s new owners began dismembering the ranch, selling off portions to various corporations and individuals. The then Texas Game & Fish Commission purchased the tract now comprising the Matador WMA in 1959. "At that time A. S. Jackson was the state's wildlife manager for the Panhandle, and the owners of the Matador allowed him to design the shape of the WMA around the Pease River, which is why it is 10 miles long but only 4 miles wide," says area manager Dave Dvorak. The WMA's western boundary joins a remnant of the Matador Ranch.

Colorful rock formations along the Pease River compete for attention with wildlife and scenic views.

GEOGRAPHY AND NATURAL FEATURES

The Matador WMA contains some extremely rugged country. The dominant red soil is typical of the Rolling Plains, as are the highly eroded breaks and canyons feeding into the Pease River bottom. Sandy soils cover some rolling hills, particularly on the eastern portion of the area, and the river bottom.

Diverse topography and soils, along with the junction of the Middle and Tongue (or South Pease) Rivers, contribute to diversity of plants and animals on the area. Mesquite dominates, but sand sagebrush, Havard (shinnery) oak, redberry juniper, and sand plum are common as well. Cottonwood, hackberry, and western soapberry line the rivers. Native grasses include several varieties of bluestems and gramas; forbs include ragweed, croton, and wild buckwheat.

White-tailed and mule deer share the area with bobwhite quail, cottontail and jackrabbits, mourning doves, coyotes, Rio Grande turkeys, feral hogs and many avian and reptile species. But the most common mammals are ones you might not expect. "We probably have more pounds of rodents than we have pounds of deer," says Dvorak.

The outstanding singularity of the Matador WMA is the Middle Pease River. "As far as I know, we are the only property on the Middle Pease that maintains permanent water," says Dvorak. "The river comes up about a quarter of a mile inside our west boundary, and about a quarter of a mile after it leaves the area, it goes underground. We also have some live springs on the place. This is something that has developed within the last 15 to 20 years. This place is continuing to change. It does add immeasurably to the diversity of the place."

Archery hunting mule deer on the Matador WMA is challenging, but a surprising number of hunters succeed.

RECREATIONAL OPPORTUNITIES

The Matador WMA is open for the following activities year-round except during public gun deer and hog hunts, when the entire area is closed to anyone not holding a permit.

CAMPING

Camping is restricted to two primitive campgrounds in the headquarters area. The first sits atop a knoll about a quarter of a mile past the headquarters. There is a composting toilet and nonpotable water at this site, but no other amenities. A quarter-mile farther on is a camping area with small mesquite trees, composting toilet, and a few picnic tables. During Special Permit hunts, campgrounds are reserved for the use of hunters.

PRO'S POINTERS. Facilities are minimal. Bring your own water and be prepared to pack out all your trash. Ground fires are allowed, but no firewood is available.

WILDLIFE VIEWING

There are no designated wildlife-viewing spots. However, diverse habitat types and ample water along the river and at windmills mean you will almost certainly see a variety of mammals, reptiles, and birds on the Matador WMA. From April until August, a breeding population of Mississippi kites is found on the area. Green and great blue herons nest along the river, and a wealth of migratory neotropical birds—bluebirds, scissor-tailed flycatchers and Bullock's orioles—pass through in spring and fall.

A unique wildlife-viewing opportunity can be had by meeting staff personnel at area headquarters at sunup during summer months. A number of live traps that may hold a variety of crawling creatures are checked each morning.

PRO'S POINTERS. "Deer and turkeys can often be seen at the food plots. Excellent places for birding are along the river and at ponds formed

by the overflow from windmills, especially the Stonewall windmill in the North Middle Pasture, the Dogleg windmill in the Dogleg Pasture, and both windmills in the OX Pasture," says Dvorak.

HIKING

Hiking is allowed on the 73 miles of barely improved roads on the area and on an unknown number of miles of unimproved or "pasture" roads. You may also drive any of the roads shown on the official map of the area, but some require four-wheel drive or high clearance vehicles due to deep sand or water crossings.

PRO'S POINTERS. One good driving/hiking tour begins at the Entrance Pasture road across from the area headquarters and goes north across the Entrance, Suitcase, and OX Pastures. The OX Pasture offers fairly level terrain, sandy soil, and extensive stands of shinnery oak along both sides of OX Creek.

For a more strenuous hike, take the first road to the left past the Parsons Food Plot. This road runs the ridges above Cow Hollow Creek; steep canyons line either side. Another

scenic but hilly trail is the marked horse trail in the North Middle Pasture.

A longer hike, but one with spectacular views, begins at the Entrance Pasture and proceeds across the Suitcase and OX Pastures to the Shorty Pasture. Shortly after entering the Shorty Pasture, walk 50 yards up the hill to the north to a bluff overlooking the valley of the Middle Pease River. Return to the road, cross the river, and pass the Shorty windmill and then a utility line. Just after entering the North Middle Pasture, the road turns west and parallels the area's north boundary. Walk 100 yards to the rugged red hills to the left. Here you may startle a deer feeding in the mesquite flat below the hills. Farther on, the land drops into deep canyons frequented by mule deer and bobwhite quail. There is an excellent view of the canyon country from the Long Canyon windmill.

One of the best scenic views is

from the bluffs on the east side of the Pease crossing in the Dogleg Pasture. As you approach the crossing and the road curves left and drops steeply, go straight ahead onto a narrow point of land. Stop! The bluff drops straight down about 25 yards ahead. Below is the heavily vegetated river bottom, criss-crossed with trails made by wandering cows, deer, and hogs. To the northwest is an impressive rampart of red bluffs on the other side of the river.

BICYCLING

Biking is restricted to the 73 miles of roads shown on the area map. In general, the most level terrain is along the main road running from the headquarters to the far western boundary in the Sisk Pen Pasture. This road parallels the river for most of its length.

PRO'S POINTERS. Unless you enjoy biking on abominably rough, washboarded gravel roads, drive to

Boot Hill (a small knoll with a metal fence post topped by a boot) in the South Middle Pasture before beginning your bike ride.

Another mostly level ride takes you through the Entrance, Suitcase and OX Pastures. However, avoid the road along the eastern boundary of the OX, Suitcase, and Entrance Pastures because of deep sand.

If you enjoy using your lower gears, try riding the horse trail through the North Middle Pasture. Or take the first road to the south past the Parsons food plot, ride to windmill number 6, then loop through the eastern end of the Sisk Pen Pasture back to your starting point. Both these rides include steep hills.

"Roads on the area are primitive and hard to get around on," advises Dvorak. "Some are impassable when wet, but we have a lot of sandy roads

The view of the Pease River bottom from bluffs in the Dogleg Pasture is spectacular.

that dry out quickly and then are in good shape for a while. The river crossings are no problem when wet, but they can be treacherous when dry due to deep sand."

EQUESTRIAN TRAIL

A designated horse trail about 10 miles long begins at pens near the campground and follows the vehicle road through the Bull Trap, Mouth of River Trap, North Middle and South Middle Pastures. The trail is signed, and riding is allowed on the road surface only.

PRO'S POINTERS. Water is available at windmills along the trail. Use of the equestrian trail has been minimal; if you want solitude while you ride, this is the place.

HUNTING

Consult the *Public Hunting Lands Map Booklet*, the *Outdoor Annual*, and the *Applications for Drawings on Public Hunting Lands* for the current year for species, seasons, and bag limits.

Bobwhite quail hunting has long been the main user activity on the Matador WMA. The Rolling Plains of Texas and Oklahoma are perhaps the last stronghold of wild bobwhite quail in the United States, and in

years with favorable conditions, quail numbers on the area can be high. Dove hunting is excellent at times, and many dove hunters travel long distances just to be able to hunt in a remote area with few other people about. A hunting license and an Annual Public Hunting Permit are required. Feral hog archery hunting is allowed, and rabbits and hares may be taken while dove and quail hunting.

The Matador WMA is one of only two public hunting areas in Texas where you can bowhunt mule deer with only a hunting license and an Annual Public Hunting Permit (most years; check your *Public Hunting Lands Map Booklet* for current regulations). Gun hunts for white-tailed or mule deer and feral hogs may also be available by drawing.

PRO'S POINTERS. Dvorak offers these tips for hunters. "Virtually everything is tied to the river. It's the key to this whole area. For deer and feral hogs, hunt the river and the canyons that feed into it. Also key on areas where prescribed burns have been conducted recently; they will be greener and will attract wildlife. For doves, hunt water holes on the river. The entire area is quail habitat; they can be anywhere."

FISHING

Don't make a trip to the Matador WMA just for the purpose of fishing. There are some permanent holes on the Pease River that hold catfish, bass, and perch, but numbers are very limited. While you are permitted to keep legal-size fish, Dvorak points out that much fishing pressure could force imposition of a catch-and-release-only rule to protect the limited resource.

PRO'S POINTERS. "The small pond on the right side of the road in the Mouth of River Trap is full of small bass; kids love it. Those fish will bite anything you throw in there—I've caught them on a bare hook," Dvorak says.

LITTLE OAKS WITH MIGHTY ACORNS

The OX Pasture supports an extensive stand of Havard oaks (*Quercus havardii*), diminutive trees that are only a few feet high but have roots that can reach 50 or more feet underground in their search for water. In an odd twist on the old saying that mighty oaks grow from tiny acorns, these tiny trees produce giant acorns that may be the diameter of a quarter.

Speaking of a forest of the little trees that stretches from West Texas into New Mexico, Texas naturalist Roy Bedichek wrote, "I venture the statement, without research, that in no other forested section, Amazon Valley not excepted, is there to be found a higher fruit to wood ratio than in this Lilliputian jungle. . . . Vegetatively considered, it is as much a natural curiosity as the Painted Desert or the wonderful areas of Yellowstone."

Perhaps to protect the trees from being killed by grazing animals, the leaves are toxic to wildlife and domestic livestock while young and tender, losing their poisonous nature when mature. The acorns, when present, are an excellent wildlife food.

To see one of the nation's largest—although shortest—oak forests, visit Monahans Sandhills State Park, on I-20 6 miles northeast of Monahans. Havard oaks cover most of the park and thousands of square miles surrounding it. Interpretive exhibits and a nature trail tell the tale of the mighty acorns that held their ground and grew up to become tiny trees.

No one seems to know the origin of the boot atop a small knoll dubbed Boot Hill, but it is replaced regularly.

1,492 acres in three tracts
Route 1, Box 46
Paducah, TX 79248
806/492-3405

DRIVING TIMES FROM:
Amarillo: 1 hour (Armstrong Unit);
1.5 hours (Taylor Lakes Unit)
Austin: 8 hours (either unit)
Brownsville: 15 hours (either unit)
Dallas: 6.5 hours (Armstrong Unit);
5 hours (Taylor Lakes Unit)
El Paso: 6.5 hours (Armstrong
Unit); 8.5 hours (Taylor Lakes Unit)
Houston: 10.5 hours (Armstrong
Unit); 10 hours (Taylor Lakes Unit)
San Antonio: 9.5 hours (either unit)
DIRECTIONS: Armstrong Unit—
From Dimmitt, go west on Texas 86
for 9.7 miles, then south on FM
1524 about 2 miles. Turn west on
County Road 618 and go 1 mile to
its intersection with County Road
503, then follow it to the left for a
quarter of a mile. Dimmitt Unit—
Access is restricted to Texas Parks
and Wildlife personnel. Taylor
Lakes Unit—From Clarendon, go
southeast 7 miles on U.S. 287.
OPEN: Year-round for day use,
except during public hunts.
ACTIVITIES: Taylor Lakes Unit—
wildlife viewing, hiking, hunting;
Armstrong Unit—wildlife viewing.
FACILITIES: At the Taylor Lakes
Unit a wildlife-viewing blind is
provided, and a nature trail is
planned. There are no facilities at
the Armstrong Unit.
SPECIAL REGULATIONS: All users
must register at the information
station. Hunting on the Taylor Lakes
Unit is restricted to the mourning
dove and early teal seasons. Some
draw hunts for geese and quail are
offered.
ADVISORIES: At the Armstrong
Unit, wildlife viewing must be
conducted from county roads; you
are not allowed to go onto the unit.

*Playa lakes, natural depressions that hold
water much of the year, nurture important
wildlife habitat in the Texas Panhandle.*

The Dimmitt Unit is off limits to all
but Texas Parks and Wildlife per-
sonnel, as access can be gained only
by crossing private land. Carry your
own supply of potable water.
LODGING IN AREA: Motels are
available in Clarendon and Dimmitt.
LOCAL POINTS OF INTEREST:
Caprock Canyons State Park, Palo
Duro Canyon State Park, Buffalo
Lake National Wildlife Refuge,
Muleshoe National Wildlife Refuge.
DISABILITY ACCESS: The wildlife-
viewing blind on the Taylor Lakes
Unit is wheelchair-accessible.

HISTORY

Apaches ruled this land until the
18th century, when Comanches and
Kiowas expanded into the area.
Indians prevented settlement until
after the Red River War of 1874-75.
One of the three original towns in the
Panhandle, Clarendon, was estab-
lished a few miles from the Taylor
Lakes Unit in 1878.

The 530 acres in the Taylor Lakes
Unit were owned by the Reed family
from 1878 until Texas Parks and
Wildlife purchased the property in

1993. The land was used for cattle grazing and farming of cotton, wheat, peanuts and vegetables. The 322-acre Dimmitt unit was farmed until its purchase in 1990. Due to lack of a dedicated right-of-way, access is restricted to Texas Parks and Wildlife personnel only. Public use of the area will not be permitted until this situation is resolved. The Armstrong Unit is operated by TPWD under a conservation easement and lease agreement. Its principal use has been as farmland.

GEOGRAPHY AND NATURAL FEATURES

The Armstrong and Dimmitt Units are located in the High Plains Ecological Area. Before settlement, the land was covered by a short-grass prairie whose principal vegetation was blue grama and buffalograsses.

The Armstrong Unit contains 480 acres leased for row crop agriculture, a 52-acre playa lake, and 108 acres of grassland surrounding the lake. The Dimmitt Unit contains a 77-acre playa lake and 345 acres of former farmland reseeded with grass and forbs. A 1,200-foot shelter belt was planted in 1993 to provide cover for wildlife.

The Taylor Lakes Unit is part of the Rolling Plains Ecological Area. It contains about 214 acres of former cropland being returned to grassland, 231 acres of pastureland, and four lakes and wetlands containing about 85 acres.

The sky dominates the impression one gets at all three areas. The land is flat to gently rolling, but by their nature playa lakes occupy what are significant depressions for the area. Once you descend into the lake area, you lose sight of the surrounding plains, leaving the sky the overwhelming feature of the landscape.

Playa lakes are one of the most important features of the plains of north Texas. Shallow and likely to dry up when rainfall is low, they have

limitations as reservoirs but are valuable for wildlife. Drawdowns due to irrigation or a falling water table followed by rises in water level create ideal conditions for plant growth in the lake bed, which becomes an important source of cover and food for waterfowl in particular. Playa lakes in the Texas Panhandle and Rolling Plains furnish stopover habitat for migratory birds and roosting sites for species that winter in the region. In addition, the margins of playa lakes are often left unfarmed due to boggy conditions, and the resulting weeds adjacent to both water and food sources create ideal habitat for species such as pheasants.

RECREATIONAL OPPORTUNITIES

While a nature trail is planned for the Taylor Lakes Unit when funding is secured, and limited hunting is allowed at the same site, at present wildlife viewing is the principal use of the two areas with public access.

WILDLIFE VIEWING
TAYLOR LAKES UNIT

"There is a series of four natural lakes, water table lakes, immediately adjacent to U.S. 287," says area manager Dave Dvorak. "We have an observation blind just off the highway. This is a major wintering area for 6,000 Canada geese as well as ducks, swans, and other waterfowl. Birding is great. In an hour, we've counted 22 different species of birds buzzing about—including one interior least tern—without using our binoculars."

West of the main lake, the land rises to the area boundary and has some broken areas. A mesquite flat lies between the lake and the breaks, and white-tailed deer frequent the area. Tracks reveal that feral hogs are also present.

PRO'S POINTERS. This is not a place to have a wilderness experience. Heavy truck traffic on the highway and occasional freight trains detract from the feeling of being in the wild. However, this is a good place to contemplate the extent to which wildlife can become habituated to human activities.

The viewing blind, a roofed tin enclosure with benches and viewing ports, is only 50 yards from the parking lot. It perches on the eastern shore of Taylor Lake #1 and commands a view of the entire lake.

A wildlife viewing blind overlooks the main lake on the Taylor Lakes Unit of the Playa Lakes WMA and is wheel-chair accessible.

Should you find a lack of waterfowl on Taylor Lake #1, hike around the lake to the west about half a mile, following mowed paths. Taylor Lake #2 and D&J Lake both are likely to hold considerable numbers of Canada geese and ducks. When approaching either lake, walk slowly and use the surrounding brush for concealment to avoid spooking the birds into flight. There is ample vegetation around both lakes to allow you to get into good viewing position, although some belly-crawling may be necessary.

HUNTING
TAYLOR LAKES UNIT

The area is open for mourning dove hunting each day of the season in the north zone. Teal may be hunted each day of the early teal season. A hunting license and an Annual Public Hunting Permit are required. Hunters must sign in and out at the information hut in the parking lot adjacent to U.S. 287.

Hunts for all legal waterfowl, including ducks, geese, and sandhill cranes, may be offered on selected dates in November, December and January. One party of no more than four persons will be selected for each hunt date. See the current *Public Hunting Lands Map Booklet* for dates available and the procedure to follow.

PRO'S POINTERS. The Taylor Lakes Unit offers a rare opportunity in Texas, the chance to hunt greater Canada geese, which are about three times the size of the more common lesser Canadas. Two blinds for hunting waterfowl are provided. Bring your own material for constructing temporary blinds. Shooting hours end at noon during the drawn hunts, but some local farmers will allow free hunting on winter wheat fields. Scout the local area and ask permission to hunt where you see geese or sandhill cranes feeding.

WILDLIFE VIEWING
ARMSTRONG UNIT

Snow geese, Ross's geese, lesser Canada geese, and sandhill cranes all utilize this lake, and the grass buffer around the lake is pheasant habitat.

PRO'S POINTERS. Morning viewing is best from County Road 618 north of the lake; in the afternoon, to avoid looking into the sun, watch from County Road 503 to the west. Since you will be some distance from the lake, good binoculars are necessary.

A short hike and some belly-crawling will get you close to waterfowl on Taylor Lake #2 and D&J Lake.

INSIDER'S CORNER

SANDHILL CRANES

One of the most beautiful sounds in nature is the call of the sandhill crane. Its long, haunting "krooo-ooo-ooo" evokes a sense of wild things and wild places better than perhaps anything else with the possible exception of a coyote's howl.

Sandhill cranes winter as far south as the Texas coast, but the greatest concentration is found in the Texas Panhandle. Shallow playa lakes provide ideal roosting places for these birds, the water providing protection from predators.

Two kinds of sandhills winter in Texas—Canadians and lessers. There is little apparent difference between the two. Those classified as Canadians tend to be slightly larger, males weighing about nine pounds compared to seven or eight pounds for the lessers. Canadians breed on the tundra of central Canada, while lessers migrate even farther north, some going on to Alaska and others crossing the Bering Strait into Siberia. Both

Canadians and lessers stop over in Nebraska's Platte River Valley to fatten on waste corn for their trip north. Cranes from the Muleshoe National Wildlife Refuge in Texas make up a large share of this group. As many as 500,000 sandhill cranes may be present along the Platte from February into April.

Lesser sandhill cranes are by far the most abundant, numbering perhaps 300,000. Their numbers seemed to have increased over the last decade, heightening concerns about crop damage and competition for food between cranes and geese. Crane-hunting seasons have been opened in a number of Central Flyway states in an attempt to control their numbers.

However, not enough is known about sandhill cranes to allow wildlife biologists to manage their numbers effectively. Data seems to indicate that today's cranes store only half the fat during their Nebraska stopover as they did in the 1970s. However, until recently scientists lacked the tools they

needed to follow individual cranes throughout their annual journey in order to gather needed information. This changed when platform transmitting terminals (PTTs) were developed. These small, one-ounce transmitters can be monitored from orbiting satellites, allowing the cranes to be tracked anywhere. As of 1999, 21 cranes had been radio-marked in a continuing study.

The satellite telemetry research will help reveal the cranes' breeding grounds, migration routes, and wintering areas; help determine what factors influence their stay in the Platte River Valley; aid in estimating the population and assist in learning which species are most subject to hunting pressure.

You can learn more about sandhill cranes and follow the progress of the study at the following website: 159.189.96.215/perm/cranemov. This site also allows you to listen to the sounds cranes make and even follow the progress of individual cranes during migration.

PINEYWOODS

PINEYWOODS

All ethics so far evolved rest upon a single premise: that the individual is a member of a community of interdependent parts. His instincts prompt him to compete for his place in that community, but his ethics prompt him also to co-operate (perhaps in order that there may be a place to compete for).

The land ethic simply enlarges the boundaries of the community to include soils, waters, plants, and animals, or collectively: the land.
—ALDO LEOPOLD

1   ALABAMA CREEK WMA

2   ALAZAN BAYOU WMA

3   ANGELINA-NECHES/DAM B WMA

4   BANNISTER WMA

5   CADDO LAKE STATE PARK/WMA

6   MOORE PLANTATION WMA

7   NORTH TOLEDO BEND WMA

8   THE NATURE CENTER

9   OLD SABINE BOTTOM WMA

10 SAM HOUSTON NATIONAL FOREST WMA

11 WHITE OAK CREEK WMA

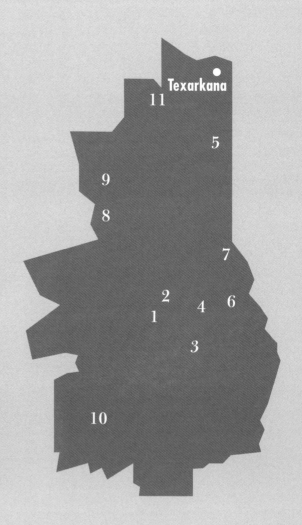

14,561 acres
1805 E. Lufkin Ave.
Lufkin, TX 75901
936/639-1879

DRIVING TIMES FROM:
Amarillo: 9.5 hours
Austin: 3.5 hours
Brownsville: 8.5 hours
Dallas: 3 hours
El Paso: 13.5 hours
Houston: 2 hours
San Antonio: 5 hours
DIRECTIONS: From Lufkin, take
Texas 94 west for 12.7 miles to FM
2262; then take FM 2262 south 4.1
miles to an information station at the
area boundary.
OPEN: Daily.
ACTIVITIES: Driving tour, camping,
wildlife viewing, hiking, bicycling,
hunting, fishing.
FACILITIES: Primitive campgrounds.
SPECIAL REGULATIONS: Hunters
are required to possess an Annual
Public Hunting Permit, although
some Limited Public Use Permit
hunting is currently allowed. Turkeys must be taken to a check station
within 24 hours. All legal firearms
and archery equipment may be used
during the general deer season and
for feral hog hunting January 15
through March 15, with the follow-

ing exception: During the archery-
only season, crossbows may be used
only by a person having a permanent
upper limb disability. All legal
firearms may be used to hunt feral
hogs during the deer archery season.
No buckshot is allowed. Trapping
for furbearers and predators is
allowed November 1 through March
31. Horses are allowed year-round.
Teal may be hunted all day each day
of the early teal season; otherwise,
waterfowl shooting hours end at
noon. For other special regulations,
see the section entitled "Special
Regulations in Effect on U.S. Forest
Service Units" in the current *Public
Hunting Lands Map Booklet*.
ADVISORIES: Copperheads, water
moccasins, poison ivy, mosquitoes,
and ticks are present. Do not leave
vehicles unattended along Forest
Road 510-F because of the possibil-
ity of theft. Carry your own supply
of potable water.
LODGING IN AREA: Motels are
available in Lufkin.
LOCAL POINTS OF INTEREST: Lake
Livingston State Park, Huntsville
State Park, Texas State Railroad,
Fort Boggy State Park, Jim Hogg
State Historical Park.
DISABILITY ACCESS: Not
wheelchair-accessible.

HISTORY

Davy Crockett National Forest, which
includes Alabama Creek WMA, was
Caddo Indian territory until the
1830s, when Anglo settlement began.
Logging began in the area about 1880.
By the 1930s the "cut out and get out"
policies of the timber companies had
removed most of the marketable
timber. In 1936 Congress approved
the creation of Davy Crockett National
Forest, and the U.S. Forest Service
began reforestation efforts. A state
game management area, the Alabama
Creek Area, was established in 1954,
but the agreement governing it was
allowed to expire in 1972. Agreements
signed in 1981 and 1984 led to the
creation of the present Alabama Creek
WMA.

GEOGRAPHY AND NATURAL FEATURES

The WMA is bounded on the west by
FM 357 and on the east by the Neches
River, a narrow, winding, sluggish
stream with steep banks. FM 2262
runs north to south through the area,
dividing approximately the eastern
one-third from the rest. The bulk of
the area is level to gently rolling
uplands bisected by shallow creeks.
Steeper slopes border the Neches
River. Much of the soil is sandy,
especially on the portion of the area
east of FM 2262.

Regrowth pines, mostly in even-
aged communities older than 55 years,
dominate the area. Loblolly, shortleaf,
and longleaf pines are the chief species. Most hardwood and mixed pine/
hardwood areas follow the course of
the Neches River. Beaver activity has
resulted in some small, scattered
wetlands.

The principal animals on the area
include white-tailed deer, feral hogs,
gray squirrels, eastern wild turkeys,

This campsite on the bank of the Neches River, reached via an unsigned road off Forest Road 510-B, is a favorite with fishers.

The Rock Hole camping area is the prettiest on the area and, as a result, receives heavy use, especially on weekends.

other parts of Davy Crockett National Forest contain developed campgrounds and recreational areas, the portion comprising the Alabama Creek WMA is largely primitive. A variety of activities are allowed, but there are no facilities provided.

DRIVING TOUR

During the spring dogwood season, the U.S. Forest Service maintains a self-guided driving trail in the Davy Crockett National Forest. This trail includes stops in the Alabama Creek WMA.

PRO'S POINTERS. Obtain a printed guide to the driving trail from the U.S. Forest Service office 1 mile west of Apple Springs on Texas 94. Office hours are 8 A.M. to 4:30 P.M. Monday through Friday, and there is no outside rack for brochures. The best month for viewing dogwoods in bloom is March. For more information, contact the district ranger at 409/831-2246.

CAMPING

Camping is permitted anywhere within the forest except during deer-hunting season. Camping is restricted to designated campsites from the beginning of archery season until the end of the general season. Except at campsite #5, which is closed during hunting season, camping is permitted at the following primitive campgrounds during hunting season and at any other time of year:

1. From Apple Springs, go south on FM 357 for 2.5 miles to Forest Road 509 and go east on 509. At 2.6 miles, follow Forest Road 509-C 0.5 mile to a T intersection, then go left 0.1 mile to a camping area between two ponds of about half an acre each. Tall pines shade the campsites. The first pond you reach is round and has a place where you can hand-launch a canoe. On the far side are more campsites and a long, narrow pond. Both ponds contain bass. Unfortunately, this area appears to be the most used and abused on the WMA. Known

and beavers. A variety of neotropical migrant songbirds and waterfowl use the area seasonally. In addition, there is a small population of red-cockaded woodpeckers, an endangered species.

RECREATIONAL ACTIVITIES

As part of a national forest, Alabama Creek WMA is governed by U.S. Forest Service rules, which allow for maximum recreational use. While

locally as the Rock Hole, it is a popular picnicking and fishing spot and is heavily trashed.

2. From the intersection of Forest Roads 509 and 509-C, continue east on 509 for 2 miles. The campground is located on the north side of the road and is totally shaded by tall pines.

3. From the intersection of Texas 94 and FM 2262, go south on FM 2262 for 4.9 miles. Turn left onto Forest Road 510-A (signed Holly Bluff Road on the highway). At the top of the hill 1.6 miles down Forest Road 510-A, there are a couple of shaded pullouts on the left. Continue another 0.1 mile to shaded riverbank campsites. Small boats can be hand-launched here. Trash indicates this area receives heavy usage, especially on weekends.

4. From the intersection of Texas 94 and FM 2262, go south on FM 2262 for 5.3 miles. The campground, on the east side of the highway, has some sites shaded by large pines. Back-in sites can accommodate large RVs, and the site is mostly level.

5. From the intersection of Texas 94 and FM 2262, go south on FM 2262 for 6.8 miles to Forest Road 510-B, which is just south of the road signed Boys Camp Road. Follow Forest Road 510-B east for 1.7 miles to an unsigned road to the right. Follow this road another 0.5 mile to a riverbank camping area. Well shaded, this campground is near the southern boundary of the area and is a favorite with trotliners. Walking upriver about a quarter of a mile takes you to a hill overlooking a beaver marsh, which offers good birding.

PRO'S POINTERS. Avoid the campgrounds on Forest Road 509-C and on the Neches River on weekends. None of the campgrounds have water, fire rings, or any other amenities. Birders or hunters wishing to access the Holly Bluff Swamp have a campground close by on Forest Road 510-A.

WILDLIFE VIEWING

The varied habitat types on the WMA—upland pine, wetland, and riverine—plus its location on the migration route of numerous birds make Alabama Creek a good birding site. In addition, the presence of the endangered red-cockaded woodpecker on the area attracts people who want to see this rare species. There are no facilities provided for wildlife viewing.

PRO'S POINTERS. Forest Road 510-B offers good birding almost any time of year. In spring, several species of warblers may be seen along the road, including Kentucky warblers, hooded warblers, black-and-white warblers, and yellow-rumped warblers. Other species you may see include indigo buntings, fox sparrows, red-headed woodpeckers, and Louisiana water thrushes. "Birding along the road is good because the cover is so thick through there, when they do come out, they will be close," says Texas Parks and Wildlife biologist Richard Pike.

A swamp along Forest Road 510-B begins 2.0 miles east of FM 2262. Plentiful dead snags in the swamp—especially near the water-control structures beside the road at mile 2.4—hold nesting prothonotary warblers in the spring. Beavers plugged the water control structures of what was to be a green-tree reservoir and killed the trees.

The Holly Bluff Swamp area offers excellent wildlife viewing. In summer you may see broad-winged hawks roosting around the swamp in big, mature pines with open limb areas. White-eyed vireos, prothonotary warblers, Mississippi kites, various egrets and herons and butterflies use the area in summer; wood storks may be present from mid- to late summer. In winter the marsh holds mallards, wood ducks, gadwalls, hooded mergansers, widgeons and numerous hunters. Alligators will be active during the warm months, including the early teal season. Holly Bluff Swamp lies east of FM 2262 off Forest Road 510-A. Park at a point 1.4 miles from the highway and walk south down the hill about 150 yards to an old, overgrown pipeline route. Then walk west for about a quarter of a mile to the swamp. This is not a marked trail, but just follow the base of the hill west and you can't get lost.

Red-cockaded woodpeckers are most easily spotted very early in the morning and very late in the day. They will be noisily exiting and entering their nest cavities, making them easier to spot. Trees with cavities are usually identified with a blue-green band (in the process of being changed to white) entirely around the trunk. Look at such trees for streaks of fresh sap—shiny, moist, runny, and honey-colored—which indicates the cavity is currently being used. Most red-cockaded woodpecker sites have cavity trees near the road, so there is no need to walk into the area. Keep quiet and move slowly to avoid spooking the birds.

Most of the red-cockaded woodpecker habitat viewable from roads is on the western part of the WMA. From the intersection of Texas 94 and FM 357 in Apple Springs, go south on FM 357 for 2.5 miles to Forest Road 509. Follow Forest Road 509 east. At 1.3 miles, the pines on the left, some with blue (changing to white) bands painted around them, are red-cockaded woodpecker habitat. At 2.0 miles, take Forest Road 541 to the right. Additional red-cockaded woodpecker colonies occur along Forest Road 541 at miles 0.2, 2.2, 2.6, and 3.0. At the intersection with FM 357/2262 at 3.5 miles, turn left and go about 1.5 miles to Forest Road 531. Turn left; red-cockaded woodpecker sites are at miles 0.3, 1.0, 1.8, and 4.0.

HIKING

Alabama Creek WMA is mostly level, and most of the roads are gravel or natural sand surface and well shaded, making this a good place to walk. There are no designated hiking trails within the WMA.

PRO'S POINTERS. For a loop walk of about 3.5 miles, park at the campground on FM 2262 across from its intersection with Forest Road 532. Walk west on 532 for 1.2 miles to the intersection with Forest Road 509; turn left and follow 509 for 1.2 miles back to FM 2262, then walk north along the highway about 1.1 miles to the campground.

For a longer walk that takes you past a number of red-cockaded woodpecker sites, park at the intersection of Forest Roads 531 and 541. Walk south on 541 for 2.6 miles to FM 357/2262, then follow it east (to your left) about 1.5 miles to Forest Road 531. Following 531 for 3.2 miles will bring you back to your beginning point.

Forest Road 510-B provides views of upland, swamp, and riverine habitats on a one-way walk of 2.8 miles. Soon after leaving FM 2262, you pass through a pine plantation, an area that was logged and then replanted. The trees will be thinned periodically to reduce crowding. Beginning about 0.6 mile down this road is one of the better dogwood viewing areas on the WMA. At 1.1 miles is a clearing where there was once a dwelling. The opening has been seeded with plants suitable for wildlife, especially wild turkeys. At 1.7 miles, you can choose to go either to the right or the left. The road to the right leads 0.5 mile to the Neches River. Forest Road 510-B goes to the left and continues another 1.1 miles, passing by a swamp before ending at the river. Primitive campgrounds are located at the ends of both roads.

BICYCLING

There are no designated bike trails. However, bike riding is allowed on any of the roads on the area, including those closed to motor vehicles.

PRO'S POINTERS. The routes recommended in the hiking section, above, also make good bike rides. A longer ride that passes through all the habitat types on the area begins at the intersection of FM 357 and Forest Road 509. Follow 509 east. At 3.2 miles is a touching memorial to Dustin Brown, who struck the scarred tree in his automobile and was killed. At 5.3 miles, 509 intersects FM 2262. Forest Road 510-B continues to the Neches River across the highway; see a description of the route in the hiking section, above.

HUNTING

All hunting on Alabama Creek WMA is by Annual Public Hunting Permit or Limited Public Use Permit. See the *Public Hunting Lands Map Booklet* and the *Outdoor Annual* for the current year for legal species, seasons, and bag limits. White-tailed deer, feral hogs, waterfowl, and squirrels are the main species present in huntable numbers. Wild turkey numbers have declined in recent years. In keeping with U.S. Forest Service policy, hunting is permitted for many other game animals, but the species discussed below are present in sufficient numbers to provide a quality hunt.

All persons 17 years of age and older who possess a centerfire or muzzleloading rifle, a handgun, a shotgun with shot larger than #2 steel or #4 lead or archery equipment with broadheads must possess an Annual Public Hunting Permit. Persons 17 and older with guns using rimfire ammunition, shotguns with smaller size shot than listed above and archery equipment with field points must possess either the Annual Public Hunting Permit or a Limited Public Use Permit.

PRO'S POINTERS. "Deer occur all over the area, but generally speaking, there are more deer east of FM 2262," says area manager Micah Poteet. "Deer tend to feed heavily on acorns, and proportionally there are more hardwoods on the east side of the WMA. I suggest that people scout along the drainages looking for rubs, scrapes, and hard mast producers. Deer will travel the drainages, especially if there is a good acorn crop. Deer prefer the sweeter acorns from white oak or post oak trees. Land along the Neches River especially seems to produce more acorns. In addition, cattle are not grazed on the east side and should not be present on the area at all during deer-hunting season."

Poteet also advises deer hunters to look for areas where pines have been killed by Southern pine beetles. In such areas, all the pines will have been cut out to stop the spread of the beetles. "The undergrowth in these areas will be very thick, making them favored bedding spots for deer, especially older bucks," he explains. "Look for one- to three-acre spots with all the pine trees cut out. At one end of the clearing will probably be a few old, dead pine trees.

"For both archery and gun hunters, I suggest placing a treestand over a trail," says Poteet. Lean-on or climbing stands work best, since fasteners or screw-in steps may not be used.

The rut in this area begins in late October and peaks in mid- to late November, but there will be less competition for hunting spots later in the season. As on most national forest lands, orange-clad hunters mob the woods the first two or three weekends of the gun season.

Feral hogs occur on the area in moderate numbers. "Hogs move on and off the area and up and down the river," says Poteet. "During winters when we have mast production, we will likely have more hogs, because there are lots of pastures around the area that do not produce acorns."

Hogs will more likely be found on the east side near the river, where acorns are more plentiful. The moist, soft ground around the edges of the swamps will also attract some hogs. Baiting is not allowed for either deer or hogs.

"Stand hunting is the method most used," says Poteet. "Most hog hunting is incidental to deer hunting. If you find a lot of fresh rooting, set a stand over that area. The area is too thick and too big for drives." Firearms may be used during the archery deer season to hunt hogs only.

Spring turkey hunting for gobblers with shotgun, archery and crossbow only is permitted; baiting is not. "Turkey habitat and numbers have declined on Alabama Creek in recent years due to forest management practices, especially the lack of prescribed burning. There are turkeys there, but it's not great turkey hunting," says Poteet.

"Look for recently burned areas that are fairly open," Poteet advises. "If an area has really thick cover, they won't be in there. The area within a loop formed by Forest Roads 532 and 509 and FM 2262 seems to be naturally more open and may be more attractive to turkeys. We're hoping burning will be used more in the future, and the turkeys will return." Harvested turkeys must be taken to a check station within 24 hours. Check stations are located in Centerville, Groveton and Trinity and on the

South Boggy Slough Hunting Club off Texas 94 between Apple Springs and Lufkin.

Holly Bluff Swamp is the main place to hunt waterfowl, but ducks also use the flooded area along Forest Road 510-B. Wood ducks, gadwalls and mallards are the main ducks. Teal may be present during the early teal season if open areas are flooded. "Holly Bluff Swamp is very heavily hunted," says Poteet. "Most hunting is done by wading out into the area and hunting over decoys. Snags and natural vegetation provide cover. The swamp will be full of hunters by 5 A.M. Get there early—no later than 4 A.M."

Holly Bluff Swamp lies 1.4 miles east of FM 2262 off Forest Road 510-A. Park along the road and walk down the hill about 150 yards to an old, overgrown pipeline route. Then walk west for about a quarter of a mile to the swamp. The swamp is full of submerged logs that tear up waders; walk carefully and carry a good flashlight. Teal may be hunted all day, but shooting hours end at noon during the regular duck season.

Woodcock are present in respectable numbers on the area, but

flushing them out of the head-high blackberry vines in pine beetle clearings will be a challenge. "Woodcock are best hunted with a pointing dog," says Poteet. "When they flush, they fly erratically and duck behind trees; you have to be quick."

Gray squirrels are numerous in the Neches bottom and in creek drainages; fox squirrels prefer the mixed pine and hardwood uplands. "Look for acorns when hunting either," advises Poteet. "Squirrel populations fluctuate with the mast crop; numbers increase the year after a good acorn year."

Rabbits, hares, and furbearers and predators—mostly raccoons—may be hunted with dogs, although not many people do. Rabbits occur mostly in the upland areas. Hunters are allowed to take one furbearer per day incidental to other hunting.

FISHING

Fishing is limited mostly to the Neches River, but its narrow, twisting channel suffers from low flows and is prone to being blocked by fallen trees. Bass and catfish are stocked in some small ponds on the area, but these receive heavy fishing pressure.

PRO'S POINTERS. Bank fishing opportunities are limited; most fishers set trotlines for flathead (yellow) catfish. One popular area is the primitive camping area off Forest Road 510-B. To reach it, go south 6.4 miles on FM 2262 to Forest Road 510-B. It's just past Boys Camp Road; the sign is obscured by vegetation. At 1.7 miles down Forest Road 510-B, take the unsigned road to the right and follow it 0.5 mile to the river.

Channel catfish are stocked periodically in a small pond on the north side of Forest Road 510-B about 0.6 mile east of FM 2262, making this a good place to take a youngster fishing.

Moist conditions around the Holly Bluff Swamp produce an abundance of flowers that attract butterflies.

INSIDER'S CORNER

PAINTING THE WOODS RED

First-time visitors to national forests in Texas often expect to see vast unbroken stretches of public land. A worker at Davy Crockett National Forest tells of one woman who came into the district ranger office asking how she could obtain a permit to build a house in the national forest. When told this was not allowed, she replied that she had passed many private dwellings along the highway. Then she pointed to her official Texas highway map, which shows the national forest as a huge solid block of land.

This woman, like many others, failed to realize that national forests and grasslands in Texas are composed of many separate tracts of land that are not all contiguous. The area shown on highway maps as Davy Crockett National Forest conforms to the maximum bound-aries Congress established for the forest. Congress authorized the purchase of any lands within those boundaries from willing sellers, but many landowners chose not to sell. Therefore, the boundaries of the national forest as it actually exists is quite different from what is shown on highway maps.

Traveling through a national forest, one might well think that someone had run wild through the forest with cans of spray paint. However, these paint markings are a convenient way for foresters to locate the boundaries of different tracts of land. Boundaries of national forests are marked with red rings painted around trees. Yellow signs are also used to mark WMA boundaries. At property corners, there are usually three witness trees which are used to help locate the actual corner, which may be an iron pin, a rock, or some kind of monument. These witness trees are often marked with red paint as well.

A variety of colors are used for other purposes. Blue-green or white blazes in national forests in East Texas identify red-cockaded woodpecker sites. Timber compa-nies use paint to mark the bound-aries of blocks of timber they own. Each company uses a specific color to mark its boundary.

Irregular boundaries and scattered tracts of land mean recreational users must pay close attention to their whereabouts to prevent trespassing on private land. If you see red, check for yellow national forest boundary signs. These signs face outward. If you can read the sign, you are on private property.

There's one other color to watch for—purple. By Texas law, landown-ers may use purple paint instead of posted or no trespassing signs. Do not enter an area if fence posts or trees are painted purple.

ALAZAN BAYOU WMA

1,973 acres
1805 E. Lufkin
Lufkin, TX 75901
936/639-1879

DRIVING TIMES FROM:
Amarillo: 10.5 hours
Austin: 5 hours
Brownsville: 9.5 hours
Dallas: 4 hours
El Paso: 15 hours
Houston: 3 hours
San Antonio: 6 hours
DIRECTIONS: From the intersection of Loop 287 and U.S. 59 on the northeast side of Lufkin, take U.S. 59 north 8.8 miles to FM 2782 (formerly County Road 628). Follow FM 2782 west 2.1 miles to the main entrance; 2.4 miles to the campground and observation platform entrance.
OPEN: Daily.
ACTIVITIES: Camping, wildlife viewing, hunting, fishing.
FACILITIES: Primitive campground, wildlife-viewing platform.
SPECIAL REGULATIONS: All users must register on-site. Waterfowl shooting hours end at noon. Trapping is allowed November 1 through March 31. Use of horses is allowed only during designated periods. Camping is restricted to designated campsites. Designated firearms may be used for hunting feral hogs. Buckshot is not allowed. Carry your own supply of potable water.
ADVISORIES: Water moccasins, alligators, and deer flies are present.
LODGING IN AREA: Motels are available in Lufkin and Nacogdoches.
LOCAL POINTS OF INTEREST: Martin Dies, Jr. State Park, Jim Hogg State Historical Park, Texas State Railroad, Sabine National Forest, Angelina National Forest, Davy Crockett National Forest.
DISABILITY ACCESS: The wildlife observation platform is wheelchair-accessible.

Extensive plantings of corn and milo on the Alazan Bayou WMA benefit deer, doves, and wild turkeys.

HISTORY

In prehistoric times the Hasinai Indians, a Caddo tribe, occupied the lands along the Angelina River. Some of the early Spanish settlements in East Texas were in the Nacogdoches vicinity a few miles northeast. Nacogdoches became one of the seminal sites in the agitation for independence first from Spain and then from Mexico.

The county remained primarily agricultural and isolated until the arrival of railroads in 1882. Better transportation spurred the development of the timber industry and a growth in population.

The area that is now Alazan Bayou WMA was privately owned and used for farming and timber production until its purchase by Texas Parks and Wildlife in 1991. Evidence of a dairy and farm operation remains.

GEOGRAPHY AND NATURAL FEATURES

Loco Bayou and Moral Creek run through the area, which is bordered on the south by the Angelina River.

Rolling uplands on the north fall away into bottomlands along the river and associated drainages. The 1,300 acres of bottomland hardwoods contain pockets of swamp, and this entire portion is subject to seasonal flooding. About 300 acres of former bottomland hardwoods cleared for farming are being reforested. Some 100 acres of cleared, leveed bottomland are flooded each winter. Another 15-20 acres of upland fallow fields support extensive food crop plantings. These plots border the Stephen F. Austin State University Experimental Forest to the west and are intended as a food source for wild turkeys stocked there.

Bottomland hardwood trees include overcup oak, nuttal oak, sweet gum, water oak, and willow oak. Wildlife species present include gray and fox squirrels, white-tailed deer, mourning doves, feral hogs, rabbits, and waterfowl.

RECREATIONAL OPPORTUNITIES

CAMPING

Six primitive campsites with picnic tables, tent pads, barbecue grills, fire rings, and lantern posts are available for use. A drive-through loop allows parking at the sites, some of which have shade from small trees.

PRO'S POINTERS. The campground is on the west side of the area. From U.S. 59, go west on FM 2782 for 2.4 miles to the information station, where on-site registration is required. Follow the entrance road about 200 yards to the campground.

WILDLIFE VIEWING

Richard Pike, TPW biologist and liaison between Texas Parks and Wildlife and the U.S. Forest Service, says Alazan Bayou WMA is probably the least appreciated of the good birding spots in East Texas. "It has some western birds on it as well as the eastern species," he says. The area contains bottomlands, marshes, and open fields and attracts a variety of birds. A wildlife-viewing platform at the end of the western entry road overlooks a marsh.

PRO'S POINTERS. One good birding area is a small marshy area along the west boundary of the WMA. A variety of birds roost there in summer—wood storks, white ibises, great blue herons, little blue herons, green-backed herons, great egrets, snowy egrets, cattle egrets, yellow-crowned night herons, anhingas, wood ducks, and cormorants. River otters may also be present. Watch out for large hogs, alligators, and water moccasins. To reach the area, walk southwest from the observation platform about a quarter of a mile. There is no trail, but maps at the information stations show the location of the marsh.

The wildlife-viewing platform offers the opportunity to see the same kinds of birds as above in summer. White-tailed kites may also be present. In winter, red-tailed and red-shouldered hawks, northern harriers, and goldeneyes can be seen. American bitterns use the marsh in spring and summer. For a closer look, walk the levees around the marsh below the platform. The best waterfowl viewing is from late winter until March. Wood ducks and mallards will be in the bottoms. The marsh will attract blue-winged teal, widgeons, gadwalls, scaup, ringnecks, and a few coots. Sandpipers and snipe feed in the muddy flats.

To reach the wildlife-viewing platform, park at the campground parking area and follow the trail 0.4 mile to the structure.

On the hilltop area in spring and summer you may see dickcissels, scissor-tailed flycatchers, blue grosbeaks, indigo and painted buntings, and Bell's vireos. "Sparrows and buntings will be in the grassy, weedy areas," says Pike. "In the trees around the viewing platform, look for Baltimore and orchard orioles. In wintertime sedge wrens, LaConte's sparrows, white-crowned sparrows, white-throated sparrows, and Lincoln's sparrows will be common."

In the hardwood bottom, spring species include red-eyed vireos, yellow-throated vireos, prothonotary warblers, northern parulas, Louisiana water-thrushes, Kentucky warblers, hooded warblers, and summer tanagers. To access the bottom, enter the area at the road that leaves FM 2782 and goes south 2.1 miles west of U.S. 59. A parking area lies a mile down that road; from that point walk along the road into the bottomland. Sloughs in the bottom may hold wood storks during summer.

HUNTING

Hunting is permitted for a wide variety of species, but white-tailed deer, feral hogs, waterfowl, and squirrels provide the best opportunities for success. Youth hunts for waterfowl and squirrels are offered. Hunting will probably continue to be by Annual Public Hunting Permit. Worthy of note is that there is no closed season or bag limit on feral hogs, and legal weapons for hogs include archery, muzzleloaders, shotguns (slugs only) and .22 caliber firearms. For information on methods, species, seasons, and bag limits, see the *Public Hunting Lands Map Booklet* and the *Outdoor Annual* for the current year.

PRO'S POINTERS. Deer hunting is by archery only. "The bottoms are the best places to hunt when you have a good mast crop and they are dry," says area manager Ski Clark. "Use a treestand in the bottoms. Deer prefer the acorns from white oaks; key on those. Once the mast is gone, or before the acorns drop, most of the forage will be in the fields. A small lightweight tripod works well in the fields. Later in the season, try setting up near a food plot. We plant a deer and turkey mix as well as wheat and white clover. The edges of the woods bordering the fields are also good, as are the creek crossings and gaps in the fence on the west side. Scout and you will find lots of trails."

Stands may be left in place 72 hours. The rut for white-tailed deer generally begins in late October and peaks in the first two weeks of November.

Feral hogs can be hunted 365 days a year with .22-caliber firearms, muzzleloaders, shotguns with slugs, and archery equipment. "Hogs will be anywhere within the fences," says Clark. "If there is a good acorn crop, they will be in the bottoms. If there is no acorn crop, they will be in the open fields and along Moral Creek (which has been erroneously labeled Alazan Bayou in previous map booklets). Many times you will find hogs right up next to the road. The area around Loco Bayou, which runs through the western part of the area, is also good for hogs. When the bottom is flooded, look for hogs and deer on two islands that remain dry." The islands are shown on the area map posted at the information stations; both are in the bottomland hardwood section adjacent to the Angelina River.

Clark advises, "Baiting is generally allowed for hogs from the end of the north zone duck season until July 31, but check the *Public Hunting Lands Map Booklet* yearly."

Hunting hogs with dogs is not allowed. "The best methods are stand hunting and drives through the switchcane thickets and brushy places out in the fields where hogs bed during the day," Clark says.

Mallards and wood ducks furnish the chief waterfowl hunting opportunities in years when there is an acorn crop and sufficient water to flood the bottomlands. Call ahead and see what the conditions are. Water levels are usually not high enough to attract teal during the early teal season, but there will be some present in the late season. The marsh is too small to make Alazan Bayou a good duck-hunting area, but there will be enough widgeons, gadwalls, green-winged teal, ringnecks, scaup, gold-eneyes, and pintails to furnish shooting for a limited number of hunters.

"Use decoys and calls in the marsh area," Clark says. "The key to successful hunting in the bottoms is to find the ducks by scouting. You can also jumpshoot wood ducks and mallards in the bottoms. Duck shooting hours end at noon, but you can scout in the afternoon." Plenty of natural cover is available, but building temporary blinds using dead vegetation is permitted.

The 100-acre marsh below the wildlife-viewing platform is an easy walk from the parking lot, but as a result, it gets hunted hard. Walking in a half-mile to the marsh on the west side will get you away from most other hunters. Access to another marsh area is via the road through the center of the area. Park at the parking area a mile in and walk down the road another mile to a swampy area be-

tween the road and Moral Creek. Hunters may also access the area by boat by putting in at public boat ramps on either U.S. 59 or Texas 7 and running the Angelina River, but they must sign in at one of the information stations on the area first.

Until an ongoing hardwood reforestation project is completed, many of the open fields on the area will be planted with food crops such as sorghum, corn, sunflowers, dove proso, browntop millet, buckwheat, iron and clay cowpeas, and sunflowers. These areas attract some doves, but not many.

Squirrels are numerous, mostly grays. Fox squirrels will be mostly on the west side next to the Stephen F. Austin State University experimental forest. The pine ridge on the east side near the power transmission line is good for fox squirrels, which prefer more open areas. Gray squirrels favor the bottomland hardwoods and seek out acorns. Most squirrel hunters sit quietly and listen for squirrels barking, then sneak up on them. Good squirrel crops lag a year behind good acorn crops; call ahead for conditions.

Rabbits are numerous on the area, but thick cover makes it hard to hunt them. The use of dogs is permitted and would probably be the best method. Trapping is allowed for furbearers and predators, and predators can be hunted with dogs year-round; night hunting is not permitted during deer season.

FISHING

Fishing is allowed, but few people fish on the area. Most fishing is by people who boat up from the river into Loco Bayou to trotline for catfish. Moral Creek has some bream and catfish, and the Angelina River, which is not within the WMA, has catfish, sand bass, and crappie. However, there are no notable fishing holes on the area.

A wildlife viewing platform lies less than half a mile from the campground parking area and overlooks a marsh area.

INSIDER'S CORNER

THE WOOD STORK

Alazan Bayou WMA offers the opportunity to see the rare wood stork, listed as an endangered species by the U.S. Fish and Wildlife Service. A number of the birds spend at least part of the summer on the area, feeding in sloughs and marshes.

Wood storks are large wading birds, reaching perhaps four feet in height with a wingspan of about five feet. They are white with black primary and secondary wing feathers and tail. The slightly curved beak is also black.

Wood storks feed in shallow water such as that found in the bottomlands of Alazan Bayou—freshwater marshes, narrow creeks, and pools. Depressions in swamps where fish become concentrated during falling water levels are a favorite hunting ground. Storks search for small fish using grope-feeding, also known as tacto-location. The stork probes the water with its bill partly open, and when a fish touches the bill, the stork snaps it shut in the amazingly short time of 25 milliseconds.

As of 1999, there were approximately 11,000 adult wood storks in the United States. Their declining numbers are believed to be due to the loss of feeding habitat due to human alteration of wetlands. Ideally, wood stork habitat will have alternating periods of flooding, which brings fish into an area, and drought, during which fish become concentrated in a small area. Due to their feeding technique, wood storks require a higher concentration of prey than do other wading birds. A breeding pair of wood storks is estimated to consume about 440 pounds of fish during the nesting season.

Wood storks seem to respond well to water management in artificial impoundments if flooding and deflooding take place at appropriate times. Drawing down water levels during the nesting season provides a rich food supply at a critical time and helps assure nesting success.

Wood storks frequent dead trees in bottomland sloughs during the summer.

16,360 acres
1342 S. Wheeler
Jasper, TX 75951
409/384-6894

DRIVING TIMES FROM:
Amarillo: 10.5 hours
Austin: 5 hours
Brownsville: 9.5 hours
Dallas: 4 hours
El Paso: 15 hours
Houston: 2 hours
San Antonio: 5.5 hours
DIRECTIONS: From Jasper, take U.S. 190 west for 11 miles. Information on the WMA is available at District 6 Wildlife Division office or Martin Dies, Jr., State Park headquarters.
OPEN: Daily.
ACTIVITIES: Camping, wildlife viewing, hiking, bicycling, hunting, fishing.
FACILITIES: Primitive campgrounds, interpretive nature trail.
SPECIAL REGULATIONS: Hunters are required to possess an Annual Public Hunting Permit. Airboats are prohibited. No buckshot is allowed. Waterfowl shooting hours end at noon. Trapping is allowed November 1 through March 31. The use of horses is prohibited. Camping is allowed only by free permit issued by the U.S. Army Corps of Engineers; call 409/429-3491.
ADVISORIES: Mosquitoes can be abundant at any time of year. A boat is required for access to the bulk of the area. Carry your own supply of potable water.
LODGING IN AREA: Motels are available in Jasper.
LOCAL POINTS OF INTEREST: Martin Dies, Jr. State Park, Sabine National Forest, Angelina National Forest, Big Thicket National Preserve.
DISABILITY ACCESS: Portions of the nature trail are wheelchair-accessible.

The lakes and rivers of Angelina-Neches WMA attract a variety of birds, including the great egret.

HISTORY

Caddo and Atakapan Indians occupied these lands before settlement. Bevilport, just north on the Angelina River, was one of the first Anglo settlements in the area. It was an important riverboat port for Texas colonists, shipping cotton and cattle hides to New Orleans.

The area was heavily logged from the early 1900s to the 1940s. However, most of the activity was high-grading, which took only the prime timber and left many trees uncut. As a result, there is much mature timber still standing. This distinguishes this area from Moore Plantation and Bannister WMAs nearby, which were clearcut and contain mostly even-aged trees.

The U.S. Army Corps of Engineers developed plans for three dam sites in the 1940s. Site "B" was chosen for construction; hence the commonly used name, Dam B. Lake B. A. Steinhagen was flooded in 1954. Built primarily for water retention, it is now also used to provide flood control and freshwater flow to prevent saltwater intrusion into the lower Neches River system. Texas Parks and Wildlife began managing the wildlife on the lake and surrounding lands in the mid-1950s under license from the Corps of Engineers.

GEOGRAPHY AND NATURAL FEATURES

The principal features of the Angelina-Neches/Dam B WMA are the confluence of the Neches and Angelina Rivers in the center of the area—known as "The Forks"—and the shallow, muddy lake that covers about 7,000 acres. Some 6,000 acres of land adjoin the lake and rivers and are connected to the main bodies of water by a maze of sloughs and oxbow lakes. This is an easy place to get lost, even for those familiar with the area.

The land itself is generally low and flat. Flooding is common during the winter and spring. Bottomlands and river floodplains are dominated by water oak, cypress, and sweet gum. Terraces above the floodplain support loblolly and shortleaf pine, red oak, and sweet gum. A difference in elevation of only six inches or so often marks a change in the type of trees.

Due to selective cutting during the logging period, this WMA preserves a mature hardwood bottomland ecosystem. Away from the rivers, huge trees canopy a very open understory.

White-tailed deer, feral hogs,

squirrels, and a variety of waterfowl are the principal game species. Surprisingly, squirrel hunting is probably more popular here than deer hunting, particularly among local people. Many families have traditional "squirrel camps" dating to before construction of the reservoir.

Recreational Opportunities

In keeping with Corps of Engineers policy, a wide range of recreational activities is allowed on the WMA. Only hunters are required to possess an Annual Public Hunting Permit. Nonconsumptive users are not required to have a Limited Public Use Permit.

Camping

The Angelina-Neches/Dam B WMA offers the rare opportunity for a Huckleberry Finn–type wilderness experience—living on the river and off the land and water. The Corps of Engineers maintains six primitive campsites on the Angelina River between its confluence with the Neches and the community of Bevilport about 8 river miles upstream. These sites are accessible only by boat and offer no facilities. However, the scenery and isolation are unmatched, especially if you choose one of the three sites upstream of Bee Tree Slough, which is heavily used by fishers and hunters to access the interior of the WMA.

PRO'S POINTERS. These free campsites are available by reservation only by calling the Corps of Engineers at 409/429-3491. Call ahead—all sites may be reserved by hunters during squirrel and deer seasons. These campsites are ideal for people who want to hunt and fish from a primitive camp.

Wildlife Viewing

A wide range of aquatic and avian species can be seen with relative ease at this WMA—alligators, ospreys, bald eagles, swallow-tailed kites,

coots, gallinules, herons, ducks, prothonotary warblers, deer, alligator snapping turtles, beavers, and nutria. Guided nature tours are given on the area by Texas Parks and Wildlife personnel; inquire at Martin Dies, Jr., State Park, which adjoins the WMA. Call 409/384-5231.

PRO'S POINTERS. Wildlife viewing on the Angelina-Neches WMA can be as easy as walking across a bridge from the camping area at Martin Dies, Jr., State Park or as complicated as a canoe trip on the Angelina River. The Island Hiking Trail from the park campground is a three-quarters of a mile hike. A bridge then joins onto the WMA trails, which offer two loop trails, one of three-quarters of a mile and the other about 2.5 miles long. The longer trail goes through all of the ecosystem types on the area—buttonbush flat, cypress-tupelo swamp, palmetto flat, hardwood bottom, mixed pine-hardwood intermediate site, and pine upland. Benches on the bridge at the beginning of the trail have labeled pictures of birds and animals likely to be seen.

The short trail goes through an area where pine beetles killed the trees and offers the chance to view a natural regeneration area. This trail does not go through pine ridge or palmetto flat habitats.

Look for prothonotary warblers in cavities in dead trees along the hiking trail during their nesting season from March through June.

For an up-close look at many birds and animals, take one of the "Canoeing the Forks" trips available through Martin Dies, Jr., State Park. Participants meet at the boat ramp at the park, then bus to Bevilport, where they board canoes for the half-day trip down the Angelina River. Side trips go into Bee Tree Slough, Moon Lake and Cow Slough, with interpretive talks along the way. Wildlife can be approached much closer than in motorized boats. Bring good binoculars and wear quick-drying clothing and footwear suitable for use in and

around water. There is a fee for this tour, and reservations are required; call 409/384-5231.

One of the highlights of the tour is Bee Tree Slough. This sluggish stream is the key to accessing the interior of the WMA between the two rivers. Its entrance is a little over a mile upstream from the confluence of the Neches and Angelina, on the west bank of the Angelina in the middle of the second large westward bend in the river upstream of the Neches. Unmarked, it is easily overlooked by those unfamiliar with the area. A short distance inside the slough is its namesake, a large cypress snag that once held bees.

One of the attractions of Bee Tree Slough is a heron rookery where a thousand or more tricolored, little blue and night herons, and snowy and cattle egrets nest in live cypress trees.

Guided tours are available of a huge rookery area along U.S. 190 just south of the WMA during May and June. Contact Martin Dies, Jr., State Park for information.

For self-guided wildlife-viewing trips along the rivers, avoid the open water. Viewing is better along the Angelina because of the number of sloughs, the amount of standing timber, and the numerous dead snags used by nesting birds.

Hiking

The WMA Hiking Trail has two loops, one of 2.5 miles and another of 0.75 mile. See a description of this trail under Wildlife Viewing, above. The trail begins with a big bridge over a slough separating the state park from the WMA; large alligators frequent this area. An information kiosk at the trailhead has interpretive displays on the area's natural history. Brochures available at the kiosk are keyed to numbered posts along the route; approximately 100 points of interest and plants are explained. On the big bridge, benches have labeled pictures of animals likely to be spotted.

PRO'S POINTERS. "This trail is the entire management area compressed into a 2-mile walk," says area manager Gary Calkins. "It took us several months to lay out the trail to go by all the different trees and bushes." The longer trail passes through all six habitat types found on the WMA; the shorter one omits pine ridge and palmetto flats habitats.

BICYCLING

Bicycling is allowed on the WMA Hiking Trail. See the Wildlife Viewing and Hiking sections, above, for a description.

PRO'S POINTERS. Pleasure bikes are sufficient for this easy trail. Mountain bikes are allowed, but they are not needed and are discouraged because of possible damage to the trail.

HUNTING

The Angelina-Neches/Dam B WMA is managed for maximum hunter opportunity. Not all species allowed to be taken are present in sufficient numbers to provide a quality hunt. Those species discussed below are the ones most likely to be present in huntable numbers. For information on legal species, seasons, and bag limits, see the *Public Hunting Lands Map Booklet* and the *Outdoor Annual* for the current year.

Hunters are required to possess an Annual Public Hunting Permit. Youth-only hunts are offered for deer and waterfowl, and there is a youth-adult squirrel hunt. Centerfire rifles are allowed during the general deer season for both deer and hogs, and there is an extended hog season. Alligator hunting is by special permit only; there is an early deadline for applications for this hunt. See the *Applications for Drawings on Public Hunting Lands* booklet for the current year.

PRO'S POINTERS. Only the June Day compartment is accessible by road. "There are no trophy deer there, but it offers the opportunity for an enjoyable hunt," says Calkins.

Moss-draped cypress trees glow when backlit by the sun. The Angelina-Neches/Dam B WMA offers a wealth of such photo opportunities.

"Once you get back off the road, there is open understory with lots of sloughs and ridges." To reach this compartment, take Texas 92 north from U.S. 190. State maintenance ends at mile 2.7 and the road becomes County Road 3725. Continue another 3 miles and turn right onto County Road 3775. After 1.5 miles, take the left fork. In another 0.3 mile, go left again. Continue another 0.7 mile to an information station.

"The West compartment has lower deer density but some nice bucks," Calkins adds. "It is surrounded by hunting clubs that have lowered the deer numbers." This compartment is accessible only by boat. It is about 6 miles west by northwest of the boat ramp in the state park, at the far end of the lake.

The Spring Creek compartment has by far the highest deer density. Hunters can now access the compartment from Martin Dies, Jr., State Park by using the hiking trail. However, hunting is not allowed along the trail, and it's a long walk into the heart of the compartment. Hunters may also camp at one of the primitive campsites on the Angelina River and walk into the compartment.

The Forks compartment has lots of deer and some really good-quality bucks. "Access is good because you can motor around there in a boat, but trying to find the right island to hunt on can be tough," says Calkins. "I advise people to boat in and still hunt on an island, or put up a temporary stand over mast-producing trees."

Feral hog numbers are extremely high on the north end of the Forks compartment and on the Spring Creek compartment, spotty in the West and June Day compartments. As on most WMAs, hunters are encour-

aged to kill all the hogs they can. Key on mast-producing trees in hardwood bottoms.

Teal hunting is excellent in both the east and west logjam areas. These are places where the cypress trees have never been harvested, resulting in lots of "fingering" along the lake edges. The east logjam is along the shore of the Spring Creek compartment beginning about a mile north of the Walnut Ridge unit of Martin Dies, Jr., State Park. The west logjam is in the West compartment on the east shore of the lake about 4 miles northwest of the park.

"We have mallards, wood ducks, pintails, redheads, widgeons, and a few scaup," says Calkins. "It depends on the winter, but normally duck-hunting opportunities are almost unlimited because the area has so many coves and potholes. Ducks have lots of places to move if there is pressure." Permanent blinds are not allowed. Access is by boat only except for one slough off County Road 3725 on the June Day compartment. "Anywhere open water is broken up by buttonbush or lotus, you will have ducks," says Calkins. One such area is called "cut-through creek" because a slough slices through the tip of a peninsula. This area is the peninsula northwest of

Martin Dies, Jr., State Park shaped like a Y with its open end pointing southeast. It's unmistakable on the map. Because of its convenient access to the park, this area attracts many hunters.

Squirrel hunting is outstanding, because mature hardwood bottoms produce a great deal of mast. The best areas for squirrels—mostly grays—are the West, June Day, and Forks compartments. "Squirrel hunting is so good that people had traditional squirrel-hunting camps along the Angelina River. It was an old tradition to camp out and hunt squirrels," says Calkins.

Both still hunting and hunting with dogs are effective. "There are so many squirrels here that you can still hunt them successfully," says Calkins. "Find a hardwood bottom or mixed hardwood-pine site and ease through it, watching for movement." County regulations on limits and season apply. The youth-adult squirrel hunt the weekend before archery season begins is open to all, and .22-caliber firearms are allowed.

The few rabbits and hares on the area are concentrated in the Spring Creek compartment. For best success, use dogs and hunt around blow-down openings.

Furbearers and predators may be hunted with dogs or mouth-blown calls. Raccoons abound. "Hunt them with dogs at night or shine for them outside of gun deer season, but call the game warden first," Calkins advises. Trapping furbearers is allowed. There are a few coyotes and bobcats in the Spring Creek compartment and a few bobcats on the northern end of the Forks.

FISHING

No Annual Public Hunting Permit is needed for fishing. Bass, crappie and catfish are the main species.

PRO'S POINTERS. Fish for crappie around downed timber or cypress

Fishers find that dabbling with jigs around cypress trees is often the ticket to a delicious crappie fish fry.

trees. Use jigs on a seven-foot rod with four to five feet of line and "dabble" around logs or stumps. Bass tend to be in the backwater sloughs in black water; Bee Tree Slough is popular, as are the ends of the east and west logjams. "Bass fishing in the main body of the lake is not good because of the turbidity of the water," Calkins says. Catfish will be in the open lake or in deep holes in the river channels. Local fishers tend to concentrate on gaspergoos and flathead catfish, but blue and channel cats are present as well.

"Frog gigging is big on this lake," says Calkins. "You can get some big frogs, mainly in the logjams. Frogs are also found in the water around lily pads and floating vegetation. Use a headlight and gig them at night."

Alligator hunts are usually the middle two weekends in September. Success rate is about 60 percent. "I'll recommend where people might want to set their hook and line," says Calkins. "We try to target specific alligators that have become a nuisance or areas of numerous or large gators. One year my wife caught an 11-footer that was causing problems with boaters."

INSIDER'S CORNER

THE GRAY SQUIRREL

Gray squirrels occur almost exclusively in East Texas, roughly in the area bounded by a line from Victoria to Seguin to Paris. They are also known as cat squirrels after their nervous nature and perhaps their quickness as they dart from tree to tree. A gray squirrel weighs about a pound, half as much as the other bushy-tailed inhabitant of East Texas woodlands, the fox squirrel.

Gray squirrels are primarily inhabitants of hardwood bottoms and seldom venture into upland areas. They prefer a large area forested with mature hardwoods with crowns closely spaced so they can leap from tree to tree without ever touching the ground. Acorns and pecans are the main items on the menu for gray squirrels, although they will eat buds and flowers, grapes, berries, and insect larvae as well as frogs and lizards.

Destruction of bottomland hardwoods adversely affects gray squirrels by eliminating their food supply. In recent years prices for hardwood timber have increased, leading to more cutting of hardwood trees. A common harvesting practice is high-grading, in which only the older trees are cut. Unfortunately for the squirrel, these mature trees are the best food producers and are more likely to have limb and trunk cavities the squirrels prefer for nesting. One scientist calculated that it takes eight water oaks and 18 red oaks per acre to keep two squirrels supplied with all the acorns they need on an annual basis, allowing for competition for food from other animals such as deer, turkeys, and feral hogs. Not surprisingly, then, a population density of two squirrels per acre is considered plentiful.

Gray squirrels are noisy animals whose presence does much to enliven the woods. They bark almost continuously when undisturbed. Running and jumping from tree to tree, playing chase around tree trunks, and perching on limbs while busily husking nuts or acorns, they do indeed seem "nervous as a cat."

28,307 acres
1342 S. Wheeler
Jasper, TX 75951
409/384-6894

DRIVING TIMES FROM:
Amarillo: 10.5 hours
Austin: 5 hours
Brownsville: 9.5 hours
Dallas: 4 hours
El Paso: 15 hours
Houston: 3 hours
San Antonio: 6 hours
DIRECTIONS: From Lufkin, take
Texas 103 east for 25 miles. Turn
south on FM 1277 and go 3 miles to
Forest Road 300.
OPEN: Daily.
ACTIVITIES: Camping, wildlife
viewing, hiking, bicycling, hunting,
fishing.
FACILITIES: Primitive campgrounds.
SPECIAL REGULATIONS: Only
hunters are required to possess an
Annual Public Hunting Permit.
Turkeys must be taken to a check
station within 24 hours. No buckshot is allowed. Waterfowl shooting
hours end at noon. All legal firearms
and archery equipment may be used
during the general deer season and
for feral hog hunting January 15
through March 15. Trapping is
allowed November 1 through March
31. For other special regulations see
the section entitled "Special Regulations in Effect on U.S. Forest Service
Units" in the current *Public Hunting Lands Map Booklet*.
ADVISORIES: Mosquitoes can be
abundant at any time of year. Carry
your own supply of potable water.
LODGING IN AREA: Motels are
available in Lufkin and Broaddus.
LOCAL POINTS OF INTEREST:
Martin Dies, Jr. State Park, Sabine
National Forest, Angelina National
Forest, Big Thicket National Preserve.
DISABILITY ACCESS: Not
wheelchair-accessible.

*Like other WMAs that are on national forest
land, Bannister WMA is crisscrossed by public
roads that offer good access for wildlife viewing
and nature photography.*

HISTORY

The area now comprising the Bannister WMA was occupied by the
Hasinai Indians prior to Anglo
settlement. A Spanish mission was
established on Ayish Bayou in 1717
to try to guard the frontier with
French-owned Louisiana. Permanent
settlers began moving into the area in
the late 1700s, and the first sawmills
were built soon after.

Isolated and far from the seats of
government, East Texas developed a
tradition of lawlessness that lingered
well into the 20th century. Remnants
of this tradition still pose occasional
problems for wildlife managers in the
area today.

Development came late to San
Augustine County. Small farms dominated until the arrival of railroads after
1900, at which time large-scale logging began. By the 1930s the timber
was exhausted and the timber companies moved out, causing the local
economy to collapse. The U.S. Forest
Service purchased the land and began
reforestation efforts using labor supplied by the Civilian Conservation

Corps. A CCC installation, Camp Bannister, was located on the northwestern portion of the WMA.

The National Forests of Texas and the Texas Parks and Wildlife Department signed a Memorandum of Understanding in 1983 that allowed for joint management of national forest lands. The Bannister WMA was created in 1984. The WMA occupies 28,307 acres of the 153,174 acres in the Angelina National Forest. Some 7,000 acres within the WMA are privately owned and abide by its regulations.

GEOGRAPHY AND NATURAL FEATURES

The Bannister WMA sits on a peninsula projecting into Sam Rayburn Reservoir but is separated from the lake by private or national forest land. The terrain is nearly level to gently rolling and is laced with numerous creeks. The area is almost totally forested with loblolly, shortleaf, slash, and longleaf pine.

The Turkey Hill Wilderness Area, a 5,286-acre block fairly representative of the original long-leaf pine systems of East Texas, makes up the northeast corner of the WMA. The area was logged, but forest regeneration was typical of the original habitat. The Turkey Hill Wilderness Area is closed to all but foot and horse traffic and is not intensively managed for wildlife.

RECREATIONAL OPPORTUNITIES

As part of the national forest system, recreational activities on Bannister WMA are governed by U.S. Forest Service rules. Hunters are required to possess an Annual Public Hunting Permit. Camping is restricted to designated campsites only during the archery and gun deer-hunting seasons; at other times, camping is allowed elsewhere. Hiking and recreational horseback riding are allowed year-round.

In keeping with its status as part of a national forest, Bannister WMA offers a wide range of recreational activities. In fact, the principal administration of the area is as a national forest, with Texas Parks and Wildlife acting in an advisory capacity regarding wildlife management. Since Bannister WMA is an eastern wild turkey restoration site, many roads on the area will be closed to vehicles during the brooding season from January through June. Hiking and bicycling are still permitted on these roads. For more information, call the U.S. Forest Service at 409/639-8620 or the Jasper office of Texas Parks and Wildlife at 409/384-6894.

CAMPING

The Turkey Hill Camping Area along Forest Road 307A has bulldozed pullouts scattered for a mile and a half along the road. There is a choice of open or shaded sites. This campground is located 4.9 miles north of FM 83 via Forest Road 300. Other campgrounds are located 1.3 and 1.9 miles north of FM 83 on Forest Road 300. One campground is accessible via a paved road, Forest Road 374, off Texas 147 about 2 miles north of Broaddus. This campground, and one on Forest Road 300C, are closed from January through June because turkeys nest in the area.

PRO'S POINTERS. The best time to camp is spring and fall. Heat and humidity make the area quite unpleasant during the summer. Fewer insects, especially mosquitoes, are present in spring.

Except for portable toilets provided during the first two weekends of the general deer season, no facilities are present at any of the campgrounds. You are expected to remove all your litter.

The campgrounds along Forest Roads 307A and 374 are best suited for recreational vehicles. While camping is allowed anywhere on the national forest except from October until January, opportunities for

parking along the road are very limited anywhere except at the designated campgrounds. Backpackers may camp anywhere except during hunting season, when all camping is restricted to designated campgrounds. Hunting is allowed in the Turkey Hill Wilderness Area, so the restriction against camping there during hunting season applies.

WILDLIFE VIEWING

The red-cockaded woodpecker, an endangered species, may be seen on the area. These birds prefer large, mature pine trees with high branching on the canopy and an open understory. Visiting areas inhabited by the red-cockaded woodpecker is discouraged in order to prevent disturbing the birds. Look for stands of pines with blue-green paint bands around them; these indicate colonies.

Other species you may see are white-tailed deer, eastern wild turkeys, and feral hogs. Deer and hogs tend to concentrate along the drainages.

Birding is excellent on the area, as the prescribed burning practices encourage use by neotropical migrants. Included among the birds you may expect to see are red-shouldered, sharpshinned, Cooper's, harrier and red-tailed hawks; great horned, barred, and screech owls; American crows; black and turkey vultures; hooded warblers; white-eyed and red-eyed vireos; summer tanagers; indigo and painted buntings; blue jays; cardinals; blue-gray gnatcatchers; tufted titmice; brown-headed nuthatches; Carolina wrens and chickadees and pileated woodpeckers. Bald eagles and ospreys may sometimes be seen moving between Sam Rayburn and Toledo Bend Lakes.

PRO'S POINTERS. To sample all the habitat types on the area, drive Forest Road 300 from FM 1277 on the northwest side of the area to White City in the extreme south. The best birding is north and west of Texas 147 because the forest is more open; huge bottoms and hardwood stands make it easier to see birds. The habitat is better as well, that area having been intensively managed for longleaf pine, red-cockaded woodpeckers, and turkeys.

HIKING

No established hiking trails exist outside the Turkey Hill Wilderness Area, but hiking is allowed anywhere on the WMA. During the months of November, December, and January, wearing blaze orange clothing is required for safety. Walking in the forest south of Forest Road 300 just west of Texas 147 is not recommended due to abandoned wells in the area that may be open.

PRO'S POINTERS. Costs associated with court-ordered management of the red-cockaded woodpecker have resulted in less maintenance on the trails in the Turkey Hill Wilderness Area. These trails are recommended for experienced backpackers only. One access point and parking lot for a trail into the wilderness area is located along Forest Road 307 6 miles from FM 83 (access is via Forest Road 300). Another is on Forest Road 300 about 1.3 miles north of its intersection with Forest Road 307. No water is available along any of the trails.

For most people, the gated roads offer the best walking routes. These are closed to vehicles during the turkey-nesting season. Forest Road 356, which runs east from Forest Road 300 about 2 miles north of FM 83, is probably the prettiest.

BICYCLING

Bicycling is allowed along any of the forest service roads. All are suitable for the casual bike rider. As with walking, some of the nicest rides are on the gated roads while they are closed during the spring turkey nesting season.

PRO'S POINTERS. Trails in the Turkey Hill Wilderness Area are closed to all wheeled vehicles, which includes bicycles. Forest Roads 300

and 300A are joined by a short section of FM 83 to make a good loop for a ride of about 9 miles.

HUNTING

In keeping with U.S. Forest Service policy, hunting regulations are set for maximum hunting opportunity. That is to say, the fact that hunting for a particular species is allowed is not an indication the animal is abundant on the area. Animals present in greatest numbers on the Bannister WMA are white-tailed deer, eastern wild turkeys, feral hogs, various furbearers, and predators. Youth-only hunts may be offered. For information on seasons, bag limits, and dates for youth hunts, consult the *Public Hunting Lands Map Booklet* for the current year.

All persons 17 years of age and older who possess a centerfire or muzzleloading rifle, a handgun, a shotgun with shot larger than #2 steel or #4 lead or archery equipment with broadheads must possess an Annual Public Hunting Permit. Persons 17 and older with guns using rimfire ammunition, shotguns with smaller size shot than listed above, and archery equipment with field points must possess either the Annual Public Hunting Permit or a Limited Public Use Permit.

Both archery and rifle hunting for white-tailed deer are available to holders of an Annual Public Hunting Permit. Archers are permitted to take either-sex animal; rifle hunters may take one buck only unless an antlerless permit (one per person) is obtained from the U.S. Forest Service by calling 409/639-8620 before October 1.

Feral hogs may be hunted during the deer seasons and from January 15 through March 15. All legal firearms and archery equipment, including crossbows, may be used to hunt hogs during the general and extended seasons; during the archery season, only persons with a permanent upper limb disability may use a crossbow.

Other legal game includes teal, ducks, geese, doves, quail, squirrels, rabbits and hares, furbearers, and predators. Furbearers may be trapped from November 1 through March 31; statewide regulations apply.

PRO'S POINTERS. Deer density is low on the Bannister WMA, but that translates into better quality. This WMA also offers challenging hunting for those who desire it. "If you really want to hunt, try the Turkey Hill Wilderness Area," advises area manager Gary Calkins. Calkins, who has guided hunters in Colorado, says the hunting experiences are similar due to the lack of vehicle access into this area roughly 4 miles square. Hunters will either have to walk in and pack their deer out or use horses.

For hunters who prefer easier access, "The area north and west of Texas 147 is really good hunting," Calkins advises. "There are good deer in there, but the key is the area is more open and is easier to hunt. It's a beautiful place to hunt—it makes you feel you are really hunting. The place is a circus on opening weekend, but after that you will have it to yourself."

The area between FM 83 and White City is loaded with deer, but the area is irregular and surrounded by private property, so you have to be careful to watch where you are. National forest boundaries are marked by red rings painted around trees, and WMA boundaries are marked with black and yellow Texas Parks and Wildlife signs. If you can read the sign, you are outside the area.

Density of feral hogs is low. The best place to hunt for a hog is along the creeks running into the Turkey Hill Wilderness Area from FM 705. You can also access this area from Texas 147. As with deer, a major part of the challenge of hunting the wilderness area is retrieving harvested animals without the aid of a vehicle.

Eastern turkeys are scattered. There is good turkey habitat throughout, but density is low to moderate, and you will have to work to find one.

Turkey hunting began on the area in spring of 1998. Gobblers only may be hunted only during the eastern spring turkey season.

"Look for mature stands of mixed hardwoods and pines with an open understory," advises Calkins. "You can locate gobblers by driving the roads and giving crow or owl calls to make them gobble."

When gobblers do not respond to this method, the technique favored by veteran turkey hunter Carl Harris of Elysian Fields is to roost a gobbler at dusk, then return to hunt him the next morning. Harris waits until the bird gobbles, yelps to make him answer, then yelps sparingly or clucks and purrs once the tom flies down from the roost. When this method works, the hunt is usually over within a few minutes after legal shooting time begins.

Waterfowl hunting on the area is very limited. "You may get a few wood ducks on ponds along Forest Road 300 midway between Texas 147 and FM 1277, but in general I'd advise hunting waterfowl somewhere else," says Calkins.

Similarly, hunting for doves, rabbits, and hares is limited. The edges of clear-cut areas may hold a few rabbits, and those with croton will attract doves.

Squirrel hunting is good in the Sandy Creek bottom between Texas 147 and FM 1277. "Look for mast-producing trees," advises Calkins. The best squirrel-hunting area on the WMA is virtually ignored. "I don't know anybody willing to walk into the Turkey Creek Wilderness Area for a squirrel," says Calkins.

FISHING

There are some perch in potholes on Sandy Creek that hold water year-round, but other streams are not reliable.

PRO'S POINTERS. Fish somewhere else. Sam Rayburn and North Toledo Bend reservoirs are close by.

INSIDER'S CORNER

EASTERN WILD TURKEY RESTORATION

Wild turkeys are one of the outstanding success stories of wildlife restoration. Nearly wiped out by market hunters by 1900, wild turkeys have responded well to restocking efforts—but only after a slow and painful learning curve.

Eastern wild turkeys, a separate subspecies from the more common Rio Grande birds found throughout most of Texas, historically ranged where annual rainfall exceeded 35 inches. This placed their range in Texas almost entirely within the Piney Woods.

Restocking efforts began in 1924 using Rio Grande turkeys and, later, pen-raised birds. These efforts continued until 1978 without success. It became obvious that only wild-trapped eastern birds had the "woods smarts" to survive. Since 1979, all restocking in Texas has been with wild-trapped turkeys. Today the gobble of wild turkeys once again rumbles through the woods from the Red River to the Big Thicket. Populations have increased to the point that hunting eastern wild turkeys is now allowed throughout much of their former range.

Eastern wild turkeys will likely never be present in numbers as large as they once were. Loss of habitat is the reason. Easterns have very specific habitat requirements regarding food, water, and cover.

They prefer to roost in mature pines, but they need grassy or brushy cover for nesting and brood-rearing. Mature stands of mixed pines and hardwoods or hardwood bottomlands are prime habitat. Both of these have nearly disappeared from East Texas due to human activities.

Open areas near timber and water are important to turkeys in the spring. Gobblers prefer open spaces to display their beauty to hens during the breeding season, their way of attracting a mate. Fast-growing poults need a high-protein diet, which they obtain by feeding on grasshoppers and other insects abundant on weeds and grasses in openings.

Managing habitat for wild turkeys is perhaps the best way to help increase their numbers. The best habitat is provided by diverse land-use types with at least half in mature timber interspersed with openings. Hardwood trees provide mast, which is vital for turkey food supplies, and rotation for timber harvest of hardwoods should be greater than 70 years, since older trees are the best producers. Pine regeneration areas should contain adjacent areas differing in age by at least five years and should be thinned at five- to ten-year intervals to open the canopy and allow a mixed understory to develop. Prescribed burns produce more food and control understory growth.

7,681 acres
325 Meadowview Rd.
Longview, TX 75604
903/757-9572

DRIVING TIMES FROM:
Amarillo: 9 hours
Austin: 5 hours
Brownsville: 10.5 hours
Dallas: 3 hours
El Paso: 14 hours
Houston: 4 hours
San Antonio: 6.5 hours
DIRECTIONS: From Marshall take Texas 43 north 13 miles to FM 2198. Turn right and go 0.5 mile to the Caddo Lake State Park entrance.
OPEN: Daily.
ACTIVITIES: Camping, wildlife viewing, hunting, fishing.
FACILITIES: None; however, the adjoining state park has complete camping facilities.
SPECIAL REGULATIONS: Any person entering upon the land area of the WMA must possess either an Annual Public Hunting or a Limited Public Use Permit. No Annual Public Hunting Permit is required for fishing from a boat. All persons on the land area of the WMA during daylight hours at time when hunting with firearms is permitted must visibly wear safety orange. Persons in campsites, hunting turkey or migratory birds are exempt from this requirement. Permanent duck blinds

existing before October 16, 1992, are allowed; all other blinds must be temporary.
ADVISORIES: Heat, humidity, and mosquitoes make the area unpleasant during July and August. Carry your own supply of potable water.
LODGING IN AREA: Motels are available in Marshall and Jefferson.
LOCAL POINTS OF INTEREST: Caddo Lake State Park, Starr Family State Historical Park, Martin Creek Lake State Park, Atlanta State Park.
DISABILITY ACCESS: Not wheelchair-accessible.

HISTORY

Whangdoodle Pass, Hog Wallow, Whistleberry Slough, Hell's Half Acre, Willowson Woodyard, Government Ditch—place names on Caddo Lake fire the imagination. Such names are a clue that this cypress-studded, moss-draped, flooded forest has been a place of mystery and legend throughout its history.

Indian legend held that the lake was formed by the Great Spirit stamping his foot in anger—an earthquake. Some have speculated that the lake was formed by the great New Madrid earthquake of 1811, which formed Reelfoot Lake in Tennessee, but this appears not to have been the case.

Adding to its mystique is the fact

that Caddo Lake was once the only natural lake of any size in Texas. (That distinction was blurred, and use of the past tense made necessary, when Big Cypress Bayou was dammed in 1914, making Caddo for all practical purposes an artificial lake.) That Texas now ranks near the top of the 50 states in surface area of inland waters is a testament both to the industry of 20th century dam builders and to the special character of Caddo Lake.

Before 1800, the Caddo Lake area was most likely an intermittently flooded swamp. In the early 1800s a tremendous logjam on the Red River, the Great Raft, began backing water up. More debris collected and enlarged the raft to nearly 100 miles long and solid enough to cross on horseback, eventually causing it to block the mouths of other bayous and spill water from the Red River system into Caddo and other area lakes. Caddo Lake became one of the largest natural lakes in the South, even though its existence depended on the Great Raft remaining in place. Efforts to remove the raft to allow navigation of the upper Red River eventually succeeded in 1874.

By the early 1900s Caddo Lake had shrunk to the point that it was less than eight inches deep in most areas, and large portions of former lakebed were converted to farm fields. In 1914 a weir was built in Louisiana that once again raised the lake level; it now averages about seven feet deep. These changes in water level had a profound impact on the ecosystem. (See Insider's Corner, below.)

Caddo Lake and Big Cypress Bayou were important in early Texas history. Anglos rapidly pushed out the Caddo Indians in the 1830s. After the town of Jefferson was founded upstream on Big Cypress Bayou in 1842, steamboats took advantage of the elevated water levels caused by the Great Raft and made their way to

Kayaking and canoeing are popular on Caddo Lake, and several establishments in the Uncertain area offer rentals.

Jefferson through Caddo Lake. Government Ditch, now part of the WMA, was dug to improve access to the Red River. Port Caddo, a riverboat landing where the present state park is located, was an important port for early Texas.

Some of the most enduring stories of Caddo Lake stem from this early period. Robert Potter, a hotheaded North Carolinian, moved to Texas in 1835 to escape troubles at home. The Texas Revolution was brewing, and Potter was actively involved, serving for a time as Secretary of the Navy. After the war he built a home at Potter's Point, near the eastern edge of what is now Caddo Lake State Park/WMA. He became embroiled in the Regulator-Moderator War and in 1842 was killed in Caddo Lake as he tried to escape attackers by swimming away.

Death also played a part in another Caddo Lake drama, the burning of the steamboat *Mittie Stephens* in 1869, which occurred near Swanson's Landing, just east of the WMA, probably on the Louisiana side of the border. Sparks from the stacks caught hay bales on deck on fire, and the ship burned to the waterline. The 107 passengers on board did not realize the water was only three feet deep; 61 drowned or were crushed when pulled into the sidewheel paddles as the crew tried to drive the ship ashore.

Another enduring—and false—story centering around the lake holds that railroad magnate Jay Gould, angered by Jefferson's snubbing of his plans to build a railroad there, wrote "the end of Jefferson" in a hotel register and bypassed the town, nearly killing it. In fact a railroad was built to Jefferson years before Gould bought the line, and he did not visit the town until many years after the alleged incident.

The "Poker Cabin" on the northern part of Caddo Lake State Park/WMA was removed to make room for a lakeside campground.

Whether fact or legend, such stories serve to illustrate the powerful grip this mysterious lake has on people's imaginations and the role the lake has played in area history.

In 1992 Texas Parks and Wildlife purchased most of the area that is now Caddo Lake State Park/WMA. NOTE: This area is *not* the same as the adjacent Caddo Lake State Park, nor does it function as a state park or offer the amenities of a park. The word *park* is part of the name because of legal requirements stemming from the source of some of the funds used in the purchase.

In 1993 Caddo Lake was designated as "a wetland of international importance, especially as waterfowl habitat" under the Ramsar Convention. The entire United States has only 15 such sites, and Caddo Lake is the only one in Texas. The Caddo Lake Initiative, begun in 1993, encompasses a series of projects designed to protect the environment while providing for economic development of the area; Texas Parks and Wildlife is a partner in this effort.

GEOGRAPHY AND NATURAL FEATURES

Caddo Lake State Park/WMA contains a permanently flooded bald cypress swamp and seasonally flooded bottomland hardwoods. The swamp covers about 3,000 acres and the bottomland hardwoods about 2,600 acres. The balance of some 1,400 acres contains uplands with pine, oak and hickory trees. Much of the land surface consists of islands in the lake.

Big Cypress Bayou, the main source of inflow, is joined by a labyrinth of other creeks, sloughs and bayous. Cypress trees draped with Spanish moss dominate one's impressions of the lake. On still, clear days when trees and sky are reflected in the water, Caddo Lake seems suspended between earth and heavens, more part of myth than fact.

Coves and backwaters on the lake are known by a bewildering variety of colorful names—Goose Prairie, Mossy Break, Carter's Chute, Old Folks Playground. Despite its reputation for swallowing intruders, never to give them up, Caddo Lake is navigable by the average boater. This is made possible by a map of the lake showing the boat lanes that have been cleared through the timber. These lanes are marked by numbered posts so closely spaced there is never a doubt which way to go. Maps are available at Caddo Lake State Park and at Fyffe's Corner Grocery at the park entrance.

Water lillies found in the area bring color and fragrance to the Caddo Lake Swamp.

RECREATIONAL ACTIVITIES

Caddo Lake State Park/WMA offers primitive camping, wildlife viewing, hunting, and fishing in a setting whose beauty is matched by few other places in Texas.

CAMPING

Primitive camping is allowed at four sites on the WMA. All offer access to Caddo Lake.

PRO'S POINTERS. By far the most appealing camping area is Goat Island. Accessible by boat only, two camping areas about 100 yards apart are shaded by huge pine trees. This camping area is kept in extremely clean condition by a volunteer group that has an annual Halloween campout there.

Another campground is at the site known as the Poker House for an old structure formerly located there. This campsite offers water access for canoes and small flatbottom boats to the Carter's Lake area and the Goat Island campsites mentioned above. Fishing in the area is good in the winter and spring for largemouth and bream. From Texas 43, go east on FM 805 to County Road 3414; turn right and continue to the entrance.

A future campsite on Greening Road has a boat ramp suitable for small trailered boats. The heavily shaded campground offers access to the north side of Goat Island and Boat Road 3. From Texas 43, go northeast 2.1 miles on Johnston Road; turn right onto Greening Road and follow it 1.2 miles to a fork. Take the road to the left and continue past the houses about a quarter of a mile to the end of the road.

On the east side of the WMA, a campground off County Road 3632 allows hand-launching of canoes and small boats. This is a very scenic area with lots of shade. From Gray, follow FM 727 south 2.9 miles to County Road 3632. Go down 3632 about a mile, then turn left onto a graveled road and follow it about a quarter of a mile to a gate. Go through the gate and follow the paved road another 200 yards or so to the camping area.

The best time of year for camping is from April through June, before heat, humidity, and mosquitoes increase to uncomfortable levels. In October, November and December the area is heavily used by hunters. If you venture outside camping areas during hunting season, you must wear safety orange even if you are not hunting.

WILDLIFE VIEWING

Wildlife viewing on Caddo Lake State Park/WMA can be especially rewarding if you do it from a paddled boat, which will allow you to approach many birds and animals without spooking them. Waterfowl, neotropical migrants, deer, beavers, raccoons, eagles, various turtles, and alligators are all present on the area. Checklists for birds, amphibians and reptiles, mammals and vegetation are all available from the headquarters of Caddo Lake State Park, adjacent to the WMA.

PRO'S POINTERS. The best birding area is reached by putting your boat in at the state park boat ramp and heading north on Big Cypress Bayou to Hell's Half Acre, where you'll veer left onto Boat Road 3 (Carney Canal).

This area has the densest stands of older cypress trees, and there's less boat traffic to disturb wildlife.

In the spring this is a good area to see neotropical migrants such as the prothonotary warbler. Wood storks may also be present in spring. Egrets and herons of many different kinds are plentiful, and bald eagles winter around the lake. They are more commonly seen around the open water off Potter's Point. Wood ducks are year-round residents, and fall brings mallards, gadwalls, widgeons, and teal.

An alternative route is to go right at Hell's Half Acre and continue on Big Cypress Bayou to Bradley Bridge on Clinton's Chute; from this point you can take Boat Road 4 south to the village of Uncertain, where there are several restaurants on the shore.

Use caution when traveling the boat roads. In many places they are only two to three feet deep, and you may encounter submerged logs, stumps, or even trees that have fallen across the path. If you venture off the boat roads, be especially watchful for cypress knees; they can inflict severe damage on a boat or motor.

Keep a sharp eye out for deer and squirrels on the islands. There are numerous beaver lodges on the lake, but any swimming head spotted in the lake will likely belong to a nutria or muskrat. Red-eared turtles perch on logs. Alligator snapping turtles are rare but tend to stay in the flowing waters of Big Cypress Bayou. Alligators will be in shallow areas of the lake and sometimes sun on the bank during the day from May through September. Look for mud slides where alligators—or possibly beavers—have been entering the water.

Hunting

Hunting is permitted for deer, eastern wild turkeys, feral hogs, quail, waterfowl, doves, squirrels, furbearers, predators, frogs, rabbits, and hares by holders of an Annual Public Hunting Permit. Special Permit antlerless/

The yellow-crowned night heron, along with many other wading bird species, can be seen in the area.

spike buck hunts are used as needed to harvest excess animals. Youth hunts may also be available. See the *Public Hunting Lands Map Booklet,* the *Applications for Drawings on Public Hunting Lands,* and the *Outdoor Annual* for the current year for seasons and bag limits.

PRO'S POINTERS. "Deer density on the area is probably a deer to 10 acres," says area manager Charles Muller. "Anywhere on the area, you will find deer. The areas along FM 805 and Greening Road seem to hold lots of deer, as do the islands in the lake." Muller advises using a portable tree stand and concentrating on the edges of the water, where there is more food. Keep in mind that no motorized vehicles are allowed on the area outside the campgrounds or designated roads.

Feral hog numbers are limited on the area. Baiting is not allowed.

Eastern turkeys are also present in limited numbers. "The best turkey habitat is off FM 805, Greening Road, and FM 727," Muller says. However, during the first three seasons turkey hunting was allowed, no turkeys are known to have been harvested.

"Ducks are the big thing here," Muller says. One of the prominent features of Caddo Lake is the elaborate and well-camouflaged duck blinds scattered all over the lake. Such blinds existing on October 16, 1992 were permitted to remain and may be repaired, but no new permanent blinds may be built. In addition, hunters are advised to avoid these blinds, since people who built them feel they have exclusive right to their use. All duck blinds must be at least 300 yards from any other duck blind.

"Most of the ducks will be in open pockets in the timbered areas," says Muller. "Use a camouflaged boat, tie up to a tree, set out decoys, and hunt out of the boat." Duck hunting on Caddo Lake has declined in recent years due to the construction of new, larger reservoirs in the area, which seem to draw off a lot of ducks. However, duck hunting on Caddo Lake WMA remains popular because hunting is allowed during all legal hours seven days a week. In addition, the beauty of the area and the long tradition of duck hunting there appeal to many hunters.

Rabbit hunting is excellent on land anywhere on the area. Cottontails prefer the brushy edges along timbered tracts, breaks between fields and timber and briar thickets. Swamp rabbits tend to be in the wetter, lower areas. Walk them up or hunt them with dogs.

Squirrels—mostly grays—occur all over the area. Islands in the lake are popular venues, especially where there are stands of overcup oaks. These oaks are found right along the edge of the water, mingled with the cypress. It is unlawful to shoot a rifle or handgun across the waters of Caddo Lake. Both shotguns and .22-caliber rimfire weapons are legal for squirrels. Most people hunt by sitting still and listening for squirrels barking or dropping cuttings from nuts, then moving quietly into shooting position. Hunting squirrels with dogs is very popular on Caddo WMA.

135

Raccoon hunting is still popular around Caddo Lake. Hunt along the access roads. Keep in mind that the area boundary is marked with white paint blazes on trees and signs every 150 to 250 yards.

Caddo Lake has a lot of bullfrogs, no closed season, and a limit of 25 per day. "People start hunting frogs in late January and early February and hunt them through June," says Muller. "They spotlight and gig them or grab them by hand out of a boat. You can hunt along the boat roads or use a go-devil or canoe to get close to the shore."

FISHING

Caddo Lake has catfish, crappie, largemouth bass, and chain pickerel, but unlike most lakes in Texas, bream are a favored quarry. "Bream grow very large here, from three-quarters of a pound to a pound—filleting size," says Muller. Crickets and worms are the baits of choice. "Most people fish for bream from March through June in the shallows just off the shore, when the bream are on their beds," he says. "You'll find the most bream down around Uncertain in the lake."

In the spring, fish shallows in the lake for spawning bass. After the spawn, the fish move into the bayous and into the lake near Uncertain, where the lake is a little deeper. "Fish disappear from the shallow waters north of Big Cypress Bayou from July through September because of low oxygen levels due to the decomposition of plant materials and high temperatures," explains Muller.

THE MYSTERY OF BIG AND LITTLE

One of the most noticeable features of Caddo Lake is the disparity in size of the bald cypress trees from one part of the lake to another. In some places the trees are very large—as much as 400 years old. These trees are widely spaced, flat-topped and gnarled as befits their age. In other parts of the WMA all the trees are small—10 inches or so in diameter, and about 90 years old. Middle-aged and middle-sized trees in still other areas are about 175 years old. The unique thing is that all the trees in an area tend to be of similar age and size, unlike other natural forests, where big and little, young and old are intermixed helter-skelter.

The explanation lies in how the lake was formed—and in how bald cypress trees take root and grow. Bald cypress seedlings must take root and live their first year or two in very moist—but not flooded—soil with an open canopy above. This fact, coupled with the rise, fall, and subsequent reflooding of Caddo Lake, explains the varying ages of bald cypress trees around the lake and the uniformity of age within the various stands.

The oldest trees began growing before Caddo Lake was formed. These trees were able to survive the rise and fall of the water level over the years. When the Great Raft formed and flooded the land that became the lake, most of the bottomland hardwoods already present were killed. On the upper end of the lake, where water levels fluctuated but remained shallow, bald cypress trees were able to take root and grow. This accounts for the stands about 175 years old. The younger trees, those about 90 to 100 years old, sprouted and grew during the time between the destruction of the Great Raft and the reflooding of the lake in 1914.

The constant level of Caddo Lake as it now exists makes it possible to enjoy this unique area, but it raises a sobering possibility. Although bald cypress trees can live to be 1,700 years old, and there are many trees now only about 100 years old, very few new trees have been able to become established in the last century. Unless a way is found to establish new trees, Caddo Lake could someday be devoid of the very thing that gives it its unique character—the stately, moss-draped bald cypress.

Alligators are present on Caddo Lake but will generally leave you alone if you leave them alone. This four-foot 'gator was captured in a nearby city park and released on the WMA.

27,034 acres
1342 S. Wheeler
Jasper, TX 75951
409/384-6894

DRIVING TIMES FROM:
Amarillo: 10.5 hours
Austin: 5 hours
Brownsville: 9.5 hours
Dallas: 4 hours
El Paso: 15 hours
Houston: 3 hours
San Antonio: 6 hours
DIRECTIONS: From Jasper, take U.S. 96 north 27 miles to Pineland. Take FM 1 and then FM 2426 east about three miles.
OPEN: Daily.
ACTIVITIES: Camping, wildlife viewing, hiking, bicycling, hunting, fishing.
FACILITIES: Primitive campgrounds.
SPECIAL REGULATIONS: Only hunters are required to possess an Annual Public Hunting Permit. Turkeys must be taken to a check station within 24 hours. No buckshot is allowed. Waterfowl shooting hours end at noon. All legal firearms and archery equipment may be used during the general deer season and for feral hog hunting. Trapping is allowed November 1 through March 31. For other special regulations see the section entitled "Special Regulations in Effect on U.S. Forest Service Units" in the current *Public Hunting Lands Map Booklet.*
ADVISORIES: Mosquitoes can be abundant at any time of year; bring insect repellent. Carry your own supply of potable water.
LODGING IN AREA: Motels are available in Jasper, Brookeland, and Pineland.
LOCAL POINTS OF INTEREST: Martin Dies, Jr. State Park, Sabine National Forest, Angelina National Forest, Big Thicket National Preserve.
DISABILITY ACCESS: Not wheelchair-accessible.

HISTORY

Prior to settlement, this area was a transition zone between the Caddoan and Atakapan Indian cultures, and archeology has revealed much evidence of their presence. (All archeological and historic sites are protected under antiquities laws and should not be disturbed.)

European settlement began with Spanish land grants in the late 1700s and continued under Anglo empresarios. Native stands of longleaf pine created an open understory that appealed to early settlers, and many old homesites are on the area. These are easily identified by the presence of exotic vegetation.

Isolated and far from the seats of government, East Texas developed a tradition of lawlessness that lingered well into the 20th century. Remnants of this tradition still pose occasional problems for wildlife managers in the area today.

Beginning in the 1880s and continuing into the 1920s, the area was logged by timber companies, which took only the larger trees. In this era of irresponsible exploitation, no thought was given to reforestation. Not until the 1930s, when the U.S. Forest Service purchased the 160,609 acres that comprise the Sabine National Forest, did efforts begin to restore and manage the forest resources.

In 1983 the National Forests in Texas and the Texas Parks and Wildlife Department signed a Memorandum of Understanding that allowed joint management of some national forest lands. In 1984 the Moore Plantation WMA was created, totaling some 27,034 acres. The largest block is national forest land, but Temple Inland and Louisiana Pacific/Kirby together own about 3,568 acres. These private lands are managed under the same rules as the public lands.

GEOGRAPHY AND NATURAL FEATURES

Moore Plantation WMA is typical Pineywoods—nearly level to gently rolling, with sandy soils. Pine trees dominate, with faster-growing loblolly and shortleaf trees introduced for harvest being most common. Most of the stands of trees are in excess of 50 years old; some are quite large, as are some of the hardwoods also found on the area. Driving down the narrow, winding gravel roads lined on either side with majestic pines gives one the feeling of being in Colorado—but with Houston's humidity and without the mountains. The terrain is somewhat more rugged on the southern part of the area, along the drainages of Six-Mile and Big Sandy Creeks.

The average annual rainfall of 55 inches and a mild climate promote rapid growth of vegetation, and prescribed burns are conducted when possible to keep the understory as clear as possible. This has important implications for wildlife, especially eastern wild turkeys, which prefer an open understory.

Moore Plantation sits between Sam Rayburn and Toledo Bend Lakes, but except for a few small coves of Sam Rayburn Lake that extend onto the area under U.S. 96, it has no access to either lake.

RECREATIONAL OPPORTUNITIES

As part of the national forest system, recreational activities on Moore Plantation WMA are governed by U.S. Forest Service rules. Only hunters are required to possess an Annual Public Hunting Permit. A Limited Public Use Permit is not required for nonconsumptive users. Camping is restricted to designated campsites only during the archery and gun deer-hunting seasons. Hiking and recreational horseback riding are allowed year-round.

Located on national forest land, Moore Plantation WMA is managed for both wildlife and timber production. Open areas allow sunlight to reach the forest floor and produce foods used by a variety of wild creatures.

Since Moore Plantation is an eastern wild turkey restoration site, many roads on the area will be closed to vehicles during the brooding season from January through July. Hiking and bicycling are still permitted on these roads. For more information, call the U.S. Forest Service at 409/787-3870 or the Jasper office of Texas Parks and Wildlife at 409/384-6894.

CAMPING

From October through January, camping is restricted to three designated hunter camps on the area. The rest of the year, camping is allowed anywhere on the area, according to standard national forest policy. Motor vehicles must stay on the designated roads, but backpackers may camp anywhere. However, most people seem to prefer the hunter camps.

PRO'S POINTERS. The best time to camp is spring and fall. Heat and humidity make the area quite unpleasant during the summer. Fewer insects, especially mosquitoes, are present in spring.

Except for portable toilets provided during the first two weekends of the general deer season, no facilities are present at any of the campgrounds. You are expected to remove all your litter.

While all three campgrounds are pleasant openings surrounded by pine trees, they differ somewhat. The northernmost, 1.5 miles north of FM 2426 on Forest Road 152, has a small knoll in the middle of a small clearing. Beside the road just a few hundred yards south is a small pond good for perch fishing.

The middle campground is 0.9 mile south of FM 2426 on Forest Road 114, which is 3.8 miles east of FM 1 in Pineland. This is a large campground with a level, firm surface, as it occupies a former oil well pad. This is the best site for large recreational vehicles.

Two miles farther south on Forest Road 114 is the southern campground, which is somewhat more appealing than the other two. Campsites jut into the surrounding forest from a central cleared area; almost all sites are fully shaded. A narrow entrance and soft surface in places makes this campground better suited for tent campers or those with small recreational vehicles or trailers.

Wildlife Viewing

The red-cockaded woodpecker, an endangered species, may be seen on the area. There are about 30 areas designated as habitat. These birds prefer large, mature pine trees with high branching on the canopy and an open understory. Some colonies are marked with signs and offer the opportunity to view the birds from a distance if care is taken not to disturb them. One such area is on the west side of Forest Road 114 about 0.8 south of FM 2426. Others are on the south side of FM 2426 at its intersection with Forest Road 114 and from half a mile to a mile east of that point. To have the best chance of seeing a red-cockaded woodpecker, be there at daybreak or sunset, when the birds will congregate around nest cavities and chatter noisily. Trees with nest cavities are marked with a blue-green band completely around them.

Other species you may see are white-tailed deer, eastern wild turkeys, and feral hogs. Deer and hogs tend to concentrate along the drainages; turkeys are more common in the central part of the area along Forest Road 114 and along FM 201 in the south.

Birding is excellent on the area, as the prescribed burning practices encourage use by neotropical migrants. Included among the birds you may expect to see are red-shouldered, sharpshinned, Cooper's, harrier, and red-tailed hawks; great horned, barred, and screech owls; American crows; black and turkey vultures; hooded warblers; white-eyed and red-eyed vireos; summer tanagers; indigo and painted buntings; blue jays; cardinals; blue-gray gnatcatchers; tufted titmice; brown-headed nuthatches; Carolina wrens and chickadees and pileated woodpeckers. Bald eagles and ospreys may sometimes be seen moving between Sam Rayburn and Toledo Bend Lakes.

PRO'S POINTERS. "A beautiful trip is to take FM 83 north from Pineland and turn east on Forest Road 133," says area manager Gary Calkins. "Take Forest Road 152 past the northern hunter camp, go west on FM 2426 to Forest Road 114, then follow it south to FM 201. Follow it east back to U.S. 96. That will take you through a portion of every habitat type on the WMA. Along Forest Road 133 are immature pine plantations. Then you enter more mature upland pine stands, then younger commercial pine plantations. This route passes by several of the red-cockaded woodpecker habitat management areas." Total length of this trip is about 17.5 miles.

Hiking

The Trail Between the Lakes is the only established trail on the area. This is a 28-mile U.S. Forest Service trail between Toledo Bend and Sam Rayburn Reservoirs. Classified as moderately difficult, it runs roughly southwest to northeast across the middle of Moore Plantation WMA. You may access portions of the trail from Forest Road 152 at 0.9 miles north of FM 2426; where Forest Road 152A intersects Forest Road 152 at 2.1 miles north of FM 2426; from FM 2426 at 3.6 miles east of its intersection with FM 1 in Pineland; and from Forest Road 114B about half a mile west of its intersection with Forest Road 114, south of the southern campground. There is no water along the trail; only experienced, well-equipped backpackers should attempt the entire trip. Work crews maintain the trail every two months or so. Maps are available at the U.S. Forest Service office in Hemphill.

Far less difficult to walk and easier to access are the many gated roads, which are closed to vehicular traffic from January through July. Hikers on these roads are more likely to see wildlife. Winter food plots along many of the roads still attract animals in the spring. Well-maintained roadbeds make walking easy.

PRO'S POINTERS. Forest Road 152A offers a 2-mile (one-way) walk through several types of forest habitat before dropping off into a big bottom. Off Forest Road 136 just west of Yellow Pine is Jones Cemetery road, a pretty walk of about a mile.

Hikers are allowed to walk anywhere on the area even during hunting season. During the months of November, December, and January, wearing blaze orange clothing whenever outside campgrounds is required.

Bicycling

Bicycling is allowed on any of the Forest Service Roads. In general, these roads are best suited for touring bikes, as the terrain does not offer the challenge preferred by mountain bikers.

PRO'S POINTERS. Bikes are not allowed on the Trail Between the Lakes. For suggested routes, see the Wildlife Viewing section, above.

Hunting

In keeping with U.S. Forest Service policy, hunting regulations are set for maximum hunting opportunities. That is to say, the fact that hunting for a particular species is allowed is not an indication the animal is abundant on the area. Only those species discussed below are present in numbers sufficient to make hunting them worthwhile.

Animals present in greatest numbers on Moore Plantation are white-tailed deer, eastern wild turkeys, feral hogs, various furbearers and predators. Youth-only hunts are offered for deer and waterfowl, and there is a youth-adult squirrel hunt. Both archery and rifle hunting are available for white-tailed deer to holders of an Annual Public Hunting Permit. For information on species, seasons, and bag limits, consult the *Public Hunting Lands Map Booklet*, the *Applications for Drawings on Public Hunting*

Lands, and the *Outdoor Annual* for the current year.

All persons 17 years of age and older who possess a centerfire or muzzleloading rifle, a handgun, a shotgun with shot larger than #2 steel or #4 lead or archery equipment with broadheads must possess an Annual Public Hunting Permit. Persons 17 and older with guns using rimfire ammunition, shotguns with smaller size shot than listed above, and archery equipment with field points must possess either the Annual Public Hunting Permit or a Limited Public Use Permit.

PRO'S POINTERS. "The better deer are north of FM 2426," says Calkins. "There aren't many there, but there are some good bucks, including some that will score in the mid-150s. On the south end of the area, we are above the carrying capacity of the habitat."

An abundance of deer and large trees makes for good archery hunting. "Hardly any archery hunters use this area, so you will have your choice of spots," advises Calkins. "Hunt along the drainages, and pay attention to which type of hardwoods are producing mast—oaks or beeches. Find a drainage with white oak acorns dropping, and you can figure on doing some good there. Archery

hunting may be better near the end of the season, because the acorns start to drop then." Hunters are allowed to put up stands that will not damage trees (no screw-in steps) and leave them in place for 72 hours. The first weekend of the general season, there is a voluntary check station at the hunters' camp just south of FM 2426 on Forest Road 114.

"I don't recommend coming the first two weekends of the general season—this place is a circus," says Calkins. "The Thanksgiving and Christmas holidays are wonderful times. Around Thanksgiving is the second peak of the rut, there are few people, and the deer are moving around and recovering from the pressure of the opening two weekends."

A spring turkey season in April allows hunters the opportunity to take an eastern wild turkey. The Moore Plantation WMA was one of the first to be restocked with turkeys. However, numbers are still relatively low, and the dense forest makes hunting difficult. "Look for mature stands of mixed hardwoods and pines with an open understory," advises Calkins. "You can locate gobblers by driving the roads and giving crow or owl calls to make them gobble."

Feral hogs are disliked by wildlife

managers almost as much as turkeys are treasured. There is no bag limit on hogs. No dogs or baiting are allowed. Hogs are nomadic and may be found anywhere on the area, but drainages are the best places to begin. Look for tracks and signs of fresh rooting.

Dove hunting is fair on first-year clearcuts with croton growing. Locate these areas by scouting. Rabbits and hares may also be hunted successfully in these areas.

Furbearers and predators, especially coyotes and bobcats, are plentiful. Bobcats prefer the area north of FM 2426. The use of dogs to hunt furbearers and predators is allowed outside of deer season. Raccoon hunting is good. No electronic calls are allowed. Predators may be hunted at night except during the general deer season, but call the game warden first.

"Squirrel hunting is really good in the hardwood and mixed hardwood-pine bottoms," says Calkins. "You'll have to walk to get into those areas for the most part. Hunting them with dogs is the most productive method. Early to mid-December is the time to get juvenile and subadult squirrels that are big enough to have some meat on them but are not tough."

Fishing

Only very limited fishing is available. Six-Mile Creek and associated drainages may have ponds that will hold a few perch. There are some old stock and mill ponds on the area as well, and lake fishing is available where Pompanaugh Creek comes under U.S. 96 onto the area. Just south of the northern hunters' camp, next to Forest Road 152, a small pond offers the opportunity to catch perch.

PRO'S POINTERS. Sam Rayburn Lake and Toledo Bend Reservoir are both just a few miles away and offer some of the best fishing in the state. Go there.

Primitive camping areas on Moore Plantation WMA are popular with hunters during the spring turkey season.

NO SMOKING CAN BE HARMFUL TO A FOREST'S HEALTH

One of the most significant changes humans have made in the natural world has been the suppression of fire. In presettlement times natural wildfires swept prairies and forests alike from time to time. These fires performed valuable functions and were a vital part of the ecosystem. Fires recycled nutrients to the soil. They kept forest understories relatively free of brush and vines. On prairies, wildfires removed dead grasses that could shade out new growth, and the fires also killed woody plants and kept them from invading and taking over grasslands. By continually setting back plant succession, fires encouraged the growth of forbs, or weeds, that are valuable food sources for many animals.

Humans had a different view of fire, at least until recent times. Fire destroyed crops and buildings. Humans regarded fire as an enemy to be eliminated if possible, or at least controlled. The result over 200 years of occupation has been a major restructuring of the environment. Fire was removed from an ecosystem that had developed with fire as one of its major components. Natural plant communities disappeared, and as they went, so did the wildlife dependent upon them. Plants that had been suppressed by fire expanded their range; mesquite and ashe juniper are perhaps the best examples.

Wildlife managers now include fire as one of the tools they use to maintain or enhance the productivity of habitat. Prescribed burns can improve the quantity and quality of plants available for wildlife food. Burning helps keep forest understories low—a condition favored by such game animals as quail and turkeys.

Unfortunately, prescribed burns cannot always be applied when and where needed. This is especially true in the national forests of Texas, which are surrounded by heavily populated areas. Smoke from prescribed burns can have serious impacts on the health of people living in the area. A fire that burns too hot can destroy desired vegetation and perhaps get out of control. Therefore, stringent conditions must be met before burns can take place. Temperature, humidity, fuel load, and wind direction and speed must all be within designated parameters before burns can be conducted. Often this means that burns cannot be conducted when needed to benefit wildlife.

One of the species sometimes negatively impacted is the eastern wild turkey. Turkeys prefer a relatively open understory. When prescribed burns cannot be conducted as needed, the understory becomes choked with vegetation rather quickly, and turkeys have to move elsewhere. Hunting is also more difficult in thick forest, making it harder for hunters to harvest the number of animals that will keep wildlife populations in balance with the food supply.

Burned is better for the habitat and the wildlife, but increasingly in today's world the needs of humans come first.

3,650 acres
1805 E. Lufkin Ave.
Lufkin, TX 75901
936/639-1879

DRIVING TIMES FROM:
Amarillo: 11 hours
Austin: 5.5 hours
Brownsville: 10 hours
Dallas: 4.5 hours
El Paso: 15.5 hours
Houston: 3.5 hours
San Antonio: 6.5 hours

DIRECTIONS: From Center, go east on Texas 7 for 13.4 miles to FM 2787. Go south on FM 2787 for 2.1 miles to FM 139. Go south on FM 139 for 2 miles to FM 2572. Follow FM 2572 for 1.6 miles and turn right onto an unsigned road, entering the WMA at the Swede Johnson Lake Recreation Area. The area may also be accessed by boat from Toledo Bend Reservoir.

OPEN: Daily.

ACTIVITIES: Camping, wildlife viewing, hiking, hunting, fishing.

FACILITIES: Primitive campground, 550-acre impoundment, boat roller.

SPECIAL REGULATIONS: All users must register on-site. Waterfowl shooting hours end at noon. Trapping is allowed November 1 through March 31. Use of horses is allowed only during designated periods.

ADVISORIES: Water moccasins and alligators are present. Beware of wasp and hornet nests on branches hanging low over the water. Submerged logs and thick vegetation make the use of a Go-Devil advisable in the impoundment. Roads may be impassable when lake levels are high. Carry your own supply of potable water.

LODGING IN AREA: Motels are available in Nacogdoches.

LOCAL POINTS OF INTEREST: Martin Creek Lake State Park, Sabine National Forest, Angelina National Forest.

DISABILITY ACCESS: None.

HISTORY

Caddo Indians occupied this area until well after European settlement began. Two main factors delayed development by settlers. First, the Mexican government prohibited settlement by American colonists within 20 leagues (60 miles) of the border with the United States. However, squatters and outlaws moved in, giving the area a reputation for lawlessness. This reputation was bolstered by the second factor hindering development: the Regulator-Moderator War of the 1840s. The roots of this war lay in disputed land claims stemming from the Mexican era. Armed conflicts between organized groups became so bad that at one point President Sam Houston reputedly suggested, only partly in jest, that the county's municipalities be

Cypress trees, buttonbush, and water hyacinth are the dominant plants in the 550-acre impoundment on the North Toledo Bend WMA.

declared free and independent governments and the residents allowed to fight it out.

Shelby County was a land of small farms well into the 20th century, with most farmers depending on corn, cotton, and livestock. Modernization was slow to penetrate the area, and poverty was widespread. The area remains predominantly rural and agricultural to the present.

The land that is now Toledo Bend WMA was purchased by the Sabine River Authority beginning in 1963, prior to the construction of Toledo Bend Reservoir. Texas Parks and Wildlife has managed the WMA under license from the Sabine River Authority since 1973.

GEOGRAPHY AND NATURAL FEATURES

The area consists of a peninsula with a highly irregular, deeply indented shoreline projecting into the extreme upper end of Toledo Bend Reservoir and includes part of that lake and its shoreline. The Sabine River, which marks the boundary between Texas and Louisiana, is immediately east of the area.

The land is generally low and swampy, with sandy ridges on the north end descending into poorly drained bottomlands on the south. Numerous oxbow lakes and sloughs pepper the area. Vegetation is typical of similar areas in East Texas, with pines on upland areas and water oak, willow oak, bald cypress, and other bottomland hardwood species in low areas. Much of the lowland area is subject to inundation when Toledo Bend Reservoir rises above its conservation pool level of 172 feet, which occurs fairly often. A marsh area on the southeastern part of the WMA results.

A levee and water-control structure impound water on about 550 acres on the southern end of the area, adjacent to Toledo Bend Reservoir. Water exchange is controlled by a riser set at 172 feet. The water level in the impoundment cannot be dropped below lake level, which hampers efforts at moist-soil management and water hyacinth and hydrilla control. As a result, the impoundment can become heavily choked with vegetation and may experience depleted oxygen levels and resulting fish kills in summer. A boat roller across the levee gives access to the impoundment from Toledo Bend Reservoir.

Swede Johnson Lake, on the north end of the area, covers about 60 acres and is dotted with scattered cypress trees. It is easily accessible by small boat from the road entering the area and is quite scenic.

Due to the variety of habitat types in close proximity, Toledo Bend WMA enjoys considerable wildlife diversity. White-tailed deer, gray and fox squirrels, cottontail and swamp rabbits, feral hogs, wood ducks, mallards, and a variety of other avian species occur on the area.

RECREATIONAL OPPORTUNITIES

CAMPING

Primitive camping is allowed in a cleared area on the north end of the WMA. There are no facilities, and all trash must be packed out. None of the campsites are shaded.

PRO'S POINTERS. The camping area is conveniently located to Swede Johnson Lake. To reach it, take the unsigned road into the area from the Swede Johnson Lake Recreation Area on FM 2572 and drive 0.7 mile into the area.

WILDLIFE VIEWING

Birding can be excellent year-round. In summer, the area holds wood ducks, cattle egrets, great egrets, anhingas, snowy egrets, great blue herons, green-backed herons, black-crowned and yellow-crowned night herons. Wood storks may stop over in late summer. Winter birds are mostly waterfowl—mallards, wood ducks, gadwalls, widgeons, pintails, green-winged teal, blue-winged teal, scaup, and hooded mergansers—and a variety of hawks. Prothonotary warblers nest on the area in spring.

PRO'S POINTERS. "Swede Johnson Lake will be covered with gadwalls at times," says area manager Ski Clark. "There are lots of natural cavities in trees on Swede Johnson Lake and on the impoundment, which attracts prothonotary warblers."

Texas Parks and Wildlife biologist Richard Pike advises looking in upland areas in spring and summer for dickcissels, scissor-tailed flycatchers, blue grosbeaks, and indigo and painted buntings. "Sparrows and buntings will be in the grassy, weedy areas," says Pike. "Look for Baltimore and orchard orioles in the trees. In wintertime sedge wrens, white-crowned sparrows, white-throated sparrows, and Lincoln's sparrows are common. In the hardwood bottoms, spring species include red-eyed vireos, yellow-throated vireos, prothonotary warblers, northern parulas, Louisiana water-thrushes, Kentucky warblers, hooded warblers, and summer tanagers."

The entry road from FM 2572 offers access to both the upland areas and the margins of Swede Johnson Lake and the impoundment. At 0.4 mile inside the area, a primitive ramp on the east side of the bridge allows launching small boats, or you can go 0.1 mile down the road to the left to the shore of Swede Johnson Lake and launch canoes or jonboats. About a mile past the bridge, a locked gate blocks one road to the impoundment 2 miles farther on. To the right of the gate is Long Field Road, which passes through an open area on its way to the impoundment but tends to be very muddy and impassable to vehicles. Visitors are free to walk or bicycle either road.

HIKING

There are no designated hiking trails. Hiking is allowed on all roads within the area, which total about 3 miles.

PRO'S POINTERS. The best hike is along the main road into the area from FM 2572. For a walk of about 3 miles one way, park at Swede Johnson Lake Recreation Area and follow the road into the area a mile to the locked gate, then bypass the gate and continue another 2 miles to the impoundment. Or park at the locked gate for a shorter walk. You will be more comfortable in long pants and waterproof shoes due to lush vegetation and muddy spots in the road.

HUNTING

Deer, feral hogs, squirrels, and waterfowl are the main species hunted here. All hunting is by Annual Public Hunting Permit. Youth and youth-adult hunts are available. For seasons, species and bag limits, see the *Public Hunting Lands Map Booklet* and the *Outdoor Annual* for the current year.

PRO'S POINTERS. Deer may be hunted during both the archery and gun seasons. "There are quite a few deer out there," says Clark. "When the marshes are low, deer will be on the edges of the marsh. When acorns are dropping, find the oak flats and hunt them. Otherwise, still-hunt along the edges of open fields along the main road. Another good spot begins at the bridge near Swede Johnson Lake and runs southwest along the slough—there's usually deer sign along there." Many sweet gum trees in the bottoms will support climbing stands, and there are also some pine ridges with climbable trees. Natural openings and mowed areas provide good visibility for stand hunters. The rut peaks during the first two weeks in November. Baiting is not allowed.

Feral hogs may be hunted concurrently with deer and from January 15 through March 15. "Hogs seem to move through the area and can be thick in there at times, but overall the numbers are moderate," says Clark. "Look up and down the sloughs, in the oak flats and around the edges of the marshes and wet areas. There's

usually a lot of sign in the fields." Clark suggests using drives through thick areas to push hogs out of the heavy cover. Another method is to still-hunt, listening for hogs to squeal or grunt and then going to them. Baiting is not allowed.

Waterfowl hunting is dependent on water levels in Toledo Bend Reservoir. "During the early teal season, if we have water, we will have birds, but this may not be the case," says Clark. "The lake needs to be at 169 to 170 feet in order to have shallow water in the marsh in the southeastern part of the WMA."

Late-season duck hunting is generally better. "Gadwalls and widgeons arrive about the middle of the second split," Clark says. "Mallards and pintails show up toward the end of the season. Wood ducks will be here all the time. We also get some scaup, ring-necks, and a few canvasbacks."

Access is the chief problem for waterfowl hunters. If Toledo Bend Reservoir is low, the boat rollers on the levee may be difficult to use. The Long Field Road runs to the impoundment from the locked gate a mile inside the area, but it is a very bad road, and many vehicles get stuck. Some people use bicycles to pull small trailers with their gear in along the road behind the locked gate; this seems to be the surest route. The northwest end of the impoundment can be very good hunting.

To access the area from Toledo Bend, follow FM 139 south from Joaquin to County Road 3385. Follow 3385 for 0.9 mile to County Road 3485. Turn right onto County Road 3485 and go another 0.2 mile to an intersection with a sign that says "Williams" and turn right onto an unnamed road. Continue on that road another 0.8 mile through a heavily developed lakeside residential area to a private boat ramp. There is a launch fee. Go northeast and then north around the first big point to a creek channel. Turn into the creek channel

and follow it to the marsh area. If the water level is at 172 feet or higher, you can get into the marsh with almost any boat, but if the level is 170 or below, you will need a very shallow-draft boat or a Go-Devil. Low water levels can offer the best duck hunting and fewer hunters.

Squirrels are plentiful and get hunted hard by locals. "The pine ridges have mature oak trees on them that produce lots of acorns; those are good spots for squirrels," says Clark. "The ridges between the fingers of the impoundment are good for squirrels, mostly grays."

Swamp rabbits are abundant. If the open fields have been mowed, rabbits are huntable in the short grass; otherwise, thick cover makes them difficult to see. The use of dogs is permitted and is probably the best method. Trapping is allowed for furbearers and predators, and predators can be hunted with dogs year-round. Night hunting is not permitted during deer season.

FISHING

Bass, crappie, and catfish are present in the impoundment. However, hydrilla and water hyacinth infestations may lead to fish kills in summer due to oxygen depletion. The upper end of Toledo Bend Reservoir is in the WMA.

PRO'S POINTERS. Red-ear bream up to 1.5 pounds may be caught during the summer spawn. Fish for crappie at the water-control structure near the boat roller when water is going in or out of the impoundment. Spring and early summer are the best times for bass in the impoundment.

Fishing guide Mike Wheatley says the portion of Toledo Bend Reservoir within the WMA is best fished in winter and spring. "In late spring and early summer the hydrilla grows and makes it very difficult to get around, because the water is so shallow," he says. "Black bass start biting in late winter; the best bait at that time of year is a jig and pig or a jig and craw worm. Spinnerbaits work well on warm days when the fish get active."

During the spawn, Wheatley switches to a Rogue or Sluggo jerkbait. "Usually the full moons in March and April are the two best times to fish that area," he says.

Crappie are very good during the same time period, Wheatley says. "A lot of people use a trolling motor and go from cypress tree to cypress tree with a tube jig or minnow on a long fly rod. Most of the trees are in four to six feet of water, so you have to use a slip cork and ease the bait out by the tree to avoid spooking the fish."

Catfish are often caught by crappie fishers using shiners around the cypress trees. "Most people fishing for cats fish the Sabine River channel along the border of the WMA," Wheatley says. "Limblines and cut bait seem to work the best on channel and blue cats, live bait on yellow cats. In the early spring, limbliners will often use Ivory soap cut into half-inch squares for bait. It gives off a white flash and is bouyant, making it appear to be alive."

Fishers have a choice of three places to launch. From the Louisiana side, follow Louisiana 191 south from U.S. 84 in Logansport about 7 miles to Oak Ridge Park and a boat ramp. Go north on the river about a mile and a half to Float Road Pass (signed), and turn left into it.

From the Texas side, put in at the boat ramp in Swede Johnson Recreation Area (see directions, above) and go south in the river to Float Road Pass. Turn right into the area.

From the Williams private ramp (see directions in the hunting section, above), go northeast around a big point, then turn north and continue about a quarter of a mile to Float Road Pass. Turn into the channel and follow it.

INSIDER'S CORNER

ALIEN ASSAULT

Perhaps exotic water plants are the best illustration of the saying "Beauty is in the eye of the beholder." Water hyacinth, a native of South America, was introduced into Florida about a hundred years ago. This free-floating plant with waxy, glossy leaves produces a beautiful purplish blue flower, making it popular with gardeners wanting to dress up their ponds.

Unfortunately, water hyacinth's growth rate is among the highest of any known plant. It can double in size in as little as 12 days. With a favorable climate in the southern United States and no natural enemies in its new home, water hyacinth spread quickly and became one of the most despised weeds in the world. Thick growths floating on lakes and rivers can completely block boat traffic. But its impacts extend beneath the surface as well. Solid mats of water hyacinth—up to 200 tons per acre—can block sunlight and prevent oxygen from getting into the water. Decaying plants can deplete oxygen levels in water to the point that fish cannot survive.

As bad as it is in some Texas reservoirs, including the impoundment at North Toledo Bend WMA, water hyacinth seems almost benign compared to the latest invader from South America, giant salvinia. This attractive fern imported for use in aquariums and water gardens now wreaks environmental and economic havoc on four continents. Capable of

doubling in size every three to five days, floating mats of giant salvinia can choke any size lake. Giant salvinia spread across half a million acres of Africa's Kariba Lake. In 1998 the plant was found in Texas' largest lake, Toledo Bend, which is less than half the size of Kariba Lake.

Unfortunately, chemical control seems to be the only way to kill the pest, and efforts have been limited by environmental concerns. Giant salvinia has been found in other Texas lakes and seems likely to continue its spread across the state. One of the chief means of spread is by buds that break off and cling to watercraft and boat trailers and are then carried to other bodies of water. Another culprit is plant nurseries that sell giant salvinia— not realizing that possessing, purchasing, or selling a prohibited exotic aquatic plant is a violation of state law. Releasing prohibited plants into any Texas water is also against the law.

For now, the best defense against these invasive aliens seems to be education. Boaters and fishers should wash their boats, trailers, and towing vehicles carefully to remove all traces of plants before launching into another body of water. Plant suppliers must refrain from selling such plants. Most importantly, however, consumers must resist the temptation to acquire exotic plants simply because they are pretty. Pretty is as pretty does, and a plant that renders its habitat unfit for other living organisms is an ugly thing no matter how beautifully it blooms.

82 acres
11942 FM 848
Tyler, TX 75707
903/566-1626

DRIVING TIMES FROM:
Amarillo: 8 hours
Austin: 4 hours
Brownsville: 10 hours
Dallas: 1.5 hours
El Paso: 12.5 hours
Houston: 4 hours
San Antonio: 5.5 hours
DIRECTIONS: From Loop 323 in Tyler, take Spur 248 south about 3.2 miles to FM 848. Turn right and go 0.5 mile to the entrance.
OPEN: Daily 8:30 A.M. to 4:30 P.M.
ACTIVITIES: Nature trail, wildlife viewing.
FACILITIES: Visitor center, nature trails, indoor classroom, outdoor meeting area, restrooms.
SPECIAL REGULATIONS: Park at the designated parking area only. Pets are not allowed. Foot traffic only is allowed on designated trails only; trails must be entered at designated points. Firearms and alcoholic beverages are prohibited. Campfires and gathering of firewood are prohibited. Usage limited to 200 persons daily. Group tours by reservation only.
ADVISORIES: Poison ivy, ticks, chiggers, fire ants, copperheads, and water moccasins are present. Carry your own supply of potable water.
LODGING IN AREA: Motels are available in Tyler.
LOCAL POINTS OF INTEREST: Tyler State Park, Governor Hogg Shrine State Historical Park, Lake Tawakoni State Park, Purtis Creek State Park, Texas State Railroad, Jim Hogg State Historical Park, Texas Freshwater Fisheries Center.
DISABILITY ACCESS: Visitor center, meeting areas, and restrooms will be wheelchair-accessible by 2002.

An outdoor pavilion serves as an outdoor classroom at The Nature Center, whose chief purpose is outdoor education.

HISTORY

The present site of the Nature Center was purchased between 1855 and 1860 by Dr. Lazariah Smith and wife Nancy as part of a 1,250-acre plantation. Dr. Smith died from injuries suffered in a fall from a mule in 1864, and his wife operated the plantation until 1868, when she divided the land among the four children, retaining the homeplace for herself. In 1886 the property was sold to the Hill family and was later divided among the Hill children. The 82 acres now comprising the Nature Center was purchased by Texas Parks and Wildlife in 1955 for use as a state quail hatchery.

For the next 30 years the facility was used for the hatching and rearing of a variety of gamebirds for release into the wild. Species produced here included bobwhite quail, sand grouse, French redleg partridges, mottled ducks, wood ducks, pearl mallards, turkeys, and pheasants. Only the latter ever survived in the wild to any appreciable degree. In 1986 hatchery operations ceased, and the facility was converted to office space.

In 1995 efforts began to develop the site into an ecological education center. A visitor center and classrooms and other improvements are being funded by environmental fines levied on an industrial polluter and by donations from a variety of other groups.

GEOGRAPHY AND NATURAL FEATURES

The Nature Center contains surprising diversity for such a small area. Adjacent to the highway is a prairie area, which grades into a small pine upland. Between the visitor parking lot and the visitor center are a pond and a small wetlands area, both constructed. Farther into the area, the Quail Creek hardwood bottom is bordered by more pine uplands.

Of all the wildlife management areas in Texas, the Nature Center has been impacted most by human activities. The site contains a number of buildings used daily for various purposes. Much of the site was cleared for agricultural or avicultural operations, and the forested areas were logged repeatedly. However, the

site still supports a wide variety of plants and animals. Water oaks, bluejack oaks, post oaks, southern red oaks, shortleaf pines, black walnuts, and mockernut hickories are all present among the more than 220 species of plants identified on the area. The former state champion huckleberry tree is located along the Upland Trail. Raccoons, foxes, cottontails, coyotes, white-tailed deer and a variety of birds inhabit the site.

RECREATIONAL OPPORTUNITIES

The principal mission of the Nature Center is to serve as an outdoor educational classroom that will help people understand their place in natural systems. Teachers are encouraged to bring school groups to the Nature Center. Hunter and angler education classes and Kidfish events are also held. A variety of other educational programs ranging from demonstration gardens to wildscaping to aquatic plant ecology are planned. Self-guided nature trails are available.

NATURE TRAILS

The 0.2-mile Upland Trail begins at the parking lot in front of the old quail hatchery building, passes along the edge of the prairie area, and loops through a loblolly pine grove. The former state champion huckleberry tree—now in decline—is on this trail and is marked by a plaque. Numbered signs correspond to an illustrated guide available at the visitor center; this guide serves both the Upland and Quail Creek trails.

The 0.9-mile Quail Creek Trail begins behind the visitor center, passes by a small wetland, and skirts a grassland area before dropping into the creek bottom. Most of the trail is in this bottomland habitat. Large trees shade the route, and an access point to the creek allows a close-up look at aquatic life.

PRO'S POINTERS. Both trails are mostly level and easy to walk. Some

places along the Quail Creek Trail may be muddy; waterproof shoes are advised. These wet areas are good places to look for deer, raccoon, and coyote tracks.

Wildflowers blanket the prairie areas in the spring. Black-eyed Susans, erect dayflowers, southern dewberries, goldenrod, and ashy sunflowers are abundant. Mexican plums, black cherries, red mulberries, muscadine grapes, American

The Nature Center contains an amazing variety of habitats for its size; just a few steps take one from prairie to pine upland to hardwood bottomland habitats.

June visitors can expect to see painted and indigo buntings, grosbeaks, blue jays, mockingbirds, sparrows, warblers, starlings, crows, doves, hummingbirds, and scarlet tanagers. Red-winged blackbirds hang out on the pond. Eastern phoebes build nests under ledges on the buildings. Killdeer nest on top of the visitor center in June and water at the pond. Red-tailed hawks nest in the tall pines west of the pavilion and hunt in the grasslands. Scissor-tailed flycatchers nest in a large sycamore tree each year."

September and October are peak fall months for migratory birds, and many monarch butterflies stop in to feed on goldenrod.

The fruits of the smooth sumac can be steeped to make tea, and birds find them tasty as well.

beautyberries, persimmons, smooth sumacs, and American elderberries provide soft mast for birds and mammals alike and brighten the area both in bloom and in fruit. Fallen trees along the route illustrate the process of decomposition; some support impressive growths of fungi.

Among the interesting plants along the Quail Creek Trail are smooth sumac, with its large clusters of brightly colored fruit resembling heads of maize; eastern hop hornbeam, whose drooping sacs of fruits resemble flowers of the ornamental shrimp plant; and the devil's walking stick, named for the rows of sharp thorns sprouting from the trunk. However, its most unusual feature is not so obvious: This plant has one of the largest leaves in the world. Each "branch" supports what appears to be a collection of separate leaves but is really one huge compound leaf that may be as much as four feet long and three feet wide.

"To really get the full benefits of the trails, you need to come at all four seasons, because they are different at each time of year," says wildlife technician Annice Storey. "The amount of diversity along the trails is amazing. There's a hardwood forest along the Quail Creek Trail with lots

of huge white oak trees, and it's so quiet you can hear the creek running."

Returning to the visitor center from the outdoor pavilion area, the trail passes by an upland demonstration area where pheasant holding pens used to be. The four cement ponds once used for watering birds demonstrate how to use similar ponds to attract and water wildlife on your own property.

WILDLIFE VIEWING

The Nature Center is surrounded by land that is being developed rapidly; it serves as a refuge for a variety of animals. White-tailed deer are present year-round. Other common species include skunks, coyotes, raccoons, hawks, owls, and various songbirds.

PRO'S POINTERS. Annice Storey lives on the site and takes morning walks regularly, giving her the opportunity to observe wildlife at all times of the year. "The best time to see mammals is in the spring," she says. "Deer are here year-round, mostly in the more wooded back part of the area. Coyotes are here from March into early May. Chuck-will's-widows use the area in April and May. Great horned and barred owls may be seen along the creek. In April, May, and

PLANTS OF THE NATURE CENTER: TRASH OR TREASURE?

Humans tend to value elements of nature in proportion to their perceived usefulness—that is, economic value. A majestic pine tree is seen in terms of how many board feet of lumber it will yield, the stately oak in terms of cords of firewood, the lowly mesquite in terms of savory briskets it will smoke.

While some plants are valued in terms of their aesthetic appeal, even this approach has its limits: A city dweller's wildflower is a farmer's weed. Nor do animals escape classification by prejudice: White-tailed deer and quail are protected as game animals and highly valued, while coyotes and skunks are thought of as varmints worthy only of eradication. If skunks were as tasty as quail or sported huge antlers, how different might their status be!

Inevitably, classification leads to the perception of "trash" species as being of little importance. In many cases the end result is extinction of that species and a reduction in biodiversity. Aldo Leopold, the father of the modern conservation movement, had strong words to say on the subject in *A Sand County Almanac*. "The outstanding scientific discovery of the 20th century is not television, or radio, but rather the complexity of the land organism. Only those who know the most about it can appreciate how little is known about it. The last word in ignorance is the man who says of an animal or plant: 'What good is it?' If the land mechanism as a whole is good, then every part is good, whether we understand it or not. If the biota, in the course of aeons, has built something we like but do not understand, then who but a fool would discard seemingly useless parts? To keep every cog and wheel is the first precaution of intelligent tinkering."

In short, Leopold said, you never know when you might need something you cast aside as worthless.

A trio of plants found at the Nature Center illustrates the bias with which humans view the natural world. Smooth sumac is used by both humans and animals. A tea made from sumac leaves can be used for medicinal purposes; its fruits steeped in warm water make a sweet, flavorful tea. From its flowers, bees produce amber-colored honey with a fine flavor. Various animals eat the fruits and use sumac thickets for cover. Obviously this plant is a valuable one.

Hop hornbeam, whose fruits form clusters of bladderlike green sacs that look like hops, is also called ironwood because the heartwood is extremely hard. Indians made bows from it; the wood was once widely used for tool handles, wagon wheel rims, and spokes. This is another valuable plant based on its uses to humans, though it is less sought after today than in horse and buggy days.

But what of the devil's walking stick, also called Hercules' club? What good can a plant be whose trunk is covered with long, sharp spines? Whose wood is not used to make useful things? Is it only an ornamental, a curiosity? Certainly it is curious. The devil's walking stick lacks branches, despite its appearance. Shooting out from its trunk are rachis, the axes of the large leaves. These structures substitute for branches, although temporarily—the leaves are deciduous. In effect, the rachis are throw-away branches. It appears that the plant developed this structure as a way of being "firstest with the mostest." Without the need to expend energy on growing branches, the devil's walking stick is able to gain height more rapidly than other woody plants, capturing all-important sunshine, shading out competing plants, and assuring its own survival.

What good is it? Too often the asking of that question presages the demise of a plant or animal, for if it is found lacking in present utility, it may be deemed to have no future value, and therefore not worth saving.

Who among us is qualified to make that judgment?

To assume that role would require omnipotence. Leopold observed, "Whatever may be the equation for men and land, it is improbable that we as yet know all its terms. Recent discoveries in mineral and vitamin nutrition reveal unsuspected dependencies in the up-circuit: incredibly minute quantities of certain substances determine the value of soils to plants, of plants to animals. What of the down-circuit? What of the vanishing species, the preservation of which we now regard as an esthetic luxury? They helped build the soil; in what unsuspected ways may they be essential to its maintenance?"

Writing more than 50 years ago, Leopold penned words that—soberingly—still ring true today. "In our attempts to save the bigger cogs and wheels, we are still pretty naive. A little repentance just before a species goes over the brink is enough to make us feel virtuous. When the species is gone we have a good cry and repeat the performance."

5,158 acres
11942 FM 848
Tyler, TX 75707
903/566-1626

DRIVING TIMES FROM:
Amarillo: 8 hours
Austin: 4 hours
Brownsville: 10 hours
Dallas: 1.5 hours
El Paso: 12.5 hours
Houston: 4 hours
San Antonio: 5.5 hours
DIRECTIONS: From Tyler, take U.S. 69 north 11 miles to Lindale. At Lindale, at the intersection of U.S. 69 and FM 16, turn right. Go about 1 mile to FM 2710. Take FM 2710 northeast 5 miles to its intersection with County Roads 452 and 4106. Go straight ahead on County Road 4106. After 0.5 mile, 4106 takes a left at its intersection with County Road 4128. Follow 4106 about a mile to the entrance of the WMA; at that point go straight ahead through an open gate to the information kiosk.
OPEN: Daily except during Special Permit hunts.
ACTIVITIES: Wildlife viewing, hiking, bicycling, hunting, fishing.
FACILITIES: Primitive boat ramps, primitive hunters' camp, hiking trails, information kiosk.
SPECIAL REGULATIONS: All visitors must register. Parking is allowed at designated parking areas only. Horses may be used by prior arrangement. Waterfowl hunting hours end at noon. Trapping is not allowed. Use of buckshot is not allowed.
ADVISORIES: Mosquitoes, poison ivy, and poisonous snakes are present on the area. Flooding may occur during rises of the Sabine River. Access is limited due to lack of roads. Wear waterproof footwear. Carry your own supply of potable water.
LODGING IN AREA: Motels are available in Tyler and Lindale.
LOCAL POINTS OF INTEREST: Tyler State Park, Governor Hogg Shrine State Historical Park, Lake Tawakoni State Park, Purtis Creek State Park, Texas State Railroad, Jim Hogg State Historical Park, Texas Freshwater Fisheries Center.
DISABILITY ACCESS: Not wheelchair-accessible.

HISTORY

Smith County was home to Caddo and later Cherokee Indians. Anglo settlement did not begin in earnest until after the Cherokees were forced from the area in 1839. Development on what is now the WMA was restricted due to frequent flooding of the area. In recent times the land was used primarily for petroleum production and hunting.

Approximately half of Old Sabine Bottom WMA was purchased in 1993 and 1994 to prevent its acquisition by interests who wanted to log the hardwood timber. The Texas Department of Transportation funded the purchase of additional acreage as mitigation for future highway projects. A small tract was donated by private owners.

The area is one of 14 bottomland hardwood preservation sites in Texas rated "Priority One" by the U.S. Fish and Wildlife Service. Together with the Little Sandy National Wildlife Refuge located just across the Sabine River, it comprises one of the largest intact bottomland hardwood forests in Texas.

GEOGRAPHY AND NATURAL FEATURES

The Old Sabine Bottom WMA is composed almost entirely of bottomland hardwoods within the floodplain of the Sabine River. It takes its name from the fact that it lies principally between the present Sabine River and an old channel. The terrain is quite

Open pastureland on the western end of the Old Sabine Bottom WMA forms a stark contrast to the balance, which is subject to periodic flooding.

flat, with generally less than 1 percent slope. Numerous shallow sloughs and small lakes, remnants of old river channels, pockmark the area.

An area of about 221 acres on the extreme western end of the WMA is open pastureland. The rest is dominated by an oak-elm-hackberry forest with an understory that includes redbud, possum-haw holly, dewberry, blackberry, greenbriar, poison oak, and Virginia creeper. Giant cane, dwarf palmetto, and various sedges are also present.

The area is subject to flooding several times a year; however, this flooding is not the violent type with rushing waters. Instead, backwater from the Sabine River typically rises slowly and quietly into the area as the river spills into numerous drainages. Witnessing one of these events borders on the mystical. Water silently creeps into places dry only hours before, winding among trees and rising slowly higher until it spills through culverts and finally inundates the entire area. The process is so quiet and so gradual as to be almost eerie.

One oilfield service road enters the area and has two short side roads associated with it. Otherwise, access to the area is via a network of footpaths

that follow old jeep trails dating from the time when the area was leased for hunting. The remains of old hunting cabins and blinds dot the area; all are in disrepair and are unsafe to enter.

Wildlife on the area includes squirrels, white-tailed deer, feral hogs, rabbits, and waterfowl. Neotropical migrants are common in spring. Beavers are numerous and active, as are timber rattlesnakes and water moccasins. Eastern wild turkeys were stocked on nearby property and are increasing in number.

Note that access to the area from County Road 4106 is via a 100-foot-wide corridor. Private land is on both sides of the road until you cross the old channel of the Sabine River. From that point the first parking area lies about another mile down the road. *Do not leave the main road until you are sure you are on the WMA.*

RECREATIONAL OPPORTUNITIES

Old Sabine Bottom WMA has made great strides toward being user-friendly, especially for nonconsumptive users. Roads, trails, and parking lots are well signed: see the map posted in the information kiosk at the entrance. Wildlife viewing, hiking,

bicycling, hunting, and fishing are offered.

Because the area is subject to flooding from the Sabine River any time water is released from lakes upstream, *always* call ahead before visiting. The area manager monitors river flow using the Sabine River Authority's website and can predict conditions two to three days in advance.

WILDLIFE VIEWING

Neotropical migrants, wood ducks, mallards, snowy egrets, barred owls, white-tailed deer, and beavers are the main wildlife species. Posters in the entrance information kiosk show some animals to watch for.

PRO'S POINTERS. "This is a great place to see prothonotary warblers from late March into early May, because they nest here," says area manager Larry LeBeau. "This riparian habitat with bottomlands provides all the elements they need. They are cavity nesters, and this area has lots of snags—dead trees with limbs broken off. That's what they use for their homes. Wood ducks use similar habitat. They nest side by side on the area—the nest boxes for wood ducks you see at ponds have separate entry holes and compartments for both species. Walk along the Channel Trail and look along the old oxbows adjacent to the trail. About a mile and a half down that trail is King Lake, which has both wood ducks and prothonotary warblers."

Wildlife technician Steve Lange adds, "A lot of snowy egrets and great blue herons use King Lake during September and early October for roosting before they migrate south. King Lake is also the largest roosting site for ducks. It's not uncommon to see 500 to 700 ducks on the lake at night." King Lake can also be reached from FM 1804 on the Channel Trail,

Beavers are mainly nocturnal and seldom seen, but ample evidence of their presence exists.

a walk of about a mile, or from the Duck Marsh parking area along the King Lake Trail, about three-quarters of a mile.

The Beaver Slough Trail passes just north of some sloughs that are wood duck and warbler habitat. The actual beaver pond, which is about 2.75 miles from the Oak Tree parking area, is also habitat for these birds.

The Long Lake Trail traverses similar habitat. Long Lake is about half a mile northwest of the Duck Marsh parking area and continues for about a mile along the south side of the trail.

Indigo buntings, summer and scarlet tanagers use the area, but they are top-canopy dwellers, and since the canopy is high overhead, they are difficult to spot. Good binoculars are a must.

The quality of fall waterfowl viewing depends on the water conditions at migration time. If the bottomland is dry, the birds won't stop. Mallards and wood ducks will be abundant in years when the area has flooding and there are are acorns on the ground. December is the best month as a rule. Check with the area manager before visiting.

HIKING

Old Sabine Bottom WMA is a hiker's paradise. It has 24 miles of trails, all signed. These are the River Trail, Channel Trail, Short Trail, King Lake Trail, Long Lake Trail, Turkey Trail, Beaver Slough Trail, East Trail, and Palmetto Bend Trail. Except for the River Trail, which follows the terrace of the present Sabine River, and a brief segment of the Channel Trail's western end, all are in bottomland habitat. The trails follow old jeep roads and are well shaded. All interconnect, making possible a variety of loop walks along various segments of different trails.

PRO'S POINTERS. Consult the area map at the entrance information kiosk for trail locations. Some trails begin at designated parking areas (where you

are required to park); reaching others requires a short walk from a parking area along another trail. Wear waterproof footwear when hiking these trails, as they cross many low, muddy areas. There is no drinking water along any of the routes.

The western terminus of the River and Channel trails is at an entry point on FM 1804 about half a mile south of the Sabine River. The trails begin by crossing an old native pasture. Walking this section of the trails is a lesson in plant succession. Low areas are dominated by wetland plants, but with a two- or three-foot change in elevation, vegetation changes to various grasses, wildflowers and trees. The single trail from the parking area splits in about a quarter of a mile into the two main trails. The River Trail is

4 miles one way; the Channel Trail 3.75 miles. However, you can walk an approximately 3-mile loop by following either trail about 1.25 miles to the Short Trail and using it to connect to the other. This walk passes through open grasslands, along the Sabine River, by King Lake, and through bottomlands along the old channel of the Sabine, giving a good overview of all the habitat types on the area. When the water is high, King Lake will cover the trail, forcing you to backtrack.

For another popular walk, park at the Duck Marsh parking lot and walk northwest along the Turkey Trail to the King Lake Trail, then go west on the King Lake Trail to the Channel Trail, then southeast along the Channel Trail to the main road. Follow the

road back to the Duck Marsh parking lot. This approximately 3.25-mile walk passes by Long Lake, King Lake, and the old channel of the Sabine.

For an all-day hike of about 16 miles, park at the Oak Tree parking area and follow the Beaver Slough Trail east about 3 miles to where it crosses the Palmetto Bend Trail. Turn left onto the Palmetto Bend Trail to reach Beaver Slough in another half a mile. This large beaver pond has many dead snags that serve as nest sites for prothonotary warblers and

Abundant duckweed on sloughs and oxbow lakes attracts mallards and wood ducks during the winter; the sight of brilliantly colored ducks descending through the trees like falling leaves is almost magical.

152

wood ducks. From Beaver Slough, continue east; in about another 1.25 miles the Palmetto and Beaver Slough trails meet, and you can either loop back or continue on the Palmetto Bend Trail another 2 miles to its end, then backtrack. The last section of the trail passes through an area with a heavy growth of dwarf palmettos.

For an easy walk, park at any of the parking areas along the main road and walk its graveled surface. The walk from the Sabine River parking area to the Oil Patch parking area is about a mile one-way and passes just steps from the river at its midpoint; footpaths lead to the riverbank.

BICYCLING

Biking is allowed on any of the 24 miles of trails shown on the area map posted in the entrance information kiosk as well as on the main road, which totals 3.75 miles. See the section on hiking, above, for descriptions of some of the trails.

PRO'S POINTERS. "For touring bikes, the main road will be best," says LeBeau. This road has an all-weather surface. It goes from the entrance to the Sabine River; a side road follows the river upstream to an oil well pad, passing very near the riverbank at its midpoint.

"The best time of the year for mountain biking is from July into September, because the trails will probably be dry," says LeBeau. "The River Trail will normally be dry any time, because it is on the river terrace. The East Trail and the Palmetto Bend Trail will probably be the driest at other times." The trails are kept reasonably cleared, but there may be downed trees across them in places, and they may be grown up in grass. If you like mud, try the Old Channel Trail or the Beaver Slough Trail, especially the latter.

HUNTING

Hunting is available by Annual Public Hunting Permit for white-tailed deer, feral hogs, waterfowl, squirrels, rabbits, and hares. Special Permit hunts are held for deer. For species, seasons, and bag limits, see the *Public Hunting Lands Map Booklet,* the *Applications for Drawings on Public Hunting Lands,* and the *Outdoor Annual* for the current year.

PRO'S POINTERS. Deer and feral hogs may be taken during archery season. Hunters must sign in but are free to hunt anywhere on the area. "This is a high-traffic area during bow season," says LeBeau. "Hunting during the week rather than on a weekend will give you an advantage. The farther you walk, the better chance you will have of seeing animals. Hunt where the least number of people are. However, you don't always have to walk far; some of the best hunting places on this area are only 200 yards from the main roads, but they are between parking areas, and most people don't hunt them."

Lange adds, "Everything here is based on food. We have a bottomland hardwood habitat, but only certain groups of trees produce in a given year. For example, we may have only water oak acorns. Wherever the acorns are, that's where you will find the game."

Archery hunters have the opportunity to hunt the prerut and the rut. "The rut is generally the last week in October and the first week in November," says Lange. "Look for scrapes and rubs paralleling the watercourses. When the leaves are off the trees, you can see much farther through the understory, and it's tempting to hunt away from the drainages where visibility is better. But deer travel parallel to the drainages, often moving between switchcane thickets and the edge of the drainage. The switchcane is 6 to 7 feet tall and looks like bamboo. It stays green during the winter, so it's easy to find."

For Special Permit hunts, the area is divided into nine compartments ranging from 400 to 500 acres each. "We do allow ATVs," says LeBeau, "because it can be 10 or 12 miles to a compartment. We will let people choose compartments when possible. Compartments 7, 8, and 9 are accessible only by ATV or by foot. All animals must be checked in at the check station during Special Permit hunts; we will help people bring game in from the field."

One reason hunts at Old Sabine Bottom are popular is that Texas Parks and Wildlife personnel working Special Permit hunts camp out with the hunters. Primitive camping is allowed at the check station during the draw hunts. "We have a campfire, bring a barbecue pit, and cook feral hog for the hunters and always have a pot of beans going," says LeBeau. "We try to help people have a traditional deer camp experience, and they really seem to enjoy it." Don't spend too much time in camp, however; LeBeau points out that deer pattern hunters very well, and the better bucks tend to move between 10 A.M. and 2 P.M., when most hunters are in camp.

Feral hogs may be hunted during archery season and the fall squirrel season, and there is a gun hog season from late January through February during which any legal weapon may be used. Baiting is not allowed. "One of the first things to look for is fresh rooting," says Lange. "Pigs almost always travel parallel to the water, looking for the softest soil that allows the easiest foraging. It's fun to stalk hunt them here. Find a fresh trail and walk, look, listen for pigs going through the switchcane—you can hear them rooting and squealing." Most breeding activity takes place during the January and February hog season, so boars are more likely to be moving during the day then, looking for sows. Open sights on a shotgun loaded with slugs is the best choice of weapons. Hogs may be taken with .22-caliber firearms during the squirrel season, but this requires accurately placing a shot just behind the ear.

The quality of gray squirrel hunting is very dependent on mast production. The year after a good acorn crop, squirrel hunting can be outstanding. Any firearm except centerfire is allowed for squirrel hunting. "Some people walk and listen for squirrels barking, but I like to sit on just one area," says Lange. "If you see a couple of squirrels in a tree, there will likely be quite a few around. Don't pick up shot squirrels right away. Let the area calm down after a shot. Just sit tight on one tree and you can kill a mess of squirrels.

"Preseason scouting is very effective on squirrels," continues Lange. "Look for pieces of acorns dropped to the ground." Lange also advises concentrating effort at dawn and dusk.

Waterfowl hunting begins with the early teal season, but the area generally remains dry until late October or early November, and that's when waterfowl start to arrive, mostly mallards and wood ducks. "Even in October, the trees will still be using water, so it takes a while before the soil starts holding water," says LeBeau. "The best waterfowl hunting will be in December and January. At that time the canopy is gone, and the ducks can see the potholes and feeding areas in the bottom really well, and they come into them in droves." Ducks feed on acorns amid the standing timber as well as on duckweed growing in the sloughs. A waterfowl hunting map showing all the bodies of water on the area in relation to trails, roads, and parking areas is available at the information kiosk.

"When the water is up, hunters can access the WMA by boat," points out Lange. There is a primitive boat launch where FM 1804 crosses the Sabine River and another where the main road reaches the river. "Most hunters put in a boat and follow the sloughs back into the area and hunt the freshly flooded timber. Most

people who hunt here have camouflaged boats and boat blinds. Often they wear waders and hide their boats and wade out into the flooded timber, put out decoys, and start calling." Don't stop hunting if shooting slows after an early flurry of wood ducks. "Wood ducks usually come in earlier than mallards, because they stay right here on the area," Lange explains. "Mallards may not arrive for as much as three hours after legal shooting time begins."

Fishing

Catfish, crappie, and largemouth bass are the main species taken on the area and in the Sabine River.

PRO'S POINTERS. "Spring rises on the river are the time to go catfishing," says LeBeau. "You'll catch blues, channels, and yellow cats. Most people trotline and limbline with live river minnows. Channel cats love crawfish in the springtime—you can dipnet them out of borrow ditches along highway rights of way. Use a single hook and put it right through the meat of the tail. Channel cats follow the banks, so limblines work well. Even trotlines are set parallel to the bank, because the water is slower moving there."

King Lake holds largemouth bass and crappie. The crappie bite is best during the spring spawn; the bass bite better in the summer. Bass fishing is good enough on King Lake that some people dolly a small jonboat in to the lake and then fish along the edge of the timber with jigs. In spring, when the water is high and running through the culverts just inside the entrance to the area, the old river channel is good for crappie and catfish. Put your bait right where water from the culverts eddies and makes a bend on the east side of the main road.

162,854 acres
P.O. Box 868
Livingston, TX 77351
409/327-8487

DRIVING TIMES FROM:
Amarillo: 10 hours
Austin: 3 hours
Brownsville: 7.5 hours
Dallas: 3.5 hours
El Paso: 13.5 hours
Houston: 1 hour
San Antonio: 4.5 hours
DIRECTIONS: From Huntsville, take I-45 south about 10 miles to New Waverly. Follow FM 1375 west 2.5 miles to the U.S. Forest Service district office.
OPEN: Daily.
ACTIVITIES: Camping, wildlife viewing, horseback riding, off-road vehicle riding, hiking, bicycling, hunting, fishing.
FACILITIES: Improved and primitive campgrounds, concessions, swimming area, boat ramps, multiuse trails, mountain bike trails, hiking trails, wildlife-viewing areas, target ranges.
SPECIAL REGULATIONS: Hunters are required to possess an Annual Public Hunting Permit or a Limited Public Use Permit. Target shooting is allowed only in designated areas. Waterfowl shooting hours end at sunset during the early teal season and at noon during the general waterfowl season. Dogs may be used to hunt feral hogs from January 15 to March 15. Camping is restricted to designated campsites only during the archery and gun deer seasons. Trapping is allowed November 1 through March 31. The use of horses is allowed year-round. Deer must be taken to hunter check stations during opening weekend of the gun deer season. For other special regulations see the section entitled "Special Regulations in

The Lone Star Hiking Trail crosses Winter's Bayou via this iron bridge near Montague Church on FM 1725.

Effect on U.S. Forest Service Units" in the current *Public Hunting Lands Map Booklet.*
ADVISORIES: Poison ivy, poisonous snakes, and mosquitoes are abundant. Summer heat and humidity are high. The national forest is composed of numerous noncontiguous parcels of land; avoid trespassing on private property. Boaters on Lake Conroe beware of submerged stumps. Carry your own supply of potable water.
LODGING IN AREA: Motels are available in Huntsville, Conroe, Coldspring, Cleveland, and other nearby towns.
LOCAL POINTS OF INTEREST: Huntsville State Park, Lake Livingston State Park, Fanthorp Inn State Historical Park, Lake Houston State Park, Fort Boggy State Park, Big Thicket National Preserve.
DISABILITY ACCESS: Restrooms and some campsites in developed campgrounds are wheelchair-accessible.

HISTORY

Prior to European settlement this part of Texas was home to several Indian tribes who hunted, farmed corn, and traded with western tribes such as the Comanches. As Europeans extended their settlements up the Trinity and San Jacinto Rivers, the Indians were displaced. Settlers raised cotton, corn and livestock.

Lumbering began after the Civil War as railroads began to penetrate East Texas. Lands now in the national forest were logged between the 1880s and 1930s. Most logging was high-grading, which took only the larger trees, and no effort was made to reforest cut-over areas. By the 1930s the loss of timber resources and the advent of the Great Depression created severe economic hardship in the area.

The purchase of lands for the national forests in Texas began in the mid-1930s. Buying land within proposed national forest boundaries was authorized, but the right of eminent domain was not used to acquire land. Therefore, land was purchased only from people willing to sell it to the government. The result was a patchwork of private and public land spread over three counties. Land acquisition continues to the present.

For half a century little effort was made to regulate hunting and improve wildlife habitat. Not until 1981 did Texas Parks and Wildlife become involved in wildlife management in national forests in Texas, and hunting on Sam Houston National Forest

lands continued to be largely unregulated until 1993, when the area was made part of the public hunting program.

GEOGRAPHY AND NATURAL FEATURES

Sam Houston National Forest WMA is the largest wildlife management area in Texas. It stretches approximately 50 miles east to west and about 35 miles north to south. However, the image of the national forest presented on most maps is misleading, since it is shown as a solid block. This area conforms to the boundaries authorized by Congress, but only the part of the forest west of New Waverly resembles anything like a contiguous mass. East of I-45 the holdings are highly fragmented.

Most of the area is level to gently rolling and is completely forested. The upper reaches of Lake Conroe, on the San Jacinto River, lie within the WMA's western portion. Winter Bayou slices across the southeastern part of the area. Little Lake Creek parallels FM 149 on the western part of the forest. Double Lake is a 23-acre impoundment within the recreation area of the same name. Otherwise, the only sources of water are small creeks and ponds.

The native longleaf pines cut by loggers were replaced with loblolly and shortleaf pines. Hardwoods are found in a few scattered upland sites. Most of the pine trees were planted during reforestation efforts during the 1930s and are contained in even-aged stands.

The area is crossed by a number of pipelines and power lines as well as numerous old logging roads. Some of these, as well as small openings, are planted as wildlife food plots. In addition, a network of U.S. Forest Service roads, county roads, and state and national highways reaches most tracts of public land. Highly irregular boundaries coupled with numerous inholdings of private land sometimes make it difficult to know when one is on public land, especially in the portions of the WMA east of I-45. The portion of the national forest west of New Waverly has larger contiguous blocks of public land and is, for the most part, the most appealing part of the area for recreational uses.

Sam Houston National Forest WMA contains two developed U.S. Forest Service recreation areas, the Little Lake Creek Wilderness, the Big Creek Scenic Area, nearly 70 miles of designated off-road vehicle trails and the 130-mile Lone Star Hiking Trail.

White-tailed deer, squirrels and eastern wild turkeys are the principal game animals found in the forest. Feral hogs, bobcats, gray foxes, and river otters are also present. Numerous bird species may be seen, including bald eagles, neotropical migrants, and the endangered red-cockaded woodpecker.

RECREATIONAL OPPORTUNITIES

CAMPING

In keeping with U.S. Forest Service policy, camping is allowed anywhere on national forest land *except* during the archery and gun deer-hunting seasons. During this time, camping is restricted to 10 designated camping areas. Of these, three are open year-round and offer some facilities, while the balance are primitive campgrounds consisting basically of mowed areas.

PRO'S POINTERS. Most developed of the campgrounds is Double Lake Recreation Area, which has over 60 campsites equipped with picnic tables, tent pads, lantern holders, and campfire rings or cooking grills. Sites with water, electrical, and sewer hookups are available. Restrooms with showers serve the area. Entry and camping fees are charged. A concession stand (open seasonally) offers groceries and rents boats for use on the 23-acre lake. Only electric motors are allowed on the lake. To reach this camping area, take Texas 150 west from Coldspring about 2 miles to FM 2025. Go south on FM 2025 for 0.4 mile to the entrance.

The Stubblefield Lake Recreation Area, also a fee area, has campsites with no hookups and restrooms with showers. To reach this area, follow FM 1375 west from New Waverly about 10 miles to Forest Road 215 (Stubblefield Road). Go north on Forest Road 215 for 0.6 mile, then veer right at its intersection with Forest Road 208 and continue on 215 about another 2 miles to the campground.

The Kelly's Pond camping area charges no fee but offers only picnic tables, lantern posts, and trash bins. It surrounds a small pond. To reach this area, follow FM 1375 west from New Waverly about 10 miles to Forest Road 204, which joins the highway opposite Forest Road 215. Go south on Forest Road 204 for 0.7 mile to Forest Road 271, then turn right onto 271 and follow it 1.2 miles.

Primitive hunter camping areas are located throughout the forest. These areas and directions for reaching them are as follows:

- A strip of forest 150 feet wide along both sides of Forest Road 271. See directions to Kelly's Pond, above.

- A strip of forest 150 feet wide along both sides of Forest Road 208H. To reach this area, follow FM 1375 about 10 miles west of New Waverly to Forest Road 215. Follow 215 north for 0.6 miles to its intersection with Forest Road 208, which goes straight ahead. Follow 208 another 3.6 miles to Forest Road 208H; turn right and continue 0.3 mile through a clear-cut area to pullouts among the trees.

- A cleared area off Forest Road 234 is on the left 0.1 mile south of its intersection with FM 1375. Forest Road 234 is 4.1 miles west of I-45 at New Waverly.

The Double Lake Recreation Area offers developed campsites, but many primitive campsites are also available.

- The Four Notch hunter camp is located on Forest Road 213. To reach the area, take U.S. 190 east from Huntsville 4 miles to FM 2929. Follow FM 2929 south 4.1 miles to its intersection with FM 2296. Cross FM 2296 and continue on Four Notch Road (unsigned) for 2.4 miles to Forest Road 213; the camping area is about a mile east on 213.

- The Big Woods hunter camp is on Forest Road 202. To reach this camp, take FM 150 west from Coldspring about 8 miles to the Evergreen community. Half a mile west of Evergreen, turn north onto John Warren Road, which becomes Forest Road 202. The hunter camp lies on the right side of the road 5.4 miles from FM 150.

- Neblett's hunter camp serves an isolated block of forest southeast of Maynard. To reach it, take FM 1725 east from Maynard for 4 miles to FM 3081. Turn south onto FM 3081 and go 1.5 miles to Forest Road 228. Turn left and follow 228 for 1.7 miles to the camping area.

- The Shell hunter camp is on Forest Road 274. From Cleveland, go north on FM 2025 about 6 miles to FM 945. Go west on FM 945 for 2 miles to Forest Road 274; turn left and go 0.5 mile to the camping area.

- Tarkington hunter camp is a strip of land 150 feet wide just east of Forest Road 217A. From Coldspring, go west on Texas 150 for 2 miles to FM 2025. Follow FM 2025 south 5.1 miles to FM 2666. Go east on 2666 about three-fourths of a mile to Forest Road 217A. Turn right and go 0.4 mile, then turn left and go about 0.2 mile to the camping area.

- A Lone Star Hiking Trail primitive camp on Forest Road 220 also serves as a hunter camp. From the intersection of Texas 150 and FM 2025 west of Coldspring, go south on FM 2025 for 2.9 miles to Forest Road 220. Turn left and follow 220 for 0.8 mile to the camping area along Double Lake Branch.

WILDLIFE VIEWING

One of the striking things about Sam Houston National Forest, especially the portion west of New Waverly, is the abundance of red-cockaded woodpecker sites. Over 400 adults of this endangered species inhabit the forest, the second-largest population west of the Mississippi River. In addition, a wide variety of other species may be seen.

PRO'S POINTERS. The distinguishing feature to look for on the red-cockaded woodpecker is the ladder-back pattern; the male's red cockade is very small and generally visible only during the breeding season.

There are two designated viewing

sites where Dawn Carrie, wildlife biologist for the U.S. Forest Service, says a red-cockaded woodpecker sighting is almost guaranteed. "A red-cockaded woodpecker (RCW) interpretive site is just south of the intersection of FM 2025 and FM 2666. There's a parking area, a sign, and an active colony of birds. Be there just before sunrise or an hour before sunset and you are almost certain to see birds." Birds may be active around nest sites any time of day during the nesting season from April to June.

Another RCW interpretive site is on FM 1375 about 2.4 miles west of the U.S. Forest Service district office. In addition, there are dozens of colony sites scattered along forest service roads. These may be easily identified by the blue-green bands painted around trees with nesting cavities and the relative lack of under-

Double Lake is a 23-acre impoundment that offers fishing; boat rentals are available seasonally.

story. Sites are along FM 149 at 0.7, 3.9 and 4.2 miles south of its intersection with FM 1375. Forest Road 208 has sites at points 0.6 and 2.0 miles north of FM 1375. Forest Road 204 has numerous sites but is heavily traveled and quite dusty. (Forest Service Road 204 is signed Stubblefield Road where it crosses FM 1375 about 5 miles west of the U.S. Forest Service district office.) Other sites—nearly 170 in all—are scattered throughout the forest. These sites are also good places to spot red-headed woodpeckers, which tend to inhabit the same type of habitat as the red-cockaded woodpecker.

There is no bird list for the national forest, but birding is excellent. "On the east side, Big Creek Scenic Area is great for neotropicals in April and May," says Carrie. "Migrants such as Blackburnian warblers, bay-breasted warblers, American redstarts, magnolia warblers, and scarlet tanagers may be spotted. The Lone Star Hiking Trail goes through this

area, which also has other trails." To reach the trailhead parking lot, go east on FM 2666 for 2.5 miles from its intersection with FM 2025. Turn left onto Forest Road 221 and go 0.5 mile to Forest Road 217. Turn right and follow 217 for 0.9 mile to the parking lot. A signboard for the trail system is just across the footbridge.

In Big Creek Scenic Area "Louisiana waterthrushes nest right around the bridge just off the parking lot," says Carrie. "You may also see wood thrushes, Acadian flycatchers, summer tanagers, Swainson's warblers, barred owls, screech owls, hooded warblers, Kentucky warblers and pine warblers. Hooded warblers are everywhere in streamside thickets." A 5-mile stretch of the Lone Star Hiking Trail runs from the Double Lake Recreation Area to the Big Creek Scenic Area and offers good birding along its length.

To view species attracted to more open areas, try the Sunoco tract, an area once mined for iron ore that is now weedy and grassy. Forest Road 2112 leads into the area off FM 2025

3 miles south of its intersection with FM 2666. If the gate is closed, walk-in access is still permitted. "Here you can see indigo and painted buntings and blue grosbeaks," Carrie says. "The Sunoco tract has lots of wintering sparrows—swamp sparrows, song sparrows, white-throated sparrows, Lincoln's sparrows, Henslow's sparrows. For the latter, you have to form a line, walk, and flush them out."

Yellow-throated warblers frequent willows along the shore of Lake Conroe. One good place to see them is at the boat ramp off Forest Road 205, which runs south from FM 1375 about 2 miles west of the U.S. Forest Service district office. "You may also see bald eagles in this area—6 to 10 winter on the lake," says Carrie. "We also have a nesting pair."

Anywhere you find mature pines—trees 70 to 80 feet tall and 14 inches or more in diameter—you are likely to see a Piney Woods resident, the brownheaded nuthatch. Listen for their squeaky call.

"Lake Conroe is not great for birding because grass carp eat the vegetation and we get few ducks on the lake," advises Carrie. "We do get Forster's terns all winter and black terns in spring and fall, as well as Bonaparte's gulls. There are quite a few wood ducks in coves and up the creeks. You can bird from a canoe up the West Fork of the San Jacinto River near the Stubblefield Recreation Area, or follow the Stubblefield nature trail."

The Scott's Ridge boat ramp off Forest Road 212 in the far southwest corner of the forest, off FM 1097, is a good place to see bald eagles near their roost in early morning from December to February. A heron rookery in the cove will have great and little blue herons, great egrets, and snowy egrets.

Carrie says people who like to observe herptiles will not be disappointed. "We have canebreak rattlesnakes, Louisiana milk snakes, Texas rat snakes, copperheads, and lots of frogs and toads."

River otters can be seen in the East Fork of the San Jacinto River and in Double Lake, usually in winter when are there fewer people about. Also look for them along the Lake Conroe shore and in Winters Bayou. "You'll see a lot of wildlife from a canoe," Carrie advises. "Put in off Forest Road 274 on Winters Bayou, about three-quarters of a mile north of FM 1725. Don't attempt it during low water. Call 409/344-6205 for the current water level."

Hiking

Sam Houston National Forest is a hiker's paradise. In addition to the 130-mile Lone Star Hiking Trail, there are shorter trails through the Big Creek Scenic Area and the Little Lake Creek Wilderness. In addition, some 69 miles of multiuse trails are available for hiking as well as equestrian, mountain bike, motorcycle, and all-terrain vehicle use. Foot traffic only is allowed on the Lone Star Hiking Trail.

PRO'S POINTERS. The Lone Star Hiking Trail runs from the southeastern corner of the forest near Montague Church, on FM 1725 northeast of Cleveland, to the western edge near Richards. This primitive trail is a cleared path that sometimes is just a green tunnel through the undergrowth and at other times follows pipeline rights-of-way, roads, old tram roadbeds, and game trails. It does cross private property from time to time. Aluminum markers nailed to trees indicate the route. Loop trails have orange tape across the center of the markers, and crossovers between the main trail and loop trails are marked with white tape. The trail is best shown on the 1:126,720 scale map of the forest for sale at the U.S. Forest Service district office. An information sheet about the trail is also available there.

Camping is allowed anywhere along the trail except during the archery and gun deer-hunting seasons, when camping is restricted to the designated sites listed in the camping section, above. Suggested camping areas are indicated by three aluminum markers nailed to a tree. Water is not available along the trail except at Stubblefield and Double Lake Recreation Areas. All trash must be packed out.

Short sections of the trail may be easily hiked by accessing the trail where it crosses highways and forest service roads. The western trailhead is located on Forest Road 219 immediately south of its intersection with FM 149. Another good access point is the parking lot on FM 149 about 1.2 miles south of its intersection with FM 1375. The trail crosses the highway again at 3.6 miles south of FM 1375, where there is a parking lot for the Little Lake Creek Wilderness. The wilderness area has a lot of beaver ponds, which makes for good birding. The Stubblefield Recreation Area has an access point at the far end of the camping area. A trailhead with parking lot is on FM 2666 about 1.2 miles east of its intersection with FM 2025, and another is nearby at the parking lot for the Big Creek Scenic Area on Forest Road 217. "Big Creek is a great place—it has short loops as well as longer trails and is very pretty," says Carrie. "It's also possible to camp at Double Lake Recreation Area and hike the 5 miles to Big Creek."

Carrie also recommends the section of the Lone Star Hiking Trail from Montague Church on FM 1725. This section of trail crosses Winter's Bayou via an iron bridge. Snowbells bloom along the route in March. It's about a 6-mile walk to FM 945 and back.

Less appealing to hikers is the network of multiuse trails, which are open to off-road vehicles and horseback riders as well as hikers. All these trails loop back to the starting point and are marked with square aluminum or plastic markers. Red arrows indicate the permitted direction of travel. Trailheads for the multiuse trails are located on Forest Road 233 about 2.5 miles north of FM 1375, and on Forest Road 208 about 1 mile north of FM 1375.

Bicycling

The only designated bicycling trail (in fact, the only one of its kind on any of the national forests and grasslands of Texas) is the Double Lake Mountain Bike Trail, an 8-mile single-track path that loops around the Double Lake Recreation Area.

PRO'S POINTERS. This sandy trail is usable in almost any weather, although there are a few places that can get muddy after rains. There are no steep hills. Use caution when crossing paved roads. Other hazards are fallen trees, low branches, exposed roots, and soft spots at corners.

Bicycles are allowed on the multiuse trail, but it is too rough for most bikes. "Most people ride on the graveled roads and pipeline rights-of-way," says Carrie.

One graveled road to avoid is Forest Road 204 because of heavy traffic and choking dust. Much more pleasant are Forest Roads 258, 208, 216, and 234. For a 4.6-mile one-way trip to Lake Conroe and the Stow-a-Way Marina, which has a restaurant, follow Forest Road 234 south from its intersection with FM 1375 about 1.7 miles west of the U.S. Forest Service district office. Along the way are roadside pullouts with access to the lakeshore. To reach the marina, go straight ahead at mile 3.7, where the forest road joins a paved road.

Mechanical vehicles are not allowed in the Little Lake Creek Wilderness Area.

Equestrian Trails

Horseback riding is allowed anywhere in the national forest except on the Lone Star Hiking Trail and in the Big Creek Scenic Area. The multipurpose trail, forest service roads, and pipeline rights-of-way are open to horses.

PRO'S POINTERS. "A lot of pipelines on the eastern side of the forest intersect, making for nice loops," says Carrie. For more information on equestrian use, contact Marilyn Kinney with the Sam Houston Forest Equestrian Association at 409/264-2550.

Target Shooting

Sam Houston National Forest WMA has four target-shooting areas. Any legal firearm is allowed on three; the other is for shotguns only. No permit is required for using these areas. No targets or target holders are provided, only a place to shoot. Roads to these areas are signed, but signs may be missing.

PRO'S POINTERS. One shooting area is at the end of Forest Road 208A. To reach this area, follow Forest Road 215 (Stubblefield Road) north from FM 1375 about 6 miles west of the U.S. Forest Service district office. After 0.6 mile, go straight ahead on Forest Road 208. Continue for 2.5 miles to Forest Road 208A, turn right, and go 1.3 miles to the shooting area.

Another shooting area lies on the west side of Forest Road 202 about 2 miles north of the Big Woods hunter camp (see directions above).

A third target range is on Forest Road 255 south of FM 1725. From the intersection of FM 3081 and FM 1725, go south on FM 1725 for l mile to Forest Road 255. Turn right onto 255 and follow it for 0.5 mile, bear right, and go another 0.2 mile to the shooting area.

The shotgun-only shooting area is at the end of Forest Road 280. From the intersection of Texas 150 and FM 2025 west of Coldspring, go south on 2025 for 2.1 miles to Forest Road 280. Turn right and follow 280 for 0.6 mile, turn right, and continue another 0.5 mile to the shooting area.

Hunting

U.S. Forest Service policy is to provide for maximum hunting opportunity. Hunting is allowed for a wide variety of species, but only those discussed below are present in sufficient numbers to make a successful hunt likely. For information on legal species, seasons, and bag limits, see the *Public Hunting Lands Map Booklet* and the *Outdoor Annual* for the current year. Youth-only and youth-adult hunts are generally available.

All persons 17 years of age and older who possess a centerfire or muzzleloading rifle, a handgun, a shotgun with shot larger than #2 steel or #4 lead or archery equipment with broadheads must possess an Annual Public Hunting Permit unless they are in one of the designated target practice areas. Persons 17 and older with guns using rimfire ammunition, shotguns with smaller size shot than listed above, and archery equipment with field points must possess either the Annual Public Hunting Permit or a Limited Public Use Permit unless they are in a target practice area.

PRO'S POINTERS. "There are good deer all over the place, but getting them in sight is a problem. They really hole up," says area manager Chris Gregory. "Burned areas or hardwood bottoms offer the best hunting. Areas where timber has been cut to contain pine borer infestations will be good for a year or two after the trees were felled."

Gregory advises avoiding hunting the first two and last two weekends of the gun season. "Hunt mid-season or mid-week to avoid crowds," he says. "This is not a place where you can come, drive around one day, and figure out where to find deer. There are nice deer for East Texas here, but they are hard to find. It takes a lot of walking and scouting. Get a mile or so away from a road, and you will have a better chance of seeing deer. Find places where deer funnel through between feeding and bedding areas. We don't have big topography changes, so finding deer is more a matter of finding habitat than specific sites."

Gregory says the rut is usually a trickle that may peak around the end of October but may run into December.

All deer must be taken to a check station on the opening weekend of the gun season. Locations are shown on the map in the *Public Hunting Lands Map Booklet.* During the gun season, antlerless deer may be taken only by obtaining a permit before October 1; call 409/639-8501.

Hog hunters should concentrate on hardwood bottoms with acorns in winter. During the special feral hog season from January 15 to March 15, hogs may be hunted with dogs. "There are lots of big hogs near the Big Woods hunter camp, on the south side of Forest Road 202," Gregory says. "In winter they will be in the flooded flats along the creeks." Hog-trapping permits good for six weeks are awarded by drawing. Contact the U.S. Forest Service office at 409/639-8501.

For eastern spring turkey hunting, Gregory recommends hunting on the east side of FM 2025 north of FM 2666. Another likely area for turkeys is just east of Huntsville north of U.S. 190. Gobblers are most likely to come to a call immediately after flying down from the roost in the morning, but they will not usually be very vocal. Successful hunters generally locate a gobbler's roost in the evening by listening to him gobble at fly-up, then return to hunt the next morning by setting up within a hundred yards or so of the roost.

Dove hunting will be best on the Sunoco tract, which has food plots and a pond. To reach it, go south on FM 2025 for 3 miles past its intersection with FM 2666, then take Forest Road 2112 into the area. This road is gated and will be locked during September, but hunters may walk in. Another area that may have doves is an isolated block of land off FM 3081. Take 3081 south from FM 1725 about 4 miles, then take Forest Road 230 into the area.

Squirrels are most numerous in the bottoms along the East Fork of the San Jacinto River, between the river and FM 2025. Also try the Caney Creek bottom between FM 1375 and FM 1791 on the west side of the forest.

Limited waterfowl hunting is available on the upper end of Lake Conroe. "People hunt around the islands south of the FM 1375 bridge, but there are not many ducks on the lake," says Gregory.

FISHING

Fishers are not required to have an Annual Public Hunting Permit. Most fishing is on Lake Conroe, but some ponds on the area have fish. Most of these ponds are small quarter-acre ponds built for livestock and wildlife use.

PRO'S POINTERS. "A lot of people fish in the Stubblefield Recreation Area by the bridge," says Gregory. There is another pond about 200 feet inside the gate at the end of Forest Road 234B, which is about a mile south of FM 1375. Camp Lutcher Pond, which is at the end of Forest Road 204G, can be reached by automobile. Other people continue on down to the end of 204 and fish in Lake Conroe. Small boats can be hand-launched here. On the Sunoco

tract, follow Forest Road 2112 and go left at every fork until you reach a big pond about 1.5 miles from the road. This pond may hold catfish.

Butch Terpe, a full-time guide on Lake Conroe for over 10 years, says the lake offers good largemouth bass, white bass, catfish, and crappie fishing. "In the fall, some largemouths will be shallow around boat docks, riprap, bulkheads, and breakwaters as well as stumps in coves. The FM 1097 bridge structure and the FM 1375 causeway riprap areas are good for bass from fall through winter." Terpe advises fishing submerged humps off points in 18 to 20 feet of water. Jigging slab spoons in winter on deepwater points and humps has produced a number of good bass, including a 12.4-pound one for Terpe.

"During the spawn, from February through April, bass fishing is really good in the backs of coves in Peach Creek and Caney Creek," he reveals. "I like to use lizards, plastic worms, and sometimes a jig. Crawworms work really well. Black, blue, tequila sunrise and pumpkinseed are good

You are almost assured of seeing a red-cockaded woodpecker at one of the two designated viewing sites, but your chances will be much better early and late in the day.

colors. Around rock structures near bridges, use shallow-running crankbaits or minnow-imitating jerkbaits."

Following the spawn, fish move to deeper water off points. "Fish stumps or brush piles in 4 to 10 feet of water using Carolina- or Texas-rigged worms," Terpe advises. "Use a short leader, no more than two feet at most, so you can sense your bite a little faster."

Catfish action is good in fall and winter under the FM 1079 and FM 1375 bridges, in Caney Creek, and in the main San Jacinto River channel in 18 to 35 feet of water. Night crawlers, chicken livers and prepared stinkbaits all work well from summer through winter. "The only time catfish are in the shallows is in spring during the spawn," Terpe says. "Any of the coves in spring may have catfish. They also like the sandy bottom around bulkheads and boat docks in the major coves."

Crappie in winter favor the FM 1097 bridge pilings as well as the roadbed of an old railroad tram across Caney Creek. "The water is 20 to 22 feet deep on top of the roadbed and drops off to 35 feet on the sides," Terpe says. "Stumps and brush piles along it hold crappie. Minnows will always be the best bait, but jigs work, too. The best time for crappie is after the spawn when they begin to feed aggressively, from late March until mid-June. They will be in 10 to 20 feet of water, stacked around submerged brush piles around major points on the lake." Almost every point has brush piles placed there by fishers.

White bass gather to spawn in late February, and the action continues through March. Terpe advises fishing submerged points and humps around the mouths of creeks and coves. "Slab spoons or trolling rigs work well in 15 to 22 feet of water," he says.

INSIDER'S CORNER

THE RED-COCKADED WOODPECKER

Sam Houston National Forest is one of the few places in Texas where you may have a chance to see the endangered red-cockaded woodpecker. The forest is home to 168 known breeding groups and about 420 adult males. The birds won't be easy to spot: They are only about the size of a cardinal, and the red patches on either side of the male's head are hidden unless the bird is agitated. The ladder-rung markings on its back are a more distinctive feature.

The red-cockaded woodpecker (RCW) has declined in numbers due to two main factors: timber management practices and the suppression of fire. Timber harvesting has resulted in a shortage of nesting habitat for the RCW. It is the only North American woodpecker that nests exclusively in living pine trees. It prefers older trees infected with heart rot, which decays the inner wood of the tree and makes it easier to excavate. The RCW also drills a series of holes in the tree, which ooze sticky resin; this deters nest predators such as rat snakes. Logging removes the older, mature trees, eliminating nesting sites.

Historically, pine forests in East Texas were characterized by many large, widely spaced trees and an open, grassy understory. Frequent natural fires kept hardwoods and brush from developing. In today's managed forests, replanting results in closely spaced stands of trees, and the suppression of fire leads to a thick understory. Both prevent the RCW from foraging for insects.

Many other species dependent on a fire-maintained ecosystem have also declined, including the eastern wild turkey, American kestrel, and bobwhite quail.

Forests can be managed in ways that will provide income from timber while at the same time protecting RCW habitat. Instead of clear-cutting, thinning and selective harvest can be used to re-create a more natural habitat. Prescribed burning can be used to keep the understory clear and benefit a variety of species. These techniques are being used on publicly owned lands in East Texas. Private landowners are encouraged to join in the effort by becoming participants in a regional habitat conservation plan. Texas Parks and Wildlife offers technical and financial support for conservation projects through a landowner incentive program.

25,777 acres
Route 2, Box 236C
Omaha, TX 75571
903/884-3800

DRIVING TIMES FROM:
Amarillo: 8.5 hours
Austin: 5.5 hours
Brownsville: 11 hours
Dallas: 2.5 hours
El Paso: 13.5 hours
Houston: 4.5 hours
San Antonio: 7 hours
DIRECTIONS: From Mount Pleasant, take I-30 east 18 miles to U.S. 259. Go south 4 miles on U.S. 259 to Texas 77, then east 1 mile to the area headquarters.
OPEN: Daily except during Special Permit hunts.
ACTIVITIES: Wildlife viewing, hiking, horseback riding, hunting, fishing.
FACILITIES: Office, hunter camping area, hunter check station, boat ramps, equestrian trails.
SPECIAL REGULATIONS: Entrance to the area is permitted only at designated entry points; hunters must sign in and out. Furbearers may be hunted with dogs from December 1 through March 31. All hunters must register on-site and must have a registration form in their possession while hunting. Horses may be used by prior arrangement. Waterfowl hunting hours end at noon. Only hunters are required to possess an Annual Public Hunting Permit. Nonconsumptive users are not required to possess a Limited Public Use Permit.
ADVISORIES: Mosquitoes, buffalo gnats, poison ivy, and poisonous snakes are present on the area. Flooding may occur in wet weather. Access is limited due to lack of roads. Carry your own supply of potable water.

Visitors to White Oak Creek WMA are mystified by this bridge to nowhere, which was placed in the wrong location by the U.S. Army Corps of Engineers because the plans showed it there.

LODGING IN AREA: Motels are available in Mount Pleasant, Daingerfield, and Naples.
LOCAL POINTS OF INTEREST: Caddo Lake State Park, Starr Family State Historical Park, Lake Bob Sandlin State Park.
DISABILITY ACCESS: Not wheelchair-accessible.

HISTORY

White Oak Creek WMA lies in the northeast corner of Texas, on land once occupied by Caddo Indians. Later, France and Spain both claimed the area, and France maintained a military post on the Red River a short distance north of the area for about 50 years after 1719. After the United States purchased the Louisiana Territory in 1803, the region was administered as part of Arkansas. Anglo settlement began in the mid-1830s; in 1836 the Republic of Texas claimed the area and formed Red River County there.

The area remained primarily agricultural until World War II, when increased demand for iron and steel led to the establishment of a steel plant at Daingerfield. Later known as Lone Star Steel, this plant was a major employer until the 1990s.

White Oak Creek WMA came into being as a result of increased environmental awareness. After the

U.S. Army Corps of Engineers proposed building Cooper Lake farther upstream on the Sulphur River in 1955, groups opposed to the destruction of bottomland hardwood habitat filed suit, delaying the project. Not until a supplemental environmental impact statement was filed in 1981 was construction allowed to proceed, and then only on condition that over 25,000 acres of similar habitat be acquired and set aside as mitigation. Acquisition of the land was authorized by Congress in 1986. In 1994 Texas Parks and Wildlife contracted with the Corps of Engineers to manage White Oak Creek WMA. The federal government pays approximately 76 percent of the cost of operating the area, and the state pays the remainder.

GEOGRAPHY AND NATURAL FEATURES

White Oak Creek WMA contains 25,777 acres, most of which is bottomland hardwood habitat, one of the most productive for wildlife. The area runs for about 25 miles along the Sulphur River and its tributary White Oak Creek, containing about 17 miles of the river and 25 miles of the creek within its bounds. The area varies in width from about a mile to about 7 miles.

The upper end of the WMA is dominated by White Oak Creek and

associated bottomlands. It is very thickly forested with large oak trees and tangled undergrowth and is almost swampy in places. Most of this part of the area is bordered by private property consisting of old agricultural fields now in improved pasture.

The section of the WMA between U.S. 259 and U.S. 67 is bottomland at the confluence of the creek and river and is subject to seasonal overflows from the streams. This thickly forested area is laced by numerous gated roads built and numbered by the Corps of Engineers. These roads are closed to vehicles even though gates may have been forced open. Hardwoods and pines cover the uplands and hardwoods the bottomlands. There are cutover areas dating from the period just prior to acquisition of the land by the Corps of Engineers; these have generally grown up into thick tangles of brush, vines and small trees. These areas provide good deer habitat but are so impenetrable as to be virtually unhuntable.

Most of the western end of the WMA and the Fork Bottom, where the river and the creek come together, was at one time part of the Broseco Ranch. This ranch was managed for hunting for many years, and only hardwood and pine trees over 20 inches in diameter were logged. This allowed hardwoods to mature into their prime mast-producing years and greatly benefitted wildlife. When it became obvious the land would be taken for the project, trees as small as 10 to 12 inches were harvested. This had mixed results on habitat quality. Some mast production was lost, but the canopy was opened up, allowing more sunlight to reach the ground and producing more forage and browse.

The area east of U.S. 67 lies along both sides of the Sulphur River and

Areas along White Oak Creek flood when the Sulphur River backs water up into the area. This scene is in the Hill Hole area.

includes significant natural hardwood bottoms with very large oak trees as well as a wetland area managed for waterfowl. The section of WMA north of the Sulphur River and east of U.S. 67 offers very good wildlife viewing and duck hunting but at present has no access except by foot.

White Oak Creek WMA is highly unusual among Texas WMAs in that it has the capability to manage the water in its wetland areas totally for the benefit of wildlife. On most WMAs, there is no dedicated water source, and often water levels in reservoirs are managed for flood control or water supply rather than for the production of waterfowl habitat. Since the timing of draw-downs and flooding is critical, moist-soil management on many WMAs is hit-or-miss. On White Oak Creek WMA, the Sciarra Wetland System of about 600 acres in three moist-soil compartments has its own 235-acre lake, Caney Creek Reservoir, whose sole purpose is to provide the water needed to manage the wetlands properly.

Recreational Opportunities

White Oak Creek WMA offers wildlife viewing, hiking, horseback riding, hunting and fishing. However, access to the vast majority of the area is difficult due to lack of roads and the bottomland character of the land.

Reaching some of the access points requires traveling back roads that are not well signed. Following are directions for reaching major access points, beginning at the western end of the area.

- Follow FM 1993 north from I-30 for 2.1 miles to County Road NE 31A at Cooper's Chapel. Follow 31A for 1.9 miles to an intersection with County Road NE 35. Continue straight ahead on 31A another 0.6 mile to the parking area.

- Proceed as above, except at the intersection with County Road

NE 35, turn right. Go 0.75 mile to an unnamed road, turn left, and go 1 mile to the parking lot on the hill above the creek. Hill Hole is just downstream.

- The final entry point north of I-30 is reached by following FM 1993 north for 2.1 miles to County Road NE 31A at Cooper's Chapel. Continue 0.2 mile to County Road NE 44. Turn right and go 1.8 miles to County Road NE 35, turn right, and go 0.4 mile to the parking area.

- In the center of the area, there are boat ramps on White Oak Creek and the Sulphur River where U.S. 259 crosses.

- An entry point to what is called the Twin Lakes area lies east of U.S. 259 between White Oak Creek and the Sulphur River. To reach it, take U.S. 259 south off I-30. About 50 yards south of the access road for the interstate, turn east onto an unnamed road and go 3.4 miles to the parking area.

- A boat ramp and two other access points are off County Road 4307. Reaching them requires following a roundabout route, since the county road cannot be accessed from I-30. From I-30, take U.S. 259 north to FM 561. Turn right and follow FM 561 0.6 mile to County Road 4307. Turn right and go 5.2 miles to County Road 4331. Turn right and go 0.7 mile to a parking area and boat ramp on the Sulphur River. The parking area is very muddy when wet, and there is a large boghole at the upper end of the ramp, which is very steep. Use of this area is advised only in dry weather and only for persons who have a four-wheel-drive vehicle and are experienced in putting a boat into the water. Do not attempt to launch a boat here by yourself. The other entry points along County Road 4307 are 7 miles and 8.6 miles from FM 561, respectively. These entry points can also be accessed from U.S. 67 north of Naples. Go north on U.S. 67 for 5 miles from its intersection with Texas 77. Turn left onto County Road 4307. The first entry point is 1.1 miles from the highway, the second 2.7 miles, and County Road 4331 leading to the boat ramp on the Sulphur River is 4.5 miles from U.S. 67.

- A boat ramp is at the U.S. 67 bridge over the Sulphur River, 4.4 miles north of the intersection of the U.S. 67/Texas 77 intersection.

- The easternmost entry point gives access to the duck marsh and green-tree reservoir. From the intersection of U.S. 67 and County Road 2512 about 5 miles north of Naples, follow 2512 east for 0.4 mile to County Road 2513. Turn right onto County Road 2513 and go 1.8 miles to the entry point. This road takes several sharp bends and crosses a railroad track along the way.

"I encourage people to bring a compass with them," says area manager John Jones. "It's easy to get turned around when it's overcast. The area runs east and west, so if you walk north or south eventually you will hit the creek, the river, or a boundary fence, all of which will take you to a road."

WILDLIFE VIEWING

The combination of riverine, bottomland hardwood, mixed pine-hardwood uplands, and wetland systems in close proximity results in an abundance of wildlife, especially birds. No bird list exists for the area, but 273 species are known to occur in these types of habitats in East

Wild roses dot the roadsides in places on the White Oak Creek WMA.

Texas. Wading birds, ducks, and neotropical migrants will be the most commonly seen. Viewing wildlife on White Oak Creek can be very rewarding but requires a lot of walking to access the best areas.

PRO'S POINTERS. The best birding opportunities are in the river and creek bottomlands and in the wetland areas. In the spring and summer you can expect to see American egrets, snowy egrets, wood ibises, bitterns, blue-green herons, red-winged blackbirds, prothonotary warblers, indigo buntings, and painted buntings in the wetland areas. As the moist-soil compartments dry up, the mud flats attract stilts, dowitchers, sandpipers, yellowlegs, avocets, and killdeer. Owls, pileated woodpeckers, and hawks are common everywhere on the area. When the river spills over its banks, it washes carp into the compartments, and bald eagles may be seen catching carp and ducks.

To reach the wetland area, begin at the entry point parking lot at the end of County Road 2513. From there a mowed path leads east three-fourths of a mile to the levee around the green-tree reservoir, one of the three moist-soil compartments. The green-tree reservoir is forested with mature oaks. At the point where the mowed path joins the levee, turn left and continue atop the levee to compartments 2 and 3, a total distance of

about a mile. To the left of the levee is Jennings Lake Slough, which holds large numbers of wood ducks. The borrow pits near compartments 2 and 3 hold teal in the fall.

To visit Caney Creek Reservoir, turn right atop the levee at the green-tree reservoir and go about a mile to the lake. There you will see waterfowl, cormorants, egrets, a rookery for cattle egrets, great blue herons, and some white ibises. If you wish you can follow the levee to the left along the south side of the lake and loop around between compartments 2 and 3 to the mowed path in from the entry point; this is about a 5-mile walk.

In fall and winter the most common birds on the area are teal (mostly blue-winged), wood ducks, mallards, pintails, widgeons, gadwalls, shovelers, ringnecked ducks, and coots.

HIKING

There are no designated hiking trails. For easy walking, the best hiking area is in the wetlands area. Walk the levees around the compartments as described above under wildlife viewing. Hiking is also allowed on the equestrian trails (see below).

PRO'S POINTERS. A pleasant walk along upper White Oak Creek begins at the Hill Hole parking area. From the parking lot, cross the road to the walk-in gate and follow the path along the fenceline to the creek about 300 yards down. There you'll find steep-banked Hill Hole, long known as a good catfishing spot. Large trees shade the area, and a path follows the creek bank.

Another good hike is in the Twin Lakes area. From the sign-in station, follow the mowed path about half a mile to where oxbow lakes—old sections of the river channel—hold water. I saw a turkey fly as I pulled into the parking area, and deer tracks were present the entire length of the road. Wild roses and blackberries bloom along the old stream banks. Fireant mounds are large and numerous. Wear good hiking shoes or boots and long pants on this hike, as vegetation gets very tall and rank. Watch out for snakes.

EQUESTRIAN TRAILS

Equestrian trails on the area are being developed and may be used by prior arrangement with the area manager; call 903/884-3800. An Annual Public Hunting Permit or a Limited Public Use Permit is required. The equestrian trails follow the mowed path that parallels the boundary fence.

PRO'S POINTERS. The 11-mile Heard Trail begins at the hunter check station behind the area office. It follows the area boundary fence east and continues to U.S. 67. Most of this trail is within the transition zone between the upland and bottomland areas, but some loops go down to White Oak Creek, so riders will see wooded areas, wetland areas, and open fields.

A longer route is planned that will go up White Oak Creek all the way to Hill Hole, about 15 miles one way. Ask the area manager.

HUNTING

White Oak Creek is managed for maximum hunting opportunities, offering archery and gun deer and hog hunting as well as dove, quail, waterfowl, rabbit, squirrel, and furbearer hunts. Youth-only deer and youth-adult squirrel hunts are offered. For species, seasons, and bag limits, see the *Public Hunting Lands Map Booklet, Applications for Drawings on Public Hunting Lands,* and *Outdoor Annual* for the current year.

PRO'S POINTERS. Dove hunting is limited on the area because no grain is grown in the surrounding area, so hunting season really kicks off the first two weeks in October. It begins not with archery deer hunting, as you might expect, but with the first of two squirrel seasons. "We have a lot more local squirrel hunters than deer hunters here, so we give them the first two weeks of October and from mid-November through mid-January,"

says Jones. "Good squirrel seasons follow a year behind good acorn crops. Hunt areas with big oaks, because they produce the most mast as a rule and are more open, making for easier walking as well."

Archery deer hunts are first-come, first-served; hunters may go anywhere on the area they like. A portable stand of some kind is a must, but lean-on stands work best. "There may or may not be acorns on the ground at that time, but there is a lot of other stuff for deer to eat—poison ivy, greenbriar, ash, locust," says Jones. Key on trails and food sources.

Gun deer hunts are by Special Permit. "We have a 'trickle rut' here—does breed from October all the way through February," says Jones. "The heaviest breeding activity is usually in November, and that's when we have most of our hunts. It's not an easy place to hunt, because the road system is limited. The more successful hunters walk a lot. Compartments range from 2,000 to 4,000 acres. There are lots of deer here; success depends on finding where they are going. Look for heavily used trails, scrapes and rubs, and bedding areas. You want to find a place along or near those trails with some sort of firing lane—it's pretty thick. Bedding areas may be grassy, or they will bed up in honeysuckle thickets or brush piles. Look for places where the vegetation has been tromped down. We usually have quite a few standby positions available during the gun deer hunts, especially during the middle of the week."

Compartments are assigned on a first-come first-served basis, but hunters are allowed to choose their compartments when possible. Hunters are taken to their compartments and shown the area and its boundaries.

During hunts, hunters may camp in the primitive camping area at the area office. A big barbecue cooker and heater, coffeepot, and tin shed are available for everyone's use.

"Feral hogs may show up any-

where, but as a rule they will be in the worst, most uninhabitable, most unpleasant areas on the place," says Jones. "Brush piles and cane thickets are where they lay up in the daytime. On any hunt, you can take a feral hog as long as you use the weapon and load legal for the species being hunted. February and March are a general season for hogs; any legal means and methods are allowed, but no dogs. The more successful people walk them up, flush them out, and shoot them." One place where really big hogs have been spotted is the Twin Lakes area between White Oak Creek and the Sulphur River.

"Waterfowl hunting is the big deal here," Jones says. "Teal hunting is limited due to the lack of open areas and shallow water—this is mallard and wood duck country." Jennings Lake Slough, on the north side of the wetlands system, is good for wood ducks. It's an easy walk from the wetlands levee. Begin at the entry point parking lot at the end of County Road 2513 and follow the mowed path east three-fourths of a mile to the levee around the green-tree reservoir. Turn left and continue atop the levee; Jennings Lake Slough is on the left.

The easiest way to access the area for duck hunting is by boat. Put in at the U.S. 67 boat ramp and go downriver about 2 miles to Jennings Lake Slough. If the water is up, boaters can come up Jennings Lake Slough to within 100 yards of the wetlands compartments; otherwise, it's a walk of about a quarter of a mile.

Only temporary blinds are allowed. "Most people just wade out into the compartments and back up into the bushes, which are scattered throughout," says Jones. "It would also be possible to tow a kayak or rubber raft behind a boat and carry it in from the river."

Ducks can be anywhere. Some people hunt mallards and wood ducks on the green-tree reservoir by finding a little opening and putting decoys out. Ducks will also be all up and down the river and the creek. "Go up or down the river until you find a backwater area, tie up your boat, put out decoys, and hunt on the river itself," Jones advises. "When the creek gets out of its banks, flooded fields are great duck habitat. The area east of U.S. 259 on the south side of White Oak Creek is good for that kind of hunting." While waterfowl shooting hours end at noon on the creek and the rest of the WMA, hunting is allowed all day on the Sulphur River, since it is classified as a navigable stream.

Jones invites duck hunters to come by the area office and look at topographical maps and aerial photographs. Those who do will be rewarded with directions to what Jones says is some of the best duck habitat in East Texas: a couple of places called Joe Wilson's Hole and Cameron Deadening.

Jones encourages raccoon hunting with dogs from December through March. "Raccoons are hard on our turkey population—they eat a lot of turkey eggs," he says. "But call the WMA office or the game warden's office in Mount Pleasant to let us know you will be hunting at night."

FISHING

Fishing is allowed on both the creek and the river; state regulations apply. Catfish, crappie, white bass, and largemouth bass may be caught in the river and in the borrow pits in the wetlands area. When the river is flooding, trotlines or setlines in flooded fields and backwater areas work well for catfish. Little Grassy Lake, which is reached by walking about a quarter of a mile north of White Oak Creek from the Hill Hole parking area, is good for crappie and white bass. Hill Hole is good for catfish. Walk about 300 yards downstream from the Hill Hole parking area.

INSIDER'S CORNER

MANAGING FORESTS FOR TIMBER *AND* WILDLIFE

John Jones is a trained forester, and he hopes to make White Oak Creek WMA a model for East Texas landowners who need to generate income from their timber but don't want to adversely impact their wildlife habitat. "You can have timber production without having negative impacts on habitat over a long period of time. They are not mutually exclusive," says Jones. "That's what forest management is all about—keeping a balance between timber production and wildlife habitat."

In much of East Texas, logging means clear-cutting large blocks of timber and replanting with fast-growing pines. This practice results in a lack of habitat diversity and wildlife. In the case of slow-growing bottomland hardwoods, says Jones, "Once you clear-cut, hunting and fishing are ruined for a hundred years. But that doesn't have to be the case. We have the opportunity on this property to show landowners how to manage their timber. That will involve delineating timber stands by type and age classes and setting up a rotational harvesting system, either by diameter limit or a selective marking system. Income from the timber is spread out over time, but the habitat is kept in good shape and in production, allowing the landowner to get income from hunting as well as timber."

Jones acknowledges that it's tempting for landowners to sell their timber, and logging interests prefer to clear-cut for reasons of economy. But he also knows that many landowners would prefer to protect their wildlife if they only knew how. "The resource is here. I want to show landowners what they can do before getting to the restoration stage."

In a very brief essay, "Deadening," in *A Sand County Almanac*, Aldo Leopold described the tragedy inherent in pushing a resource past its limits.

"The old oak had been girdled and was dead.

There are degrees of death in abandoned farms. Some old houses cock an eye at you as if to say 'Somebody will move in. Wait and see.'

But this farm was different. Girdling the old oak to squeeze one last crop out of the barnyard has the same finality as burning the furniture to keep warm."

PRAIRIES AND LAKES

A thing is right when it tends to preserve the integrity, stability, and beauty of the biotic community. It is wrong when it tends otherwise.
—ALDO LEOPOLD

1   Aquilla WMA

2   Big Lake Bottom WMA

3   Caddo National Grasslands WMA

4   Cedar Creek Islands WMA

5   Cooper WMA

6   Gus Engeling WMA

7   Keechi Creek WMA

8   M. O. Neasloney WMA

9   Pat Mayse WMA

10   Ray Roberts Public Hunting Area

11   Richland Creek WMA

12   Somerville WMA

13   Tawakoni WMA

9,826 acres
406 N. Avenue R
Clifton, TX 76634
254/582-2719

DRIVING TIMES FROM:
Amarillo: 7.5 hours
Austin: 2 hours
Brownsville: 7.5 hours
Dallas: 1.5 hours
El Paso: 11 hours
Houston: 4 hours
San Antonio: 3.5 hours
DIRECTIONS: From Whitney, go south on FM 933 for 5.7 miles to FM 310. Follow FM 310 about 2.5 miles to the headquarters office at the east end of the dam. The office is closed to the public.
OPEN: Year-round for day use.
ACTIVITIES: Wildlife viewing, hiking, bicycling, hunting, fishing.
FACILITIES: Boat ramps, restrooms, parking areas.
SPECIAL REGULATIONS: Access to the area is by foot only at designated points along state and county roads, or by boat from Aquilla Lake. Driving on the area is not permitted. Muzzleloaders and shotguns are the only firearms permitted. Waterfowl hunting is not permitted in the waterfowl sanctuary, which includes the entire part of the management area from FM 1534 northwest to Texas 22. Hunting is not permitted south of the lake from the Dairy Hill boat ramp on FM 1947 to the area's southwestern boundary on FM 310, nor in the area below the dam. Hunters are required to possess an Annual Public Hunting Permit.
ADVISORIES: Bridges across county roads affording access to the area are load zoned for two or three tons in many cases. Large recreational vehicles should not attempt to cross these bridges. Carry your own supply of potable water.
LODGING IN AREA: Motels are available in Hillsboro and Whitney.
LOCAL POINTS OF INTEREST: Lake Whitney State Park, Fort Parker State Park, Old Fort Parker State Historical Park, Meridian State Park, Dinosaur Valley State Park, Acton State Historical Park, Cleburne State Park, Cedar Hill State Park.
DISABILITY ACCESS: Restrooms and boat docks are wheelchair-accessible.

HISTORY

This area was within the historic ranges of the Tonkawa and Comanche Indians. Anglo settlers arrived beginning in the 1830s and 1840s; a cemetery abutting the WMA dates from 1846. Farming has always been the chief use of the land, with the principal crops in the 20th century being cotton, grains, oats, peanuts, and hay. Numerous small farms occupied the land that is now the WMA; farming ceased about 1979 following construction of the lake by the U.S. Army Corps of Engineers. In 1994, Texas Parks and Wildlife entered into a 25-year lease with the Corps of Engineers for management of the area as public hunting lands.

This old cemetery lies just outside the boundary of the Aquilla WMA and offers a view of the dam in the background.

GEOGRAPHY AND NATURAL FEATURES

The Aquilla WMA is unusual among Texas wildlife management areas, because it is sited at the confluence of two distinct geographic regions, the Eastern Cross Timbers and the Blackland Prairie. The wooded Cross Timbers historically furnished firewood to farmers on the mostly treeless Blackland Prairie.

Hackberry Creek and Aquilla Creek join at the dam after receiving the flow of lesser tributaries such as Jack's Branch, Rocky Branch and Little Aquilla Creek. The V-shaped lake covers about 3,280 acres at conservation pool level.

Rolling hills and narrow stream valleys support cedar elm, post oak, pecan, and mesquite woodlands interspersed with old farm fields being invaded by a variety of woody plants and grasses. The Corps of Engineers seeded much of the open land with switchgrass, which has choked out many native grasses. While much of the area surrounding the lake is flat and featureless, there are some elevated areas, primarily along FM 1947, which runs northwest to southeast and crosses the Hackberry Creek arm of the lake.

Bottomlands along Aquilla and Hackberry Creeks are thickly vegetated in the riparian areas, but old fields bordering the creeks provide more open, savannah-type habitat. A network of unpaved county roads laces the WMA and the surrounding farmlands, furnishing numerous access points. Many of these roads dead-end at the WMA boundary, but the roadbeds continue onto the area and in some cases disappear under the lake. These abandoned roadbeds and pasture roads kept relatively clear by the cattle lessee on the area furnish convenient walking trails for hikers, wildlife watchers, and hunters.

Huntable populations of white-tailed deer, Rio Grande turkeys, mourning doves, various ducks, fox

Wildflowers typical of the Blackland Prairie surround Aquilla Lake in spring.

from local hunters and fishers, but annual wildlife surveys indicate the wildlife resources on the area are stable. Its location within a two-hour drive of population centers such as Dallas-Fort Worth and Waco and the ease of access make the area ideal for nonconsumptive uses as well.

WILDLIFE VIEWING

Bluebirds are abundant on the area from February through June, and some 45 nesting boxes provide good viewing locations. Watch for them on fenceposts along roads. About 280 species of birds are known to occur in the vicinity, although the area itself has no official checklist. Many are seen only during spring and fall migrations. These include the eastern wood peewee, white pelican, black-and-white warblers, Wilson's warblers, and various ducks. At most times of the year you can expect to see such species as great blue herons; great egrets; vultures; red-tailed hawks; killdeers; mourning doves; screech owls, great horned and barred owls; belted kingfishers; red-bellied, red-headed, downy, and ladder-backed woodpeckers; common crows; Carolina chickadees; tufted titmice; Carolina wrens; mockingbirds; starlings; house sparrows; eastern meadowlarks; red-winged blackbirds; brown-headed cowbirds; and cardinals. Waterfowl and shorebirds are present in greatest numbers during winter.

PRO'S POINTERS. "We have an abundance of bird life," says area manager José Cano. "Aquilla WMA is not touted as a great birding area, but that's because people have not found it."

One easily accessible place to view birds is from the observation area atop the dam, near the area office. Hawks, which are numerous in the fall, tend to hunt the grassy area between the dam and the water's edge. Resident ospreys and an occasional bald eagle may also be seen from the dam. Waterfowl use the

squirrels, cottontail rabbits, jackrabbits, and feral hogs are found on the area. The principal fish species in the lake are black bass, channel and flathead catfish, and crappie.

RECREATIONAL OPPORTUNITIES

Due to lack of available staff, the Aquilla WMA is one of the least-regulated areas in the public hunting program. The area receives heavy use protected cove at the south end of the dam, and wild turkeys can sometimes be seen on the flat north of the cove.

For shorebirds and waterfowl, the best place is the County Road 2446 access point, where Hackberry Creek comes into the lake. The area is very secluded, and birds feel more secure there. Beavers have a lodge in the lake there, but they tend to be nocturnal. To reach the area, drive northeast from the area office on FM 310 about 4 miles, then follow County Road 2446 half a mile past a farmstead to a parking area on a bluff overlooking the lake. The hill quickly falls off into the creek bottom, and the shallow upper end of the lake is ideal habitat for waterfowl. A large number of white pelicans also frequent the area in spring and fall. An interesting springtime spectacle is the carp spawn, when the gold-colored fish thresh the water into a frenzy.

A rookery for great blue herons is in the tall snags to the southeast of the FM 1534 bridge, which stretches across the Aquilla Creek arm of the lake. You can view the birds from the highway shoulder with binoculars or walk in on the promontory that juts into the lake quite near the rookery.

"To view woodland species, I suggest walking down the old road-bed that begins at the access point parking area at the end of County Road 2437," says Cano. "Trees overhang the road, and it's easy walking. About a quarter of a mile down, the road tees, and you can either walk northwest to a cove where the shorebird watching is good, or go southeast through a post oak wood-land area that skirts old fields." County Road 2437 is reached by taking FM 310 from the area office northeast to FM 1947, then going north on FM 1947 about 3 miles to the county road. The parking area is about half a mile down.

HIKING

There are no marked hiking trails, but you are free to hike anywhere on the area. The extensive network of old roadbeds on the area and pasture roads used by the cattle lessee will take you to every part of the area. Hikers should beware of hunting activity during the various seasons.

PRO'S POINTERS. For a circular, mostly level route of about 3 miles, begin at the parking area at the end of County Road 2437. Follow the old roadbed that is a continuation of the county road. Large trees overhang the path. After about half a mile, the route turns left and runs parallel to the lakeshore for about another mile, then turns northeast and proceeds to an access point on FM 3440. (FM 3440 is a relict roadbed and is only 0.4 miles long; therefore, it will not appear on most maps. It is a quarter of a mile north of the FM 1947 bridge over the Hackberry Creek arm of the lake.)

For a trip of about 2 miles, begin at an access point parking lot on County Road 2122E about three-quarters of a mile south of FM 1534. Go south on the county road about 200 yards to a gate at the area bound-ary fence. Cross over the gate and follow the dirt road through a dense post oak woodland. Open coastal bermuda fields on private property border most of the route's southern side, but the entire route is well shaded. The road makes several turns but never leaves the boundary fence.

A scenic route especially beautiful during the spring wildflower season begins at the observation area near the office and travels atop the dam northeast about half a mile to the spillway. A haying contractor keeps the dam mowed, making travel easy. At the edge of the spillway, you can look across and see the Vaughn Cemetery on the other side. A shorter dam-top journey takes you from the observation area to the outlet struc-ture in the center of the dam and back.

BICYCLING

There are no designated biking trails on the WMA.

PRO'S POINTERS. See the hiking section, above, for suggested routes. A mountain bike is probably best suited for traveling most of the old roadbeds on the area.

HUNTING

There are no sign-in stations and no check stations for hunters using Aquilla WMA. Anyone with an Annual Public Hunting Permit may hunt at any time for legal game as specified in the *Outdoor Annual* and the *Public Hunting Lands Map Booklet* for the current year. Hunting seasons, regulations, and bag limits are the same as those for Hill County with the following exceptions: Hunt-ing is allowed with archery equip-ment, muzzleloaders, and shotguns only; bag limit for white-tailed deer is one buck only (no does); bag limit for Rio Grande turkeys is one gobbler. Turkeys may be hunted in spring only. Feral hogs may be hunted from September 1 until the end of spring turkey season.

PRO'S POINTERS. "Deer occur over the entire area," advises Cano. "Any of the parking areas for walk-in gates gives access to deer habitat. Those who want to go to a little more trouble and get away from other hunters can boat or canoe from the Hackberry Creek boat ramp on County Road 2428 and go across to the southeast side of the lake, which has no public access from the other side. On the north side of the area, there is no access except by boat up Hackberry Creek.

"This area offers excellent hunting for someone willing to take the trouble to get there. There's one old homestead that still has pieces of tin that one can hide behind. I wouldn't make a blind or take a treestand. I'd hunt right there."

Portable treestands are recom-mended for deer hunters, and there are trees large enough to support them throughout the area. However, leaving a treestand in place during a hunt carries the risk of having it stolen. Building permanent stands is not permitted, nor is baiting.

Deer use the post oak trees for cover, travel paths and feeding on acorns, so post oak woodlands are good areas to key on. Find and hunt trails, especially in areas where adjacent farms have wheat fields. Deer use the WMA for refuge and feed in the fields.

Turkey hunting is allowed during the spring season only, and the bag limit is one gobbler only. Shotguns and archery only are allowed. Small flocks occur all over the area. One seems to favor the southwest end of the dam. Turkeys have also been spotted off County Road 2122E south of the walk-in access point and in the tall timber northwest of the old iron bridge on County Road 2415S. Access this area from the walk-in gate just east of the Texas 22 bridge over Little Aquilla Creek or from the walk-in gates along County Road 2415. Turkeys stay along Rocky Branch west of County Road 2428 and along Jack's Branch to the east. Directly across from the Hackberry Creek boat ramp is a flock you can access by canoe, or you can walk in from the County Road 2446 access point.

Feral hogs are known to be on the area, but they seem to move in and out and can be hard to find. Their presence on the area may fluctuate with the availability of food on the surrounding farmland. Numerous plum thickets on the area provide excellent cover.

Feral hog hunting regulations on the Aquilla WMA are some of the most liberal on any public hunting lands. While hogs may be hunted with archery equipment only during the deer archery season, from September 1 through the end of the spring turkey season they may be hunted with archery, shotgun, or muzzleloader. The prime area for feral hogs based on reported

sightings from hunters seems to be the waterfowl santuary between FM 1534 and Texas 22.

Mourning doves take advantage of the milo, oat and wheat fields on the northeast side of the area. Some 20 small farm ponds are scattered over the area and provide good locations for afternoon dove shoots. The open fields along FM 3440 seem to be a flyway. In the same vicinity, the parking area at the end of County Road 2437 gives access to open fields frequently overflown by doves.

The eastern end of the WMA is best for dove hunting. "Some of the better hunting has been during the second or third week of the season, because farmers cut their grain crops then," says Cano. "Some will leave stubble and waste grain in the fields until later in the fall before plowing it under and planting winter wheat. This makes for some good dove hunting."

Waterfowl hunting consists mainly of ducks, as the only geese are occasional migrants making an overnight stop. Mallards are one of the main species of ducks using the lake, but wood ducks, gadwalls, pintails, widgeons, shovelers, ring-necked ducks, and lesser scaup are common.

Aquilla Lake is a water supply for surrounding communities and is normally drawn down during the summer, allowing vegetation to grow on exposed flats which then flood with fall rains, creating ideal habitat for ducks. Note that the area between FM 1534 and Texas 22 on the Aquilla Creek arm of the lake is a waterfowl sanctuary and is closed to waterfowl hunting.

"My favorite waterfowl hunting area is where Hackberry Creek comes into the lake," says Cano. "However, there are a lot of secluded coves on the west side of the lake, so if you don't mind walking in with your decoys, you can do well there." Mallards seem to favor the Hackberry Creek area, while teal seem to prefer the cove near the southwest end of

the dam and the lake around the Hackberry Creek boat ramp.

No permanent blinds are permitted, but building temporary blinds out of natural vegetation is allowed.

Quail hunting is permitted on the WMA, but quail populations in the area have followed the downward trend common in Central Texas. Even where there is good habitat, birds are scarce. Introduced switchgrass has crowded out most of the plants that would be good quail food.

Squirrels, hares, and rabbits may be hunted with shotguns only. There is no closed season or bag limits on these species. The best squirrel area is the tall timber along Aquilla and Little Aquilla Creeks from the iron bridge on County Road 2415S to Texas 22. Most of the pecan and burr oak trees are in this area. Note that while you may not hunt waterfowl in this area, all other legal species are fair game.

Fishing

Bass, catfish, and crappie are the principal species in the lake. "Largemouth bass do very well in this lake," says Cano. "When the Corps of Engineers built this lake, they took the suggestion of local fishing clubs and left a lot of natural timber standing in the lake. They cleared only the basin right around the dam, and what vegetation they did knock down, they piled up. This created lots of brush piles in the lake you can find with a depthfinder."

PRO'S POINTERS. Easy access to areas with standing timber is from the Dairy Hill boat ramp on Spur 1947 at the south end of the FM 1947 bridge and from the Old School boat ramp at the end of County Road 2127. From the latter, run into the main lake and then head almost due north to the standing timber around the FM 1534 bridge. This is a favorite spot of local bass fishers.

Sand or white bass were not present in the lake originally but mysteriously appeared, perhaps the

product of unauthorized transplantings from nearby Lake Whitney. People usually catch white bass on what are locally called ghost minnows, which are clear with a silver stripe down the side. Live bait is available at Peoria Station, a store at the intersection of Texas 22 and FM 1947. "After the spring spawn, white bass will school on the main part of the lake. I've seen them beating the water to a froth and wondered, where are the fishers?" says Cano. "I've also seen a lot of white bass near the inlet to the water treatment plant, because a lot of shad hang around those inlets. Put in at the Dairy Hill boat ramp and run southwest about a mile and a half to the water-treatment plant intake structure."

Because it receives runoff from surrounding cultivated fields, Aquilla Lake's waters are generally murky, which helps make it a good catfish lake. Photographs on the wall at the Peoria Station store attest to large flathead and channel cats taken from the lake. Trotliners like the lake because there are many places with tree stumps that provide places to tie lines to. Bank fishing is also popular. Fishing off the dam is allowed as long as you don't block the entrance gates to the area between the dam and the water, but parking is very limited. Most people park at a paved parking area beside the stilling basin below the dam and walk over, but it is a long hike. Fishing is good in the stilling basin itself when water is being released.

"A good catfishing spot is the gravel bar at the north end of the FM1534 bridge," says Cano. "There's a dropoff just off the bank there. It's such a popular spot that the Corps of Engineers has put a couple of portable toilets there." An access road allows driving right to the water's edge, which adds to the area's appeal. Traditional catfish fare such as stinkbait, chicken livers, and dead shrimp are the baits of choice.

"Aquilla is an excellent crappie lake because of the abundance of structure and all the small creeks that come into the lake," says Cano. "People fish those creeks, especially where trees have fallen into the creek and provide natural structure." The iron bridge area on County Road 2415S 2 miles south of Texas 22 is popular. Bank fishers also favor the numerous small, easily accessible coves around the lake. Boat ramp areas usually have good bank fishing areas nearby. Most people fish for crappie using small minnows under a cork, but boat fishers try their luck with jigs around stickups in the lake.

The County Road 2446 access point leads to the shallow upper end of the lake, where waterfowl are abundant.

CARP: ULTIMATE GAMEFISH OR LAKE LEPER?

The same fish can be trash or treasure, depending on one's point of view. And few fish generate more disagreement among fishers than the common or German carp.

Carp are nonnative fish introduced to Texas in 1879 by, of all people, the Texas Fish Commission. Overfishing had reduced native fish populations to the point that the commission felt that something had to be done. The concepts of habitat management and controlled harvests would not become accepted knowledge for another half-century, so it was decided to stock Texas streams with shad, herring, rainbow trout, and salmon. These attempts failed. Enter the carp, which in another irony was being touted by the U.S. Fish Commission. A carp hatchery was set up at Barton Springs in Austin, and the hatchlings soon swam in most Texas river systems.

"This is *the* fish for Texas," trumpeted the Texas fish commissioner. However, the carp provided neither the sport nor the food that Texas fishers sought. Difficult to catch and with oily, bony flesh, carp fell out of favor in only a handful of years.

However, bowfishers regard carp as worthy targets. Catfish and bass fishers occasionally take a carp by accident. And a small but growing number of people actually fish for carp, which can easily reach 15 to 20 pounds and are tough fighters.

Part of the mystique of carp fishing is the bait. Fly fishers, with their myriad fuzzy little lures tied in a bewildering variety of patterns to "match the hatch," have nothing on carp fishers when it comes to exotic attractants. One of the most common carp baits is corn flakes moistened with strawberry-flavored soda pop and formed into doughy balls. But this is too easy for the confirmed carp addict. It's like a fly fisher using a factory-made woolly booger instead of one laboriously tied by hand at home in the wee hours using secret techniques.

Following is a generalized recipe for a carp bait. If you find you don't like carp fishing, it's also said to work on catfish.

Homemade Carp Bait

1. Begin your search for ingredients at a health food store. (This alone discourages many people from taking up carp fishing, since you don't see many fishing boats parked in front of health food stores.) Look for ingredients like cooked soya flour, maize meal, or semolina (used to provide bulk); and attractors such as dried brewers' yeast, paprika, or cinnamon. Other attractors are essential oils used in aromatherapy—black pepper or geranium—and liquid amino acids such as extract of liver and spleen.

2. To prepare the bait, mix the attractors with eggs and then add enough bulking material to make a dough wet enough to roll into balls but dry enough not to stick to your fingers. (Use the attractors in very small amounts—too highly flavored baits repell carp rather than attract them.)

3. Drop the balls into boiling water. Boil for about two minutes, and then spread on paper towels to dry overnight. The bait balls can be frozen until used.

It sounds like a lot of trouble, but then you don't need a $20,000 boat pulled by a $30,000 pickup to catch carp, either.

What do you do with a carp after you've caught it? The standard recipe is to place the fish between two cedar shingles, bake it until done, then throw the fish away and eat the shingles.

You can learn all about carp fishing on the carp website: www.carp.net.

1,794 acres in four tracts;
additional acreage owned as
an undivided interest
809 E. Clifton
Athens, TX 75751
903/677-9588

DRIVING TIMES FROM:
Amarillo: 8.5 hours
Austin: 3.5 hours
Brownsville: 9.5 hours
Dallas: 2 hours
El Paso: 15 hours
Houston: 2.5 hours
San Antonio: 5 hours
DIRECTIONS: From Loop 256
around Palestine, take FM 320 west
about 8 miles to FM 645. Take FM
645 north about 1.5 miles to County
Road 3452. Go west on 3452 1.2
miles to County Road 2901. Turn
right and follow 2901 for 1.9 miles
to a sign on the left marking the
entrance to an access road to the
WMA. Follow this road to the parking area and walk in approximately
1 mile. See below for additional
access points.
OPEN: Daily.
ACTIVITIES: Wildlife viewing,
hiking, hunting, fishing.
FACILITIES: Information kiosks.
SPECIAL REGULATIONS: All users
must register on-site. Dogs are
prohibited except for one dog for
each person hunting waterfowl,
squirrels, or rabbits. Waterfowl
shooting hours end at noon. Trapping and horses are not allowed.
ADVISORIES: Some property in this
WMA is owned outright by TPW,
but other parcels are co-owned.
Only property owned 100 percent
by TPW is shown in the *Public
Hunting Lands Map Booklet*. To get
to some of this property requires
crossing land in which TPW owns
an undivided interest. While on
these lands you may encounter

individuals who own or have purchased trespass rights to the land
from co-owners. These individuals
may use ATVs and are not bound by
Texas Parks and Wildlife rules for
the WMA. However, Texas Parks
and Wildlife–sanctioned users must
comply with all area rules. Users
should be aware that the Big Lake
Bottom WMA is close to a large state
prison complex. Almost the entire
area is subject to flooding. Carry
your own supply of potable water.

LODGING IN AREA: Motels are
available in Palestine, Crockett, and
Fairfield.
LOCAL POINTS OF INTEREST:
Texas Freshwater Fisheries Center,
Texas State Railroad, Confederate
Reunion Grounds, Fort Parker State
Park, Old Fort Parker State Histori-
cal Park, Jim Hogg State Historical
Park, Fairfield Lake State Park, Fort
Boggy State Park.
DISABILITY ACCESS: Not
wheelchair-accessible.

*Partridge pea, a valuable wildlife food, is
abundant in open fields on Big Lake Bottom
WMA.*

HISTORY

Before Texas Parks and Wildlife acquired the land within the Big Lake Bottom WMA, it was used primarily for grazing and hunting. Most of the pines on the area were logged at some time in the past.

Texas Parks and Wildlife began purchasing tracts of bottomland hardwoods for the WMA in 1990. Development of the area for public use began in earnest in 1999. Until that time the area was accessible only by permission of adjacent landowners or by boat from the Trinity River, since there were no roads or easements to Texas Parks and Wildlife-owned land. Three access points were established in 1999; directions for reaching them are included in the following section. The eventual goal is to acquire 100 percent ownership of all land within the WMA boundaries.

GEOGRAPHY AND NATURAL FEATURES

Over 90 percent of the WMA is bottomland hardwood habitat in the Post Oak Savannah. The land is generally quite flat and within the flood plain of the Trinity River, and flooding occurs several times a year.

Oaks dominate the overstory, with overcup oaks being the most common species, followed by water and willow oaks. The understory, which is quite thick in most places, contains redbud, possum-haw holly, dewberry, greenbriar, poison oak, and a variety of other vines and grasses. White-tailed deer, feral hogs, wood ducks, mallards, squirrels and rabbits occur on the area. Eastern wild turkeys have been stocked on the area.

Big Lake Bottom WMA is bordered on the west and south by the Trinity River and on the north and east by privately owned lands or lands co-owned by Texas Parks and Wildlife. River access is prohibited.

The area was little used until the establishment of the following access points:

1. From Loop 256 around Palestine, take FM 320 west about 8 miles to FM 645. Take FM 645 north about 1.5 miles to County Road 3452. Go west on 3452 for 1.2 miles to County Road 2901. Turn right and follow 2901 for 1.9 miles to a sign on the left marking the entrance to an easement road to the WMA. Follow this road to the parking area. Walk approximately 1 mile to the WMA. Note that private property borders this road on both sides. Two entry gates enter the WMA. From the east gate a trail leads east about a quarter of a mile to a block of land owned by Texas Parks and Wildlife. From the west gate a trail leads west about half a mile to the south of Big Lake and eventually to the largest tract of Texas Parks and Wildlife–owned land in the WMA. These trails are signed.

2. Take FM 645 south from FM 3452 for 1.9 miles to County Road 2904. Turn right and go 1.9 miles to County Road 2906. After 0.2 mile the pavement ends. Continue straight ahead another 0.2 mile to the entrance on the right. This entrance accesses a 60-acre tract owned by Texas Parks and Wildlife.

3. Reach the third entry point by driving south on FM 645 from County Road 2904 for 2.9 miles to County Road 2907. Turn right and go 1.2 miles to County Road 2909; follow it straight ahead for 0.2 mile, at which point it turns left 90 degrees at its intersection with County Road 2910. Follow 2909 for 0.4 mile from that intersection, then go straight ahead on an unsigned road another 0.6 mile to an entry gate on the left. Follow this easement road, bounded by private property on both sides, to the parking area. From there walk due west into the WMA; Keechie Creek (not to be confused with Keechi Creek) lies approximately half a mile from the parking area.

RECREATIONAL OPPORTUNITIES

Visitors may view wildlife, hike, hunt, and fish. However, periodic flooding, lack of facilities such as hiking trails, and difficult access are serious impediments to public use. This situation will improve as total ownership of lands within the WMA is achieved and development continues.

WILDLIFE VIEWING

Birders can expect to see a variety of wrens, sparrows, and neotropical migrants, primarily during the spring and summer months. Due to the watery environment, this is a good place to see green tree frogs, bullfrogs, gray tree frogs, water moccasins, canebrake rattlesnakes, copperheads, ratsnakes, and banded water snakes.

PRO'S POINTERS. The best areas for wildlife viewing are the tracts accessed from the entry points #2 and #3 above. Both have creek bottoms and some edges around clearings.

HIKING

There are no designated hiking trails on the area. The only trails are those between noncontiguous tracts. Some pass through property that is owned by undivided interest.

PRO'S POINTERS. The few trails on the area were designed with hunter access in mind. Trail maintenance is minimal, and areas off the trail are thickly vegetated. Hiking here is allowed but not recommended.

HUNTING

All hunting is by Annual Public Hunting Permit at present. This may change should all the property become 100 percent owned by Texas Parks and Wildlife. Youth hunts are also available. See the *Public Hunting Lands Map Booklet* and the *Outdoor Annual* for the current year for species, seasons, and bag limits.

Big Lake Bottom WMA is managed for maximum public hunting opportunity. White-tailed deer, feral

hogs, and squirrels are the main species. Both archery and gun hunting are allowed for deer and feral hogs.

PRO'S POINTERS. "Deer are pretty evenly distributed over the area," says area manager Kay Fleming. "Hunt drainages and food sources. During archery season, there may be grapes, but there probably won't be acorns. However, most of the acorns on the area are overcup acorns, which are not a deer favorite. Find an area with willow oak or water oak acorns to increase chances of success. In the bottoms, deer will probably be feeding on leafy plants and sedges." Portable stands are allowed, but they must be removed daily and cannot damage the tree. Lean-on or climbing stands are best.

The rut falls in early November, but it may not increase chances of seeing a buck. "There are few bucks and lots of does," Fleming says. "Bucks have been overharvested in the county as a whole, and there is a lot of hunting pressure. This particu-

lar area has not been hunted as much because of lack of access in the past; if you can get back into the area a good distance, your chances of success are better, but getting a deer out will be difficult." Mountain bikes are allowed; a small trailer attached to one can ease the job of game retrieval.

Feral hogs occur all over the area but are not abundant. The use of dogs is not allowed for hunting hogs and deer. "Hunt the thickest areas along the creeks," advises Fleming. "The most successful hunters walk hogs up."

For the best squirrel hunting, look for stands of water oaks and willow oaks. "The area on the extreme east end, off County Road 2909, will probably be good for squirrels," says Fleming. "However, most of the area is riverbottom and should be good squirrel habitat.

"Hunt squirrels while the leaves are still on the trees. Sit quietly, listen, and watch for movement in the trees. Once the leaves are off, squirrels will see you coming and hide."

Waterfowl hunting is challenging and not very productive. "Most of the time when waterfowl are here, it will be too wet to get into the bottom from land," warns Fleming. Big Lake, probably a former channel of the Trinity River, lies at the eastern end of the largest area of land completely owned by Texas Parks and Wildlife. Private homes along the shore of Big Lake make hunting along the lake inadvisable due to safety concerns.

FISHING

Fishing is allowed in Keechie Creek, which crosses the tracts of land accessed from County Roads 2906 and 2909, and in the Trinity River.

PRO'S POINTERS. White bass run up the creeks in spring, but this is not a prime place to fish. Access is difficult due to fallen trees across channels and a thick understory.

Access to the WMA from County Road 2901 passes through this area, which may be flooded and impassable at times.

ARE YOU OUT OF YOUR GOURD?

One of my most treasured possessions is an ordinary fruit jar in which I keep, from year to year, cantaloupe seeds. These seeds produce one of the juiciest, sweetest, best-tasting cantaloupes I've ever eaten. But saving seeds from each year's best melons is the only way to enjoy this variety. Thin-skinned, the cantaloupe bruises easily and does not ship well. But its biggest disadvantage, and the one which no doubt led to its commercial demise, is the fact that one day it is green, and the next day it is falling-off-the-vine ripe. These cantaloupes must be enjoyed straight from the vine; they cannot endure waiting around in warehouses and supermarket produce departments.

I got my start collecting seeds in the form of a juicy melon handed to me by a local old-timer, who admonished me, "Save the seeds. You can't get these anymore." I've since passed seeds on to others.

The fate of many native Texas plants depends on similar efforts. One such plant, the Texas gourd, is fairly common on Big Lake Bottom WMA. The plant has large, yellow flowers that open only in the morning. The tennis-ball-sized fruits are oblong and not particularly pretty. Despised by farmers for invading their crops, the Texas gourd was considered for a time for listing as an endangered species.

Although collecting plant materials on wildlife management areas is prohibited, there is a way to ensure that the Texas gourd and other native Texas plants do not disappear from the Lone Star State: the Seeds of Texas Seed Exchange. Members who grow native Texas plants save the seeds and trade them among themselves, helping to ensure that a species will not be wiped out by some local disaster or, more likely, widespread indifference. Currently about 600 varieties of seeds are stockpiled by members.

Many people save seeds from rare plants simply because of their novelty. However, there are scientifically valid reasons for doing so. One of the problems with commercially produced seed is lack of genetic diversity, which can result in plants that are susceptible to disease. The Irish potato famine of the 1800s was due to a blight among potato plants descended from just two varieties brought to Europe over 200 years earlier. Russian and American corn farmers suffered huge crop losses in the 1970s after disease wiped out corn from seeds developed from one single plant. Preserving native varieties of plants may some day provide the genetic diversity needed to maintain the world's food supply.

If you are interested in helping to save native Texas plants, you can join the Seeds of Texas Seed Exchange by writing to them at P.O. Box 9882, College Station, TX 77842. Members receive a seed directory (updated annually) and periodic newsletters. Each annual directory lists descriptions of all seeds offered by members as well as complete information on who to contact to obtain the seeds. Members do not have to offer seeds in order to join, but only members may obtain seeds through the exchange.

16,140 acres in two units
185 SE 31st St.
Paris, TX 75460
903/785-0482

DRIVING TIMES FROM:
Amarillo: 7 hours
Austin: 5.5 hours
Brownsville: 11 hours
Dallas: 2 hours
El Paso: 13 hours
Houston: 5.5 hours
San Antonio: 7 hours
DIRECTIONS: Bois d'Arc Creek
Unit—From Bonham, take U.S 82
east to Honey Grove. Go north 10
miles on FM 100 to FM 409.
Ladonia Unit—From Honey Grove,
take Texas 50/34 south about 11
miles to Ladonia. Follow Texas 34
west about 5 miles, then county
roads to various tracts.
OPEN: Daily.
ACTIVITIES: Camping, wildlife
viewing, hiking, hunting, fishing.
FACILITIES: Campgrounds, boat
ramps.
SPECIAL REGULATIONS: Waterfowl
shooting hours end at noon. Trapping for furbearers only is allowed
during designated periods. Use of
horses is allowed year-round. Camping is restricted to designated areas
only from October through early
January. Hunters must possess an
Annual Public Hunting Permit. All
deer hunters are required to register
at an information station. For other
special regulations, see the section
entitled "Special Regulations in
Effect on U.S. Forest Service Units"
in the current *Public Hunting Lands
Map Booklet.*
ADVISORIES: The Ladonia Unit is
highly fragmented, and boundaries
are poorly marked. Extreme care is
required to avoid trespassing on
private land. Poisonous snakes are
common on the Bois d'Arc Creek
Unit. Carry your own supply of
potable water.

*Caddo National Grasslands WMA contains both
open grasslands and bottomland hardwoods.*

LODGING IN AREA: Motels are
available in Paris and Bonham.
LOCAL POINTS OF INTEREST:
Bonham State Park, Cooper Lake
State Park, Sam Bell Maxey House
State Historical Park.
DISABILITY ACCESS: Restrooms
and campsites at the East Lake
Crockett campground are
wheelchair-accessible.

HISTORY

The area now comprising the Bois
d'Arc Creek Unit of the Caddo
National Grasslands WMA was once
home to Caddo Indians, but these
had reportedly abandoned the area
by 1836, when the first Anglo settlers
arrived. Reflecting the early and rapid
settlement of the area, the present
boundaries of Fannin County were
set in 1839 by the Congress of the
Republic of Texas. Bonham, the
county seat, located a dozen miles
southwest of the WMA, began as Bois
d'Arc but was renamed in 1844 in
honor of a defender of the Alamo.

Agriculture was the primary
economic activity in Fannin County
from the beginning, with production
of most crops peaking around 1900
and slowly declining thereafter.

Population followed a similar trend.
The Great Depression of the 1930s
and the drought of that same period
further wounded the local economy.

By the 1930s much of the land in
the region had been severely damaged by poor farming practices,
which led to erosion. The federal
government purchased the Caddo
National Grasslands with the aim of
restoring the land. The grasslands are
presently administered by the U.S.
Forest Service. The Texas Parks and
Wildlife Department has been managing the wildlife on the area since
1984.

The Caddo National Grasslands
have been an important recreational
area for people from the Dallas-Fort
Worth area since 1935. Fishing in
Davy Crockett and Coffee Mill Lakes
is particularly popular. During the
nearly 50 years before Texas Parks
and Wildlife took over management
of the wildlife on the area in 1984,
deer hunting was unregulated. As a
result, deer were seriously overharvested. In 1983, the last year of
unrestricted hunting, the number of
hunters averaged from 1,500 to 2,000
per day during a five-day season—a
hunter to every 9 to 12 acres!

GEOGRAPHY AND NATURAL FEATURES

Caddo National Grasslands WMA suffers from a badly split personality. The 13,360-acre Bois d'Arc Creek Unit is part of the Post Oak Savannah. The 2,780-acre Ladonia Unit is 20 miles away and is part of the Blackland Prairie. In addition, landholdings are fragmented: the Bois d'Arc Creek Unit consists of six separate tracts and the Ladonia Unit has a dozen. In the Ladonia Unit in particular, boundaries are poorly marked and management is difficult. The area is used principally for grazing. Visiting the Ladonia Unit is not recommended due to the difficulty of locating the various tracts and the resulting possibility of inadvertent trespassing on private land.

The Bois d'Arc Creek Unit encompasses rolling hills with two sizable lakes and four flowing streams. About half the area is upland hardwoods such as post oak, black jack oak, white oak, red oak, and hickory, and shrubs such as eastern red cedar. The remainder of the area is equally divided between open grasslands and bottomland hardwoods. The grasslands have mainly native bluestem, switchgrass, and forbs. Bottomland hardwood species include a variety of oaks—swamp chestnut, cherrybark, water, and willow—as well as elm, ash, sugarberry, and pecan. Due to logging in the 1930s and 1940s, most of the hardwoods are just now reaching the age of prime productivity. The Bois d'Arc Creek Unit has white-tailed deer, fox squirrels, and gray squirrels. Waterfowl use the lakes in fall and winter. Eastern turkeys have been stocked on the area.

The relatively flat Ladonia Unit has heavy black soil covered mainly in grasses; trees and shrubs occur mainly along the drainages. Doves and quail are the main game species found.

RECREATIONAL OPPORTUNITIES

CAMPING

Three camping areas are managed by the U.S. Forest Service on the Bois d'Arc Creek Unit; a fee is charged only at the West Lake Crockett campground. All are accessed from FM 409. They are heavily used by local fishers and family groups. In spring and summer, almost the entire campground area may be covered with tents, vehicles, and people pitching horseshoes.

PRO'S POINTERS. For more solitude, head to the primitive campground southwest of Monkstown. Go a mile west of Monkstown on FM 273, then turn south on County Road 2325. At 1 mile the graveled county road bends sharply to the right. Go straight ahead here on the caliche Forest Service road to the campground a quarter-mile past the cattleguard. This pleasant place is shaded by huge oak trees, and a small pond lies a couple of hundred yards beyond. Wild turkeys frequent the area. A second primitive campground, well shaded, is southeast of Monkstown and is reached via FM 2216 and County Road 2415. Another is located on a discontiguous parcel in the far southwest portion of the Bois d'Arc Creek Unit. There are no campgrounds on the Ladonia Unit.

WILDLIFE VIEWING

The Ladonia Unit is typical blackland prairie habitat and offers the opportunity to see dickcissels, eastern meadowlarks, sedge wrens, and scissor-tailed flycatchers. The Bois d' Arc Creek Unit contains Post Oak Savannah and a greater variety of wildlife.

PRO'S POINTERS. The Ladonia Unit is highly fragmented, and poorly marked boundaries make it difficult to locate. If you choose to visit this area, you may park at gates and walk in, but be careful where you go, as private property is all about. Birding from public roads through the area is possible, however.

Multiuse trails radiate from Crockett and Coffee Mill Lakes on the Bois d'Arc Creek Unit. Along them you can see northern cardinals and blue jays year-round. In the summer, several varieties of warblers and thrushes can be heard in the treetops. Beavers and an occasional river otter can be seen around both lakes.

EQUESTRIAN TRAILS

The three multiuse trails on the Bois d'Arc Creek Unit are open to horseback riders. See descriptions of these trails in the hiking section below. Horses and horse trailers are not allowed in the campgrounds, so special access points have been provided.

PRO'S POINTERS. An unmarked parking area for equestrian use is on the west side of Lake Crockett. Follow FM 409 about a quarter-mile past the West Crockett campground to the first green gate on the left. Left unlocked, the gate permits access to a parking area for horse trailers adjacent to the trail. At the Coffee Mill Lake area, park horse trailers in the parking area at the intersection of FM 409 and FM 100. "We do have certain areas behind locked gates that I will open for use as campgrounds by horseback riders," says ranger Tom Palmer. "Call me ahead of time at 903/378-2103 to make arrangements."

Free-range horseback riding is allowed in any unlocked pasture. Many of these pastures have wire gaps between them; riders may pass through any gap or gate that is not locked.

HIKING

Three multiuse trails are open to horseback riders, hikers, or bicycle riders. Motorized vehicles are prohibited. The trails are mostly level and pass principally through wooded areas. None are wheelchair-accessible.

PRO'S POINTERS. Trail 1 loops 7.6 miles from the information board at

the western Lake Crockett campground almost to Coffee Mill Lake. Well marked with signs, the trail has a natural surface of sandy loam, but it can get slick in wet weather. Waterproof footwear is advised, as there are a few minor drainages to be crossed.

Trail 2 is accessible from the entry road to the Coffee Mill Lake camping area. This 6.2-mile loop follows the lakeshore and passes through mixed pine and hardwood uplands. A third trail of 8.4 miles was under development at the time of writing. It will be accessible from trail 2 or from a proposed equestrian campground.

Trail maps may be obtained by calling the U.S. Forest Service Decatur office at 940/627-5475 or the Caddo National Grasslands Caddo Work Center at 903/378-2103. The latter is on FM 409 about a mile west of FM 100 and is normally staffed from 7 A.M. to 3:30 P.M. on weekdays, but someone is usually there on weekends as well.

BICYCLING

Three multiuse trails are open to bicycle riding.

PRO'S POINTERS. See the hiking section, above, for a description of the trails.

HUNTING

Deer hunting attracts the greatest number of hunters, although significant numbers of squirrels and waterfowl are also harvested. Most hunting is by Annual Public Hunting Permit. Turkey hunting, by Special Permit, was offered for the first time in the spring of 2000. Dove-, quail-, and rabbit-hunting opportunities are very limited. See the current *Public Hunting Lands Map Booklet* and the *Applications for Drawings on Public Hunting Lands* for legal species, seasons, and bag limits.

All persons 17 years of age and older who possess a centerfire or muzzleloading rifle, a handgun, a shotgun with shot larger than #2 steel or #4 lead or archery equipment with

A small pond lies near a primitive campground off County Road 2325 southwest of Monktown.

broadheads must possess an Annual Public Hunting Permit. Persons 17 and older with guns using rimfire ammunition, shotguns with smaller size shot than listed above, and archery equipment with field points must possess either the Annual Public Hunting Permit or a Limited Public Use Permit.

PRO'S POINTERS. Because of the possibility of trespassing on private land, hunting on the Ladonia Unit is not recommended unless you are very familiar with the area. Hunting pressure is very heavy during the gun season, especially during the first two weeks. Bowhunters will find the area much less crowded. "The best deer-hunting opportunity is on the northern portions of the Bois d'Arc Creek Unit around Monkstown—Forest Service units 19 and 22," says area manager Richard Hines. "The better hunting is in the Bois d'Arc Creek bottomland forest. Be sure and take a compass—it's easy to get turned around in there." Bois d'Arc Creek cuts across both Forest Service units 19 and 22 from southwest to northeast. Access to these areas is via County Roads 2325 and 2415. Another good area is north of FM 409 in the Coffee Mill Lake area, where cover is very thick. Hunters who have hunted the area in the past need to be aware that registration was required for all deer hunters starting in the fall of 1999.

Feral hogs also favor Units 22 and 19 and Bois d'Arc Creek. Baiting is not allowed. The best technique is to look for fresh rooting and wallows and still-hunt the area. Listen for pigs feeding or fighting and stalk them.

Waterfowl hunting is best on Davy Crockett and Coffee Mill Lakes. The main species harvested are pintails, gadwalls, mallards, scaup, and teal. "You will need a boat," says Hines. "Anywhere you can find a cove is good. Hunt out of a covered boat or

pull your boat to a point, put decoys out, pull the boat around the point and cover it with camo, then walk back and hunt on the point. Using downed vegetation or driftwood to make a blind is permitted, but the best thing is to use burlap and poles to make a temporary blind." Waterfowl shooting hours end at noon.

Both gray and fox squirrels are present in good numbers on the Bois d'Arc Creek Unit. "The better areas are east of FM 2029 along Coffee Mill Creek and south of FM 409 on the

northwest side of the area," advises Hines. "These areas have mostly post oak and blackjack oak trees. If you can find a post oak with a heavy crop of acorns and cuttings under the tree, go back before daylight and set up. Within an hour after daylight you will have gray squirrels working. The hunt will be over by 10 or so because they get less active as the day heats up. Fox squirrels tend to start later and move more around the noon hour, so you can get a later start and still be successful."

Developed campgrounds are operated by the U.S. Forest Service along FM 409.

FISHING

Perch, crappie, catfish, and large-mouth bass are the main species found on Caddo National Grasslands WMA.

PRO'S POINTERS. "There's great bluegill fishing on Coffee Mill Lake in the shallow areas and weedbeds in late April and May when they are bedding," says Hines. "Crappie are present in both lakes. Fish stickups and flooded buttonbush thickets in the upper end of the lakes when they are up."

Lake Crockett, about 450 acres, has the same species as above and is also stocked with Florida bass. Fishers should check the slot limit posted at the boat ramp.

INSIDER'S CORNER

SILENT FALL

Bottomland hardwoods are some of the most productive wildlife habitat in the world, and the reason falls from the sky each autumn: acorns. Acorns are one of nature's most brilliant inventions, a bite-sized bounty of energy easy to find, eat, and digest. Woodpeckers, blue jays, wood ducks, mallards, raccoons, squirrels, white-tailed deer, and wild turkeys all depend heavily on acorns for survival. Acorns are the cake of the plant world—everything likes to eat them.

Oak trees have long symbolized strength and longevity. For these seemingly invincible trees, however, the long-term outlook is not good. Logging, deer browsing, wildfire suppression, drought and competition from faster-growing trees take a heavy toll on oak survival and regeneration.

Acorns fall into two basic groups, depending on whether they come from a tree in the white oak or the red oak family. Acorns from white oak trees—those with leaves with rounded lobes—mature in one growing season and taste sweet. Acorns from red oak trees, which have pointed, spine-tipped leaves, take two seasons to mature and taste bitter due to a high tannin content. However, red oak acorns are three times as rich in fat as white oak acorns, which makes them a prime food.

Experienced hunters know to concentrate on white oak trees dropping acorns when hunting for squirrels or deer, because the animals will search out and eat those acorns first. White oak acorns also get eaten quickly because they sprout soon after hitting the ground and use up their sweet fat reserves. Red oak acorns,

on the other hand, are dormant after dropping and do not sprout until spring. This makes them an ideal food to be stored away by squirrels and other animals for use during the winter.

Hunters know that squirrel populations in particular boom the year following a good acorn crop. Oak trees tend to produce bumper crops of nuts only every three to four years. This seems to be an evolutionary response to nut predation. If there were large acorn crops every fall, the populations of squirrels, birds, deer, mice and other acorn eaters would increase until there would be no way the trees could produce enough acorns to feed all the animals and have enough left over to grow new trees. So the trees starve off many of their predators by producing few acorns most years.

Over time, red oaks are more successful survivors than white oaks. New white oak trees tend to grow near parent trees since the acorns sprout so quickly. Red oaks, in contrast, increase their range due to their acorns being carried away and stored for later use. Squirrels are the key players. They eat only the tops of the red oak acorns, where the concentration of tannin is much lower, and bury the bottoms. Since the seed leaves and embryo are at the point of the nut, these half-acorns sprout and grow almost as often as whole ones.

Some scientists predict a parallel to Rachel Carson's silent spring a century or more from now—a silent fall in which the plop of tiny acorns dropping from mighty oaks may no longer be heard. Since acorns are the number-one natural wildlife food east of the Rocky Mountains, the implications are serious indeed.

159 acres in three islands
809 E. Clinton
Athens, TX 75751
903/677-9588

DRIVING TIMES FROM:
Amarillo: 8 hours
Austin: 4 hours
Brownsville: 10 hours
Dallas: 1.5 hours
El Paso: 12.5 hours
Houston: 4 hours
San Antonio: 5.5 hours
DIRECTIONS: From Athens, take U.S. 175 north to Texas 334. Take Texas 334 west through Gun Barrel City. Two of the islands are just south of the causeway over Cedar Creek Reservoir between Gun Barrel City and Seven Points. The third island is 6 miles north in the lake.
OPEN: Daily.
ACTIVITIES: Wildlife viewing.
FACILITIES: None.
SPECIAL REGULATIONS: Landing on the rookery islands near Gun Barrel City is not permitted. Viewing is allowed only from boats.
ADVISORIES: Water in the vicinity of the islands is very shallow in places; use caution to avoid grounding. Carry your own supply of potable water.
LODGING IN AREA: Motels are available in Gun Barrel City and Seven Points.
LOCAL POINTS OF INTEREST: Tyler State Park, Governor Hogg Shrine State Historical Park, Lake Tawakoni State Park, Purtis Creek State Park, Texas State Railroad, Jim Hogg State Historical Park, Texas Freshwater Fisheries Center.
DISABILITY ACCESS: Not wheelchair-accessible.

RIGHT:
Telfair Island hosts thousands of nesting egrets, cormorants, and herons each spring.
ABOVE, RIGHT:
Due to the lack of predators on the islands, chicks hatch unmolested in nests that are sometimes only inches off the ground—and from neighboring nests.

HISTORY

The three islands were acquired by the Tarrant County Water Control and Improvement District Number One in the 1960s as part of the land acquisition for Cedar Creek Reservoir. In 1990 Texas Parks and Wildlife obtained a 99-year lease on the islands in order to protect seasonal waterbird rookeries.

GEOGRAPHY AND NATURAL FEATURES

The two main islands of interest are the ones near Gun Barrel City. They sit just south and in plain sight of Texas 374 and lakeside homes around Cedar Creek Reservoir, between the communities of Gun Barrel City and Seven Points.

The islands rise about 10 feet above the water and are about a quarter of a mile apart. Telfair Island, about 11 acres, is to the west and harbors the largest nesting colony. It has more shrubs and trees that the birds use for nesting. Bird Island is about 4 acres. Both are losing area fairly rapidly due to erosion. The northernmost island, Big Island, occupies about 144 acres and is totally wooded. At the present time birds are not known to nest there.

On Telfair and Bird Islands, nests fill almost all available trees, and some birds nest on the ground beneath the trees. Egret, cormorant, and heron nests are freely mingled. Black cormorant and white egret chicks occupy nests side-by-side. Birds nest among branches drooping almost to the waterline and as high in the trees as branches will support them. Droppings cover the ground beneath the trees and whiten the trees themselves.

The soil, highly enriched by droppings, supports a cover of bermudagrass so dense and spongy that walking across it is like walking across a waterbed. Cowpen daisies also prosper on the nitrogen-rich soil. Chinaberry trees on the western end of Telfair Island are almost totally ignored by the birds. They seem to prefer the abundant honey locust and

occasional crepe myrtle for nesting. Most nests are within four feet of the ground.

Fire ants are abundant. Armadillos and nutria are known to occur on the islands as well. There are no predators living on the islands, explaining the birds' willingness to build nests on and very near the ground.

RECREATIONAL OPPORTUNITIES

While the primary purpose of the islands is to protect the nesting colonies of birds, and entry onto the land is therefore prohibited, the birds can easily be viewed from boats.

WILDLIFE VIEWING

The principal bird species nesting on the islands are snowy egrets, cattle egrets, tricolored herons, little blue herons, great egrets, olivaceous cormorants, and mallards.

PRO'S POINTERS. Access by boat is easy from public boat ramps along the Texas 374 causeway; there is a $2 launch fee. The islands are immediately south.

"Birds use the islands year-round, but nesting starts the first part of April and extends until the end of August," says area manager Kay Fleming. "Mallards, which may be tame ducks from subdivisions around the lake, nest on the ground in June."

The birds nest mostly in honey locust and ashe juniper trees. "The trees they are nesting in are the ones that can stand the abuse," Fleming says. Even so, most of the nest trees are devoid of leaves, making the islands resemble a World War I no-man's land, with naked tree trunks and limbs sticking up from barren ground. The lack of vegetation, and the fact that birds nest right up to the water's edge, make viewing with binoculars from a boat easy. "There's no set limit on how close you can approach the birds; just stay in your boat," says Fleming.

INSIDER'S CORNER

BANDING TO BEAT THE BAND

Cedar Creek Islands WMA is the site of a long-term bird-banding project headed by Dr. Raymond C. Telfair, a Texas Parks and Wildlife wildlife biologist from Tyler. Each year a number of wildlife biologists visit the islands to band birds. Approximately 1.5 million bands are issued annually to banders taking part in the North American bird-banding program, which is jointly administered by the U.S. Department of the Interior and the Canadian Wildlife Service. A permit is required.

Bird banding is an important tool for both researchers and wildlife managers. Each time a bird is banded, the bander records the location and date, the age and sex of the bird, and other information specific to that bird, such as whether it was a wild bird, was hand-reared, was sick or injured, or had been transported to that location. Coded numbers on bands reveal, among other things, the flyway and state where the bird was banded. For example, the numbers 383 tell that a bird was banded in the Central Flyway, in Texas. This information is then sent to the Bird Banding Laboratory in Laurel, Maryland, in the United States or in Hull, Quebec, in Canada.

When banded birds are recaptured, information as to when and where it was found is useful in determining the distribution and movements of that species, life-span and cause of death, reproductive success and population growth. This information assists in decisions about conserving and managing bird populations. Banding studies have helped locate the nesting and wintering grounds for many species as well as their migration routes. This knowledge is essential if habitat critical to their survival is to be protected.

Bands are recovered in a variety of ways. Some banded birds are captured in the course of other banding projects, their data recorded, and then released. Hunters recover bands from harvested waterfowl. Perhaps not surprisingly, many songbird bands are recovered by the owners of domestic cats—along with a few feathers!

For information on bird banding, call the U.S. Geological Survey Wildlife Research Center at 301/497-5790 or visit their website at www.pwrc.usgs.gov. Or contact the Inland Bird Banding Association at http://aves.net/inlandbba/ibbamain.htm.

14,480 acres
Route 2, Box 236C
Omaha, TX 75571
903/884-3800

DRIVING TIMES FROM:
Amarillo: 7 hours
Austin: 5.5 hours
Brownsville: 11 hours
Dallas: 2 hours
El Paso: 13 hours
Houston: 6 hours
San Antonio: 6.5 hours
DIRECTIONS: From Sulphur Springs, take Texas 19 north 14 miles to County Road 4795. Turn left and go 0.8 mile to Tira Boat Ramp Road, just before the dam. Turn left and go a quarter of a mile to the area office.
OPEN: Daily.
ACTIVITIES: Wildlife viewing, hiking, hunting, fishing.
FACILITIES: Office, boat ramp, and restrooms at Johns Creek access point.
ADVISORIES: In wet weather, some roads may not be passable even with four-wheel drive. Always accessible are County Roads 2065, 2070, 4753, 4754, and 4804 and the Johns Creek boat ramp road off FM 1528. Carry your own supply of potable water.
LODGING IN AREA: Furnished cabins are available at the South Sulphur Unit of Cooper Lake State Park. There are motels in Sulphur Springs, Commerce, and Cooper. Closest to the WMA is Fisherman's Landing Motel at Klondike, at the intersection of Texas 24 and FM 2890.
LOCAL POINTS OF INTEREST: Cooper Lake State Park, Sam Bell Maxey House State Historical Park, Lake Bob Sandlin State Park, Governor Hogg Shrine State Historical Park, Lake Tawakoni State Park, Daingerfield State Park, Tyler State Park, Bonham State Park.
DISABILITY ACCESS: Restrooms at Johns Creek access point are wheelchair-accessible.

HISTORY

Occupied in historic times by Caddo Indians, the area that is now Cooper WMA was settled by Anglos in the 1830s. The South Sulphur River, which runs through the middle of the WMA, is also the boundary between Delta and Hopkins Counties. Jernigan Thicket, a heavily wooded area just northwest, was a noted hideout for outlaws in the mid-1800s. An early bridge spanned the South Sulphur River just east of the area and was heavily used by cotton farmers to the north who used the steamboat port at Jefferson for shipping.

Although Cooper Lake (originally designated Jim Chapman Lake) was authorized by Congress in 1955, it is one of the newer impoundments in Texas due to a series of court actions that delayed the beginning of construction of the dam until late 1986. As a result of these court actions, mitigation lands around Cooper Lake and downstream at White Oak Creek were provided for; these lands totaling some 40,000 acres are permanently earmarked for wildlife management. Texas Parks and Wildlife manages these lands under a 50-year contract with the U.S. Army Corps of Engineers. Under this arrangement, the Corps of Engineers pays 75 percent of the costs associated with the WMA and Texas Parks and Wildlife the remainder.

GEOGRAPHY AND NATURAL FEATURES

Cooper WMA lies within the Blackland Prairie and Post Oak Savannah geographic regions. The surrounding area is level to gently rolling. The WMA itself occupies the western half of Cooper Lake and a generally narrow band of shoreline and bottomland on the south and north shores of the lake.

The area contains significant emergent wetlands as well as bottom-land hardwoods, and these two habitat types are the most productive. Some 300 acres of wetlands are leveed, and water levels are manipulated to achieve maximum growth of waterfowl food and hunting opportunity. Smartweed and dock are the dominant plants in the wetlands, which are bordered by bottomland hardwoods where water oak, elm, hackberry, willow oak, pecan, and assorted other mast-producing trees form dense woodlands.

While the main body of the lake from the dam to the boundary of the WMA was cleared of timber, all timber with the exception of lanes cleared for boat traffic was left standing in the western half of the lake. This area provides outstanding fishing and waterfowl hunting opportunities, even though navigation is extremely difficult and can be hazardous, especially during times of low lake levels.

RECREATIONAL OPPORTUNITIES

Wildlife viewing, hiking, biking, hunting, and fishing are available on the area daily, including holidays. Hunters are required to possess an Annual Public Hunting Permit. Nonconsumptive users are not required to have a Limited Public Use Permit, but they are requested to sign in at one of the self-registration stations before entering the area.

WILDLIFE VIEWING

White-tailed deer are present on the entire area. The land between the dam and Texas 154 is a refuge where deer hunting is not allowed. The access road below the dam passes by open fields where deer may be seen early and late in the day.

Waterfowl begin to arrive in September. Blue-winged teal generally arrive first, and as it gets colder, other species begin to arrive, with mallards generally being the last. Wood ducks nest on the area and are present year-round. Some 25,000 cormorants and a few white pelicans winter here. Great blue herons, cattle egrets, snowy egrets, white ibis, osprey, bald eagles, northern harriers, Cooper's hawks, red-tailed hawks, eastern wild turkey, northern bobwhite quail, various species of rails, plovers, stilts, and avocets, sandpipers, mourning doves, terns, and gulls may be seen.

Among the songbirds, eastern bluebirds, yellow-rumped warblers, black-and-white warblers, and summer tanagers are the most common. Indigo and painted buntings are common from spring through fall, and dickcissels are abundant during that same time. Red-winged blackbirds seem to occupy every bush and stalk of grass in the wetlands year-round.

There are some river otters and a large population of beavers in the streams, but both are reclusive and mostly nocturnal. Feral hogs, coyotes, and gray and fox squirrels are present in large numbers. Bobcats are also quite common.

PRO'S POINTERS. Area wildlife technician Kevin Kraii suggests looking for wild turkeys in the area behind the dam and in the Middle Sulphur River bottom off FM 1531 near the community of Horton.

Access to this Horton Bottom area is via County Roads 2065 and 2070. Go 4.2 miles south of Texas 24 on FM 1531 and turn east onto County Road 2065; follow it to its intersection with County Road 2070. Turn left and follow the road to the sign-in station. From that point, follow the old roadbed into the WMA for about 2 miles. The old roadbed goes through a bottomland area and Post Oak Savannah and eventually reaches the lake. When the lake is low, the trail continues to Lost Ridge, which at normal water levels is a 50- to 60-acre island. Besides birds, this trail offers the opportunity to see feral hogs, squirrels, and wild turkeys. In the winter, waterfowl are abundant on the lake and in the nearby wetlands.

Access to the wetlands area is via two county roads, one unsigned, off FM 71. *Neither of these roads is passable in wet weather.* County Road 2080 is 0.7 mile east of the intersection of FM 71 and FM 1531. Follow 2080 to an intersection, turn right, and continue to the gate at the WMA boundary. Follow the old roadbed straight ahead to the wetland area. Another access point is off FM 71 on an unsigned county road 1.3 miles east of FM 1531. Just past an old house ruin, turn left onto the dirt road and follow it to the parking area. Walk along the old roadbed about half a mile to the wetland area.

Moist-soil management produces abundant food that attracts mallards, gadwalls, widgeons, blue-winged and green-winged teal, American shovelers, northern pintails, wood ducks, American coots, lesser scaup, redheads, canvasbacks, goldeneyes, buffleheads, and hooded mergansers. During migrations snow geese and white-fronted geese use the area as a stopover. A wildlife observation platform overlooking the wetland area is planned.

Wetland areas in Cooper WMA produce prodigious crops of smartweed and other plants used as food by wintering waterfowl.

Waterfowl viewing is also possible from FM 1528 where it crosses Doctors and Johns Creeks. These areas are closed to waterfowl hunting. Parking is very limited on the sides of the road at the ends of the bridges. Avoid these areas in wet weather.

HIKING

There is no motorized vehicle access on the WMA. However, at some access points old roadbeds continue into the management area, furnishing good paths for hiking.

PRO'S POINTERS. "The Horton Bottom trail is the best," says Kraii. (See a description of this trail under the section on wildlife viewing, above.) Another trail is planned for the area behind the dam. The 2- to 3-mile loop along old roadbeds will traverse Blackland Prairie and bottomland hardwood habitat. The trail will have interpretive signs at points of interest.

BICYCLING

There are no trails designated specifically for biking. However, bikes are allowed.

PRO'S POINTERS. See the section on hiking, above. Mountain bikes will be required for riding on most of the old roads.

HUNTING

For information on legal species, seasons, and bag limits, see the *Public Hunting Lands Map Booklet* for the current year. Cooper WMA is managed for maximum hunting opportunity; not all legal species are present on the area in numbers sufficient for good hunting. The species discussed below provide the most opportunity. Deer, feral hogs, and waterfowl are the main game animals hunted.

Hunters *must* sign in and enter the area at one of the designated entry points around the lake. Failure to do so could result in being ticketed by the game warden.

In the past there have been problems with individuals removing all the

Cooper Lake was cleared of timber from the dam to the boundary of the WMA, but trees were left standing in the balance to provide habitat for fish and other wildlife.

archery equipment only. During the statewide archery season, bucks and does are legal; during the general season, archery equipment only may be used, and only bucks are legal.

Feral hogs may be taken during any hunt as long as the weapon and ammunition legal for that hunt is used. There is a special feral hog season from February 1 through March 31 during which archery equipment or shotguns with buckshot or slugs may be used.

PRO'S POINTERS. Permanent stands and baiting are not allowed. Lean-on or climbing tree stands may be used, but hunters may not screw anything into trees. "For deer, I'd suggest the Middle and South Sulphur River bottoms," says Kraii. "These are the largest tracts of land on the property, and they hold the highest numbers of deer. During good mast years, November through December is when acorns will be on the ground. Hunting during October is tough because the area is generally still too green and thick with grass and trees. Find commonly used trails and set up a stand there. During the rut in mid- to late November, look for rubs and scrapes along the drainages. If you want to get away from people, you will have to walk a long way. You must enter through designated entry points, and the farther away you get from those, the farther away you will be from people."

Hunters with boats can put in at one of the state park boat ramps or the Johns Creek access point and hunt the area between Chigger and Merrit Creeks on the south side of the lake. This same area can be accessed from the parking area at the end of County Road 4804 near Peerless. The narrow strip of land along the lake between the South Sulphur River and Merrit Creek can be accessed only by boat.

Feral hogs are abundant on the entire property but tend to concentrate in the area behind the dam reserved for feral hog hunting. "This

registration cards in an attempt to discourage others from hunting. If there are no cards in the box, one may be obtained at the Corps of Engineers office at the dam on County Road 4795, at one of the state park offices at Doctors Creek or South Sulphur Park, or at the WMA office on Tira Boat Ramp road off County Road 4795.

Deer may be hunted with legal

area is very heavily wooded, with incredibly thick bottomland hardwoods on the southeast side and Blackland Prairie and Post Oak Savannah farther west," says Kraii. "The best method seems to be cooperative walking drives to flush the hogs out of the thick grass and brush." The Middle and South Sulphur River bottoms also hold good numbers of hogs. No baiting or dogs are allowed.

Dove hunting can be very good. "The best dove-hunting area is the wetland units off FM 71," says Kraii. "There are a lot of seed-producing plants in the uplands all around the lake. Hunt the treelines and the bare shoreline for birds coming to water. Sit down in the grass between the shoreline and the trees and pass shoot birds."

Waterfowl hunting attracts the most hunters. The west or upper end of the lake offers the best habitat. About 300 acres in moist-soil units are seasonally drawn down and then flooded to produce food plants such as smartweed and barnyard grass. From November through January one foot of water is maintained in the three compartments.

Access to the wetlands area is via two county roads, one unsigned, off FM 71. *Neither of these roads is passable in wet weather.* County Road 2080 is 0.7 mile east of the intersection of FM 71 and FM 1531. Follow 2080 to an intersection, turn right, and continue to the gate at the WMA boundary. Follow the old roadbed straight ahead to the wetland area. Another access point is off FM 71 on an unsigned county road 1.3 miles east of FM 1531. Just past an old house ruin, turn left onto the dirt road and follow it to the parking area. Walk along the old roadbed about half a mile to the wetland area. There are no designated hunting spots; it's first come, first served.

Another popular waterfowl hunting spot is Lost Ridge, an island cut off from the mainland during normal water levels. To reach Lost Ridge, follow County Road 2065 to County Road 2070, turn left, and follow 2070 through numerous bends to a parking lot at its end. From there, the old roadbed continues to the lakeshore. Depending on lake level, this walk can be from one and a half to 2 miles.

The upper end of the lake can be accessed from the Johns Creek boat ramp off FM 1528. Turn onto Park Road 2158, which is 4.8 miles west of the intersection of FM 1528 and Texas 154/19. Be aware there is lots of standing timber; people who do not know the lake should not attempt boating in the dark.

Walk-in access is possible from any of the sign-in boxes, but note that waterfowl hunting is *not allowed* up in the creeks; only along the lakeshore and in the wetland unit. Study the WMA map carefully.

"The best waterfowl hunting is during rising water levels and cold snaps," says Kraii. "We will generally have the most ducks on the property then. In good mast years, the rising water floods bottomlands and timber, and ducks flock to those areas. During cold snaps, northern birds come down, primarily mallards. The best duck hunting is in December and January. During the first split, we have teal and wood ducks and not much else."

The most successful waterfowl hunters are those who hunt out of camouflaged boats in flooded timber. On the wetland unit, bring in a temporary blind and set up on one of the levees. Gathering natural vegetation such as grass and cattails is allowed, but cutting tree limbs is not. No permanent blinds are allowed. Most people use two to three dozen mallard decoys; there is no need for a large spread.

Shooting hours for waterfowl end at noon.

Squirrel hunting is popular during the one fall season. Both fox and gray squirrels can be hunted along the drainages of Middle and South Sulphur Rivers, where most of the hardwoods are. The area north of Peerless is hilly, higher ground, and is good for squirrels. "Both types of squirrels tend to inhabit the same areas here," says Kraii. "There's not enough variation in habitat to make a difference." Kraii suggests hunting squirrels by slipping through the woods, sitting and listening for dropping acorns or squirrels barking. Only shotguns with no larger than #4 lead shot are allowed.

Snipe are found along the lakeshore and in the moist-soil units. "Snipe like the muddy places between the wetland unit and the lake," says Kraii. "People walk them up and jump shoot them like quail. They fly erratically and are very hard to hit. Woodcock seem to be along the Horton Bottom trail and are most numerous along the treeline bordering the wetland area. They are best hunted with pointing dogs, like quail."

FISHING

Fishers are not required to possess an Annual Public Hunting Permit. Bank access fishing for crappie and white bass running up the creeks in spring can be good. The standing timber holds largemouths of a size and number to lead some people to call Cooper Lake the next Lake Fork. A 15.17-pound bass set a new lake record in April 1999.

PRO'S POINTERS. The stilling basin below the dam offers good fishing for crappie, white bass, hybrid stripers, and catfish when water is being released from the lake. Shad are abundant in the lake and seem to be the preferred bait of local fishers.

Mike Garner and his son Terry are both licensed fishing guides on the lake. Terry caught the lake record 15.17-pound bass in April 1999; that same week Mike boated a fish over 13 pounds.

"The best time of year for bass is April and May," says Mike. "Cooper is probably the best summer lake in

the state. The water is shallow and stained, and the fish stay shallow. The average depth of this lake is only 12 to 13 feet, and there is so much cover here. The best baits are spinnerbaits and jigs. The lake record fish was caught on a chartreuse shad with gold blade. For jigs, I like ¼- and ⅜-ounce black-and-blue or white jigs with a pork trailer.

"I mainly fish in the timber," Mike continues. "In the spring and fall, fish bite all day long. In the summer, early morning is best. Pitch up close to snags and laydowns in sloughs and channels throughout the timber area. Good places are the channels and timber between boat lanes 2 and 3. Put in at the Johns Creek access point and run down the boat lane southeast to the river channel. From that point there are hundreds of creeks and channels to fish." The map of the project area, available from the U.S. Army Corps of Engineers office at the east end of the dam, shows the boat lanes and areas covered by standing timber.

"Cooper was rated the number-one crappie lake in Texas by Texas Parks and Wildlife in 1998," says Mike. "There are a lot of them, and they are big. We catch up to three-pounders on bass tackle. Crappie start turning on the end of March and continue biting through the end of May. The Doctors Creek and Johns Creek areas are especially good in spring. Tube jigs of 1/16 ounce in bright colors like red, pink, white, and chartreuse work best."

Summer crappie fishing is concentrated on the edges of the river channel and brush piles in the main lake. Approximate locations of these brush piles and the river channel are

About 300 acres are managed as wetlands on the upper end of Cooper Lake to provide waterfowl habitat.

shown on the Corps of Engineers map.

Catfish are found on the flats in timber or in the numerous open areas that were old farm fields on the west end of the lake. Cut and cheese baits and live shad work well. May through the end of July sees fishers bringing in large numbers of blues up to 30 and 35 pounds, channels up to 30, flatheads up to 60. Many are caught on rod and reel. Good bank fishing for catfish at the Johns Creek boat ramp is due to the fact that locals keep the area baited.

Sand bass hang out in the main lake on humps on the flats. "I've seen as much as 10 acres of water covered with sand bass schools," says Mike. "There's a big hill in the middle of the lake southeast of the Johns Creek access. Sand bass school between the edge of that hill and the point between Johns Creek and Doctors Creek. Sand bass start picking up the middle of May. They school in the lake, but they don't make a big run like they do in other lakes. They seem to go up the river channel into timber around the boat lanes and spawn on the logs and stumps. People think you're crazy when you tell them that, but this lake is different."

Striped bass up to six and seven pounds are in the deeper end of the lake near the dam. This area has a lot of old roadbeds and borrow pits dating from construction of the earthen dam. "Fish the edges of the borrow pits in the deeper water," Mike advises. "Stripers will school under sand bass in the summer. If you are catching pound and a half sand bass and suddenly start losing line, it's a hybrid. Fish below schools of sand bass."

INSIDER'S CORNER

HOPKINS COUNTY STEW

One of the greatest pleasures of hunting and fishing is cooking and eating meals outdoors. Taste buds and olfactory receptors simply work better outdoors, or at least it seems that way. Perhaps it's due to the cleansing effects of wood smoke on one's nose and throat, or the soothing sound of night creatures going about their business, or just the simple pleasure of feeling the warmth of the sun on one's skin. A 2-mile hike through the woods can be a good appetizer as well.

One of the most popular inhabitants of any hunting camp is the person who can manipulate ingredients in the kitchen and produce something edible. A basic rule of hunting camp etiquette is never to criticize the cook. Some hunting camps are blessed with people who come not to hunt but just for the pleasure of serving up hearty meals to hungry, appreciative eaters. If your hunting camp is not so fortunate, perhaps the following recipe will come in handy. People who've tried Hopkins County stew say it's the best. If this recipe doesn't strike you that way, consider attending the annual Hopkins County Fall Festival in Sulphur Springs the second Saturday in September and sample all the entries in the annual stew cook-off. One is sure to become your ticket to being invited back to hunting camp again and again.

Hopkins County Stew

4 slices bacon, diced
2 tablespoons butter
3 1/2- to 4-pound stewing
   chicken, cut into pieces (For a
   real outdoor stew, substitute
   squirrel, cottontail, pheasant,
   wild turkey or the doves you
   shot today on Cooper WMA.)
3 large onions, chopped
1 bell pepper, chopped
1 1/2 cups chopped celery
3 1-pound cans tomatoes
2 12-ounce cans whole kernel
   corn
3 pounds potatoes, peeled and
   diced
1 1/2 cups water
1 tablespoon salt
1/4 teaspoon paprika
1/4 teaspoon curry powder
1/4 teaspoon black pepper

Fry the bacon in a large pot or dutch oven. Remove the bacon and add the butter and meat to the bacon grease. Cook until well browned. Return the bacon pieces, add the remaining ingredients, and bring to a boil. Simmer, covered, for about an hour. Remove chicken or other meat with bones and debone it. Dice the meat and return it to the pot. Cover and cook slowly three hours more, stirring occasionally. Adjust seasonings to taste and serve with hot cornbread.

10,958 acres
Route 1, Box 27
Tennessee Colony, TX 75861
903/928-2251

DRIVING TIMES FROM:
Amarillo: 8 hours
Austin: 4 hours
Brownsville: 10 hours
Dallas: 1.5 hours
El Paso: 15 hours
Houston: 3 hours
San Antonio: 5.5 hours
DIRECTIONS: From Palestine, go north 22 miles on U.S. 287.
OPEN: Year-round for day use and camping in designated areas, except during public hunts.
ACTIVITIES: Driving tour, nature trails, camping, wildlife viewing, hiking, bicycling, hunting, fishing.
FACILITIES: Information kiosk, nature trails, wildlife-viewing blind, hunter check station, restrooms with showers, screened shelters, drinking water.
SPECIAL REGULATIONS: All users must register on-site at the information kiosk. No Annual Public Hunting Permit or Limited Public Use Permit is required for the driving tour or designated nature trails. Walking in bog areas is prohibited. Camping is permitted only in designated areas.
ADVISORIES: Bring insect repellent and sunscreen. Beware of alligators.
LODGING IN AREA: Motels are available in Palestine, Athens and Corsicana.
LOCAL POINTS OF INTEREST: Texas Freshwater Fisheries Center, Texas State Railroad, Confederate Reunion Grounds, Fort Parker State Park, Old Fort Parker State Historical Park, Jim Hogg State Historical Park, Purtis Creek State Park, Mission Tejas State Historical Park, Fairfield Lake State Park, Tyler State Park.

Gus Engeling WMA is unusual in that it provides screened shelters in a camping area along Catfish Creek.

DISABILITY ACCESS: The wildlife observation blind and the restrooms are wheelchair-accessible.

HISTORY

Before Anglo colonization, the area that became Anderson County was home to Comanche, Waco, Tawakoni, Kickapoo, and Kichai Indians. In 1826 empresario David G. Burnet, who later became the first president of the Republic of Texas, received a grant from the Mexican government to bring settlers into the area. After removal of the Indians in the 1840s, settlement proceeded rapidly, and Anderson County was organized on March 24, 1846.

By 1900 most of the land comprising the Engeling WMA was owned by M. L. Derden. Cattle and hogs grazed most of the land, with some acreage planted to cotton, watermelons, sugar cane, and vegetables.

Texas Parks and Wildlife purchased the Derden land and additional acreage between 1950 and 1960. Initially called the Derden WMA, it was renamed in 1952 in honor of the first biologist assigned to the area, Gus Engeling, who was killed by a waterfowl poacher.

GEOGRAPHY AND NATURAL FEATURES

The Gus Engeling WMA lies in the Post Oak Savannah region a few miles east of the Trinity River. It contains about 2,000 acres of hardwood bottomland floodplain and nearly 500 acres of riparian corridors along its main drainage, Catfish Creek, and the eight spring-fed branches that flow into it. These streams form wetlands that support red maple, sweet gum, and river birch in corridors coursing through the uplands. Beaver ponds sprinkle the area. Other wetland areas include over 350 acres of marshes and swamps and nearly 300 acres of sphagnum moss bogs.

Uplands comprise the balance of the acreage. Oak, hickory, elm, and gum trees canopy dry, rolling hills. Dense thickets of dogwood, beautyberry, farkelberry, yaupon, possumhaw, hawthorn, and greenbriar throng the understory, draped by muscadine and mustang grapes.

Nearly 600 plant species have been documented on the area; a field

194

checklist is available from the information kiosk. Four are of special interest. The swamp thistle and the black deathcamus, both of which occur in bog areas, are known to exist nowhere else in Texas. Wild azaleas occur around the bog at Lake 2. The dwarf pipewort, also a bog dweller, is potentially eligible for federal listing as endangered.

The original Post Oak Savannah was an area of about 8.5 million acres extending from near San Antonio to far northeast Texas. Open uplands were dominated by waist-high grass and large, scattered trees. Large oak motts or "islands" of hardwoods were scattered throughout the prairie. Timbering, fire control, damming of streams, and land clearing changed the landscape dramatically after settlement. Thick stands of native grass almost disappeared. Woody species replaced grass as the dominant vegetation type.

The Gus Engeling WMA did not undergo this transformation as extensively as did the rest of the Post Oak Savannah. It was not cleared extensively, and mature stands of hardwood timber remain on the area. The end of overgrazing and the use of prescribed burns is returning portions of the area to its presettlement condition.

Wild turkeys disappeared from East Texas due to unregulated hunting between 1860 and 1920. Attempts to stock the area with Rio Grande turkeys between 1948 and 1960 failed. In the 1970s, both Rio Grande and eastern turkeys were stocked, but populations remained small. Since 1988, eastern turkeys only have been released.

At times portions of the area may be closed to visitors in order to reduce disturbance of the eastern wild turkeys during nesting season. Signs are posted to mark areas off limits. Visitors are asked to respect the need to provide these birds with the maximum opportunity to reproduce.

RECREATIONAL OPPORTUNITIES

The Gus Engeling WMA is open for the following activities year-round except during public gun deer hunts, when the entire area is closed to anyone not holding a permit. Consult the *Public Hunting Lands Map Booklet* and the *Applications for Drawings on Public Hunting Lands* or call the area office for dates.

DRIVING TOUR

An 8-mile self-guided driving tour, which can also be hiked or biked, starts at the information kiosk across the road from the area headquarters. A booklet available here, *Wildlife Management Past, Present and Future on the Gus Engeling Wildlife Management Area,* contains a history and description of the area as well as driving tour instructions. (Help conserve resources by returning the booklet after your tour.) The 10 stops on the tour visit areas demonstrating various management practices designed to improve wildlife habitat on the area, such as disked fields, planted food plots, bluebird and wood duck nest boxes, strip clearing, and wetlands creation. Stop 10 shows how prescribed burning has returned a portion of the WMA to its presettlement condition, when the uplands were open, dominated by waist-high grasses and peppered with large, scattered trees.

PRO'S POINTERS. The driving tour is open only during daylight hours. The road is maintained in condition for ordinary passenger and recreational vehicles in all types of weather.

NATURE TRAILS

The Dogwood Trail, a 1-mile loop, skirts a free-flowing spring area along Skeet Branch Creek and goes into uplands. Obtain a trail guide keyed to signposts along the way from the information kiosk. Many of the plants identified are the same as those along the Beaver Pond Trail. The Dogwood

Trail is accessed from the main road 1.1 miles from the information kiosk.

The .5-mile Beaver Pond Nature Trail begins at a parking area 1.8 miles from the information kiosk. A trail guide is available at the kiosk. An observation blind overlooks a two-acre pond, beaver lodge, and dam on spring-fed Berry Branch. "We like beavers and let them do their thing as long as they don't back water up over our roads," says area manager Hayden Haucke. "We leave them alone even if they kill some of our hardwood timber." Alligators lurk beneath the pond's surface; caution is advised.

Mallards, scaup, and teal feed on the pond in fall and winter. Wood ducks reside on the area year-round and nest in boxes placed overlooking the water; the males are especially colorful in their breeding plumage in spring. Cavities in dead timber around the pond harbor red-headed woodpeckers, great crested flycatchers, and prothonotary warblers. The large stick nests in the tops of tall, dead trees were built by great blue herons.

Water lilies blanket the pond's surface with their pads, and in mid- to late May, yellow lotus send shafts towering skyward, each topped with a bright blossom. These large, waxy flowers are followed by showerhead-like fruits bearing round nuts, each in its own little hole. These seedheads are commonly used in flower arrangements. (Gathering of plant materials in wildlife management areas is prohibited.)

A boardwalk skirts the pond's edge for a short distance before continuing over the beaver dam and into a dense woodland, a mix of bottomland vegetation that grades into an upland site. Dead trees along the route are used by nesting woodpeckers; many living trees bear holes drilled by yellow-bellied sapsuckers, which feed on the sap and insects attracted to it.

The best time to visit is late March, when the dogwood is in bloom. In April and May, wood ducks nest; in late May, yellow lotus bloom on the beaver pond.

Numbered signposts along the Beaver Pond and Dogwood Trails correspond to information in trail guides and do not appear in numerical sequence along the trails. If you find it difficult to spot which plant is marked by a sign, look for a splotch of yellow paint.

CAMPING

Camping is allowed in three areas for holders of the Annual Public Hunting Permit, Limited Public Use Permit, or Texas Conservation Passport. In addition, organized groups may, with permission, overnight in several daycamp areas with no facilities or water. Apply for a permit at the office.

Three screened shelters beside Catfish Creek nestle in a heavily shaded area. This campground has no amenities other than latches on the screen doors. To reach this site, follow the main road into the area north from WMA headquarters 3.3 miles to County Road 473. Turn right and go 1.25 miles to the campground on the left.

A primitive camping area is also on County Road 473 just 0.4 mile east of the screened shelters above. Tent and RV camping are permitted; there are no facilities. The campground is almost totally shaded by large trees.

A third camping area is the hunter's camp 0.3 mile north of the headquarters on U.S. 287. Tent and self-contained RV camping are allowed here; there are eight RV pads. Sites have fire rings, barbecue pits, and lantern posts, but no individual water and electrical hookups. Restrooms with hot showers serve the area. Shade is plentiful. No reservation is needed.

PRO'S POINTERS. Spring has the most pleasant temperatures and the fewest insects. The Catfish Creek screened shelter area is popular with fishers who like to night fish. The hunter's camp on U.S. 287 is best for RV campers. Those who prefer isolation and excellent wildlife viewing within easy walking distance should try the primitive camping area on County Road 473.

WILDLIFE VIEWING

Wildlife is abundant on Gus Engeling WMA, with 36 mammal, 140 bird, 54 reptile and amphibian, and 53 fish species documented. Field checklists for birds, fishes, amphibians, reptiles, and mammals are available at the information kiosk.

PRO'S POINTERS. Mammals and birds are most abundant in wetland, bottomland, and riparian areas. Strip clearings along the main road attract white-tailed deer early and late in the day. June is a good month to see does with their fawns. Gray and fox squirrels populate the bottomlands and nearby upland areas. Water attracts species such as raccoons, ringtails, mink, beaver, nutria, and river otters. You may also see spotted and striped skunks, opossums, and gray foxes. Bobcats and coyotes, while elusive, are known to inhabit the area, as do feral hogs.

Dense vegetation in bottomlands and around bogs can make birding difficult, but those areas attract the most birds. Easily accessible wetlands lie on either side of County Road 473 between the screened shelter and primitive camping areas.

Fall and winter are the best times for waterfowl, although wood ducks reside on the area and can be seen year-round. Berry Lake, a scenic pond just south of County Road 473, has several wood duck boxes around it and is an easy 300-yard walk from the main road. Park at the remains of a building at the southwest corner of the main road and County Road 473 and follow the pasture road west.

For birding, the best time is May, when the neotropical migrants have arrived back on their summer nesting territory. Visitors during the first part of May have been rewarded with sightings of Kentucky and Swainson's warblers, while the prothonotary warbler is common during summer, as are indigo and painted buntings and scissor-tailed flycatchers.

The best location for bottomland species is the area between day camps 3 and 4. Follow the signs along the main road; it's about 2 miles from the information kiosk at the entrance. For wetland species, walk the Beaver Pond Nature Trail, where you can see a variety of woodpeckers, gallinules, wood ducks, and perhaps a water thrush. During September, the main access road and associated side roads provide good wildlife viewing for a variety of mammals in early morning and late evening. Drive slowly, be quiet, and stay in your car.

HIKING

A network of unpaved roads and truck trails laces the area, providing ready-made paths through every kind of habitat. Some parallel Catfish Creek; some track fencelines; others follow ridges through uplands. Hiking may not be permitted during public hunts in fall or through areas used by wild turkeys during the nesting season in spring.

PRO'S POINTERS. Although the area has about 15 springs and a number of dirt ponds, you should carry a supply of drinking water or a water purification device; potable water is available only at the office and the hunters' camp. The best hiking areas are north of U.S. 287 along the main road and associated side roads. While many of the side roads are closed to vehicle traffic, you are free to walk them unless signs state otherwise. There are no marked, designated hiking trails other than the two nature trails.

BICYCLING

A bike is perhaps the best way to enjoy the Gus Engeling WMA. The main graveled road is about 8 miles long and can be navigated by any bike. It runs north through the entire area with branches to Catfish Creek, small lakes, and bogs.

PRO'S POINTERS. Mountain bikes are better suited for the side trails, some of which are very sandy. Ample shade is available along all routes, but carry your own drinking water.

OPPOSITE PAGE:
A boardwalk carries the Beaver Pond Trail across part of a two-acre pond where a variety of wildlife and flora may be seen.
RIGHT:
The Dogwood Trail passes by springfed Skeet Branch Creek and through an upland area.

HUNTING

For information on species, seasons, bag limits and weapons restrictions, see the *Public Hunting Lands Map Booklet,* the *Outdoor Annual,* and *Applications for Drawings on Public Hunting Lands* for the current year. The main species hunted on the area include white-tailed deer, feral hogs, squirrels, and waterfowl. Most hunting is by self-registration for holders of an Annual Public Hunting Permit, but youth waterfowl hunts and Special Permit gun, archery, and youth hunts are held for deer. Some very good quality bucks have been taken on the Gus Engeling WMA. Regular Permit hunts may be held for squirrels.

PRO'S POINTERS. Haucke says you will improve your chances of

success by following these tips. "Deer are fairly evenly distributed over the management area. In general, they will go where the food is. The most productive habitat is always the Catfish Creek bottom, so that is the place to start." Range conditions can vary from year to year, however, so inquire at the office for recommended areas.

Assistant area manager Dale Prochaska advises, "The area has some openings we have created, and drainages act as corridors between those areas. Concentrate on the spring-fed creeks—Skeet, Crawford, Long Branch, Berry Branch, Kidd Spring, D.D. Spring, and Gibson Branch. If you have just a few days to hunt, spend time in the transitional

zones between the uplands and the creeks, where deer have easy access to either type of habitat."

"When there is a good bottomland acorn crop, hogs frequent the areas around the wetlands and the many tributaries of Catfish Creek," Haucke says. "In years when bottomland acorns fail and there is a good crop in the uplands, the hogs will move to those areas. Gray or cat squirrels will be found almost totally within the bottomland habitat where there are water oaks, willow oaks, and overcup oaks. Fox squirrels are generally found in the upland areas, where red oaks, post oaks, blackjack oaks, and Schumard oaks grow. Generally, areas just out of the Catfish Creek bottom along the drainages that flow into it are the most productive. A good strategy is to work the bottom for gray squirrels and loop up drainages into upland areas for fox squirrels."

Successful waterfowl hunting depends on two factors. Catfish Creek must have overbanked and put water into the hardwood bottoms, enabling ducks to feed on acorns. Also, cold weather in the Midwest area of the Central Flyway must have pushed birds down this far. At such times, the oxbows, swamps, and sloughs associated with Catfish Creek all hold waterfowl. "Basically we have just mallards and wood ducks, and people hunt them over decoys," Haucke says. "You don't need a boat, just chest waders and a good retriever. Stand next to a tree in a flooded bottom or in a swamp." Your dog will appreciate a seat strapped onto a tree and a flotation vest when hunting the flooded hardwood bottoms.

FISHING

The camping area with screened shelters along Catfish Creek is popular with fishers, as overnight camping and night fishing are allowed here. Abundant sunfish and perch in the creek make this a great place to introduce kids to fishing. All the common species of catfish are also found in the creek. Lakes 1 and 2 on the area as well as the beaver pond hold largemouth bass up to six pounds. Small boats or canoes may be hand-launched at the beaver pond beside the wildlife-viewing blind.

PRO'S POINTERS. Be aware of the danger from alligators whenever fishing. Berry Lake, a five-acre impoundment, has been stocked with Florida bass and channel catfish and is catch and release only for bass. There is no vehicle access, but the lake is within 300 yards of the parking area, so it is possible to carry a canoe or kayak in.

Catfish Creek has a very healthy population of channel and flathead catfish. There are four main access points: day camp 3, day camp 4, County Road 473, and day camp 1.

INSIDER'S CORNER

BOGGED IN BEAUTY

Even in humid East Texas, where rainfall averages 40 inches locally, the Gus Engeling WMA stands out due to its abundant wetland resources. Approximately 15 springs feed Catfish Creek and its associated tributaries. Some 2,000 acres of bottomland are rank with large trees, understory vegetation, and fallen timber. Beaver ponds and plant succession have retarded Catfish Creek's flow and formed sloughs and marshes. More than 8 miles of Catfish Creek enjoy a strong, continual flow with plentiful fish and other aquatic life. The creek chubsucker is listed as a state threatened species (likely to become endangered). This section of Catfish Creek was declared a National Natural Landmark in 1983 for its significance in illustrating the natural heritage of the United States.

For the visitor, however, the area's four sphagnum moss bogs offer an even more interesting visual feast. The largest covers 225 acres, while others are but a couple of acres. All are "really neat in spring," says area manager Hayden Haucke. "Beds of wild iris have masses of purple blooms in mid- to late April. One bog is rimmed with wild azaleas that bloom near the end of May. They aren't showy like domestic azaleas, but they are very unusual in the wild."

The bogs owe their existence to the area's combination of sandy upland hills underlain by a layer of clay, Haucke says. "Rainfall filters through the sand, hits the impervious layer, and is shunted laterally into the bogs," he explains. Where there is no outlet for the water, a bog forms. Bogs are typically very acidic and allow little decomposition of organic matter, which falls to the bottom and builds up over time.

The bogs are a transition landscape continually striving to become woodlands. "The bogs may have started as beaver ponds," Haucke speculates. "Over time, they will become a sedge wetland; then trees will begin encroaching." In order to keep the bogs in their present state, trees are periodically cleared using inmates from state correctional institutions. "There are places where the bog surface is floating and has trees several inches in diameter growing on mats," Haucke says.

A semiliquid, semisolid somewhere between water and land, the bogs support carnivorous bladderworts, sun dews, and pitcher plants. Pitcher plants entice insects to fall into a reservoir and drown. Bladderworts feed below the surface on microscopic organisms. Sun dews grow flat on the ground and take a more direct approach to predation, snaring small crawling bugs with sticky drops of liquid coating their leaves. Such extreme measures are necessary because the bog soil itself furnishes few nutrients.

The bogs provide an interesting contrast of habitats. Just yards from the swampy soil, dry upland soil supports yuccas, cactus, and sand jack oaks. Common alders form a thicket in the moister area between the two. In some areas, bracken ferns form a green sea under the trees near the bog.

To visit the bogs, contact the area office. Due to the sensitivity of these sites, visitors must be accompanied. For further information on bogs and a virtual tour of similar sites in Leon and Robertson counties, visit the website www.csdl.tamu.edu/flora/flynnbog.

Berry Lake is a good birding venue and a catch-and-release bass fishery.

1,500 acres
P.O. Box 962, Centerville, TX
75833
903/536-7122

DRIVING TIMES FROM:
Amarillo: 8.5 hours
Austin: 3.5 hours
Brownsville: 9.5 hours
Dallas: 2 hours
El Paso: 15 hours
Houston: 2.5 hours
San Antonio: 5 hours

DIRECTIONS: From Palestine, go south on U.S. 79 to Oakwood. Take FM 542 south 0.4 mile to FM 831. On FM 831, drive 4.2 miles to County Road 236, turn left, and go 4.7 miles to the area sign. From that point follow the signs 2.3 miles to the area check station.

OPEN: Only on specified dates.

ACTIVITIES: Hunting.

FACILITIES: Hunter check station.

SPECIAL REGULATIONS: Access is permitted only when Texas Parks and Wildlife personnel are present to monitor traffic on the easement road leading to the property. Trapping and use of horses are prohibited. Shotguns and firearms of no greater than .22 caliber are permitted during squirrel hunts. Muzzleloaders used to hunt deer must be at least .45 caliber.

ADVISORIES: Mosquitoes, poison ivy, and poisonous snakes are present on the area. Flooding may occur in wet weather. Carry your own supply of potable water.

LODGING IN AREA: Motels are available in Palestine, Crockett, Buffalo and Centerville.

LOCAL POINTS OF INTEREST: Texas Freshwater Fisheries Center, Texas State Railroad, Confederate Reunion Grounds State Historical Park, Fort Parker State Park, Old Fort Parker State Historical Park, Jim Hogg State Park and Fairfield Lake State Park.

DISABILITY ACCESS: Not wheelchair-accessible.

HISTORY

Archaeological surveys indicate that the land making up the Keechi Creek WMA was used extensively by prehistoric Indians, probably members of the Deadose tribe, a band of the Bidais. They were part of the Caddoan culture and lived by farming and hunting. After European intrusion, most of the Deadose were wiped out by smallpox; the rest were absorbed into other tribes, including the Keechi, Kickapoo, and Kichai.

An Indian attack on Fort Parker in neighboring Limestone County in 1833 discouraged settlement in the area until after the Texas Revolution. Battles between settlers and Indians resulted in removal of the Indians from Leon County by 1850. Farming and ranching have always been the chief economic activities, although there has been some lumbering.

The previous owner of the land now making up the WMA raised cattle and leased the land for hunting. The area was purchased in 1986 to fulfill mitigation requirements for the Brazos River Authority's construction of Lake Limestone. Mitigation funds and money from sales of the Texas Waterfowl Stamp were used. Keechi Creek WMA was the first noncoastal waterfowl habitat to be acquired using waterfowl stamp funds.

Unfortunately, the purchase appears in retrospect to have been ill-advised. First, there is no deeded public access to the area, and deed restrictions require that Texas Parks and Wildlife personnel be present any time the area is open to the public. This greatly limits its usefulness. Second, this purchase was envisioned as the first in a series of acquisitions totaling about 5,000 acres, but those purchases never happened. As a result, the area is too small to be managed effectively. The flat terrain makes it impossible to manipulate water levels in the bottomland hardwoods without flooding adjacent private property.

GEOGRAPHY AND NATURAL FEATURES

Keechi Creek WMA is about 5 miles west of the Trinity River. Keechi and Buffalo Creeks join on the area, which is primarily flat bottomland hardwoods with small, scattered upland areas. About 90 percent of the area is forested, but there are some small openings and marshes. Water oaks, willow oaks, and overcup oaks are the main trees, along with water elms, and water hickories. The area was logged about 50 years ago, but some of the larger hardwoods were left uncut. Ironwood, yaupon, and beautyberry dominate the understory.

The blue waterleaf blooms as the summer heat wears out and autumn begins to take hold.
ABOVE:
Natural ponds and green-tree reservoirs dominate the bottomlands that cover almost the entire Keechi Creek WMA.

White-tailed deer, feral hogs, and squirrels are the principal game species present. Migratory waterfowl use the marsh areas in winter. Threatened timber (canebrake) rattlesnakes and alligator snapping turtles are present on the area.

Except for a handful of acres around the hunter check station, all the land is subject to seasonal flooding. At present roads on the area are very primitive and may be impassable in wet weather. An all-weather road through the area is planned. Access to the area is restricted by deed; the entrance road passes through private property from County Road 236 to the check station.

Three green-tree reservoirs impound floodwaters from Keechi and Buffalo Creeks from October through January. These are managed for wintering waterfowl. A marsh area is managed for wintering waterfowl and for breeding wood ducks. The marsh area is dewatered in July following nesting.

RECREATIONAL OPPORTUNITIES

Hunting is available by Annual Public Hunting Permit or Regular Permit for squirrels, waterfowl, rabbits, and hares. Special Permit archery and gun deer and feral hog hunts are available by drawing. See the current issue of the *Public Hunting Lands Map Booklet* and the *Applications for Drawings on Public Hunting Lands* for seasons and bag limits.

HUNTING

Despite its small size and limited access, Keechi Creek WMA offers the opportunity for a quality hunting experience. Hunting pressure is very light and human impact negligible. The area is pristine. "This is one of the best areas in Texas for someone who likes a rugged bottomland hunt," says area manager Rick Knipe.

PRO'S POINTERS. About 95 percent of squirrels on the area are gray or "cat" squirrels. These are bottomland dwellers, and since almost the entire area is bottomland, squirrels can be found throughout. Due to the lack of natural cavities in trees, nest boxes are provided for squirrels and have been quite successful in increasing squirrel numbers. Dogs are allowed for squirrel hunting, but Knipe says the best method is to walk through the woods slowly, sit quietly, and watch and listen for squirrel activity. Gray squirrels tend to be most active early and late.

Waterfowl hunting is almost exclusively for wood ducks and mallards. "We only have two weekends of hunting—in January—and they will be here," says Knipe. "Depending on how much water we have, you can hunt green-tree reservoirs, marshes, creeks, and numerous sloughs all over the area. Low spots with water attract ducks to acorns. Hunters are furnished with a map that shows the creeks, marshes, and green-tree reservoirs, and we also have an aerial photo at the check station. We will advise hunters on possible hunting spots." This latter is especially important, since hunters must be off the area by noon, making scouting in the afternoon impossible. The area gate is opened two and a half hours before official sunrise on hunt days, and there are no assigned hunting spots. "The best way to hunt this area is to come and learn it on your first trip—find the green-tree reservoirs, scout for inundated areas, then form a strategy," advises Knipe. "The first weekend will probably be the best hunting, before the ducks are disturbed and move off. By the last day of a three-day hunt, it's hard to buy a duck."

In general there is no need for a boat. Hunters can walk in anywhere, because the water is shallow. In most cases you won't have to walk more than a quarter of a mile from a road to hunt. However, at times the entire management area is under water, and a boat would be very helpful. Call the area manager before going.

Draw hunts for either-sex archery and gun deer and feral hog hunts are conducted by randomly assigned compartments. Baiting is allowed but corn must be certified aflatoxin-free. Hunters are furnished with maps and directions to their compartments. Each hunter has an area of about 100 acres. Hunters may bring their own stands and leave them in place for the duration of the hunt. The gun deer hunts are timed to fall during the rut.

Feral hogs may be hunted using any legal weapon. Look for fresh rooting, wallows, and other signs of hog activity. Hogs tend to be most active early and late.

Because the area is lightly used, the likelihood of standby positions being available for archery and gun hunts is high.

INSIDER'S CORNER

GREEN-TREE RESERVOIRS

Words failed even renowned birding authority Roger Tory Peterson when he attempted to describe the male wood duck, North America's most highly colored duck. "Crested; bizarre face pattern; rainbow iridescence. Descriptive words fail; the illustration explains it," he wrote. Even the gaudy mallard drake pales in comparison. These ducks are, understandably, highly valued by birders and hunters alike for their beauty.

It is no wonder, then, that managing habitat for the benefit of mallards and wood ducks is a priority on many WMAs. Bottomland hardwoods, especially oaks, that can be flooded to a depth of no more than 18 inches during the dormant season provide ideal habitat. Green-tree reservoirs are the tools wildlife managers use to accomplish this.

"Green-tree reservoirs are a waterfowl management strategy," says area manager Rick Knipe. "The idea is to make acorns accessible to ducks while denying them to terrestrial animals such as deer, hogs, and squirrels." Stuttgart, Arkansas, is famous among duck hunters for its green-tree reservoirs, but a number of Texas wildlife management areas have them as well, including Keechi Creek.

Water management is crucial to the success of green-tree reservoirs. Trees will be killed if water is not drained during the growing season (generally March through September), and it is the trees, of course, that produce the acorns. Soils must have good water-holding capabilities. Terrain should be relatively flat so that a water level between 1 and 18 inches can be maintained, and a minimum of 10 acres is needed to attract ducks regularly.

Besides oaks, mast can be provided by trees such as bald cypress, sweet gum, buttonbush, hackberry, honey locust, water locust, pecan, water tupelo, and black gum. Having a variety of mast producers is important, because no one single species will produce adequate quantities of food every year.

Wood duck nesting on green-tree reservoirs can be increased by leaving dead trees standing. Wood ducks nest in cavities in trees; where few such cavities exist, they are often supplemented by nesting boxes placed around the edges of ponds.

Green-tree reservoirs generally use a system of dikes and water-control structures to regulate water levels. Areas such as Keechi Creek WMA close control structures to capture seasonal floodwaters, then open them when the growing season begins. Ironically, one of the chief problems in managing green-tree reservoirs is beavers, who frequently plug drains in an attempt to keep "their" pond flooded.

100 acres
3852 Pine Ridge Rd.
La Grange, TX 78945
979/968-6591

Driving Times from:
Amarillo: 9.5 hours
Austin: 0.75 hour
Brownsville: 5 hours
Dallas: 4 hours
El Paso: 10.5 hours
Houston: 2.5 hours
San Antonio: 1 hour
Directions: From the intersection of I-10 and Texas 80 in Luling, go south on Texas 80 for 7.9 miles to the entrance gate on the right. Follow the road for 0.9 mile to the area office.
Open: On designated dates.
Activities: Nature trail, wildlife viewing, hiking.
Facilities: Indoor classroom, picnic pavilion, restrooms, nature trail.
Special Regulations: All use must be under the supervision of Texas Parks and Wildlife employees.
Advisories: Rattlesnakes, copperheads, and coral snakes are present. Carry your own supply of potable water.
Lodging in Area: Motels are available in Luling, Seguin, and Gonzales.
Local Points of Interest: Lockhart State Park, Palmetto State Park, Sebastopol State Historical Park.
Disability Access: The restrooms, indoor classroom, and picnic pavilion are wheelchair-accessible.

History

The Neasloney WMA is the only such area in Texas that contains the grave of the person who donated it to the Texas Parks and Wildlife Department. Milfred Otto Neasloney lived on the site for approximately 10 years before donating it to the department in 1984 to be used as a wildlife demonstration area, especially for schools and youth groups. "One stipulation of the donation was that he be buried here and that there be a flagpole with flag always flying and a light shining on it at night," says area manager Bob Carroll. "Mr. Neasloney retired from the United States Marine Corps and was buried here with full military honors." The grave is located about 30 feet south of the area office.

Geography and Natural Features

The Neasloney WMA is located in the sandy post oak belt. While most of the area is fairly level, it does contain one significant intermittent drainage and some low rolling hills. An old field of about 40 acres remains treeless, but the balance of the area is thickly wooded. One stock pond furnishes water for wildlife.

Woody vegetation consists primarily of post oak, black jack oak, and hickory trees. Yaupon and deciduous holly share the understory with a rampant growth of American beautyberry. Grasses such as little bluestem and brownseed paspalum are found in the open pasture.

Significant numbers of white-tailed deer, wild turkeys, bobcats, coyotes, fox squirrels, raccoons, and feral hogs are present on the area. Javelina visit on occasion. Migratory songbirds use the area in spring and fall.

Recreational Opportunities

The principal uses of the area are for demonstration of wildlife management practices to landowners and hunter education courses for youth groups. However, visitation by the general public is permitted by reservation or whenever Texas Parks and Wildlife personnel are present. For information, call Bob Carroll at 979-968-6591.

Nature Trail

A nature trail winds about 1 mile through the wooded portion of the area and passes by the stock pond and supplemental food plot demonstration area before returning to the area office. A guidebook to the trail available at the office is keyed to 30 numbered markers along the trail.

PRO'S POINTERS. The natural-surfaced trail begins at the office and follows a drainage for part of its length. It is mostly level, easy walking, but the sandy soil is very loose when dry.

"Notice the food plots along the trail," advises assistant area manager Don Bujnoch. "We try out different plants to see how they do in this climate and soil. The intent is to show people how to use supplemental food plots to improve herd health, not numbers."

April and May are peak months for wildflowers on the area. Among the flowers to look for are asters, coreopsis, Engelman daisies, erect dayflowers, gaillardias, gayfeathers, Indian blankets, meadow pinks, Drummond phlox, Queen Anne's

A one-mile nature trail winds through all the different habitat types on the small M.O. Neasloney WMA.

TOP:
The WMA office building also houses an indoor classroom used during wildlife management field days for landowners and hunter education courses for youth groups.

ABOVE:
A coyote visiting a small farm pond on the area left this evidence of its passage.

lace, Texas vervain, and winecups. Also be alert for bull nettle's white flowers and spiny leaves, which give a nasty sting.

WILDLIFE VIEWING

There is no designated wildlife-viewing area. However, deer and other animals can often be seen along the nature trail and near the office, especially early in the morning or late in the day. A deer feeder about 150 yards northeast of the office attracts animals.

PRO'S POINTERS. The stock pond attracts a variety of animals and birds, especially during dry, hot weather. From the pond, you can also follow the perimeter fence west to a hill on the southwest corner of the property. This hill overlooks the drainage and is often used as a bedding area by deer.

Migratory birds are present in March and April. There is no bird list for the area at present, but birds you are likely to see include barred owls, mourning doves, Inca doves, cardinals, painted buntings, chickadees, several kinds of warblers, scissor-tailed flycatchers, meadowlarks, and sparrows.

The entry road and the utility right-of-way from the highway offer good close-up birding. Both run from the highway to the office building, where you can park. A bonus on the right-of-way is the possibility of seeing badgers, which have burrows in the area of the third utility pole east of the edge of the open field.

HIKING

The only designated trail on the area is the nature trail. However, you are also free to hike the entry road.

PRO'S POINTERS. To sample all the habitat types on the area, begin at the edge of the open field where the access road enters it. Turn to the right and follow the fence all the way around the property and back to the beginning. This is about a 2-mile walk. The pasture road along the fence is mowed periodically. Be prepared for walking in deep, slippery sand. Open-toed shoes or footwear with vents where sand can enter are not recommended.

BULL NETTLE

My visit to the Neasloney WMA brought back memories of childhood—unpleasant ones. The farm where I grew up was heavily infested with Texas bull nettle, and since we worked crops by hand, we came in contact with this stinging abomination regularly. Its other common names of "tread-softly" and "mala mujer" (Spanish for "bad woman") give some indication of its reputation.

Bull nettle's bright-green leaves and white flowers belie its evil nature. Its stems bristle with stinging trichomes—fragile, needlelike structures that need only brush one's skin lightly to impart an instant unpleasantness lasting for several minutes.

On our farm, bull nettle could hardly be avoided, since it grew prolifically in the fields of peanuts, corn, sweet potatoes, and watermelons. When we hoed crops to remove weeds, it was one of our chief enemies. Its very deep taproot meant we could never get rid of it completely, but we hacked away at the part above ground with a zeal fired by desire for revenge. Often, of course, it struck back, and we applied the only remedy we knew to ease the pain: We spit on the affected place and then rubbed it with a handful of sand. Apparently the sand removed the tiny trichomes. Or perhaps, as with many folk remedies, the relief was mostly mental.

Watermelons were the worst crop for attracting bull nettle, since the spreading vines prevented plowing after the plants began to spread, and the bull nettle was able to grow unmolested. The biggest and best watermelons seemed to have a knack for growing close beside bull nettle plants, and picking them guaranteed many nasty encounters.

However, as the bull nettle matured, it displayed a trait we did enjoy. Bull nettle produces seeds in triple pods that, when they dry to just the right stage, suddenly pop open and fling the seeds a short distance from the plant. These seeds have a thin, easily removed husk housing a meat with a very tasty, nutlike flavor. Gathering and eating bull nettle seeds was one of the simple pleasures of farm life that—along with the stings—lingers in memory still.

8,925 acres
185 SE 31st St.
Paris, TX 75460
903/785-0482

DRIVING TIMES FROM:
Amarillo: 7 hours
Austin: 5.5 hours
Brownsville: 11 hours
Dallas: 2 hours
El Paso: 13 hours
Houston: 5.5 hours
San Antonio: 7 hours
DIRECTIONS: From Paris, go north on U.S. 271 about 3.5 miles to FM 1499. Follow FM 1499 west 11.5 miles to the area check station.
OPEN: Daily except when closed for Special Permit hunts.
ACTIVITIES: Wildlife viewing, hiking, hunting, fishing.
FACILITIES: None.
SPECIAL REGULATIONS: All users must register on-site. Use of horses is allowed except during gun deer season. Hunters must possess an Annual Public Hunting Permit. A Limited Public Use Permit is not required for nonconsumptive users. Rifles or handguns no larger than .22-caliber rimfire or .36-caliber muzzleloader may be used to take squirrels, rabbits, hares, coyotes, and fur-bearing animals.

Pat Mayse WMA includes a 1,500-acre lake that is popular with local fishers.

ADVISORIES: Unexploded artillery rounds and rockets from World War II training exercises remain on the area. Do not approach or disturb any such objects. Avoid leaving vehicles at some access points; see below.
LODGING IN AREA: Motels are available in Paris and Bonham.
LOCAL POINTS OF INTEREST: Bonham State Park, Cooper Lake State Park, Sam Bell Maxey House State Historical Park.
DISABILITY ACCESS: The waterfowl-viewing area at Pat Mayse Dam is wheelchair-accessible.

HISTORY

The area now comprising the Pat Mayse WMA was once home to Caddo Indians. Anglo settlers began arriving in the Red River Valley as early as 1815. The Central National Road of the Republic of Texas passed through the vicinity. Agriculture was the primary economic activity in Lamar County from the beginning, with production of most crops peaking between 1900 and and 1920 and slowly declining thereafter. Population followed a similar trend. The Great Depression of the 1930s and the drought of that same period further weakened the local economy.

World War II brought the establishment of Camp Maxey, an infantry training base 10 miles north of Paris. The area was chosen because its varied terrain presented the opportunity for building facilities dealing with modern battle conditions. An artillery range, obstacle course, infiltration course, and "German village" were built. The latter was located in what is now the southeastern part of the WMA, in hunt compartment 1.

Construction of Pat Mayse Reservoir in the early 1960s led the U.S.

Army Corps of Engineers to purchase land adjacent to the lake to be managed for fish and wildlife as mitigation for losses due to construction of the lake. Texas Parks and Wildlife has managed these lands under license from the Corps of Engineers since 1971.

GEOGRAPHY AND NATURAL FEATURES

Pat Mayse WMA is in the Post Oak Savannah region. It contains 1,500 acres of lake surface, 2,500 acres of abandoned fields and pastures, and almost 5,000 acres of hardwood timber. Of the latter, approximately 1,000 acres are classified as bottomland hardwoods.

The area is generally level to gently rolling. Sanders Creek, Craddock Creek, and Sand Branch are permanent streams. Dominant trees include post oak, blackjack oak, water oak, red oak, willow oak, hickory, elm, and sweet gum. Abandoned fields contain a variety of grasses, including Bermuda, threeawn and lovegrass and a variety of forbs. Persimmon, winged elm, and eastern red cedar are invading these open areas.

RECREATIONAL OPPORTUNITIES

WILDLIFE VIEWING

The varied habitat types on Pat Mayse WMA provide the opportunity to see everything from neotropical migrants to waterfowl to bald eagles. A birding checklist is available from the Corps of Engineers office at Pat Mayse Dam, on FM 906 between Chicota and Midcity.

PRO'S POINTERS. The best birding is from spring through early summer, says area manager Richard Hines. "In woodland areas, look for scarlet tanagers and orchard orioles. Open meadows may have roadrunners, scissor-tailed flycatchers, indigo buntings, and painted buntings." Cedar waxwings are present on the area in winter, as are ducks and bald eagles. An occasional white pelican may be seen on the lake during spring and fall migrations.

Some of the best waterfowl viewing is below Pat Mayse dam in a 40-acre moist-soil management area that is part of the WMA. A wheelchair-accessible levee extends into the wetland area. Several varieties of plovers, sandpipers, herons, and egrets frequent the area.

HIKING

A quarter-mile trail adjacent to the Sanders Creek bridge on FM 1499 offers a loop through typical Post Oak Savannah and woodland. The trail passes a pond holding wood ducks, cormorants, great blue herons, and beavers. The trailhead is at the information station at the north end of the bridge on the east side of the highway. A 4-mile trail also begins here and ends at the hunter check station at FM 1499 and County Road 35650. It is marked with red and blue paint blazes. The trail runs west along the southern boundary of compartment 5C, then turns north along the boundary of compartments 8B and 8A and continues to County Road 35650. The trail traverses open meadows, Post Oak Savannah, and dense woodland. Birds likely to be seen include bobwhite quail, eastern meadowlarks, wild turkeys, warblers, and vireos. In the fall, numerous wildflowers along the trail include blazing stars, coneflowers, and asters.

In addition to the two trails described above, there are 11 miles of existing roads and trails open to hiking; horseback riding is allowed on designated roads. The area is closed to hiking during draw hunts.

HUNTING

In keeping with Corps of Engineers policy, hunting is allowed for most types of legal game that occur on the area. Most game can be hunted under the Annual Public Hunting Permit program, but there are draw hunts for

deer and eastern wild turkeys. Youth-only waterfowl and youth-adult squirrel hunts are also offered. For legal species, seasons, and bag limits, see the current editions of the *Public Hunting Lands Map Booklet* and the *Applications for Drawings on Public Hunting Lands.*

WMA boundaries are marked with white paint about every 100 feet; the 24 hunt compartment boundaries are marked with yellow paint every 100 feet. Hunters are furnished detailed maps of the area showing these boundaries. Compartments range in size from 150 to 400 acres. For gun hunts, the person whose name appears first on the list of paid hunters furnished by Texas Parks and Wildlife headquarters has first choice of hunting compartments, the person whose name appears second has second choice, and so on. Some compartments are more accessible than others; hunt managers will advise which require four-wheel drive for access.

PRO'S POINTERS. "Deer are pretty evenly distributed around the area," says Hines. "We have some upland compartments with open fields as well as some bottomland forests that are 100 percent wooded with swampy areas. Ask the hunt staff for a compartment with the type of habitat you prefer to hunt."

Highest deer densities are in the compartments adjacent to Sanders Creek—numbers 1C, 3A, 3B, 5B, 8B, and 9B. "Deer move from the bottomland areas up the drainages to the upland compartments during the public gun hunts—people push them up onto the ridges," says Hines. "If you don't get a bottomland site, take an upland compartment above one of the bottomland sites and hunt travel corridors along drainages."

Compartments 10A and 10B require a 4- to 5-mile walk to get in. Both go all the way to the lake, however, so they can be accessed by boat. Launch at Lamar Point at the end of FM 1500 and boat about a mile across the lake.

"Tree stands—the lean-on or hang-on types—work best here," says Hines. "Hunters can leave them in place while they are hunting." Baiting is not allowed.

Archery deer hunting is available by on-site registration. Visit the check station at the intersection of FM 1499 and County Road 35650; there will be an aerial photograph posted there during hunting season. "Look for drainages and travel corridors between habitat types," advises Hines.

You may be lucky enough to spot an eastern wild turkey, which have been restocked on the area and have increased to huntable numbers.

207

"We have a lot of oak areas; in good mast years food is widespread, so deer will be scattered all over the place. In scarce mast years, if you can find acorns dropping, that's the place to hunt. In dry years willow oaks in the bottomlands produce more acorns. If you don't find acorns on upland sites, check out bottomland sites. In deep woodlands, look for old fencelines and old field lines with large trees on one side and smaller trees on the other. This creates natural travel lanes through the woods. In drainages, look for places where two or more drainages join; deer tend to concentrate there. If you have a Pat Mayse Lake West Quadrangle topo map, look for ridges with saddles and hunt the saddles. Deer tend to cross there. Keep in mind that saddles are very subtle here—there's not a lot of relief."

Pat Mayse is one of the few WMAs in Texas reporting low numbers of feral hogs—the first one was killed on the area in 1998. Taking hogs during any legal hunt is allowed using the weapon and ammunition legal for that hunt.

Squirrel hunting varies according to the mast crop—good squirrel seasons lag good acorn crops by a year. Because of its large number of oak trees, Pat Mayse WMA has the potential to produce large numbers of gray and fox squirrels and has both spring and fall seasons.

For gray squirrels, "Hunt any woodland area," says Hines. "The Sanders Creek bottom produces the largest number of gray squirrels. Everything east of FM 1499 seems to be the best squirrel-producing area—the densest woods are there. I'm strictly a still-hunter. I sit, listen, and when I hear squirrels dropping pieces of hickory nut or barking, I'll gradually move to the area, look for squirrels in trees, and take one. This kind of hunting is the best way to break young hunters in. They learn how to stalk, keep quiet in the woods, and sit still." Hines suggests hunt compartments 4A, 5A, 5C, and 8B for gray squirrels.

Barely noticeable unless you know they are there, mima mounds occur only in undisturbed prairie lands such as those found on Pat Mayse WMA. See the Insider's Corner for more information.

Fox squirrels occur primarily in upland sites and more open woodlands; they typically inhabit savannah areas. Try compartments 7 and 10 for fox squirrels.

Quail are present on the area, and Hines is making a concerted effort to restore quail habitat. Between 800 and 1,000 acres per year are burned, and members of local quail hunting clubs are assisting with brush-control efforts. "In several years, we will have the habitat back where it needs to be," Hines says. "Compartments 5, 6, 7, 8, and 10 will be best for quail."

Waterfowl hunters have their choice of jumpshooting ducks on ponds within the WMA or decoying on old farm ponds in compartments 5A and 8A. Pintails, gadwalls, mallards, scaup, and teal are the main species present. "The best waterfowl hunting is on Pay Mayse Lake itself, and you do need a boat," says Hines. "There are about 1,500 acres of surface water within the WMA itself. If it is crowded on the WMA, you can hunt the rest of the lake, and you do not need an Annual Public Hunting Permit to hunt on that part of the lake outside the WMA." Hines suggests hunting out of a covered boat on points jutting into the lake or hiding your boat around a point and walking back to the point to hunt. Using downed vegetation or driftwood to make a blind is permitted.

FISHING

Catfish, crappie, chain pickerel, and largemouth bass are the main species in the lake, which also has white bass and hybrid striped bass.

PRO'S POINTERS. No Annual Public Hunting Permit is required for fishing in the lake. To fish Sanders Creek from a boat, use a canoe or jonboat that can be hand-launched at the FM 1499 bridge. To fish standing timber, run into the 800 or so acres of standing timber in the west end of the lake. Jig for crappie around the trees. In the spring, the outlet below the dam is good for striped bass and sand bass when water is being released.

Launching at the Clay Bluff boat ramp (1.2 miles west of FM 1500 on County Road 34770) or at Lamar Point (at the end of FM 1500) is not recommended due to the presence of underwater hazards and the lack of security for vehicles left in the parking lot.

For largemouth bass, local fishing guide Jim Blassingame advises launching from one of the Corps of Engineers ramps on the east end of the lake (Sanders Cove, Pat Mayse East, or Pat Mayse West) and working points on the main lake. "We keep brush piles on all the main points; find them and you'll catch fish. Any main lake point in 8 to 12 feet of water will almost always produce largemouths," he says. "Drop off to about 14 feet, and you will catch crappie and stripers, just about any time of year."

The lake also supports a couple of unusual fisheries. "Lots of people like to bowfish for carp here," says Blassingame. "We also have quite a few grass and chain pickerel—the state record chain pickerel came out of this lake. I caught and released an even bigger one; he's still out there around Pat Mayse West park." Blassingame advises fishing for pickerel in the winter months using spinnerbaits, jerkbaits, or swimming minnow type baits with a slow presentation, in the same type of cover as largemouths.

INSIDER'S CORNER

MOUNDS OF MYSTERY

One of the most fascinating features of Pat Mayse WMA almost escapes detection. Both in savannah and woodland areas, you may notice low, circular mounds from 3 to 40 feet in diameter and as much as 3 feet tall. These microtopographical features are known variously as pimple mounds, prairie mounds, or mima mounds. The latter name comes from their similarity to burial mounds made by the Mima Indians of Washington State.

An area with a number of mounds scattered among the trees is located across from the entrance to hunt compartments 5A and 8A on County Road 35650, 0.7 mile west of its intersection with FM 1499.

While the processes that made the mounds are unclear, they do seem to be associated with unplowed prairie lands. As a result, they are quite rare. In Minnesota, similar mounds have been associated with the wintering activities of Manitoba or Canadian toads, which burrow into ground loosened by pocket gophers and spend the winter there insulated from the cold. Researchers found over 3,000 toads in just one mound.

Toads—especially Canadian ones—do not appear to have made these Texas mounds. But what did? For now, that remains a mystery.

40,920 acres
121 CR 3131
Decatur, TX 76234
940/627-5475

DRIVING TIMES FROM:
Amarillo: 5.5 hours
Austin: 4.5 hours
Brownsville: 10 hours
Dallas: 1 hour
El Paso: 12 hours
Houston: 5 hours
San Antonio: 6 hours
DIRECTIONS: From Denton, take I-35 north about 10 miles to FM 3002. Travel east 7 miles to the Johnson Branch Unit of Ray Roberts Lake State Park. The WMA office is located in the maintenance area. Access points are scattered around the lake.
OPEN: Daily.
ACTIVITIES: Wildlife viewing, hiking, hunting, fishing.
FACILITIES: Boat ramps, restrooms.
SPECIAL REGULATIONS: Hunters are required to possess an Annual Public Hunting Permit. No Limited Public Use Permit is required for nonconsumptive users. Hunters must enter at designated access points or boat ramps. Shotguns and archery equipment only may be used for hunting. Hunting is prohibited on land or water within 100 yards of state park boundaries. Waterfowl shooting hours end at noon. Camping, trapping, target shooting, and use of horses are prohibited.
ADVISORIES: Carry your own supply of potable water.
LODGING IN AREA: Motels are available in Denton, Gainesville, and Sanger.
LOCAL POINTS OF INTEREST: Eisenhower State Park, Eisenhower Birthplace State Historical Park, Ray Roberts Lake State Park, Fort Richardson State Historical Park, Lake Mineral Wells State Park, Lake Lewisville State Park, Hagerman National Wildlife Refuge.
DISABILITY ACCESS: Restrooms (at state park boat ramps) are wheelchair-accessible.

HISTORY

This section of North Texas lay between territory of the Caddo Indians to the east and the Comanches to the west. Anglo settlement began in the 1840s on land granted to colonizer William Peters by the Texas Congress. Most settlers built homes in the wooded Cross Timbers. Cattle rancher John Chisum came later and ran cattle on the grasslands to the west, but farming was the principal land use for most of the area's history. Livestock raising and dairying now dominate, but in recent years increasing amounts of land have been sold for real-estate development. Urbanization poses one of the biggest problems facing Ray Roberts WMA today, along with heavy demand for all forms of recreation, especially waterfowl hunting.

Lake Ray Roberts was constructed in the early 1980s, and Texas Parks and Wildlife took responsibility for managing wildlife on the property in 1988 under license from the U.S. Army Corps of Engineers. In 1999 the name was changed to Ray Roberts Public Hunting Area in recognition of the principal use of the area. The annual waterfowl harvest is among the highest of all WMAs in Texas.

GEOGRAPHY AND NATURAL FEATURES

Ray Roberts WMA is dominated by huge Ray Roberts Lake, which occupies approximately 29,000 of the total acres. Most of the land area lies within the flood pool of the reservoir, which was formed by damming the Elm Fork of the Trinity River. Buck Creek and Range Creek are major tributaries on the area, which forms a giant horseshoe stretching some 16 miles north to south and 20 miles east to west. The shoreline of the lake is heavily indented with coves.

"Ray Bob," as it is commonly called, spans three major physiographic regions: the Eastern Cross Timbers, the Grand Prairie, and the Blackland Prairie. The latter occurs

This busy marina is just one sign of the heavy use and development that characterize the Ray Roberts Public Hunting Area. Unlike many WMAs, Ray Roberts is used almost to the point of abuse.

only in a small area on the extreme eastern portion of the WMA. Most of the eastern portion of the WMA lies within the Eastern Cross Timbers and the western part within the Grand Prairie.

Overall, the land is gently rolling. The Cross Timbers consist of oak savannah dominated by post oak and blackjack oaks. Elm, ash, pecan, and cottonwood trees are found in the bottomlands. The Grand Prairie to the west is covered principally with little bluestem on the uplands and mixed hardwoods in the bottomlands of the Elm Fork of the Trinity River. Little prairie habitat is found in the Blackland Prairie portion of the WMA, which is mostly confined to creek bottoms. Access to the area is by boat or via numerous highways and county roads. The latter weave a confusing tangle through the area.

Wildlife on Ray Roberts WMA consists mainly of smaller mammals such as rabbits, raccoons, gray foxes, coyotes, beavers, and opossums. Game animals present include mourning doves, ducks, geese, feral hogs and fox squirrels. A few bald eagles winter on the lake, and neotropical migrants use the area in spring.

RECREATIONAL OPPORTUNITIES

Ray Roberts Lake WMA offers wildlife viewing, hiking, hunting, and fishing. Waterfowl hunting and fishing are the main uses.

WILDLIFE VIEWING

Ducks offer the best wildlife-viewing opportunities. Widgeons, mallards, wood ducks, and teal are the main species, but scaup, gadwalls, canvasbacks, ringnecks, pintails, and redheads may be spotted as well. Neotropical migrants are present in spring.

PRO'S POINTERS. Waterfowl viewing is best during the winter months, when ducks are on the lake. During this time some shore and wading birds can also be seen in wetland areas along Range Creek. "The best waterfowl viewing is in the designated waterfowl sanctuary on the west side of the lake," says area manager Jennifer Barrow. "No waterfowl hunting is allowed there." FM 922 offers one good viewing site where it crosses the Elm Fork of the Trinity River east of Valley View and another farther east, at the first lake crossing west of Tioga. Park at the end of the bridge and walk through the gate to the shoreline. Bald eagles winter in the waterfowl sanctuary and other areas and may be spotted from the highway. To see the maximum number of duck species, visit from December through February.

Waterfowl watching is also good around a managed wetlands area at the northeast corner of the WMA. To access this area, go north from Tioga on U.S. 377 about a mile to Shawnee Road. Turn right and go 0.4 mile to Airport Road; turn right and go 1.2 miles to Hart Lane. Turn left and

drive 1.5 miles to the parking area. The wetlands lie east of the road and were once part of the WMA.

"In March and April it is possible to see migrating white pelicans on the main lake and in the coves," says Barrow. "For songbirds, the Culp Branch Native Prairie area is good, because it has a mixture of open space and brush." It also has both Blackland Prairie and Cross Timbers habitat. By walking in a half mile or so from the parking area on FM 455 about 5 miles east of Sanger, you can access several hundred acres of rolling hills overlooking the lake. The trees along the old roadbeds harbor numerous songbirds, while shorebirds frequent the water's edge. Several old homesites dot the area; they are easily identified by the presence of concrete slabs and exotic plants. Birds seem to like these areas as well. Plum thickets and small drainages provide plenty of cover for wildlife.

Another good birding area begins at the Hunsaker Road access point. To reach this area, go to Tioga and turn west off U.S. 377 on Gene Autry Street, across the highway from Clark's Outpost restaurant. Cross the railroad tracks and go 100 yards or so

LEFT:
Birding is excellent around the shore of Lake Ray Roberts.
RIGHT:
A brightly colored male cardinal sings to defend his territory on Ray Roberts Public Hunting Area.

to North Texas Street. Turn left and follow the gravel road along the white board fence. Continue, following the bends in the road, through a residential area for a total of 1.2 miles from the highway. At the parking area, the old roadbed continues straight ahead until it submerges beneath the lake. Large trees and open fields on either side of the old roadbed attract many songbirds. Depending on the lake level, it may be one-quarter to one-half mile to the lake, where shorebirds roam and carp spawn in the shallows in spring.

Blue heron rookeries can be seen in tall dead trees in the lake where U.S. 377 crosses it 3 miles north of Tioga and on Wolf Creek about a

mile south of FM 922 on County Road 215.

Hiking

There are no designated hiking trails on Ray Roberts WMA, and the property boundary tends to hug the lakeshore and heavily wooded drainages, so walking opportunities are limited.

PRO'S POINTERS. Culp Branch Native Prairie has old roads that make good walking routes, and there are good views of the lake from atop low hills. Just the sight of wind waves running through the grass make the walk worthwhile. The parking area and access point for Culp Branch is on FM 455 about 5 miles east of

Sanger. Another good short walk is from the parking area for the Hunsaker Road access point; see directions under wildlife viewing, above. For a walk across open fields overlooking the lake, park at the entry point at the intersection of FM 3002 and County Road 231 and walk north between the shore and the boundary fence. This area is within the waterfowl sanctuary, making it a good birding area during hunting season.

Hunting

Hunting for waterfowl (primarily ducks—few geese use the area), feral hogs, quail, doves, rabbits and hares, and squirrels is allowed by Annual Public Hunting Permit. Youth waterfowl and youth-adult quail hunts are offered. See the current *Public Hunting Lands Map Booklet* and *Outdoor Annual* for legal species, limits, and seasons. Waterfowl hunting closes at noon.

Due to its proximity to the Dallas-Fort Worth area, Ray Roberts WMA attracts more waterfowl hunters than any other state wildlife management area in Texas.

PRO'S POINTERS. Expect to have lots of company when you hunt waterfowl on Ray Roberts WMA. "We have about 1,200 duck hunters annually, many of whom are regulars," says Barrow. "It's first come, first served. In order to get a good spot, a lot of people arrive at 2 A.M., put out their decoys, then fish until shooting time." The waterfowl sanctuary north of FM 3002 on the west side of the area is closed to waterfowl hunting only.

"Most of the duck hunting takes place on the northeast side of the lake," says Barrow. "Anywhere on Buck Creek is generally good. There's a boat launch on U.S. 377

The Culp Branch Native Prairie is crossed by old roads that make good hiking trails; birding is very good in the trees along the roads.

just south of the Buck Creek bridge. Another good spot is on Indian Creek about halfway to FM 922." An access point off County Road 203 about 2 miles south of FM 922 gives foot entry. The tip of the peninsula between Indian Creek and the main lake can also be accessed from the boat ramp on the Johnson Branch unit of Ray Roberts Lake State Park. To shoot ducks in standing timber, use the access point where FM 372 dead-ends on the north side of the lake and hunt around the mouth of Wolf Creek. Widgeons, mallards, wood ducks, teal, scaup, gadwalls, canvasbacks, redheads, and ringnecks are the main species.

Hunters may not cut vegetation to make blinds. "Most people hunt out of a boat," says Barrow. "Walk-in hunters use temporary blinds or natural cover. You can have a quality hunt, but you have to get here early. Midweek during December and early January is the best time to come because all the ducks are here and there aren't as many people."

Feral hogs tend to be most numerous along Range Creek on the northeast side between U.S. 377 and Horseshoe Road and along Buck Creek between U.S. 377 and Howell Road. To reach the access point on Howell Road, take FM 121 east from Tioga about 4 miles to Buck Creek Drive. Turn right onto Buck Creek Drive and go about three-quarters of a mile to Howell Road. This area is also good for squirrels. The wetlands area east of Horseshoe Road is also good hog habitat. Archery-only hunting is allowed from January through September. Check the map booklet for current dates. Tree stands or blinds may be put up but must be taken down daily. Access points are located on both Horseshoe Road and Howell Road. (Several new access points were added for the 1999–2000 hunting season. Hunters familiar with Ray Roberts WMA from prior years will find foot access is much more convenient now.)

Quail may be present in the Culp Branch Native Prairie area and in the Range Creek upland off Hart Lane, but there are not many birds. Hunt quail somewhere else. Mourning doves, however, offer better possibilities. The open field at the intersection of FM 3002 and County Road 231 is probably the best for doves, but the Culp Branch Native Prairie close to the water can also be good. Culp Branch is the best habitat for rabbits and hares here as well. There are some wheat fields on private property on the west side of the lake, making it possible to catch birds flying to and from the lake for water. The WMA is close to a lot of public dove-hunting areas, so if there are no birds there, it's easy to try another place close by.

Squirrels may be hunted with shotgun only; there is no closed season or bag limit. "One good area is on the Buck Creek drainage along Howell Road," says Barrow. "Also try along Range Creek in the bottom along Horseshoe Road (which is signed Graham Road on the north end). In wet weather, enter from the north side from Hogtown road; in really wet weather, do not attempt this road at all." Squirrels may also be hunted in the Crossroads Road area north of Tioga; there's an access point about a mile and a half west of U.S. 377.

FISHING

Fishers are not required to register, but Barrow requests they do so to assist in the gathering of harvest information. Black bass, crappie, and catfish are the main species in the lake, but white (sand) bass are also present. The lake has an abundance of standing timber, but perhaps just as important are the flooded roadbeds and fencerows scattered all over the lake. Some brush piles were put in the lake before it was flooded. A lake map is available at Ray Roberts Lake Marina and area stores selling tackle.

PRO'S POINTERS. Charlie Steed of Gainesville, a full-time fishing guide on Ray Roberts Lake, identifies three keys to fishing this big lake: creeks, cormorants, and submerged structure. "Buck Creek, Pierce Branch, Indian Creek, Isle de Bois Creek, Walnut Creek, Spring Creek, and the Elm Fork of the Trinity River are all good. There are creeks coming into those creeks, and all have lots of standing timber and fencerows around them. There is lots of structure," Steed says.

Steed says black bass fishing is best from the end of March through mid-May. "In March, fish deep—15 to 20 feet—early in the morning, then as the day and the water warm up, work your way shallower as the fish move to the shallows to feed. During April, the fish get shallower and shallower, and by the end of April into the first part of May, you are fishing for bedding fish. This is when I catch most of my big fish."

In summer, Steed says, use Texas or Carolina rigs and fish deep-water humps. "You need a 30- to 40-foot depth around a hump that comes up to within about 20 feet of the surface," he explains. "Anchor at the top of the hump and pull the worm from the deep water into the shallower water. That way you don't have to guess what depth the fish are—you'll pull it through them."

For duck hunters in December and January fishing while waiting for shooting time, Steed suggests fishing deep-water structure next to the hydrilla beds at the mouths of Walnut, Lick, and Wolf Creeks. "Fish with big red Rattletraps, big red spinner baits, or pumpkin-pepper green glitter craw worms," he advises. "Throw shallow and work your bait slowly out to deep water."

Creeks are also the key to crappie on Ray Roberts. "In early spring, crappie will be in shallow water up in the tailends of the creeks where the water is warmer," Steed says. "In early spring, fish for crappie late in the afternoon until nine o'clock or so

213

at night, because that's when the shallow water will be warmest. By mid-April, when they start to spawn as the days get longer and warmer, you can fish shallow all day long up in the tailends of the creeks and coves in six inches to two feet of water. Use a slip cork and a jig and bank fish or wade fish, because you can't get to the water you need to in a boat."

In summer, crappie will suspend near standing timber in 25 to 30 feet of water; you'll find fish from 12 feet deep all the way to the bottom. In winter, crappie can be found even deeper near standing timber next to creek channels and especially in 25 to 35 feet of water next to the mouths of creeks. "Fish with small jigs and small minnows," Steed says. "A good minnow color is chartreuse with a red head."

Compared to bass and crappie fishing, catfishing on Ray Roberts Lake is simple. "It sounds crazy, but fish underneath the cormorants," Steed says. "Their droppings are a natural chum. Use a seine or throw net to get some shad. Cut their heads and tails off, and fish with the body using a 1/16-ounce slip sinker and a number 2 hook. The fish will be right under the big timber the birds roost in. Water depth doesn't really matter, because the fish will be where the birds are, but about 10 feet is my favorite depth. That lets you sneak the boat in and cast quietly up under the limbs without spooking the fish off, and you won't spook the other fish when you catch one." As everywhere else, stinkbaits will also work on cats.

INSIDER'S CORNER

OVEREAGER BEAVERS

Among the animals making a quiet comeback in Texas is one some people would rather stay away: the beaver. Beavers are more common in Texas than many people realize, and in many places, they have become numerous enough to be nuisances to people attempting to manage wetlands for wildlife.

A beaver's overriding concern in life is to hoard water, because water provides cover and access to food. To this end, beavers dam streams and spend a considerable amount of time maintaining and repairing their dams so as to prevent the escape of water. So ingrained is this behavior that the sound of running water stimulates beavers to plug whatever hole is allowing the water to escape.

Managers of wetlands draw down ponds during warm months to allow the growth of plants that will be used as food by ducks when the pond is refilled. Known as moist-soil management, this is a productive technique for providing food for wintering ducks. Alternatively, flooding bottomland hardwoods during the winter can give ducks access to acorns, but the water must be drained before the growing season begins in order to avoid killing the trees. Conflicts between people and beavers arise when beavers plug water-control structures and interfere with attempts to manipulate water levels. The beavers do not realize that partially draining the pond represents no threat to them. They simply cannot resist the urge to plug leaks—that's what beavers do. The simple answer is to get rid of the beavers, and for many years, that's what was done.

Fortunately, wildlife biologists have found a way to have their wetlands and their beavers, too. They install PVC pipes through beaver dams so that water from the pond can be drained to the desired level. Perforated sewer-pipe sections serve as the intake; solid sections of pipe pass through the dam and carry the outfall far enough away that the sound does not stimulate the beavers to build a new dam below it.

Texas Parks and Wildlife offers a free brochure detailing this technique entitled "An Improved Device for Managing Water Levels in Beaver Ponds." Overeager beavers no longer need pose a threat to wetlands management. The slap of a beaver's tail on the water can once again be a sound to be welcomed rather than dreaded.

13,796 acres in two units
1670 FM 488
Streetman, TX 75859
903/389-7080

DRIVING TIMES FROM:
Amarillo: 8 hours
Austin: 4 hours
Brownsville: 10 hours
Dallas: 1.5 hours
El Paso: 15 hours
Houston: 3 hours
San Antonio: 5.5 hours

DIRECTIONS: From Corsicana, go south about 25 miles on U.S. 287. Turn right onto FM 488 and go 1.8 miles to the area headquarters and entrance to the South Unit. Entrance to the North Unit is on U.S. 287, 0.4 mile south of FM 488.

OPEN: Year-round for day use and camping in designated areas, except during Special Permit hunts.

ACTIVITIES: Camping, wildlife viewing, hiking, bicycling, hunting, fishing.

FACILITIES: Office, primitive camping areas, wildlife-viewing blind, hunter check station, restrooms.

SPECIAL REGULATIONS: Entrance to the area is permitted only during daylight hours at designated entry points. Users must possess an An-nual Public Hunting Permit, a Limited Public Use Permit, or a Texas Conservation Passport. All deer and hog hunters must register on-site. Camping is permitted only in designated areas. Trapping, use of dogs to hunt feral hogs, and ATVs are prohibited. Horses may be used only by written permission obtained in advance. Waterfowl hunting is allowed only on designated days; shooting hours end at noon.

ADVISORIES: Mosquitoes, poison ivy, and poisonous snakes are present on the area. Flooding may occur in wet weather. Carry your own supply of potable water.

LODGING IN AREA: Motels are available in Palestine, Athens, and Corsicana.

LOCAL POINTS OF INTEREST: Texas Freshwater Fisheries Center, Texas State Railroad, Confederate Reunion Grounds State Historical Park, Fort Parker State Park, Old Fort Parker State Historical Park, Jim Hogg State Historical Park, Purtis Creek State Park, Mission Tejas State Historical Park, Fairfield Lake State Park, Tyler State Park.

DISABILITY ACCESS: The wildlife observation blind and the restrooms are wheelchair-accessible.

HISTORY

The land that is now Freestone County lay within the range of the Caddoan Indians, but a number of other tribes seem to have used the area for hunting and trading. The region became known as Indian country and was avoided by settlers until the 1840s. Agriculture remained the chief economic activity until the 1920s. During Prohibition, a sizeable bootlegging industry centered around the community of Young, which lies about 3 miles south of the WMA. About this same time the natural resources of the area's bottomlands began to be exploited, with most of the hardwoods being logged. In the 1960s some 3,000 acres now part of the North Unit were cleared for agriculture. The South Unit was again logged in the 1970s and 1980s. Oil and gas have been produced on the area since the 1940s.

The Richland Creek WMA was established to provide mitigation for the construction of Richland-Chambers Reservoir. This water supply lake for Fort Worth lies immediately west of the WMA; its spillway divides the two units. The Tarrant County Water Control and Improvement District Number One deeded the land to Texas Parks and Wildlife in 1987 with the stipulation that the land must be used for public use and wildlife management or it will revert to the water district. Texas Park and Wildlife is also obligated to improve habitat quality substantially on the WMA during its first 50 years of ownership.

GEOGRAPHY AND NATURAL FEATURES

The Richland Creek WMA occupies a portion of the ecotone where the Post Oak Savannah and Blackland

Richland Creek WMA is fortunate in that it is one of the few WMAs in Texas to have a reliable source of water for its wetland area.

Prairie blend. Much of the South Unit's 8,993 acres lies within the floodplains of the Trinity River and Richland Creek. This land is low, densely vegetated, and mostly level. Cedar elm, sugarberry and green ash dominate, mixed with a variety of oaks and pecan. The understory is so thick as to be almost impenetrable in places. Palmetto, cat brier, swamp privet, poison ivy, rattan, Virginia creeper, and trumpet creeper thrive in the shade of the canopy, which is nearly total.

The North Unit, in contrast, contains considerable open areas, a lake, and a wetlands area as well as 1,700 acres of bottomland hardwoods. A Ducks Unlimited MARSH project on the North Unit established about 580 acres of shallow water impoundments to allow for moist-soil management for the production of waterfowl habitat. Lack of a reliable water supply hindered this effort in the past, limiting moist-soil management to 140 acres. However, an experimental project to supply raw water from wetlands initiated with the Tarrant County Water Control and Improvement District in the late 1990s could result in the eventual development of some 2,300 acres of wetland habitat.

If the project goes as planned, by about 2015 all the open fields on the North Unit will be converted to wetlands. Raw Trinity River water will filter through constructed wetlands and be pumped into Richland Chambers Reservoir, ready to be treated for public water supply. (During a five-year experimental phase, water will be released from the wetlands back into the Trinity River rather than into the lake; water quality will be constantly monitored to assure the project works as intended.)

A pilot project at another location indicates that water from the wetlands will be cleaner than the water in the lake. "We hope to demonstrate that state agencies and water-supply districts can slow the destruction of bottomland hardwoods by reducing the need for new reservoir construction," says area manager Jeff Gunnels. "It will be a new way to get raw water without building a lake." Ideally such wetlands could be located near cities using the water. All the wetlands created by the project will be open for wildlife viewing and hunting.

RECREATIONAL OPPORTUNITIES

CAMPING

Two primitive camping areas are available for use year-round; these are reserved for the use of hunters during Special Permit hunts. The South Unit campground occupies the top of a rolling hill with scattered post oak trees 0.6 mile north of the area headquarters off FM 488. Camping is permitted anywhere in the mowed area. It is anticipated that 12 sites will have picnic tables, fire rings, grills, and lantern posts. The North Unit campground is a former oil well pad beside Zachery Lake. This approximately 50-acre pond is the borrow pit for the construction of levees around the original wetlands nearby. The campground is 1 mile north of U.S. 287 on the only road into the North Unit.

PRO'S POINTERS. People with RVs and camping trailers should use the North Unit campground, as it is level and hard-surfaced. While it has no trees and lacks charm, it does allow camping next to the lake, which offers fishing for catfish, largemouth bass, and carp. Birders may also prefer this campground for its proximity to the wetland area; the wildlife observation blind is another 1.8 miles down the road.

WILDLIFE VIEWING

Richland Creek WMA contains large areas of the two most critical habitat types in Texas, wetlands and bottomland hardwoods.

In the spring both units are covered in a variety of wildflowers—coneflowers, daisies, morning primrose, obedient plant, trumpet creeper. In some years coneflowers seem to be, besides trees, the dominant vegetation on the area and blanket huge expanses.

Access to each area is limited to a single road. Woody Road runs through the northwestern corner of the South Unit, extending 3.2 miles from FM 488 to a pipeline right-of-way that roughly parallels the Trinity River. Along the way the road passes through low, heavily wooded bottomlands and crosses several lakes and sloughs that provide good birding opportunities for wading birds.

The North Unit has a network of roads serving an oilfield, but only the main road through the center of the area is recommended for vehicular travel. It runs from U.S. 287 for 2.8 miles to a wildlife observation tower overlooking the original duck marsh. Along the way it passes a number of wetland compartments that attract and hold a multitude of wading and shorebirds.

LEFT:
Not just for looks, deer vetch adds many nutrients to the diets of area wildlife.
OPPOSITE PAGE:
Zachery Lake offers fishing, but hunting is not permitted there because of the adjacent camping area.

A bird list for the area is available at area headquarters and at the information kiosks at designated entry points.

PRO'S POINTERS. "On the South Unit, the most common springtime species are white-eyed vireos, painted buntings, indigo buntings, northern parulas, eastern wood peewees, Acadian flycatchers, Carolina chickadees, and prothonotary warblers," says Gunnels. "These birds will be primarily in the timbered, hardwood bottomland area. Park and walk down the main or side roads looking for birds. We also get migrating shorebirds in the spring in the wetland areas on the North Unit. There will be numerous species of sandpipers, greater and lesser yellowlegs, Wilson's phalaropes, Hudsonian godwits, and black-necked stilts.

From late spring into summer, wading birds feed in the wetland areas as they dry up. There could be great egrets, snowy egrets, white ibises, glossy ibises, white-faced ibises, great blue herons, tri-colored herons, and cormorants. In June we may have 300 to 400 wood storks, a state-threatened species, as well as roseate spoonbills. Birders may use the observation blind or walk the levees around the compartments. The side roads are closed to motor vehicles only—walking or bicycling on closed roads is permitted."

Various hawks migrate through the North Unit in the spring—Mississippi kites, northern harriers, red-shouldered and red-tailed hawks. Cooper's hawks reside on the area during March and April. A few bald eagles winter on the area, but they tend to stay along the river and are hard to see due to poor access.

Waterfowl dominate the winter scene, particularly in the wetlands area on the North Unit. Teal arrive in September. Significant numbers of pintails, mallards, gadwalls, and northern shovelers winter on the area. The deeper waters of Zachery Lake attract a few redheads and canvasbacks, but in general diving ducks are scarce.

"Pintails favor the Triangle Field, where the observation blind is, and the West Field, because they are shallower areas," says Gunnels. To reach these areas, take the main road into the North Unit. At 1.3 miles the graveled road turns sharply right. At that point a levee goes straight ahead. Follow the levee about a quarter of a mile to the West Field.

The hunter check station offers picnic tables, barbecue pit, and cold storage.

Unit, which is a nice way of saying you will see nothing but trees for the most part. Wear waterproof footwear and be aware that water moccasins, copperheads, and canebreak rattlesnakes are numerous. Leaving the roads will expose you to the abundant poison ivy. The most enjoyable walks will be during spring and summer on the roads and levees around wetland areas on the North Unit. Follow the main road into the area; at half a mile levees begin to branch off. You are free to hike any of these levees even though the gates across them are locked.

BICYCLING

There are no designated biking trails. However, all the roads and levees on the area are open for biking.

PRO'S POINTERS. An excellent ride on the North Unit follows the main road half a mile to compartment 2. Bypassing the gate on the levee will allow you to ride completely around the compartment.

HUNTING

Richland Creek offers an extensive public hunting program for archers, waterfowl hunters, modern rifle hunters, and muzzleloader hunters. For legal species, seasons, and bag limits, consult the *Public Hunting Lands Map Booklet,* the *Applications for Drawings on Public Hunting Lands,* and the *Outdoor Annual* for the current year. All deer and hog hunters must self-register at one of the designated entry points.

PRO'S POINTERS. "Archery deer hunting is really popular here," says Gunnels. "That is due to our high deer population. Hunting is pretty evenly distributed over the area, but one of the most underhunted areas is the open fields on the North Unit. The only way to hunt that area successfully is with a tripod. When the deer get pressured in the woods, they will go right out in the fields. There is a lot of brush there. Take a tripod and set up in thick cover over a trail

To reach the Triangle Field, continue on the main road to an intersection at mile 2. Turn left there and go another 0.8 mile to the wildlife-viewing blind.

HIKING

No designated trails are provided for hiking, but visitors are free to travel the main roads and any of the side roads they feel comfortable about.

PRO'S POINTERS. The habitat is pretty homogenous on the South

between a feeding area and a bedding area. I advise against leaving stands in the field overnight, as we have had problems with theft of stands."

In wooded areas on the North and South Units, if you can find one of the scarce oak trees on the area in a year with a good acorn crop, that is the place to hunt. Since the vegetation is so thick in the bottomlands, the best method there is to set up on a well-used stream crossing.

"There is so much food scattered over the area, only acorns concentrate deer," explains Gunnels. "It's difficult to pattern deer except at stream crossings. You can also try to find a scrape or rub line during the latter part of the archery season. The rut starts here in late October through early November, and bucks normally run does the last week of the archery season."

Since the area is so popular with archers, getting away from other hunters can pose a problem. Gunnels suggests using a bicycle to access areas behind locked gates on the North Unit. On the South Unit, hunters may drive secondary roads at their own risk. In wet years, the river can rise suddenly following heavy rains and cut off access to the main road. Vehicles have been trapped and flooded on the area. Even U.S. 287 is closed an average of twice a year by high water.

Special Permit hunts include a youth-only hunt. See the *Applications for Drawings on Public Hunting Lands* for the current year. General season Special Permit hunts are conducted by compartment, of which there are 24 ranging in size from 250 to 900 acres. "The use of ATVs is allowed and encouraged on Special Permit hunts," says Gunnels. "That lets me get people farther back into the area. I assign the more rugged or remote compartments to people with ATVs or four-wheel-drive vehicles." Hunters who have hunted the area before can request to be assigned to a specific area they like. The hunting

of mature bucks and does is encouraged.

"On the South Unit, a lot of hunters do well on pipeline rights-of-way and roads during the Special Permit hunts," says Gunnels. "A lot of rye grass grows in those areas. Mature bucks will be found in the thicker cover, where rifles with low-power scopes will work better."

Gunnels recommends that people bring a stand of some sort. Baiting is allowed on the Special Permit hunts only, but it must be certified aflatoxin free. "However," Gunnels notes, "baiting has not been productive, because the deer here don't see corn often and don't seem to know what it is. Hunters tell us the deer walk right past it."

On the North Unit, Gunnels suggests hunting the edges of woods and thickets. "Tripod stands work really well during the pressured times—deer will head for the open areas," he says. "Hunt the thickets for the bigger bucks—the thicker it is, the better they like it."

During Special Permit hunts, hunt personnel keep coffee and a fire all day at the check station. Cold storage is available, but no ice. Hunters will be instructed as to whether to field dress deer in the field or bring them to the check station for biological sampling.

"This is a rugged, heavily wooded area," Gunnels cautions. "Bring a compass and know how to use it. On cloudy, overcast days it's very easy to get turned around in thick woods with no landmarks."

Feral hogs may be hunted concurrently with archery and Special Permit deer hunts, and there are muzzleloader and archery seasons in spring. "We have a low harvest rate on hogs," Gunnels says. "Most hunters hear or see them but don't get a shot due to the thick vegetation. In dry years you'll find hogs around the lakes and wetland areas. The lakes shown on the area map generally hold water year-round except during

drought years. If you can find an oak dropping acorns in the fall, hunt hogs there. They love those acorns."

Doves come to water at the wetland areas. Sit in the grass on a levee near bare dirt at the water's edge. Dove hunting is not permitted around Zachery Lake, because it is a designated campground. Dove numbers are limited due to a lack of agriculture in the region.

Waterfowl hunting takes place mostly on the North Unit. "The majority of people wear waders and wade out into the compartment and hunt over decoys," says Gunnels. "Be careful when you walk off the levees—they have a ditch alongside that can be three or four feet deep. Out in the compartments, the water is a foot and a half to two feet deep."

Compartment 2 receives the heaviest hunting pressure. It is closest to the highway and is right by the road. It begins half a mile from U.S. 287 on the road into the North Unit, on the right side. Triangle Field (at the end of the main road into the North Unit), compartment 1 (to the west of Triangle Field), and the main channel of Alligator Creek (which crosses the road into the North Unit) are not utilized as heavily. Park and walk to those, or use a canoe or pirogue on Alligator Creek. Pea Patch Lake usually has birds and can be walked to. To reach it, drive into the North Unit 2 miles and park where the main road takes a sharp left. Walk across the road, then angle to the right and walk about a mile to the lake.

"Hunting locations are on a first-come, first-served basis, so you have to get here early to get a good spot," Gunnels says. "It helps if hunters will spread out and keep the birds stirred up. Scout the afternoon before and find where the birds are feeding." Beginning with the 1999 season, weekend waterfowl hunts will be on Saturdays only.

If the Trinity River is flooding, some low-lying natural wetland areas can be productive. Check with the WMA office for local conditions before you come. Boats are not recommended because the vegetation is too thick. Canoes or pirogues are allowed.

The area has a considerable snipe population, but few people hunt them. They may only be hunted concurrently with waterfowl hunts, and tramping around the mudflats walking up snipe would interfere with waterfowl hunters.

FISHING

Fishing is marginal on the area. Zachery Lake offers the best chance to catch catfish, largemouth bass, sand bass, crappie, or carp. Other lakes on the area dry up from time to time, but Zachery Lake gets groundwater recharge and is 38 feet deep in the middle. The banks drop off steeply, but out in the lake are some old spoil piles that hold some fish. The lake is 1 mile from the entrance to the North Unit, on the west side of the road. Areas suitable for hand-launching a small boat are at the southeast corner of the lake, near the road, and at the southwest corner, near the campground. Bank fishing may be hampered by high weeds.

PRO'S POINTERS. Since the acquisition of a permanent water supply for compartment 2, bass fishing there has improved. Bank fishing around the water inlet structure can be productive.

INSIDER'S CORNER

PALMETTO RUSTLERS

Common in the shady, swampy understory on the South Unit of Richmond Creek WMA is the dwarf palmetto, a member of the palm family native to the southeastern United States. The fan-shaped fronds stand in groups about three feet high. They appear trunkless, but this is not the case, as most of the trunk grows underground.

The terminal bud of the dwarf palmetto is edible and would seem to be a staple in the diet of Asian peoples, judging from a series of incidents on Richland Creek WMA in the spring of 1999. Several Asian people from the Dallas area were arrested on at least two occasions for illegally harvesting dwarf palmettos on the WMA. At first they claimed the plant was being used for religious purposes, but further investigation revealed the truth: the plants were being cut into small pieces, put into plastic bags, and sold for food.

"Rustlers" of one kind are another are a continuing problem on Texas wildlife management areas. They range from people who pick a single wildflower to those who hunt without a license or public hunting permit or collect rare species. In many cases wildlife management areas contain the only remnants of native plant and animal species in an area. They are biological islands surrounded by a monocultural sea of cropland, improved pasture, or urban development. The impact of a single individual's actions seem insignificant. However, when multiplied by the actions of many, serious damage can result.

The basic problem facing all wildlife managers stems from the same source: decreasing quantity and quality of wildlife habitat. It is important to remember, however, that loss of habitat is the problem, not the cause. Habitat loss can be traced directly to human activities such as reservoir construction and conversion of wildlife habitat to agricultural fields or building sites. Again, however, it is easy to confuse the problem with the cause. Loss of habitat is caused by human population growth and the resulting increased need for food, water, and shelter.

A quotation that has long been a favorite of mine is, "There are a thousand hacking at the branches of evil for every one striking at the root." Until the problem of human overpopulation is successfully addressed, wildlife biologists and game wardens will have plenty of work trying to protect the shrinking reserves of what is left of our natural heritage.

3,180 acres
Route 1, Box 61-C
Ledbetter, TX 78946
409/289-2392

DRIVING TIMES FROM:
Amarillo: 9.5 hours
Austin: 1.5 hours
Brownsville: 6.5 hours
Dallas: 3.5 hours
El Paso: 12 hours
Houston: 1.5 hours
San Antonio: 3 hours

DIRECTIONS: Nails Creek Unit—From the intersection of U.S. 290 and FM 180, 6 miles east of Giddings, go east on FM 180 for 11.8 miles to County Road 125. Turn left onto County Road 125 and continue 0.6 mile to an access point. Yegua Unit—From the intersection of Texas 21 and FM 141, go south through Dime Box about 5 miles to FM 1697. Turn left and follow FM 1697 for 1.5 miles to County Road 124. Turn left and go 1.6 miles to the access point on the north side of the Yegua Creek bridge.

OPEN: Daily except on designated dates.

ACTIVITIES: Wildlife viewing, hiking, bicycling, hunting, fishing.

FACILITIES: Boat ramps and restrooms at Corps of Engineers and state parks, nature trail, camping.

SPECIAL REGULATIONS: Driving is permitted only on designated roads. Shotguns with no larger than #4 nontoxic shot are the only firearms permitted except during Special Permit hunts. Only hunters are required to possess an Annual Public Hunting Permit. Trapping and use of horses are prohibited.

ADVISORIES: Due to the thick cover, long pants and sleeves are recommended for hunters at all times. Do not park on oilfield roads or in front of oil tank batteries, as service trucks use those roads regularly. Carry your own supply of potable water.

An old iron bridge with a sturdy plank down the middle gives entry to the area between East and Middle Yegua Creeks from access point 3.

LODGING IN AREA: Motels are available in Giddings. Camping is available at Lake Somerville State Park and at Corps of Engineers parks nearby.

LOCAL POINTS OF INTEREST: Lake Somerville State Park, Washington-on-the-Brazos State Historical Park, Bastrop State Park, Buescher State Park, Monument Hill/Kreische Brewery State Historical Parks.

DISABILITY ACCESS: Restrooms at Corps of Engineers parks are wheelchair-accessible.

HISTORY

Tonkawa Indians roamed the general area until historic times; they were removed to the Brazos Indian Reservation in 1855. A major Spanish travel route to missions in East Texas, the Old San Antonio Road, followed the general route of today's Texas 71 a few miles northwest of the area. The area seems to have been relatively isolated and unpopulated until after the Civil War, since Lee County, which contains the bulk of the

WMA, was not organized until the 1870s.

The area followed the general pattern of development of Central Texas, with cotton and corn farming dominating until after the Great Depression. Livestock grazing then became the major land use. After plans for Lake Somerville were revealed and people knew their land was going to be taken, overgrazing severely damaged much of the area. The U.S. Army Corps of Engineers purchased land for the lake in the early 1950s. In 1975 some 8,700 acres were leased to Texas Parks and Wildlife; in 1982 the acreage now comprising the WMA was placed under Texas Parks and Wildlife's Wildlife Division.

GEOGRAPHY AND NATURAL FEATURES

Somerville WMA consists of two separate units in the Post Oak Savannah. The Nails Creek Unit is 1,150 acres and is a long, narrow strip along the creek by the same name. The Yegua Unit is 2,030 acres and contains the confluence of Middle and East Yegua Creeks as well as portions of both those creeks. The two units are approximately 3 air miles apart. Neither contains shoreline of Lake

Somerville at normal lake levels. There are 14 ponds that hold water seasonally, usually during winter.

Most of the land within the WMA is part of the flood zone of Lake Somerville and is subject to periodic inundation. Nearly all the area is seasonally flooded in years of heavy rainfall. Habitat on the area is primarily level bottomland, with about 40 percent being wooded. Water oak, live oak, cedar elm, sugar hackberry, water hickory, and pecan trees are common in the bottomlands, which are very thickly vegetated. Uplands contain post oak, black hickory, blackjack oak, and yaupon. Open lands are heavily infested with seacoast sumpweed. Often growing eight feet tall, it is the most noticeable plant along roads and paths.

Wildlife on the area includes white-tailed deer, feral hogs, fox squirrels, swamp rabbits, mourning doves, and a variety of waterfowl. Black-shouldered kites and Swainson's warblers are known to nest on the area.

RECREATIONAL ACTIVITIES

The WMA is surrounded by private land, but a number of public roads allow access. Information stations and parking areas are located as follows.

These are shown on a detailed map of the WMA available at Somerville State Park headquarters.

Access point 1: Nails Creek Unit—From U.S. 290 6 miles east of Giddings, go east on FM 180 for 11.8 miles to County Road 125. Turn left onto County Road 125 and continue 0.6 mile to the access point. Another graveled parking area is an additional 0.6 mile west on County Road 125.

Access point 2: Nails Creek Unit—From U.S. 290 6 miles east of Giddings, go east on FM 180 for 9.8 miles to FM 1697. Turn left and go 0.8 mile. Oilfield service roads on both sides of the highway parallel Nails Creek and lead into the area.

Access point 3: Yegua Unit—Follow FM 141 south from Dime Box about 5 miles to FM 1697. Turn left and follow FM 1697 for 1.5 miles to County Road 124. Turn left and go 1.6 miles to the access point on the north side of the Yegua Creek bridge. An oilfield service road 0.4 mile south on County Road 124 gives access to the area between East Yegua and Middle Yegua Creeks; an old iron bridge across Middle Yegua

LEFT:
Inland seaoats are used by birds for seed and nest material.
BELOW:
Colorful wildflowers dot the nature and hiking trails of Somerville WMA.

Creek has been converted to a foot-bridge. To reach the bridge, park at the oil well pad at the end of the road and walk south to the creek.

Access points 4 and 5: Yegua Unit—From Dime Box, go south on FM 141 about 3 miles to County Road 430. Turn left. At mile 1.5, the pavement ends. At mile 2, the road turns sharply to the left. Access point 5 is at mile 2.2. Access point 4 is at mile 3.8.

NATURE TRAIL

A 3-mile interpretive nature trail follows Middle Yegua Creek on the Yegua Unit. Small signs along the way identify trees by common and scientific names. The trail passes by a wetland area, crosses the creek via a suspension footbridge (not wheel-chair-accessible), and meanders through densely wooded bottomland along the creek.

PRO'S POINTERS. This trail was very overgrown when I visited and had a number of fallen trees across it. The trail abuts private property, and access for maintenance vehicles is sometimes a problem. Wear long pants and sleeves to protect yourself from crowding vegetation, and carry a stick to clear spiderwebs from your path. "The best time to visit the nature trail is in fall or spring," says site manager Darrell Fischer. "The path will not be grown up in spring, and I try to shred it in June and August, mainly because this is the season for neotropical migrants."

To reach the trailhead, follow the oilfield service road that heads south-east off County Road 430 just south of access point 5. Go 0.15 mile and take the first road to the right, which goes to an inactive oil well pad that serves as a parking area. Trail maps are available in the black mailbox beside the willow tree with an arte-sian well at its base. The trail retraces your path back to the oilfield service road on which you entered, turns right onto it, and continues along the road about half a mile to another oil well pad. From this pad the trail heads almost due south toward the creek. The footbridge is hidden just inside the line of trees along the creek, about 100 yards from the pad. Cross the bridge and turn left, con-tinuing downstream along the creek bank.

WILDLIFE VIEWING

The nature trail (see above) offers the best birding, although there is a small wetlands area near access point 5 where waterfowl may be present in fall. Deer, coyotes, bobcats and squirrels are the most common mammals. A birding checklist for the area is available at the state park headquarters.

PRO'S POINTERS. "In spring the wetland area, the ponds, and the creeks attract a wide variety of wading and shorebirds such as egrets, her-ons, killdeer, and greater and lesser yellowlegs," says Fischer. "Nails Creek in the area of access point 1 is especially good, as is Yegua Creek from the nature trail downstream to the old iron bridge. East Yegua Creek is too overgrown to enable visitors to walk or see well." (The old iron bridge is south of the oil well pad at the end of the oilfield service road, 0.4 mile south of access point 3.)

Woodlands and open areas attract painted buntings, indigo buntings, Swainson's warblers, white-eyed vireos, cardinals, parula warblers, red-eyed vireos, yellow-throated vireos, western kingbirds, scissor-tailed flycatchers, purple martins, cliff swallows, and barn swallows.

In fall the wetlands area near access point 5 and some of the ponds will attract wood ducks, mallards, teal, and pintails. White pelicans and American kestrels are quite common in winter. The wetlands area lies along County Road 430 on the Yegua Unit; the oilfield service road just south of access point 5 passes through it. Small ponds dot meadow areas north of Middle Yegua Creek and west of access point 3 and east of access point 5 on the Yegua Unit. On the Nails Creek Unit, ponds are east of Nails Creek on either side of FM 1697, near access point 2.

HIKING

The nature trail is the only desig-nated hiking trail. However, 3 miles of oilfield service roads are open for hiking. From late summer through winter, some 14 miles of hunter access trails are mowed and available for walking. Most begin at an oil well pad parking area.

PRO'S POINTERS. The oilfield service roads are shown on the detailed map of the WMA available at state park headquarters. Note that some of these roads cross private land before entering the WMA; only those accessible from public roads are open to visitors. These are gravel-surfaced, all-weather roads. Two of the more interesting are the ones passing through the wetlands area on the Yegua Unit south of access point 5 and the one running southwest from FM 1697 along the east bank of Nails Creek. The former offers a walk of a little over 2 miles round trip that passes through the wetland area and then parallels Middle Yegua Creek. The latter passes through mostly open meadows and is a little under 2 miles round trip.

Mowed hunter access trails link the nine ponds within the Yegua Unit and the five within the Nails Creek Unit. These trails total about 14 miles and offer excellent hiking through all the different habitat types on the area. "The better trail for hiking is prob-ably on the Nails Creek Unit, from access point 1 to the oil well pad midway between FM 125 and FM 1697," says Fischer. "It's a round trip of about 2 miles. Another good walk is a 1-mile loop that starts at the graveled parking area 0.6 mile west of Nails Creek on County Road 125." This trail heads southwest across an open area, crosses Nails Creek, and parallels the creek back to the highway.

The sun sets on the Somerville WMA as viewed across Lake Somerville from the state park.

PRO'S POINTERS. There are about 3 miles of gravel oilfield service roads on the area. These roads all begin at a public road and terminate inside the WMA and have space for parking near their beginnings. Due to the lowland nature of the WMA, these roads are subject to flood damage, but they are maintained regularly and should be suitable for ordinary bikes most of the time.

Riders of off-road bikes can choose from the 14 miles of mowed hunter access trails; in fact, a bike is an excellent tool for hunters. A bike-towed small trailer can ease the transport of duck decoys and harvested game. Note that the trails are mowed only for the hunting season and may be overgrown from spring until fall. For a loop ride of about 6 miles, begin at the parking area for access point 1. Follow the mowed path southwest. At about mile 1.5, the trail turns sharply to the right and continues to Nails Creek, then runs parallel to the creek and intersects FM 1697. Turn left onto FM 1697 and follow it a mile to FM 180, turn left, and go 2 miles to County Road 125. Go left on the county road to the starting point.

HUNTING

Most hunting on Somerville WMA is by Annual Public Hunting Permit and is archery or shotgun only, although there are usually gun deer hunts by Special Permit. Youth-only waterfowl hunts are also available. For information on species, seasons, and bag limits, see the *Public Hunting Lands Map Booklet,* the *Applications for Drawings on Public Hunting Lands,* and the *Outdoor Annual* for the current year. White-tailed deer, feral hogs, and squirrels are the most common game sought, although when water is abundant, waterfowl hunting can be good. Hunters are not required to register. Baiting is not allowed on any hunt.

PRO'S POINTERS. "For archery deer hunting, I've always been partial

Note that once hunting season is over, the hunter access trails will quickly grow up in sumpweed and will be heavily rooted by hogs, making them unsuitable for walking.

BICYCLING

Somerville WMA has areas suitable for both mountain bikes and street bikes. The hunter access trails are well suited for mountain bikes. Street bikes will be better off on the oilfield service roads.

to the Nails Creek Unit between County Road 125 and FM 1697," says Fischer. "West of 1697 had more improved pastures and is not as good deer habitat. Gun hunters do take some deer there as they cross roads and clearings.

"A better bowhunting area is southwest of the graveled parking area 0.6 mile west of Nails Creek on County Road 125. A drainage crosses an L-shaped clearing with lots of cedar elms on the north side. Visibility is better due to a thinner understory, and the area is a travel lane for deer crossing from the state park into the WMA." Use hang-on or lean-on stands; screwing steps into trees is not allowed. Remove the stand after each day's hunt. A tripod stand in the treeline can also work.

"Generally acorn production is better along the edges of the hills for post oaks and live oaks; along the drainages are water oaks and willow oaks," says Fischer. "Find a tree that's dropping acorns and hunt there. Perhaps the best method is to find a trail crossing an opening or drainage and sit on it."

Draw gun hunts for bucks only are normally held the second and third weekends in November. Each unit is divided into compartments by natural features and roads. Hunters are assigned to compartments mainly based on the size of the group, but when possible allowance is made for hunters who can't walk into one of the remote compartments. No ATVs are permitted, and driving access is allowed only on oilfield roads. Ladder stands are available for loan.

Orientation for the gun hunts is held at the pavilion next to the boat ramp in the Nails Creek Unit of Somerville State Park. The pavilion also serves as a check station. A game-cleaning area in the park is provided, but when possible deer should be field-dressed before being brought to the check station. During the draw hunts, Texas Parks and Wildlife personnel will help retrieve deer.

Feral hogs may be hunted by archers from September 1 to February 15 except during gun deer hunts. "The hunting closure is to encourage nonconsumptive use," says Fischer. He advises, "Hunt the drainages, hunt the levees, hunt the mowed paths. During that time of year hogs will be rooting a lot in open areas. Also look for oak trees that still have acorns under them. The area along Nails Creek usually has lots of tracks. In October hogs really start moving into the area from private property surrounding because of hunting pressure."

On my visit I noted that a pasture road paralleling Middle Yegua Creek west of access point 3 held numerous deer tracks, and the continuation of that road across an open meadow beyond appeared to be used regularly by a number of hogs, some of them large. To reach this area from access point 3, go south on County Road 124 for 0.4 mile to a graveled oil field service road running northwest. Follow that road about half a mile to the creek. Immediately after crossing the creek and climbing out of the creek bottom, turn right onto a road (not open to vehicular traffic) that runs almost due east. The road runs along the treeline for a short way before heading across an open meadow.

"Waterfowl hunting here is mostly jumpshooting on the creeks or duck ponds," says Fischer. (Beavers have thwarted efforts at water management in the wetlands area on the Yegua Unit by plugging water-control structures, limiting hunting opportunity there.) "We have 14 ponds scattered over the area that flood starting about November 1 if we have enough natural flow in the creeks." Mowed paths connect most of the ponds to parking areas at access points. "Normally there is not much decoy hunting, and waterfowl aren't a big deal," Fischer continues, "but in years when the lake is very full and is backed up onto the WMA, open areas

flood and hold thousands of ducks. At times people have been able to launch boats off County Road 125 into Nails Creek right over the fence." Waterfowl hunters should call the WMA to check conditions before traveling; the number is 409/289-2392.

Fox squirrels are abundant on the area and are usually hunted in conjunction with doves and rabbits. "I see quite a few squirrels along the hill south of FM 1697 on the Nails Creek Unit, but there are also quite a few along the creek itself," says Fischer. "You'll also find squirrels on Middle Yegua Creek along the oilfield road near access point 5." There's a pecan orchard on the south side of the Yegua Creek Unit, but it's a walk of about a mile, and there's no good path. Some people reach it by following the creek from the old iron bridge; see directions for access point 3, above.

Rabbits and hares are present, but thick cover makes hunting them difficult except after floods that clear out undergrowth. Mourning doves may come to ponds on the area for water and provide some pass shooting. Furbearers—mostly raccoons—may be hunted from November 1 through February 15 *at night only;* dogs are allowed. Only shotguns with no larger than #4 nontoxic shot are allowed.

FISHING

Catfish and white bass are the main species, although bowfishers try for gar and carp from the Irvin Bridge across Yegua Creek on County Road 124.

PRO'S POINTERS. "White bass fishing is good from the middle of January until the first of May in both Nails and Yegua Creeks," says Fischer. "On Nails Creek, the best fishing is at the County Road 125 crossing. Park in the parking lots at the ends of the bridge and walk to the creek to bank fish. For white bass, most people use crappie jigs or minnows under a cork. Bounce jigs along the bottom. Every year a different colored jig is hot, but white and chartreuse are always good to start with." Fish for white bass on the Yegua Unit at the Irvin Bridge and also where County Road 430 crosses East Yegua Creek between access points 4 and 5.

"For catfish, the best time is when there is a rise on one of the creeks; fish come up out of the lake then," says Fischer. "Fishing is hottest when the creek is on the rise or falling a bit; when it is in full flood, there is too much current." Nails Creek has a couple of deep holes about halfway between FM 1697 and County Road 125; it's about a mile and a half walk. On Yegua Creek, walk into the area about half a mile on either creek from the Irvin Bridge to deeper holes.

INSIDER'S CORNER

WHAT HAPPENED TO THE QUAIL?

On Somerville WMA, as in most of Texas, the sharp "bob-white" call of quail is seldom heard anymore. Quail have largely disappeared from the state east of I-35. One expert has predicted bobwhites will be extinct in the southeastern United States by 2005.

Everything from lack of water to feral cats has been suggested as the cause for quail's decline, but if you want to find the culprit in the case of the disappearing quail, you need look no farther than the nearest mirror. We all share the responsibility.

The basic problem comes down to a difference between people and quail. People like order and efficiency—weed-free fields and lawns and large open expanses of parks, grazing land, or crops. Quail thrive in a messy environment—weedy fencerows and borrow ditches, abandoned farm equipment with prickly pear growing up around it, and small, brush-sprinkled fields and pastures. During the last 50 years, the trend in Texas has been toward exactly the opposite: large weed-free farms, elimination of native brush, and the planting of thousands of acres of coastal bermudagrass.

Elimination of habitat and food sources—a weed to a farmer is a grocery store to a quail—coupled with overgrazing has sounded the death knell for quail over much of Texas. Introduction of the fire ant also appears to have been a factor in eastern Texas. In drier parts of the state, overgrazing appears to play a particularly critical role, according to quail expert Dale Rollins, extension wildlife specialist with the Texas Agricultural Extension Service in San Angelo. "Bumper quail crops in West and South Texas generally occur when two years of above-average rains fall on the heels of a drought," he explains. "My theory is that dry weather reduces nest site availability, and that the availability of suitable nesting cover spread *across the landscape* may be the weak link in a quail's chain of habitat needs."

In dry years ranchers often overgraze pastures, leaving little or no dry grass standing. Quail prefer to nest in last year's stands of bunchgrass. When an adequate amount of such habitat is lacking, predators like coyotes and raccoons have an easier time finding and plundering quail nests. Poor production translates into low quail numbers.

Quail have survived in West and South Texas primarily because these areas have not been as heavily developed for industry, housing, row-crop agriculture, and improved pastures as the eastern third of the state.

With proper management, quail can be brought back. If you want more quail on your property, the key is to provide the habitat they need. The Texas Agricultural Extension Service conducts landowner workshops that teach the basic principles. For information, contact Dr. Dale Rollins, Texas Agricultural Extension Service, 7887 U.S. 87 North, San Angelo, TX 76901; 915/653-4576.

2,335 acres in three units
P.O. Box 2127
Sulphur Springs, TX 75482
903/945-3132

DRIVING TIMES FROM:
Amarillo: 7.5 hours
Austin: 4.5 hours
Brownsville: 10 hours
Dallas: 1 hour
El Paso: 12 hours
Houston: 4.5 hours
San Antonio: 6 hours

DIRECTIONS: Pawnee Inlet Unit—From I-30 in Greenville, travel south on U.S. 69 to Lone Oak. Turn west onto FM 1571 and go 2.7 miles to Spur 1571. Turn right and go 0.2 miles to the campground entrance. Caddo Creek Unit—From I-30 in Greenville, take Texas 34 south about 14 miles to the Caddo Creek bridge. The area southwest of the creek and the highway is WMA. Duck Cove Unit—From I-30 in Greenville, go south on Texas 34 to Quinlan. Take FM 35 east 1.1 miles to FM 751. Follow FM 751 south about 5.5 miles to County Road 3827. Go west on County Road 3827 for 0.8 mile to an information station.

OPEN: Daily.

ACTIVITIES: Camping, wildlife viewing, hiking, hunting, fishing.

FACILITIES: Primitive campground.

SPECIAL REGULATIONS: No trapping is allowed. Shotguns are the only firearm allowed. Horses are allowed only during specified times.

ADVISORIES: Vandalism and illegal trash dumping interfere with legal users' enjoyment of the area. Carry your own supply of potable water.

LODGING IN AREA: Motels are available in Greenville and Quinlan.

LOCAL POINTS OF INTEREST: Lake Tawakoni State Park, Governor Hogg Shrine State Historical Park, Purtis Creek State Park, Cooper Lake State Park, Lake Bob Sandlin State Park, Texas Freshwater Fisheries Center.

DISABILITY ACCESS: Not wheelchair-accessible.

HISTORY

From the time of its first settlement by Anglos in 1839 until relatively late in the 20th century, the vicinity of Tawakoni WMA remained largely rural. The lack of navigable waterways and railroads inhibited development. Not until the 1960s did the area begin to move from a primarily agricultural economy to an industrial one.

In the 1950s a growing need for water led the city of Dallas to contract with the Sabine River Authority to build the Iron Bridge Dam and Reservoir on the Sabine River. The lake was later renamed Tawakoni after a Texas Indian tribe.

From the time land acquisition was completed in 1960 until the Sabine River Authority signed a 50-year lease for Texas Parks and Wildlife to manage lands around the lake for wildlife in 1995, there was little regulation or policing of public land around the lake. Much of the land was sold, and the few parcels of public land remaining were small and

Fishers use a bridge on the frontage road of Texas 34 where it crosses Caddo Creek to fish for crappie, sand bass, freshwater drum, and catfish.

The beautiful false dragonhead, or obedient plant, blankets fields on the Caddo Creek Unit of Tawakoni WMA.

before being acquired for the reservoir. During the era of Sabine River Authority management, much of the land was severely overgrazed.

The Pawnee Inlet and Duck Cove units of the WMA border Lake Tawakoni. The Caddo Creek Unit borders a flowing stream from which it takes its name. Most of the area is covered in post oak woods interspersed with old fields in which the grasses are being invaded by honey locust, mesquite, and eastern red cedar.

RECREATIONAL OPPORTUNITIES

CAMPING

One primitive campground is provided, on the Pawnee Inlet Unit. A cleared area of about an acre has small openings among trees bordering the graveled pad.

PRO'S POINTERS. This camping area is open for use year-round, but it is mowed only prior to deer season in the fall. If camping at other times of the year, carry a weed cutter to clear campsites. To reach this campground, take FM 1571 west from Lone Oak 2.7 miles to Spur 1571. Turn right and go 0.2 miles to the campground entrance.

WILDLIFE VIEWING

The combination of prairie, woodland, bottomland, and lakeshore habitats provides the opportunity to see a variety of bird species, from red-winged blackbirds to scissor-tailed flycatchers to great blue herons to prothonotary warblers.

PRO'S POINTERS. The best time for birding is the spring. On the Pawnee Inlet Unit, dickcissels and bobolinks are fairly common. Lucky birders may see a Smith's longspur or McCown's longspur, which tend to show up in this part of Hunt County. Wading birds and shorebirds frequent the lake.

County Road 3401 on the north side of the unit provides good birding. This narrow, graveled road is

scattered. Due to development around the area, the isolated nature of the tracts, and a longstanding tradition of unregulated use of the area, illegal activities such as trespassing and trash dumping remain serious problems today.

GEOGRAPHY AND NATURAL FEATURES

The land within the Tawakoni WMA is part of the Blackland Prairie and had been farmed for some 100 years

bordered by a fringe of trees backing up to open fields. A variety of songbirds engage in territorial disputes among the trees. From the parking area on County Road 3404, a trail goes west and splits, both parts eventually winding up at the lake. The paths are not mowed unless they have been used as firebreaks for prescribed burns, but they pass through grassland, woodland, and lakeshore habitats. These paths are also planted as food plots, which may attract species such as white-tailed deer. Common loons and crested caracaras may be seen around the lake in winter.

On the Duck Cove Unit, a trail parallel to the west boundary is good for woodland birds such as vireos, woodpeckers, cuckoos, red-shouldered hawks, and warblers. The road from the parking lot passes through meadows, grasslands, and wooded areas and goes all the way to the lakeshore.

The Caddo Creek Unit is an open grassland running down to a fringe of woods along the creek. Here are found swallows, scissor-tailed flycatchers, kingbirds, and others that like to perch and chase insects. Cliff swallows and chimney swifts nest under the bridge on Texas 34.

HIKING

There are about 6 miles of unimproved, unmarked trails on the three units.

PRO'S POINTERS. One nice walk is from the Pawnee Inlet Unit campground down the trails all the way to the parking lot on the north end on County Road 3401. The lake is visible from a ridge in the middle of the area. The 2-mile route passes by a couple of ponds and through woods, wetlands, and open grassland meadows.

Isolated and unstaffed WMAs sometimes suffer the indignity of being used as dumping grounds by uncaring area residents. See the Insider's Corner for the Lower Neches WMA for ways you can help.

On the Duck Cove Unit, the road from the parking area along County Road 3827 goes north through the area, crossing a savannah area with lots of big oak trees. This area has lots of wildflowers in the spring.

HUNTING

Because of the small size of the tracts and the proximity to developed areas, hunting is restricted to the use of archery equipment or shotguns. Deer, feral hogs, and waterfowl are the primary game present. All hunting is by Annual Public Hunting Permit with the exception of youth-only waterfowl hunts. See the *Public Hunting Lands Map Booklet* and the *Outdoor Annual* for the current year for legal species, seasons, and bag limits.

PRO'S POINTERS. "The majority of the deer are on the Pawnee Inlet Unit," says area manager David Sierra. "Deer use the area fairly uniformly, but I'd suggest hunting near the lake because it is less accessible. There are also some ridges in the middle of the unit with lots of forbs growing in the grassy areas." Fire lanes on the edges of open fields are planted as food plots, and deer use the edges of woods as travel lanes, so places where fire lanes meet natural funnels would be good areas to hunt.

"Feral hogs have overrun the Pawnee Inlet Unit," Sierra says. "Most will be in the bottom near the lake. They wallow in the road from the parking area down to the lake. They particularly like the marshy areas and the oak woodland areas when there is an acorn crop."

The Pawnee Inlet and Duck Cove units offer good waterfowl hunting along the lake, and wood ducks use the creek area on the Caddo Creek Unit. Mallards, gadwalls, wood ducks, blue-winged teal, and shovelers are the main species, although there will be an occasional ringneck or widgeon. The Pawnee Inlet Unit usually has some snipe and woodcock as well. The snipe prefer the marsh; woodcock will be in wet, wooded areas.

On the Pawnee Inlet Unit, instead of turning into the campground, follow the public road to within a hundred yards or so of the water and set up on the shoreline to hunt. The shoreline is very marshy in wet years; hunting is not so good in dry years. Boat access is from ramps along FM 35 at East and West Tawakoni. There is a private boat ramp (fee) at Wind Point Park at the end of FM 1571. "There is no restriction on using dead and fallen plant material for blind building, but you cannot cut anything or build permanent blinds,"

says Sierra. "There will be plenty of natural cover available if the water level is normal, and the marshy area will extend a long way from the shore. However, the lake fluctuates quite a bit, and in dry years the shoreline can be 600 to 700 yards from where it normally is."

Hunt the Duck Cove Unit by boat. Boat ramps along FM 751 where it intersects FM 429 are within a mile of the unit. There is plenty of vegetation along the shoreline for cover.

On the Caddo Creek Unit, put in a small boat at the highway bridge on Texas 34 and float to the lake. There should be wood ducks along Caddo Creek.

In some years, both the Duck Cove and Pawnee Inlet units may have some quail. Hunt the open meadows, especially next to the treeline. The open field on the Caddo Creek Unit can be good for doves. Rabbits and hares occur on all three units; roads and meadows offer the best places to hunt. There are a lot of clover patches on the area, and rabbits will work those, but the cover makes them hard to find without a dog.

FISHING

The WMA itself includes no lake waters, so fishing is limited.

PRO'S POINTERS. Caddo Creek has a frontage road crossing it west of Texas 34, making this a natural fishing spot for people seeking crappie, sand bass, freshwater drum, and catfish.

INSIDER'S CORNER

BLOOMING SURPRISE

One of the joys of researching this book came as I was visiting WMAs in the spring. Time and again I was surprised by riotous displays of wildflowers on areas I'd only seen wearing their fall or winter clothes of brown and gold.

One of the most pleasant surprises befell me at the Caddo Creek Unit of the Tawakoni WMA. As soon as area manager David Sierra and I pulled off the highway, I was fascinated by a sea of purple bending gently in the breeze. Most of the flowers on WMAs I've seen before—bluebonnets, gallardias, coneflowers, meadow pinks, winecups, daisies, and myriads of the almost indistinguishable varieties my wife refers to as "DYFs," or damn yellow flowers.

But these purple flowers—long, trumpet-shaped blossoms with reddish purple spots, arranged in rows on a tall stem—were ones I'd never seen before. Sierra enlightened me. "They're the beautiful false dragonhead, also called obedient plant," he said. I asked about the origin of the name, and he showed me this plant's secret: Move one of the blossoms sideways to a new position, and it stays there. "You can tell which way the wind has been blowing by looking at the blossoms," he said. "They will all be pointing downwind." And indeed they were.

This plant has developed a quite successful survival adaptation. Bees and other flying pollinators can land easier if approaching heading into the wind. What better way to entice them than to have all your sweet offerings pointing right at them, a runway to the goodies?

SOUTH TEXAS PLAINS

The outstanding scientific discovery of the 20th century is not television, or radio, but rather the complexity of the land organism. Only those who know the most about it can appreciate how little is known about it. The last word in ignorance is the man who says of an animal or plant: 'What good is it?' If the land mechanism as a whole is good, then every part is good, whether we understand it or not. If the biota, in the course of aeons, has built something we like but do not understand, then who but a fool would discard seemingly useless parts? To keep every cog and wheel is the first precaution of intelligent tinkering.
—ALDO LEOPOLD

1 CHAPARRAL WMA
2 JAMES E. DAUGHTREY WMA
3 LAS PALOMAS WMA—
    LOWER RIO GRANDE VALLEY UNITS

15,200 acres
P.O. Box 115
Artesia Wells, TX 78001
830/676-3413

DRIVING TIMES FROM:
Amarillo: 10.5 hours
Austin: 3.5 hours
Brownsville: 5 hours
Dallas: 7 hours
El Paso: 10.5 hours
Houston: 5.5 hours
San Antonio: 1.5 hours
DIRECTIONS: From San Antonio go south on I-35 for about 100 miles to Artesia Wells. Take FM 133 west 8 miles to the entrance.
OPEN: Daily for nonconsumptive uses April 1 through August 31; otherwise Monday through Friday except when closed for public hunts.
ACTIVITIES: Driving tour, nature trails, camping, wildlife viewing, hiking, bicycling, hunting.
FACILITIES: Driving tour, nature trails, primitive campground with restrooms and showers, potable water, check station, office/meeting room, hunting stands.
SPECIAL REGULATIONS: All users must register on-site. Trapping and use of horses are prohibited. Overnight access is limited to the designated campground only. Killing of rattlesnakes is prohibited. Taking of any wildlife, vegetation, or artifacts is prohibited.
ADVISORIES: Summer heat can be oppressive. Rattlesnakes are numerous on the area. Most roads are passable by ordinary vehicles, but there are some sandy places. Carry your own supply of potable water.
LODGING IN AREA: Motels are available in Cotulla and Catarina.
LOCAL POINTS OF INTEREST: Lake Casa Blanca International State Park, Choke Canyon State Park.
DISABILITY ACCESS: The office, check station, restrooms, kiosks and Arena Roja Nature Trail are wheelchair-accessible.

HISTORY

The area that is now the Chaparral WMA lay within the range of the Coahuiltecan Indians until these hunters and gatherers were pushed out by Spanish, Apache, and Comanche intruders. A major Spanish travel path, the Old San Antonio Road (the Camino Real) passed through the WMA.

Since the area is between the Nueces River and the Rio Grande, ownership was disputed from the Texas Revolution until the end of the Mexican War. The "Nueces Strip" became a haven for outlaws because of the disputed ownership, and lawlessness prevailed until after the Civil War, when Texas Rangers waged a successful campaign to clean up the area. Raids by cattle rustlers from Mexico continued into the 1880s.

A massive drought in 1886 and 1887 wiped out much of the area's grassland and a growing sheep industry. Cattle ranching became the main industry. The discovery of extensive artesian water in the area in the 1880s led to the development of numerous farming communities, with ranchers selling off townsites and farmlands to immigrants from the Midwest. Commercial cool-season farming grew to the extent the area became known as the Winter Garden, famous for producing onions and other vegetables.

Between 1900 and 1910, 23 new towns were laid out in La Salle County alone. One of them, Farmington, was located near the present campground on the WMA. The town was served by the San Antonio, Uvalde, and Gulf Railroad, which hauled to market the strawberries and other vegetables grown on the surrounding irrigated farmlands. The Great Depression of the 1930s ended the farming boom, and the town disappeared. The railroad was dismantled during World War II for its valuable steel.

Until its purchase by Texas Parks and Wildlife in 1969, the Chaparral WMA was part of a ranch owned by the Light family, who acquired the property after 1900.

As one of 10 research and demonstration WMAs in the state, the Chaparral's primary mission is to provide a site for research on the South Texas ecosystem and disseminate that information to managers of private lands and the public. The Chap, as it is commonly known, is managed on an ecosystem basis emphasizing diversity of habitat and of wildlife endemic to the South Texas Plains.

GEOGRAPHY AND NATURAL FEATURES

For the most part, the Chaparral WMA is gently rolling land covered with typical South Texas brush species such as honey mesquite and various acacias. Much of the area has been subject to brush manipulation in the past. The amount of cover varies from extremely dense to fairly open, with some of the thickest brush in the southern part of the WMA, an

The sign at the entrance to the Chaparral WMA campground qualifies as metal art.

area subjected to historic chaining activity. Some pastures in the northern portion offer good examples of habitats not subjected to mechanical manipulation.

There are no natural surface water sources on the WMA, and drainages are normally dry. All water for livestock and wildlife is supplied by a network of pipelines from two wells and by stock ponds.

Soils are mostly fine, red, sandy loams that support a very diverse vegetation. This diversity, plus a very long growing season, creates an abundance of wildlife food in spite of often adverse weather and low rainfall. Prickly pear, twisted acacia, croton, partridge pea, ragweed, tallow weed, retama, huisache, blackbrush acacia, hairy grama, hooded windmill grass, lovegrasses, and sand dropseed are some of the plants used by wildlife.

Game animals on the area include white-tailed deer, javelinas, feral hogs, cottontails and jackrabbits, mourning doves, bobwhite, and scaled quail. Coyotes, badgers, and bobcats are fairly common. Mountain lions are present occasionally. Raccoons, skunks, and ground squirrels are some of the smaller mammals present. Of special interest to conservationists are four species on the Texas threatened list: the Texas horned lizard, the

Texas tortoise, the reticulated collared lizard, and the Texas indigo snake.

Nearly 200 bird species have been identified on the area. One of the most common is the roadrunner, also called the paisano, for which the area driving tour is named. Tropical birds such as the greenjay often visit. Red-winged blackbirds, cardinals, several varieties of owls, common pauraques, poorwills, pyrrhuloxias, Cassin's sparrow, long-billed thrashers, cactus wrens, vermilion flycatchers, red-tailed hawks, American kestrels, and Audubon's orioles can be present any time of year.

The entire WMA is surrounded by an 8-foot fence and is divided down the middle by another, providing four separate research areas. There are approximately 260 miles of roads and senderos, some 60 miles of which are maintained for vehicle access.

Recreational Opportunities

Texas Conservation Passport tours may be offered to see wildflowers, horned lizards, and Texas tortoises. The Chap is also the site of a Christmas bird count every year. In recent years, national highs have been recorded for pyrrhuloxia, Audubon's

orioles, Cassia's sparrow, and golden-fronted woodpeckers. Volunteers who want to help mist net and band birds are welcome. Contact the area office for information (e-mail: cwma@usta.com).

Driving Tour

The Paisano driving trail, an interpretive tour consisting of 49 numbered stops along an 8.5-mile paved loop, is open daily from April 1 through August 31. The rest of the year, the driving tour is open during office hours from Monday through Friday except when public hunts are in progress, when the entire area is closed except for a short nature trail around the headquarters. No permit is needed for the driving tour or the nature trails.

PRO'S POINTERS. To get the most out of the driving tour, you'll need a copy of the accompanying brochure, which explains each of the numbered stops. Brochures are available at information kiosks at both the area office and the campground. Visitors must sign in at one of these kiosks. The office is open Monday through Friday from 8 A.M. to 5 P.M., and the driving trail begins there, so it's best to use it as your starting point when possible. However, when the office is closed, you can access the driving tour route by entering through the campground, 1.5 miles east of the office on FM 133 (opens an hour before sunrise and closes an hour after sunset).

When entering from the campground, you will join the tour between stops 18 and 19. If you wish to start the tour at the beginning, turn left at the first intersection past the electric gate and follow the paved road to the headquarters. Otherwise, turn right and pick up the first part of the tour on your way out.

"Spring is the primary time to come out," says area manager David

On-going studies of the Texas horned lizard on the Chaparral WMA illustrate the fact that non-game species are given equal importance to game animals on Texas WMAs.

Synatzske. When Chaparral WMA receives adequate fall and winter rainfall, wildflower season can be spectacular beginning in March. By June the heat becomes unpleasant, and by August the average high is 102 degrees.

The driving tour presents an interesting mix of natural and cultural features. In addition to identifying and describing native plant species and detailing their importance to both animals and humans, the brochure explains some wildlife management practices such as strip discing to create edge and increase food supplies. The brochure also points out such features as the right-of-way of the San Antonio, Uvalde, and Gulf Railroad, remains of the Farmington irrigation system and sheet-metal drift fences used to trap small animals for study.

A wheelchair-accessible wildlife observation tower overlooking the waterhole at stop 30 provides a view of a rollerchopped area that is attractive to javelina and deer.

INTERPRETIVE NATURE TRAILS

In addition to the driving tour, the WMA offers two nature trails, each of which has its own brochure available at the information kiosks. A half-mile trail, the Arena Roja, makes a loop beginning from the area office and is geared toward plant identification. This trail is wheelchair-accessible. The natural-surfaced Camino de Fiero trail begins at the high fence west of the office parking lot and winds about 2.5 miles through the brush in a circular pattern. (A marked shortcut allows you to cut the length by about a mile if you wish.) While plant identification is also emphasized on this tour, the brochure does contains information on wildlife management features.

PRO'S POINTERS. When a public hunt is in progress, visitors may still access the Arena Roja trail, which lies entirely within the headquarters pasture (where hunting is not al-

lowed). To access the nature trails when the office is closed but entrance through the campground is allowed, take the driving tour road to the office area, park at the lot just north of the office, and walk to the trailheads.

The Arena Roja Trail is a flat, easy half-hour walk looping from the area headquarters. The 32 stops along the way feature native plants. This trail is particularly attractive during the spring wildflower season. The Camino de Fiero Trail follows a historic railroad right-of-way for part of its route. There are two rest

benches along the path but no water. At stop 32, you can see the Texas prairie acacia. Thornless—a rarity in the South Texas brush country—this plant is uncommon in South Texas because its lack of defenses allows it to be overgrazed easily. This trail is a good one for wildlife viewing because it gets away from most human activity.

When timely spring rains fall, the Chapparal WMA erupts into wildflowers. In addition to being eye candy in their flowering stage, the young plants are nutritious food for deer, and the seeds of mature plants are an important food source for many kinds of birds.

235

CAMPING

Chapparal WMA has two free camping areas. The main one, which is 1.5 miles east of area headquarters on FM 133, offers 10 covered sites with shade shelter, picnic table and fire ring/barbecue grill. This campground is served by wheelchair-accessible restrooms with hot-water showers, and potable water is available from a central spigot. About a quarter mile west of the main campground is an RV campground. Fifteen pull-through spaces allow self-contained RVs with generators to have more freedom of space while limiting noise disturbance in the main campground. There are no hookups; the light standards remain from a prison work camp and are not electrified. No dump station is available.

PRO'S POINTERS. Camping is allowed anywhere within the main campground area, not just at the sites with facilities. All camping is first-come, first-served. The campground is reserved for hunters during public hunts. Hunters are requested to use the game cleaning area rather than the restrooms for processing birds in order to avoid stopping up the drains.

WILDLIFE VIEWING

The driving tour and the Camino de Fiero nature trail both offer a chance to see wildlife, especially early or late in the day. A wildlife-viewing tower is located at the waterhole at stop 30 on the driving tour. In addition, whenever the driving tour is open, visitors are allowed to drive, walk, or bike any of the roads in the 1,200 acres open to public use during this time period. Pastures are clearly marked with signs at all entry points; driving tour visitors are restricted the two named above.

PRO'S POINTERS. "The laguna area at stop 16 is an excellent birding spot—we do mist netting there," says Synatzske. "This is probably one of the better places to see javelina, although they sometimes visit the campground. The viewing tower near stop 30 is also a good place to observe javelina as well as deer." A herd of javelinas has its home territory between stops 29 and 31, but thick brush makes seeing them tricky.

As you drive the roads, watch for areas that have been mechanically enhanced or burned within recent months. These areas tend to produce more wildlife food than surrounding, undisturbed areas, and thus attract animals. Also key on water sources. Ponds near stops 16, 28, 32, and 49 are good birding spots. "The entire driving loop is good birding, offering a variety of species," says Synatzske. "It goes through blackbrush, mixed brush, and semi-riparian and savannah habitat types." The road is also a good place to spot Texas tortoises and horned lizards, which tend to be active in May and June, at which time they may not move until mid-morning, when temperatures warm. Later in the summer they are more active in early morning and late afternoon. Rattlesnakes are also more active during the early summer.

Birds you may see include painted buntings, vermilion flycatchers, scissor-tailed flycatchers, and a variety of hawks. The Chaparral is on the northern limit of habitat for groove-billed anis, greenjays, and Audubon's orioles, birds commonly seen at the WMA. Cactus wrens, ground doves, pyrrhuloxias, and roadrunners are abundant. At times you will see white-winged, white-tipped, and mourning doves as well as scaled and bobwhite quail. "We get a lot of migrant birds in April and May. You never know what you're going to see," says Synatzske. "We've even had woodcock go through."

The best chance of seeing a Texas tortoise is on a road after temperatures warm. Be careful to avoid

On the Chapparal WMA as on most WMAs in Texas, small game animals such as rabbits and hares are a vastly underutilized resource. WMAs offer ample opportunities to take youngsters hunting for small game.

running over one; vehicles are one of the chief causes of mortality. Horned lizards become active in February as the weather warms; activity reaches a peak in April and May. In summer they bury up under shrubs in the heat of the day. They can be found almost anywhere on the area but prefer more open, grassy areas with plenty of red harvester ant mounds.

Checklists for birds, mammals, reptiles, and amphibians are available at the area office and at the kiosks.

HIKING

Other than the two nature trails, there is no designated hiking trail. Visitors are also allowed to hike the driving tour route. See descriptions for these trails above. A 5- to 6-mile trail from the campground to the Mare Pasture is planned; check with area staff.

PRO'S POINTERS. You may hike any of the roads or senderos in the Rosindo and Hogue pastures, the ones the driving tour passes through. Be aware that there are rattlesnakes on the area. Wear sturdy footwear, a hat, long sleeves, and pants to protect yourself from thorny vegetation. If you plan to hike off the driving tour road, notify area personnel of your approximate whereabouts in case you have trouble. Carry your own drinking

water, but if you run out, there are 45 miles of waterline on the area, and spigots are located at intervals along it.

BICYCLING

Bicycle riding is allowed on the driving tour road and on any of the other roads in the Rosindo and Hogue pastures. There is no designated bike trail.

PRO'S POINTERS. Ordinary bikes will be at home on the paved driving tour road, but a mountain bike is probably required on the sandy pasture roads. The entire area is mostly level.

HUNTING

The Chaparral WMA has long been known for the quality of its white-tailed deer. It also offers outstanding quail hunting when weather conditions are right.

Hunting for doves, quail, jackrabbits, and cottontail rabbits is generally by Annual Public Hunting Permit or Regular Permit on designated dates. Hunting for deer and javelina is by Special Permit. Youth hunts by drawing may also be available. For species, seasons, and bag limits, see the *Public Hunting Lands Map Booklet*, and the *Applications for Drawings on Public Hunting Lands*.

PRO'S POINTERS. Note that the area is not open for dove or quail hunting every day of the season, only on dates specified in the *Public Hunting Lands Map Booklet*. On these dates, the check station opens an hour prior to legal shooting time. "It's difficult to predict, but we have had exceptional dove hunts here," says Synatzske. "Most are mourning doves, but there are increasing numbers of white-wings and a few white-tips. When we have a lot of doves and abundant forage such as croton and partridge pea, pass shooting can be good. You can sit near a road and get a limit in 30 minutes." (Note that shooting from, along, or across a designated road is not permitted.)

Both bobwhite and blue (scaled) quail are present on the area and are legal game. "We have a number of combination dove and quail hunts, generally the first one or two weekends in November when both seasons are open," says Synatzske. "One of the weekends is our youth-adult hunt weekend in which having a youth in the party qualifies the adults to hunt.

"This place can have exceptional quail hunting, but it can be difficult to hunt because of all the brush," Synatzske explains. "We do mechanical brush treatments to create more edge and open areas. The preferred pastures for quail hunting are the West Guajalote, the South Jay, and the North Jay. These are more open and are easier to use dogs in.

"Dove and quail hunters need to be very aware of snakes, which are very active at that time of year."

The campground opens at 8 A.M. the day before a hunt begins. Scouting is allowed if someone is at the office to open the gate. "A lot of drawn hunters on deer hunts use the dove and quail hunts to scout for later deer hunts," Synatzske says.

The Chaparral WMA is famous throughout Texas for the quality of its deer. One reason is restrictive hunting limits. Regulations, which vary from year to year, are detailed in the *Public Hunting Lands Map Booklet* and covered carefully in prehunt orientation sessions. In general, antler spread and number of points determine shootable deer. Both archery and gun hunts are available.

The Chap has 120 tripod stands, but hunters can bring their own. Each group is assigned a compartment; groups are not mixed within compartments. In the past hunters were allowed to choose the pasture they would hunt in, but current procedure is for hunters to draw for pastures on the east side or west side of the high fence dividing the area, then Texas Parks and Wildlife personnel assign compartments. "Both

sides of the area are pretty even now on age structure of the deer herd," Synatzske reasons. "The main thing we try to do is avoid putting hunters in pastures where there are cattle. We also try to keep several pastures in reserve so if hunters don't like the type of habitat in their compartment, we can move them to an area more to their liking." Everyone dreams of taking a big buck on the Chaparral. "The biggest question we get is where to find a big deer," Synatzske says. "I think the best time to kill a big deer here is probably during the archery hunts in October, because it's possible to pattern the deer then. After the rut starts, there's no telling where the bucks will be. However, this is a hard place to archery hunt. I encourage people to bring their own stands and hunt on the heavier wooded drainages. That's where they'll kill deer." Tripod or ladder-type stands work best.

Hunting the heavy cover applies during the gun hunts as well. It's tempting to hunt open areas where visibility is good, but the chances of seeing deer there are poor. Even gun hunters must think like bowhunters and search out the places where visibility is limited but the deer want to be.

Since each group is assigned its own compartment, it is possible to still hunt, spot and stalk, or use drives. However, since the gun hunts are timed to coincide with the rut, one of the more productive methods is to find areas where does are feeding and put up a stand there. Rattling may also work. "You may not kill a big deer here, but if you do, you'll be proud of the way you killed it," Synatzske says. John Jurek of Markham, who took a 150s-class buck on the Chap, advises hunters, "Don't shoot the first buck you see." Younger bucks are generally less cautious and show themselves more readily; patience may give you a shot at a mature deer.

INSIDER'S CORNER

THE TEXAS HORNED LIZARD

Ironically, on an area famed for big deer, one of the most intensively studied critters will fit in the palm of a child's hand. Wildlife biologist Chip Ruthven has been collecting information about the Texas horned lizard—commonly called the horny toad—since 1995 on the Chap.

Once common across the entire state, horned lizards are now on the state threatened list. Ruthven's studies hint at the reasons. "They have been almost eliminated in the eastern third of the state," he says. "Habitat loss is probably the biggest factor, but overcollection for the pet trade in the 1940s, '50s, and '60s was a factor. Imported fire ants kill the harvester ants, which are horned lizards' main food source, and are probably a big factor in their decline, compounding the loss of habitat problem."

Horned lizards are still doing well in parts of South and West Texas and in the Rolling Plains. What many people do not realize is there are actually three species of horned lizards. "The Texas horned lizard is found over most of the state and all the way into Canada," Ruthven explains. "It has longer horns than the other two and has two rows of scales fringing its sides. The round-tailed horned lizard, found west of a line from Del Rio to Childress, does not have the fringe of scales. The mountain short-horned lizard has one row of scales fringing its sides and is found only in the Davis and Guadalupe Mountains."

Fitting horned lizards with radio telemetry equipment and following their movements has yielded much information. "We are finding out they are active a lot longer into the winter than they are farther north," Ruthven says. "The primary purpose of the radio telemetry work was to look at the effects of grazing and prescribed burning programs on the horned lizards' home range size and activity patterns. We've found they move longer distances than some people thought, up to 300 meters per day. Their home range size is generally two to three acres."

Ruthven studies the lizards' diet by finding and analyzing the contents of their scats, which are easier to find than you might expect. "The scats are about three-fourths of an inch long and as big around as your little finger—very large for the animals' size," he says. "You can see ant heads, which are not digested, in the scats, as well as parts of beetles and crickets." Unlike coyotes, which favor depositing used food in roads, horned lizards go wherever the mood strikes them. "I usually find scats while walking around doing radio telemetry work," Ruthven says.

Radio telemetry also reveals much about the little critters' daily habits. "Three of the four we followed this past year did not go into hibernation until mid-December, but some were active even after we'd had freezing temperatures. They become active in early February and in late April and May move quite a bit, which is when the bulk of the breeding takes place," Ruthven says. "Males in particular make large moves looking for females, kind of like a buck deer does. During the heat of midsummer they are not nearly so active and bury up under shrubs in the middle of the day. They are pretty well scattered over the entire area, but you are more likely to find them in the area of ant beds."

Sexing horned lizards is easy if you know what to look for. "The males have their reproductive organ at the base of their tail and have a swelling there. Females' tails are narrow at the base," Ruthven points out. When breeding, males hop on the female's back and hold on by biting one of her horns. Females dig a nest to lay the eggs in, then totally cover the nest and leave. The roundish eggs are about three-eighths to half an inch in diameter. The dozen or so eggs incubate by themselves. When the three-quarter-inch, fully formed young hatch in June and July, they are on their own. "Survivorship is low," Ruthven says. "Lots of things eat horned lizards—roadrunners, caracaras, coyotes, and snakes."

Horned lizards generally rely on their camouflage skin for protection from predators, but they do exhibit some interesting behaviors when threatened. In many cases they run a short distance to cover and then freeze. They will also inflate to make themselves look bigger, and they may raise up on one side and face all their horns toward the predator. They also have the ability to rupture an artery behind an eye and squirt blood at a predator, but how and why they do it is unclear.

4,400 acres
1607 Second St.
Pleasanton, TX 78064
830/569-8700

DRIVING TIMES FROM:
Amarillo: 10.5 hours
Austin: 3 hours
Brownsville: 4.5 hours
Dallas: 6.5 hours
El Paso: 11.5 hours
Houston: 4 hours
San Antonio: 1.5 hours
DIRECTIONS: From Tilden go north on Texas 16 3 miles, then go east on FM 3445 for 5.5 miles to the entrance.
OPEN: For nonconsumptive use, daily except during Special Permit hunts. Open for hunting on designated dates only. Fishers may access Choke Canyon Reservoir through the WMA except during Special Permit hunts.
ACTIVITIES: Nature trail, wildlife viewing, hunting.
FACILITIES: Check station, office, maintenance building, bunkhouse, primitive campground, hunting blinds.
SPECIAL REGULATIONS: Only hunters are required to possess an Annual Public Hunting Permit.

Trapping, horses, and ATVs are prohibited. Waterfowl hunters must remain within 100 yards of the lake during Special Permit hunts. Access to Choke Canyon Reservoir through the WMA is prohibited during Special Permit hunts.
ADVISORIES: Mosquitoes can be abundant at any time of year. Rattlesnakes are numerous on the area. Carry your own supply of potable water.
LODGING IN AREA: Motels are available in Three Rivers, Tilden, Pleasanton, and on Texas 72 near Choke Canyon State Park.
LOCAL POINTS OF INTEREST: Choke Canyon State Park, Tips State Park, Lake Corpus Christi State Park, Lipantitlan State Historical Park, Goliad State Historical Park.
DISABILITY ACCESS: Not wheelchair-accessible.

HISTORY

Archaeological studies indicate that Archaic peoples inhabited the area as early as 11,000 years ago. Vast expanses of prickly pear attracted annual migrations of people who feasted on the juicy fruits for weeks. European settlement was delayed because Texas and Mexico disputed ownership of the land between the Nueces River and the Rio Grande until 1848. During this time only adventurers and outlaws ventured there.

Not until just before the Civil War did settlers begin to arrive, and then mostly along the Frio River. The first permanent settlement, in 1858, began as Rio Frio and later was called Dog Town before becoming Tilden. J. Frank Dobie's family ranched in the area, and he wrote extensively about experiences and legends encountered in the surrounding brush country,

The hardy retama thrives throughout South Central and South Texas.

which was a seminal site in the development of the Texas longhorn and the Texas ranching heritage. Another early settlement was on Yarbrough Bend, about 10 miles east of Tilden. Settlers there subsisted mainly by hunting and selling the wild hogs that roamed the area.

The discovery of natural gas in the area in 1917 spurred development of ranchlands into cities and farms, but lack of water prevented farming from taking hold, and the area remained largely ranchland. Choke Canyon Reservoir was built between 1972 and 1976, and Texas Parks and Wildlife took over responsibility for the recreation and wildlife resources surrounding the lake in 1981.

The James E. Daughtrey WMA is named in honor of a state game warden killed in a car accident while pursuing game law violators.

GEOGRAPHY AND NATURAL FEATURES

The Frio, Atascosa, and Nueces Rivers join near Three Rivers, just east of the WMA. The Frio was dammed to form Choke Canyon Reservoir and the WMA occupies five noncontiguous parcels adjacent to the lake. It is significant that the WMA begins at the water's edge, for as Choke Canyon Reservoir's level fluctuates, the acreage in the WMA shrinks and expands. When the lake is low, the WMA contains closer to 9,000 acres than the 4,400 it covers when the lake is at conservation pool level.

Originally a grassland, after the suppression of fire and the elimination of the buffalo, this region developed into the South Texas brush country of today. Mesquite, catclaw, huisache, prickly pear, and other thorny plants dominate: Local wisdom holds that everything here sticks, bites, or stings.

The Daughtrey WMA consists of low, rolling, brush-covered hills and some Frio River floodplain. San

Miguel, Elm, and Opossum Creeks join the Frio from the north. Despite the arid climate, the WMA is thickly vegetated, with limited visibility over most of the area. Elms, live oaks, and hackberry trees are plentiful and large in the bottomlands. Ample cover, food, and water in close proximity add up to a very productive wildlife habitat. White-tailed deer, javelina, wild turkeys, mourning doves, bobwhite and scaled quail, rabbits, coyotes, gray foxes, bobcats, feral hogs, and other animals live on the WMA.

"I use this WMA as a demonstration area for plant succession," says area manager Macy Ledbetter. "A lot of it had been chained or root-plowed, so you can go to different areas and see what it will look like after 20 years or so. I'm also experimenting with food plots to demonstrate what will and won't work in South Texas. By replicating what ranchers do and can do, I can take them out and show them the likely results of their land practices."

RECREATIONAL OPPORTUNITIES

The Daughtrey WMA offers an interpretive nature trail, wildlife viewing, and hunting. Fishing is available on Choke Canyon Reservoir, which is not part of the WMA.

The WMA has 15 numbered compartments, each accessed by a signed gate. These compartments are located as detailed below.

Compartments 1 and 2 are on the north side of FM 3445. To reach them, drive past the entrance road to the WMA. The entrance to compartment 2 is on the highway. To reach compartment 1, follow the highway to the WMA boundary at a sharp right bend in the road, enter a gate on the left, and drive along the high fence to the entrance gate at the northwest corner of the compartment. Compartments 3, 4, 5, and 6 have signed gates along the road leading to the area headquarters off FM 3445. The

entrances to compartments 7 and 8 are on FM 99, 4.4 miles north of its intersection with Texas 72. Compartment 7 is on the west side of the highway; compartment 8 is on the east side. To reach compartments 9 and 10, continue north on Texas 99 across the lake to a road on the right, 0.1 mile past the road to the FM 99 boat ramp. Compartments 11, 12, and 13 are along Recreation Road 7, which runs northeast from Texas 72, 1.25 miles east of its intersection with FM 99. Compartments 14 and 15 lie between the lake and Texas 72 about 6 and 10 miles, respectively, east of the intersection of Texas 72 and FM 99.

Most of the graveled roads into these compartments are passable by ordinary vehicles. Close gates behind you.

NATURE TRAIL

Two acres of native, undisturbed South Texas brush are next to the hunter campground, across the road from the area headquarters. A self-guided tour booklet is available at the entrance. Some 27 plant species are identified along the trail.

PRO'S POINTERS. Spring is the best time to visit, because the area is in bloom and the temperature is pleasant. March and early April are the best months.

WILDLIFE VIEWING

A diverse habitat of brush, lake, riverine bottomland, and proximity to the Texas coast result in a rich birding area. Portions of every section of the WMA are accessible by public roads. A bird list for the area is available from Choke Canyon State Park headquarters. Wading and shore-birds, neotropical migrants, water-fowl, and species generally found only in southern portions of the state are the main attractions.

PRO'S POINTERS. There are approximately 30 hunting blinds on the WMA; these may be used for wildlife viewing any time a hunt is not

in progress. However, inspect blinds carefully for spiders, snakes, and wasps before entering. Most of the blinds are elevated, but there is a ground blind in the middle of an open area in compartment 5. To reach it, take a road leading north out of the hunter campground and go 0.4 mile to a utility line; turn right and follow the graveled road until you've gone 1.5 miles from the campground. The blind is about 100 yards on the left under a tree.

The influence of Choke Canyon Reservoir on birding on the WMA is hard to overemphasize. To fully appreciate what the lake means, drive past the area headquarters to the end of the road, where a boat ramp provides access to the upper end of the lake. Ghostly tree trunks stand in the water, waves lap at the shore, mist rises from the water, and shorebirds call—signs of a complete and wrenching transformation from the surrounding brush country. "We are the only WMA in South Texas surrounding a lake," says Ledbetter. "The WMA forms an undisturbed buffer zone around the lake, so there is a lot of wildlife there."

Altimira orioles nest in compartments 4 and 5, which has a mixture of the older mesquite trees and the open savannah areas they prefer. Vermilion flycatchers are fairly common along the road leading to the area headquarters, because it runs down a peninsula with San Miguel Creek on one side and the Frio River on the other. Caracaras are abundant; they make roosts in dead trees that are killed when the lake is high. Look for these areas along the road by the area headquarters and near the FM 99 boat ramp. Groove-billed anis can be found in compartment 4 in the open, mixed brush area near San Miguel Creek. Painted buntings prefer brushy areas such as that around the hunter campground. Look for screech, barred, and great horned owls in dead snags anywhere on the area.

In fall, the area comes alive with waterfowl: cinnamon teal, mallards, pintails, wood ducks, wigeons, blue- and green-winged teal, shovelers, and gadwalls. If late summer rains raise the lake level and flood shallows, teal will be found in coves all around the lake.

To view wild turkeys and white-tailed deer—including some truly impressive bucks—go to the Calliham Unit of Choke Canyon State Park.

HUNTING

In general, waterfowl, upland bird, and migratory bird hunting are available on specified dates to holders of an Annual Public Hunting Permit, and deer hunting is available by drawing only. See the *Public Hunting Lands Map Booklet,* the *Applications for Drawings on Public Hunting Lands,* and the *Outdoor Annual* for species, seasons, and bag limits. Youth-only deer and waterfowl hunts are available; see the above publications.

PRO'S POINTERS. Dove hunting is very limited because the WMA lacks open areas. "Birds do water in the lake, so if you can find an open, level area near the lake, you may have some shooting," says Ledbetter.

Quail hunting can be good or poor, depending on rainfall. Bob-white quail are best on the north side of the lake; compartments 1–10—particularly 4, 5, 9, and 10—are the best. "Look for old fallow fields, oil and gas production sites, roadsides, senderos—wherever there is edge," advises Ledbetter. The last hour of the day can offer excellent hunting in old fields as birds arrive from the surrounding brush to roost. Find an open field with dinnerplate-sized circles of black-and-white quail droppings and walk slowly around the field several times. The same covey may flush and return two or three times. Blue quail can be found in compartments 14 and 15. How-ever, the brush is very thick and the ground is bare, allowing the birds to

run. Good dogs are needed to do well there.

Teal may be hunted each day of the early teal season. Ledbetter suggests compartments 9, 10, and 14 for waterfowl hunting. Access the lake by public boat ramps. Compart-ments 9 and 10 may be reached by launching from the ramp on FM 99 or from the Mason Point ramp at the end of Recreation Road 7. Compart-ment 14 is best reached from the ramp at the Calliham Unit of Choke Canyon State Park. Portable blinds may be used, or grasses and weeds can be used to build blinds.

A few sandhill cranes can usually be found on the area, on the flats of the south shore of the lake in Com-partment 14. A free permit is needed to hunt them.

Rabbits and hares may be hunted concurrently with dove and quail. The area has lots of cottontails, but very few people hunt them. Hunt the roads and senderos.

Special Permit archery deer hunts are held in November. Compart-ments are assigned according to the number of people in the party, where they are staying, and whether they have a four-wheel-drive vehicle.

"Success depends on your ability to interpret deer sign," says Ledbetter. "Bucks will not be in the rut yet, so you have to locate major food sources such as persimmons or prickly pear flats and hunt travel corridors between the food sources and bedding areas. I highly recommend that people bring their own tree stands, because the permanent blinds we have are better suited for rifle hunting."

Rifle hunts are held in late No-vember and early December. Any legal weapon may be used, but only one weapon per hunter may be possessed while hunting. The Daughtrey has produced quite a few deer in the 140 to 160 class, making this WMA a leader in the quality of deer taken on public hunts.

Hunters are assigned compart-ments, given directions to the com-partment and to blinds, and told where they are most likely to see deer from that blind. "Deer will follow the draws, and all the permanent blinds are sited to take advantage of this," Ledbetter says. However, still hunting

A number of WMAs contain active oil or gas wells, and service roads furnish hiking opportunities and hunter access. Birding is often good along treelines bordering roads.

Choke Canyon Reservoir can be accessed through the James E. Daughtrey WMA, which consists of five noncontiguous parcels adjacent to the lake.

until just before dark. The bigger bucks bed in the thickest of the native brush in the day and travel the drainages to the more open areas to feed and to chase does. You need to sit back in the brush a couple of hundred yards and catch them on their way."

Gun antlerless deer, javelina, and feral hog hunts are also offered by drawing. However, with the exception of spring turkey hunts but including archery hunts, hunters may take one javelina, unlimited feral hogs, and unlimited coyotes. Hunters are allowed to kill rattlesnakes on the area. Baiting is allowed on all hunts, including spring turkeys, as long as the corn is in a *paper* bag from a known dealer, with an aflatoxin test tag.

Youth-only deer hunts are offered by drawing only and are very special on the Daughtrey WMA. They are timed to fall during the peak of the rut. "I want to provide kids with the optimum opportunity to kill a large white-tailed buck in South Texas in the hope that the experience will encourage them to continue hunting," says Ledbetter. Success rate is usually better than 50 percent. Since each youth must be accompanied by a nonhunting adult, double tripod stands and box blinds are provided.

On all Special Permit hunts, all game must be checked in at the check station, where it is weighed, measured, aged, and photographed. Researchers may do organ analysis or DNA sampling.

Spring turkey hunts are held by special permit by compartment. "Turkeys tend to roost in bigger trees along the drainages," Ledbetter says. "One technique is to find trees along a creek with an open area nearby for flydown, roost a gobbler at dark, and hunt him the next morning. Coyote and owl locator calls work really well here because we have so many of each. Use them either at dawn or dusk to locate a gobbler, then go to him." The Daughtrey WMA often leads WMAs in hunter success rate on spring turkey hunts.

or stalking are allowed. Every hunter in a compartment will be part of the same group to help ensure communication among hunters. Most compartments have several blinds to allow for differing wind directions.

"Hunt all day," Ledbetter advises, noting that a substantial portion of the better bucks taken on the area have been killed within two hours either side of noon. "Hunt the lower elevations—the draws, the drainages, the swales, the creeks. Avoid the water's edge, even though the visibility is better there. Big bucks won't venture into the open grassy areas

INSIDER'S CORNER

PASSING THE TORCH

One of the greatest threats to continuation of the hunting heritage in Texas is declining recruitment. Fewer young people becoming hunters means declining revenues for landowners and Texas Parks and Wildlife, as well as weakened public support for hunting. Since hunting-related revenues generate most of the money available for habitat acquisition and enhancement and the management of all wild species, not just game animals, a decline in the number of hunters can have a negative impact on all outdoor recreationists. Area manager Macy Ledbetter addresses that problem in several ways, one of which is holding annual youth deer hunts during the rut. Another is holding twice-yearly hunter education survival courses on the Daughtrey WMA.

"We bring kids out here for a weekend camp," he says. "The kids have to cook their own meals in a primitive camp and sleep outdoors. I show slides of animals and talk about what a wildlife biologist does. A game warden talks about his job. There's also classroom instruction on hunting and ethics. Then we take the kids into the field and teach them safety skills such as how to cross a fence with gun and how to get in and out of tripod stands. We teach safe gun handling and have a shooting range where every kid gets to shoot at least three shots on every kind of bow and gun available."

A hunter skills trail puts kids in situations where they have to recognize shoot/don't-shoot situations or decide if taking a shot is ethical under certain conditions. "You can see lightbulbs coming on in their heads," Ledbetter says.

There are fun activities, too. "We set live traps on creeks, catch and talk about animals, show them tracks and rubs. On Saturday night we tell hunting stories, blow predator calls, and listen to the animals."

Children take a written test at the check station on Sunday morning. Ledbetter has no doubt about the value of the program. "It's the best thing I've come across," he says.

Becoming an Outdoors Woman workshops are also held on the Daughtrey WMA. For information, contact Ledbetter at the address or phone above.

Texas Parks and Wildlife also operates an annual summer camp at which youngsters can earn their angler and hunter certification. For information, call the Parrie Haynes Youth Camp at 254/554-4052.

5,656 acres in
23 noncontiguous tracts
410 N. 13th St.
Edinburg, TX 78539
956/383-8982

Driving Times from:
Amarillo: 13.5 hours
Austin: 5.5 hours
Brownsville: 0.5 hour
Dallas: 9 hours
El Paso: 14 hours
Houston: 6 hours
San Antonio: 4.5 hours
Directions: The units in the WMA are scattered throughout the Lower Rio Grande Valley from the mouth of the Rio Grande to west of Rio Grande City. Specific directions to units open for public use are given below.
Open: Daily. Some units will be closed on designated dates for Special Permit hunts.
Activities: Camping, wildlife viewing, hiking, hunting.
Facilities: Primitive campgrounds and wildlife-viewing platform at the Ebony Unit.
Special Regulations: Only shotguns are allowed. During the special white-winged dove season, shooting hours are from noon to sunset. On-site registration is required of white-winged dove hunters on some units.
Advisories: Some roads may be muddy after rains. Heat, humidity, ticks, and chiggers are present in summer. Accessing some units requires crossing private property. Carry your own supply of potable water.
Lodging in Area: Motels are available in numerous local towns.
Local Points of Interest: Port Isabel Lighthouse State Historical Park, Bentsen-Rio Grande Valley State Park, Falcon State Park, Sabal Palm Sanctuary, Laguna Atascosa National Wildlife Refuge, Santa Ana National Wildlife Refuge, Lower Rio Grande National Wildlife Refuge,

Palo Alto Battlefield National Historic Site.
Disability Access: A wildlife-viewing facility at the Ebony Unit is wheelchair-accessible.

History

Originally occupied by Coahuiltecan and Karankawa Indians, the lower Rio Grande area was also among the first parts of Texas explored by Europeans. Numerous Spanish expeditions traveled along the river, which they named the Rio Bravo. By about 1750 the Spanish began to establish settlements on the south bank of the river. Land north of the river was divided into large ranchos. These early settlements survived frequent raids by Lipan Apache and Comanches. They were not so fortunate after the Texas Revolution and the Mexican War, when many families that had legally held land for generations saw it taken from them by questionable means.

Texas claimed the Rio Grande as its southern boundary after winning independence from Mexico in 1836, but Mexico continued to exert considerable control over the area between the Rio Grande and the Nueces River, which it claimed as the boundary. In 1846 an American army under General Zachary Taylor landed near the mouth of the Rio Grande and set up a base on what is now the Boca Chica Unit of the WMA. Following the war that resulted from armed clashes along the north bank of the river, the treaty imposed by the United States established the Rio Grande as the international boundary.

Ill feelings between Mexico and the United States continued to complicate life along the Rio Grande into the early 1900s. However, by that time two developments were taking shape that were to change the Rio Grande Valley and bring the peoples of the two countries closer together. The first was the introduction of large-scale irrigation in 1898; the

second was the arrival of the railroad in 1904. Within three decades most of the Lower Rio Grande Valley was cleared of native brush and converted to farmland, largely by farmers from the Midwest and immigrants from Mexico.

The citrus industry began to develop commercially from small private beginnings after 1904. By 1949 there were some 9 million citrus trees in the region, but disastrous freezes in 1949 and 1951 killed most of them. Following that time there were several tree-killing freezes, including very severe ones in 1983 and 1989. These freezes, and the loss of nesting habitat for white-winged doves that resulted, had a direct impact on the development of the Las Palomas WMA (Spanish for "the doves").

Population surveys of white-winged dove in the Lower Rio Grande Valley done before and after freezes in 1949 and 1951 showed that devastation of the citrus groves, which provided nesting habitat, resulted in greatly decreased numbers of birds. The white-winged dove hunting season was closed in 1951, 1952, and 1953. It was clear that since the citrus groves could not reliably provide nesting habitat, the preservation of native brush was the only alternative. Texas Parks and Wildlife began purchasing tracts of native brush to prevent loss of such habitat to agriculture. The first unit, the Longoria, was purchased in 1957. Purchases continued sporadically through the 1960s, but money was not always available when land came up for sale.

Public pressure led to the passage of a law establishing a white-winged dove hunting stamp in 1971. Half the proceeds from sale of the stamps was dedicated to land acquisition. Purchases have continued since then as suitable tracts became available. The first public hunts for white-winged doves were held in 1983.

Part of the historical significance

of the white-winged dove stamp is that it set a precedent for the sale of special stamps. Other special stamps introduced since include archery, muzzleloader, waterfowl, and turkey.

GEOGRAPHY AND NATURAL FEATURES

The flat and fertile plains of the Rio Grande dominates the Las Palomas WMA. The 23 units are scattered over 100 miles east to west, most within a handful of miles of the river. Some contain resacas, or oxbow lakes, that were once part of the river channel. While some contain land that was cleared for farming, others have native or reforested brush. Vegetative cover on the various units ranges from grasses to impenetrable thickets of native brush.

All the various tracts interface with private land, most of which is intensively used for agriculture. Cotton, sorghum, citrus, sugar cane, and various vegetables are the principal crops. The entire Lower Rio Grande Valley is densely populated, and farmsteads or towns lie near many of the units.

The Lower Rio Grande Valley's location and climate make it one of the most important birding locations in the world. Many tropical species achieve their northernmost range here, attracting birders from across the nation. The World Birding Center is planned for the area in the near future. The Adams, Resaca de la Palma, Brasil, and Arroyo Colorado Units of Las Palomas WMA are likely to play an important role as birding sites associated with the center.

Units of Las Palomas WMA provide habitat for approximately 19 threatened and endangered species, including bald eagles, American peregrine falcons, brown pelicans, jaguarundis, ocelots, and several kinds of sea turtles.

The Arroyo Colorado lends its name to the unit of the Las Palomas WMA bordering it.

RECREATIONAL ACTIVITIES

Wildlife viewing and hunting are the main activities available on the Las Palomas WMA. Driving directions are given below to each of the units open to the public.

Anacua Unit—From U.S. 83 in La Feria, follow FM 506 south about 6 miles to U.S. 281. Turn right onto U.S. 281 and go 1.4 miles to an unsigned road to the left just before Santa Maria High School. Turn left

and follow the road 0.8 mile to an information station.

Arroyo Colorado Unit—From Rio Hondo northeast of Harlingen, go east on FM 508 for 3.7 miles to FM 2925. Follow FM 2925 north for 5.7 miles to a dirt farm road to the left in the middle of a long curve to the right. Follow the dirt road across private property for 0.3 mile to the area entrance.

Baird, Chapote, and Taormina Units—From the intersection of U.S.

281 and FM 1015 in Progreso, follow U.S. 281 west 6.9 miles to FM 493. Go north on FM 493 for 3.4 miles to an unsigned road and turn right. Follow the road 1 mile to a T intersection, turn right onto another unsigned road, and follow it 0.6 mile to an information station at a cluster of old farm buildings. Use the first gate on the left during the white-winged dove season. The second gate on the left is open during the mourning dove season. The three units are contiguous and accessible by county roads.

Boca Chica Unit—From the intersection of U.S. 77/83 and Texas 4 in Brownsville, go east on Texas 4 for 21 miles. The area begins at the subdivision on the left and continues to the beach 2 miles on down Texas 4.

Brasil Unit—See Resaca de la Palma and Brasil Units, below.

Carricitos Unit—From the intersection of U.S. 77/83 and FM 345 in San Benito, go north on FM 345 to FM 3462. Turn right onto FM 3462 and go 0.5 mile to Kornegay Road. Turn left and go an additional 2 miles to the information station.

Chapote Unit—See Baird, Chapote and Taormina Units, above.

Ebony Unit—From the intersection of U.S. 77/83 southeast of Harlingen, go south on FM 1479 for 6.4 miles to Jimenez Road, which is not signed. Turn left and go half a mile to the information station.

Longoria Unit—From the intersection of U.S. 77 and Spur 413 at Sebastian, north of Harlingen, follow Spur 413 west 0.4 mile, at which point it becomes FM 506. Follow FM 506 west for 3.2 miles to the information station.

Penitas Unit—From the intersection of U.S. 83 and FM 1427 in Penitas, west of Mission, go south on FM 1427 for 1 mile. Turn right onto an unsigned road and go 0.6 mile to an information station.

Resaca de la Palma and Brasil Units—From the intersection of U.S. 281 and FM 3248 northwest of Brownsville, go west on FM 3248 for 1.9 miles to a dirt farm road to the north opposite the entrance to the River Bend RV Resort. Follow the dirt road north 0.9 mile across an open field, which is private property. Ignore the No Trespassing sign at the farm equipment storage area and continue another 0.2 mile to an information station.

Taormina Unit—See Baird, Chapote, and Taormina Units, above.

Tucker Unit—From the intersection of U.S. 77/83 southeast of Harlingen, go south on FM for 5.3 miles to FM 675. Go east on FM 675 for 1.1 miles to Tilden Road. Turn left and follow Tilden Road 0.7 mile to the information station.

CAMPING

Primitive camping for hunters is available at three of the units. At the Ebony and Taormina Units, camping is allowed only during the special white-winged dove season. At Arroyo Colorado, drawn hunters for the youth-only deer hunt are allowed to camp. Only primitive camping is available; there are no facilities at any of the sites.

PRO'S POINTERS. The campsite at the Ebony Unit is the caliche parking lot at the information station. Mosquitoes from the adjacent resaca (a large oxbow lake) can be troublesome. At the Taormina Unit, camping is allowed adjacent to the parking area inside the second (south) pipe gate. At Arroyo Colorado, Texas Parks and Wildlife personnel will guide hunters to the designated camping area.

WILDLIFE VIEWING

The Lower Rio Grande Valley is generally regarded as one of the great birding locations in the world. The various units of Las Palomas WMA provide habitat for a variety of birds, ranging from coastal to upland, and other wildlife such as the Texas tortoise. The blending of temperate and tropical climatic zones attracts both familiar North American species as well as those found in the United States only here. And finally, as the funnel through which birds traveling the Central Flyway between North and Central America pass, the area concentrates migratory species in sometimes unbelievable numbers.

PRO'S POINTERS. "For coastal-type species such as brown pelicans, common loons, laughing gulls, and others, the Boca Chica Unit is best," says Texas Parks and Wildlife biologist Steve Benn. "You'll see most of the open beach type birds—sanderlings, willets, migrant red knots. You may see snowy and piping plovers. Look for neotropicals in the black mangroves; they may 'fall out' onto the ground in the spring."

One of the advantages of birding the Boca Chica Unit is that part of the Lower Rio Grande National Wildlife Refuge is nearby; information about it is posted on the north side of Texas 4 at a point 14 miles from the intersection of U.S. 77/83 and Texas 4 in Brownsville. The clay ridge 3.4 miles east of this information station is a great place to look for neotropicals. Park at the Camp Belknap historical marker and walk the ridge running north and south. Much of the refuge is tidal flats.

The Arroyo Colorado, Longoria, Resaca de la Palma, and Tucker Units have quite a bit of brush and are the better properties for upland South Texas birds. "You may see long-billed thrashers, greenjays, olive sparrows, and Altamira orioles," says Benn. "Unusual but possibly present on the Longoria Unit are blue buntings. Chachalacas, white-tipped doves, least grebes, buff-bellied hummingbirds, groove-billed anis, yellow-green vireos, clay-colored robins, kiskadee flycatchers, and pauraques will occur primarily in the woodlands and brush on these units."

The Ebony Unit has a wildlife observation deck overlooking the resaca near the information station. Commonly seen are shorebirds like

black-necked stilts, greater and lesser yellowlegs, least grebes, and a variety of puddle ducks such as scaup, ruddy ducks, teal, and pintails. The observation deck is also a good place for tricolored herons, and snowy and great egrets. "There may be the opportunity to see ringed and green kingfishers. Look for them in the trees around the edge of the water," Benn advises.

Arroyo Colorado has 6 miles of interior roads available for walking. The World Birding Center will likely use this unit for birding. Unlike most of the other units of Las Palomas, which have little variety of habitat, Arroyo Colorado has six vegetative habitats and seven soil types, resulting in great diversity. This is a good place to see chachalacas, and Texas tortoises (a state-listed threatened species).

INTERPRETIVE NATURE TRAIL

The Longoria Unit has a nature trail about a quarter-mile long that is wheelchair-accessible. It passes through areas of native brush, and wildlife waterers have been installed. Although primarily a birding trail, the area is also Texas tortoise habitat, and plants on the trail attract a lot of butterflies.

PRO'S POINTERS. FM 506 runs through the center of the area. Hunting is permitted west of the highway; the eastern half of the area is for

ABOVE, LEFT:
The Boca Chica Unit of the Las Palomas WMA was once designated a state park but now is part of the WMA. It lies at the mouth of the Rio Grande.

ABOVE, RIGHT:
White-winged dove hunting furnishes family recreation for this father and son on the Ebony Unit of the Las Palomas WMA.

nonconsumptive use only. A pad for unloading wheelchairs at the parking lot on the east side is the start of the trail. Brochures keyed to numbered posts along the trail are available at the information kiosk. Benches along the trail are good places to sit quietly and wait for wildlife to appear.

When hunting is not going on, the area west of the highway offers good wildlife viewing as well. A trail leads through the brush from the information station at the parking lot to a shallow wildlife watering pond near a windmill. You may meet a Texas tortoise on the dirt path, as I did.

Note that Texas Parks and Wildlife regulations require that nonconsumptive users comply with requirements for wearing safety orange clothing whenever hunting is permitted on an area. Hunting season on most units of Las Palomas WMA extends from September through February.

HIKING

The interpretive nature trail on the Longoria Unit is the only designated trail on Las Palomas WMA.

PRO'S POINTERS. See information on this trail in the section above.

The Tucker Unit has a levee that runs east-west. Walking west from the parking lot takes you through an area with heavy brush. To the east, the levee passes between brush on one side and open fields on the other. Hikers must wear safety orange clothing during hunting season.

HUNTING

Although the name Las Palomas (The Doves) identifies the principal game species, there is also the opportunity to hunt quail, chachalacas, rabbits, hares, feral hogs, and deer on various units of the WMA. For species, seasons, and bag limits, see the *Public Hunting Lands Map Booklet,* the *Applications for Drawings on Public Hunting Lands,* and the *Outdoor Annual* for the current year.

The special white-winged dove season is generally the first two weekends in September. Hunting is allowed on designated units of Las Palomas by Annual Public Hunting Permit or Regular Permit. Registration is required on some units but not others. See the *Public Hunting Lands Map Booklet.*

Be sure to check the unit map at the information station before hunting, as not all parts of a unit may be open to hunting. Hunting on all the units is with shotgun only except during Special Permit hunts.

PRO'S POINTERS. "Scouting and weather are the keys to white-winged dove hunting on Las Palomas," says Benn. "We've opened up all the units listed in the *Public Hunting Lands Map Booklet* to hunting by Annual Public Hunting Permit so hunters will have the opportunity to scout, figure out how and where the birds are flying, and go from there. We may or may not have successful food plots on a given area. We plant either sorghum, corn, or sunflowers and promote native plants such as croton. The presence of white-wings depends on the weather. They are on the brink of migrating south in early September anyway, so it takes only a little weather system to move them out."

The first weekend of the season will likely be the time when the most white-wings are present, but hunter numbers will be high as well. Even after white-wings move out, however, there will probably be enough mourning doves to furnish good shooting. Be sure to check the bag limit set for the special white-wing season, as this governs the number of birds you may take (usually 10) and the number of mourning and white-tipped doves that may be part of the bag (generally five and two, respectively).

Shooting hours are from noon to sunset during the special white-winged dove season, allowing plenty of time for scouting the various areas to see which have birds. A unit that is hot one day may not be the next if it receives heavy hunting pressure, so daily scouting may be required. In general, look for birds flying between feeding areas and patches of brush where they roost. The edge of a field along a treeline is usually a good place to hunt. However, doves tend to follow natural features when flying, so observation will often reveal the best hunting locations within an area.

Limited numbers of quail can be found in open areas and along brush lines on the Anacua, Ebony, Taormina, Chapote, and Penitas Units. The Penitas Unit was all farm fields when purchased, so there are three small open fields where food plots may be planted for doves and quail. "The area is small enough you can decide quickly how the hunting will be," Benn says. "The old road that runs from the information station to the Rio Grande is closed to vehicles but is open to foot traffic."

Chachalacas prefer heavy brush and are most likely to be found on the Baird, Carricitos, Longoria, and Tucker units. "The best way to hunt them is to find a food source such as

You may meet a Texas tortoise on the Longoria Unit of the Las Palomas WMA; approach slowly and quietly to avoid spooking it into its shell.

an anacua or coma tree in fruit and stake it out," says Benn. "They will be around there somewhere. Or you can walk them up in the brush. One of the tricks to remember is they generally run in small groups. If one bird crosses in front of you, be ready for a second or third behind it. You won't have many chances to wingshoot them, because they live in such thick brush." The Baird Unit has a foot trail that runs north-south; hunt chachalacas along it. You may have a chance to ground-swat one when it crosses the road.

If you hunt the Longoria Unit, remember that hunting is allowed only west of FM 506.

Special Permit feral hog hunts are held on the Resaca de la Palma and Arroyo Colorado Units. "Hog hunts are by assigned stand, and baiting is allowed," says Benn. "On the Arroyo Colorado, feeders and stands are provided for all hunters, and we do prebaiting before the hunt. Hunters must hunt from assigned stands."

Youth-only deer hunts may also be offered on Arroyo Colorado by Special Permit.

INSIDER'S CORNER

THE ELUSIVE—AND RAUCOUS—CHACHALACA

One of the most unusual trophies for either birder or hunter in Texas is a dull brown, pheasant-sized bird found only in the Lower Rio Grande Valley, the chachalaca. Destruction of the dense Tamaulipan scrub brush that is their favored habitat has lessened even this limited range.

Chachalacas are sought out for their rarity, not their beauty; while I would not describe them as ugly, they are definitely not pretty, either. The body is gray-brown, and the darker tail is tipped in white. Adults have a reddish throat patch, but even this splash of color is subdued and hard to see. Chachalacas are ideally equipped to lurk in the shadows.

Although chachalacas in South Texas parks regularly feast on handouts of fruits and seeds within feet of people, the wild birds found on several units of the Las Palomas WMA are noticeably wary. They prefer to walk or hop through trees and dense ground cover rather than fly, making them even harder to spot. However, if you are lucky enough to see one, you will probably see several, as they travel in groups.

Chachalacas feed on the fruit, foliage, and flowers of native trees. To try to sight one, find a tree in fruit and sit quietly nearby. The birds also visit water sources. Sam Patten, wildlife technician on the Arroyo Colorado Unit, has devised ingenious watering devices that drip or spray water and attract a variety of birds, including chachalacas.

People who have eaten chachalacas say the meat is very greasy, making it a good candidate for barbecuing. Young birds, generally identified by their smaller size, are more tender and flavorful.

How did the chachalaca get its name? The name is inspired by the strident call of the male, which is especially evident during the spring mating season. Oddly, however, experts describe this call in quite different ways. One transcribes it as "cha-ca-lac," while another hears it as "slap er back." All agree, however, that when in full throat, the noise made by a group of chachalacas borders on being obnoxious. When courting, chachalacas sing from the treetops rather than the underbrush, making their racket all the more audible.

BIBLIOGRAPHY

An Improved Device for Managing Water Levels in Beaver Ponds. Austin: Texas Parks and Wildlife Department, 1997.

Applications for Drawings on Public Hunting Lands, 1999–2000. Austin: Texas Parks and Wildlife Department, 1998.

Armstrong, Bill. Interview with Larry D. Hodge, 1999.

Baker, T. Lindsay. *Lighthouses of Texas.* College Station: Texas A&M University Press, 1991.

Barrow, Jennifer. Interview with Larry D. Hodge, 1999.

Benn, Steve. Interview with Larry D. Hodge, 1999.

Blassingame, Jim. Interview with Larry D. Hodge, 1999.

Brewer, Clay. Interview with Larry D. Hodge, 1999.

Calkins, Gary. Interview with Larry D. Hodge, 1999.

Cano, José. Interview with Larry D. Hodge, 1999.

Carpenter, Trey. Interview with Larry D. Hodge, 1999.

Carrie, Dawn. Interview with Larry D. Hodge, 1999.

Carroll, Bob. Interview with Larry D. Hodge, 1999.

Clark, Ski. Interview with Larry D. Hodge, 1999.

Dvorak, David. Interview with Larry D. Hodge, 1998.

Fisher, Darrell. Interview with Larry D. Hodge, 1999.

Fleming, Kay. Interview with Larry D. Hodge, 1999.

Foster, Charles, Jr. Interview with Larry D. Hodge, 1999.

Fox Squirrel Management in East Texas. Austin: Texas Parks and Wildlife Department, 1979.

Frels, Donnie. Interview with Larry D. Hodge, 1999.

Fuchs, Gene. Interview with Larry D. Hodge, 1999.

General Regulations of River Use, Big Bend National Park, Rio Grande Wild and Scenic River. Washington: United States Department of the Interior, National Park Service, 1997.

Ging, Glenn. Interview with Larry D. Hodge, 1998.

Green-Tree Reservoir Management. Austin: Texas Parks and Wildlife Department, 1988.

Gregory, Chris. Interview with Larry D. Hodge, 1999.

Gunnels, Jeff. Interview with Larry D. Hodge, 1999.

Harris, Carl. Interview with Larry D. Hodge, 1999.

Haucke, Hayden. Interview with Larry D. Hodge, 1999.

Hines, Richard. Interview with Larry D. Hodge, 1999.

Hughes, John. Interview with Larry D. Hodge, 1998.

Jones, John. Interview with Larry D. Hodge, 1999.

Kitchens, Jim. Interview with Larry D. Hodge, 1996.

Knipe, Rick. Interview with Larry D. Hodge, 1999.

Kraii, Kevin. Interview with Larry D. Hodge, 1999.

Lawyer, Tim. Interview with Larry D. Hodge, 1999.

LeBeau, Larry. Interview with Larry D. Hodge, 1999.

Ledbetter, Macy. Interview with Larry D. Hodge, 1999.

Lee, Raymond. "The Desert Bighorn Sheep." Cody: *The Wild Sheep Journal*, 1998.

Leopold, Aldo. *A Sand County Almanac, with Essays on Conservation from Round River.* Oxford: Oxford University Press, 1966.

Lewis, Linda. Interview with Larry D. Hodge, 1999.

Lewis, Violet. Interview with Larry D. Hodge, 1999.

Lobpries, David. Interview with Larry D. Hodge, 1999.

Management Plan for Alabama Creek Wildlife Management Area. Austin: Texas Parks and Wildlife Department, 1997.

Management Plan for Alazan Bayou Wildlife Management Area. Austin: Texas Parks and Wildlife Department, 1997.

Management Plan for Angelina-Neches/Dam B Wildlife Management Area. Austin: Texas Parks and Wildlife Department, 1997.

Management Plan for Aquilla Wildlife Management Area. Austin: Texas Parks and Wildlife Department, 1997.

Management Plan for Atkinson Island Wildlife Management Area. Austin: Texas Parks and Wildlife Department, 1997.

Management Plan for Bannister Wildlife Management Area. Austin: Texas Parks and Wildlife Department, 1997.

Management Plan for Big Lake Bottom Wildlife Management Area. Austin: Texas Parks and Wildlife Department, 1997.

Management Plan for Black Gap Wildlife Management Area. Austin: Texas Parks and Wildlife Department, 1997.

Management Plan for Caddo Lake State Park/Wildlife Management Area. Austin: Texas Parks and Wildlife Department, 1997.

Management Plan for Caddo National Grasslands Wildlife Management Area. Austin: Texas Parks and Wildlife Department, 1997.

Management Plan for Candy Abshier Wildlife Management Area. Austin: Texas Parks and Wildlife Department, 1997.

Management Plan for Cedar Creek Islands Wildlife Management Area. Austin: Texas Parks and Wildlife Department, 1997.

Management Plan for Chaparral Wildlife Management Area. Austin: Texas Parks and Wildlife Department, 1997.

Management Plan for Cooper Wildlife Management Area. Austin: Texas Parks and Wildlife Department, 1997.

Management Plan for D.R. Wintermann Wildlife Management Area. Austin: Texas Parks and Wildlife Department, 1997.

Management Plan for Elephant Mountain Wildlife Management Area. Austin: Texas Parks and Wildlife Department, 1997.

Management Plan for Gene Howe Wildlife Management Area. Austin: Texas Parks and Wildlife Department, 1997.

Management Plan for Granger Wildlife Management Area. Austin: Texas Parks and Wildlife Department, 1997.

Management Plan for Guadalupe Delta Wildlife Management Area. Austin: Texas Parks and Wildlife Department, 1997.

Management Plan for Gus Engeling Wildlife Management Area. Austin: Texas Parks and Wildlife Department, 1997.

Management Plan for J.D. Murphree Wildlife Management Area. Austin: Texas Parks and Wildlife Department, 1997.

Management Plan for James E. Daughtrey Wildlife Management Area. Austin: Texas Parks and Wildlife Department, 1997.

Management Plan for Keechi Creek Wildlife Management Area. Austin: Texas Parks and Wildlife Department, 1997.

Management Plan for Kerr Wildlife Management Area. Austin: Texas Parks and Wildlife Department, 1997.

Management Plan for Lower Neches Wildlife Management Area. Austin: Texas Parks and Wildlife Department, 1997.

Management Plan for M.O. Neasloney Wildlife Management Area. Austin: Texas Parks and Wildlife Department, 1997.

Management Plan for Mad Island Wildlife Management Area. Austin: Texas Parks and Wildlife Department, 1997.

Management Plan for Mason Mountain Wildlife Management Area. Austin: Texas Parks and Wildlife Department, 1997.

Management Plan for Matador Wildlife Management Area. Austin: Texas Parks and Wildlife Department, 1997.

Management Plan for Matagorda Island State Park/Wildlife Management Area. Austin: Texas Parks and Wildlife Department, 1997.

Management Plan for Moore Plantation Wildlife Management Area. Austin: Texas Parks and Wildlife Department, 1997.

Management Plan for North Toledo Bend Wildlife Management Area. Austin: Texas Parks and Wildlife Department, 1997.

Management Plan for Old Sabine Bottom Wildlife Management Area. Austin: Texas Parks and Wildlife Department, 1997.

Management Plan for Old Tunnel Wildlife Management Area. Austin: Texas Parks and Wildlife Department, 1997.

Management Plan for Pat Mayse Wildlife Management Area. Austin: Texas Parks and Wildlife Department, 1997.

Management Plan for Peach Point Wildlife Management Area. Austin: Texas Parks and Wildlife Department, 1997.

Management Plan for Playa Lakes Wildlife Management Area. Austin: Texas Parks and Wildlife Department, 1997.

Management Plan for Ray Roberts Public Hunting Area. Austin: Texas Parks and Wildlife Department, 1997.

Management Plan for Redhead Pond Wildlife Management Area. Austin: Texas Parks and Wildlife Department, 1997.

Management Plan for Richland Creek Wildlife Management Area. Austin: Texas Parks and Wildlife Department, 1997.

Management Plan for Sam Houston National Forest Wildlife Management Area. Austin: Texas Parks and Wildlife Department, 1997.

Management Plan for Sierra Diablo Wildlife Management Area. Austin: Texas Parks and Wildlife Department, 1997.

Management Plan for Somerville Wildlife Management Area. Austin: Texas Parks and Wildlife Department, 1997.

Management Plan for Tawakoni Wildlife Management Area.

Austin: Texas Parks and Wildlife Department, 1997.

Management Plan for The Nature Center Wildlife Management Area. Austin: Texas Parks and Wildlife Department, 1997.

Management Plan for Tony Houseman State Park/Wildlife Management Area. Austin: Texas Parks and Wildlife Department, 1997.

Management Plan for Walter Buck Wildlife Management Area. Austin: Texas Parks and Wildlife Department, 1997.

Management Plan for Welder Flats Wildlife Management Area. Austin: Texas Parks and Wildlife Department, 1997.

Management Plan for White Oak Creek Wildlife Management Area. Austin: Texas Parks and Wildlife Department, 1997.

Management Plan for Las Palomas Wildlife Management Area. Austin: Texas Parks and Wildlife Department, 1997.

McAlister, Wayne and Martha. *A Naturalist's Guide: Matagorda Island.* Austin: The University of Texas Press, 1993.

McKinney, Bonnie. Interview with Larry D. Hodge, 1999.

Merendino, Todd. Interview with Larry D. Hodge, 1999.

Muller, Charles. Interview with Larry D. Hodge, 1999.

Ortego, Brent. Interview with Larry D. Hodge, 1999.

Palmer, Tom. Interview with Larry D. Hodge, 1999.

Patten, Sam. Interview with Larry D. Hodge, 1999.

Pike, Richard. Interview with Larry D. Hodge, 1999.

Pittman, Michael. Interview with Larry D. Hodge, 1999.

Poteet, Micah. Interview with Larry D. Hodge, 1999.

Prochaska, Dale. Interview with Larry D. Hodge, 1999.

Public Hunting Lands Map Booklet, 1999–2000. Texas Parks and Wildlife Department, 1998.

Ruthven, Chip. Interview with Larry D. Hodge, 1999.

Schwertner, T. Wayne. Interview with Larry D. Hodge, 1999.

Sierra, David. Interview with Larry D. Hodge, 1999.

Simpson, Brad. Interview with Larry D. Hodge, 1998.

Steed, Charlie. Interview with Larry D. Hodge, 1999.

Storey, Annice. Interview with Larry D. Hodge, 1999.

Sullivan, Murty. Interview with Larry D. Hodge, 1999.

Sutherlin, Jim. Interview with Larry D. Hodge, 1999.

Synatzske, David. Interview with Larry D. Hodge, 1999.

Telfair, Ray C. Interview with Larry D. Hodge, 1999.

Telfair, Raymond C. II, ed. *Texas Wildlife Resources and Land Uses.* Austin: University of Texas Press, 1999.

Texas Parks and Wildlife Outdoor Annual, 1999-2000. Austin: Texas Monthly Custom Publishing, 1999.

The Gray Squirrel in Texas. Austin: Texas Parks and Wildlife Department, 1961.

Thomas, James. Interview with Larry D. Hodge, 1998.

Thorne, John. Interview with Larry D. Hodge, 1999.

Tschanz, Eric. Interview with Larry D. Hodge, 1999.

Turney, Terry. Interview with Larry D. Hodge, 1999.

Tyler, Ron, et al. *The New Handbook of Texas.* Austin: The Texas State Historical Association, 1996.

Veatch, Cathleen. Interview with Larry D. Hodge, 1999.

Waggerman, Gary. Interview with Larry D. Hodge, 1999.

Wheatley, Mike. Interview with Larry D. Hodge, 1999.

INDEX

Abshier, Catherine ("Candy") Cain, 29
Alabama Creek WMA, 113–118
Alazan Bayou WMA, 119–122
American Bird Conservancy, 49
Angelina National Forest, 129
Angelina River, 123
Angelina-Neches/Dam B WMA, 123–127
Anvil Park, 97
Aquilla WMA, 171–176
Aransas National Wildlife Refuge, 51
Armstrong, Bill, 79, 82
Army Hole, 51, 53, 55
Atkinson Island WMA, 27–28
Austin, Stephen F., 57
Azalea, wild, 195, 199

Bailey's Fishing Camp, 44, 45
Bald cypress, life cycle of, 136
Bannister WMA, 128–131
Barrow, Jennifer, 211–213
Bats, Mexican free-tail, 88–90
Beachcombing tours, 54
Beautiful false dragonhead, 230
Beavers, problems with, 202, 214, 225
Becoming an Outdoors Woman, 243
Bedichek, Roy, 105
Bee Tree Slough, 124, 127
Benn, Steve, 246–249
Berry Lake, 196, 198
Bicycling, 7, 37, 54–55, 59, 73, 81, 93, 99, 104–105, 116, 125, 130, 139, 153, 160, 173, 183, 189, 197, 218, 224, 237
Big Creek Scenic Area, 156, 158, 159
Big Cypress Bayou, 132–135
Big Island, 186
Big Lake Bottom WMA, 177–180

Big Time Texas Hunts, 85
Big Woods hunter camp, 157
Bird banding, 187, 234
Bird Island, 186
Birding. *See* Wildlife viewing.
Black bears, 6, 9
Black deathcamus, 195
Black Gap WMA, 3–9, 20
Black Kettle National Grasslands, 99
Black, Hugo, 68
Black-capped vireo, 79, 80–81, 92
Blackland Prairie, 71, 77
Blackland Prairie Replication Site and Gene Bank, 71–72, 74, 77
Blue Elbow Swamp. *See* Tony Houseman State Park/WMA.
Bluebird Fishing Camp, 64
Boot Hill, 104, 105
Bottomland hardwoods, 123, 133–134, 150, 163, 165, 178, 185, 188, 194, 200, 216
Brewer, Clay, 11–15, 21–22
Broseco Ranch, 165
Broussard, Joseph, 33
Brown Schools of Central Texas, 84
Brown, Dustin, 116
Buck, Walter, Jr., 91
Buck, Walter, Sr., 91
Bujnoch, Don, 203
Bull nettle, 205
Burnet, David G., 28, 29

Cabeza de Vaca, Alvar Nuñez, 50
Caddo Lake, 132–133
Caddo Lake Initiative, 133
Caddo Lake State Park, 133
Caddo Lake State Park/WMA, 132–136
Caddo National Grasslands WMA, 181–185

Calhoun, 50
Calkins, Gary, 125–127, 130, 131, 139, 140
Camp Maxey, 206
Campbell, Henry H., 102
Camping, 6, 12, 17, 53, 60, 64, 72, 98, 103, 114–115, 120, 124, 129, 134, 138, 143, 156–157, 182, 196, 216, 228, 236, 246
Canadian River, 97
Candy Abshier WMA, 29–31
Caney Creek Reservoir, 165, 166
Cano, José, 172–175
Carp, 173, 176
Carpenter, Trey, 74–77
Carrie, Dawn, 158–160
Carroll, Bob, 203
Carson, Burch, 22
Catfish Creek, 194–199
Cats, impact of on bird populations, 49
Cavallo Pass, 50, 52, 53
Cedar Bayou, 52
Cedar Creek Islands WMA, 186–187
Cedar Creek Reservoir, 186
Chachalacas, 249
Chaparral WMA, 233–238
Charlie's Bait Camp, 67
Choke Canyon Reservoir, 239, 240
Choke Canyon State Park, 241
Christmas Bird Count, 47, 49, 58, 234
Citrus industry, 244
Civilian Conservation Corps, 128–129
Clark, Ski, 120–121, 143, 144
Cliburn Ranch, 66
Coffee Mill Lake, 181, 182, 184, 185
Cooper Lake, 163, 188
Cooper WMA, 188–193

Cranes, sandhill, 109
Culp Branch Native Prairie, 211, 212, 213

D. R. Wintermann WMA, 32–33
Darlington Road, 51, 54
Davy Crockett Lake, 181, 182, 184, 185
Davy Crockett National Forest, 113
Derden Wildlife Management Area. *See* Gus Engeling WMA.
Derden, M. L., 194
Desert bighorn sheep, 4, 10, 11–12, 15, 20–23
Devil's walking stick, 148, 149
Double Lake Mountain Bike Trail, 160
Double Lake Recreation Area, 156, 159, 160
Doves, white-winged, 244–245
Driving tours, 4–5, 11–12, 79, 114, 195, 234–235
Dvorak, Dave, 102–105, 107
Dwarf palmetto, 220
Dwarf pipewort, 195

Eastern wild turkey, restoration of, 131, 138
Ecosystem management. *See* holistic resource management.
Eisenhower, Dwight D., 68
Elephant Mountain WMA, 10–15
Equestrian trails, 5–6, 99, 105, 160, 167, 182

Farmington, 233, 235
Fire, suppression of, 141, 162
Fischer, Darrell, 223–226
Fishing
   bass, 42, 76, 81–82, 99, 105, 127, 136, 144–145, 154, 161–162, 168, 174–175, 179, 185, 191–192, 192–193, 198, 209, 213, 220, 225–226, 230
   bream, 136, 144, 185, 198
   carp, 209, 220, 225
   catfish, 8, 36–37, 42, 65, 76, 99, 117, 121, 127, 145, 154, 162, 168, 175, 192, 198, 209, 214, 220, 226, 230
   chain pickerel, 209
   crappie, 76, 126–127, 144, 145, 154, 162, 168, 175, 185, 192, 209, 213–214, 220, 230

saltwater, 37, 38, 42, 45, 55, 60, 67
   striped bass, 193
Fleming, Kay, 179, 187
Forests, management of, 168
Four Notch hunter camp, 157
Fredericksburg, 87–88
Frels, Donnie, 79, 80
Frog gigging, 127, 136
Fyffe's Corner Grocery, 134

Garner, Mike, 191–191
Gene Howe WMA, 97–101
Giant salvinia, 145
Gipson, Fred, 83
Goat Island, 134
Golden-cheek warbler, 79, 80–81
Gonzales, Mike, 53
Gould, Jay, 133
Granger WMA, 71–77
Great Raft, 132
Green-tree reservoirs, 166, 201, 202
Gregory, Chris, 160–161
Guadalupe Delta WMA, 34–38
Guadalupe River, 78, 81–82
Gulf Intracoastal Waterway, 39, 42, 46–47, 57, 58, 67
Gunnels, Jeff, 216–219
Gus Engeling WMA, 194–199

Habitat, destruction of, 49, 78, 238, 244
Hagar, Connie, 31
Hardwood bottomlands. *See* bottomland hardwoods.
Harmel, Donnie, 82
Harris, Carl, 131
Haucke, Hayden, 195, 197, 198, 199
Hawes family, 50, 51
Hercules' club. *See* devil's walking stick.
Hiking, 6–7, 12–14, 17, 37, 44, 54, 59, 64, 72–73, 81, 90, 92–93, 99, 100, 103–104, 115–116, 124–125, 130, 143–144, 151–153, 159–160, 166–167, 173, 178, 182–183, 189, 197, 204, 207, 212, 218, 223–224, 229, 236, 248
Hill family, 146
Hill Hole, 166, 167, 168
Hills family, 50, 51
Hines, Richard, 184, 185, 206–209
History tours, 54
Hogs, feral, 60

Hogtown, 97
Holistic resource management, 78, 233
Holly Bluff Swamp, 115
Hop hornbeam, 148, 149
Hopkins County stew, recipe for, 193
Houseman, Tony, 63
Houston, Sam, 28, 29, 68
Hughes, John, 97–100
Hunter education course, 243
Hunting
   alligator, 36, 40–41, 47, 48, 125, 127
   bobwhite quail, 99, 100, 105, 209, 230, 237, 241, 248
   chachalaca, 248–249
   exotic, 81, 85, 93
   feral hog, 36, 47, 48, 54, 59, 64, 74, 75, 81, 99, 105, 116–117, 121, 126, 130, 140, 144, 153, 161, 167, 174, 179, 184, 190, 198, 202, 208, 213, 219, 225, 229, 242, 248
   furbearer, 76, 85, 117, 121, 126, 136, 140, 144, 168, 225
   Gambel's quail, 8
   javelina, 8, 15, 242
   mourning dove, 7–8, 14, 17–18, 37, 76, 81, 99, 100, 105, 108, 140, 161, 167, 174, 191, 213, 219, 230, 237, 241
   mule deer, 8, 15, 105
   pheasant, 99
   rabbit and hare, 75–76, 99, 105, 117, 121, 126, 135, 140, 144, 213, 225, 230, 237, 241, 248
   sandhill crane, 241
   scaled quail, 8, 14, 237, 241
   snipe, 191, 220, 229
   squirrel, 65, 117, 121, 126, 131, 135–136, 140, 144, 153–154, 161, 167, 179, 184, 191, 198, 201, 208–209, 213, 225
   turkey, 75, 81, 85, 93–94, 99, 117, 130–131, 135, 140, 161, 174, 242
   waterfowl, 33, 36, 37–38, 40–42, 44–45, 47–48, 54, 59, 60, 64, 75, 99, 108, 117, 121, 126, 131, 135, 144, 154, 161, 167–168, 174, 179, 184, 191, 198, 201–202, 209, 212–213, 219–220, 225, 229–230, 241
   white-tailed deer, 15, 36, 54, 59,

74–75, 81, 85, 93, 99, 105, 116, 120–121, 125–126, 130, 135, 139–140, 144, 153, 160–161, 167, 173–174, 178, 183–184, 190, 197–198, 202, 207–208, 218–219, 224–225, 229, 237, 241–242, 248
  white-winged dove, 248
  woodcock, 117, 191, 229

Inland Bird Banding Association, 187
Internet, outdoor information on, 151, 154
Iron Bridge Dam and Reservoir, 227

J. D. Murphree WMA, 39–42
Jackson, A. S., 102
James E. Daughtrey WMA, 239–243
Jefferson, 133
Jennings Lake Slough, 167
Jernigan Thicket, 188
J-Hook, 52, 53
Jim Chapman Lake. See Cooper Lake.
Johnson Lake, 42
Johnson, C. G., 10, 23, 83
Jones, John, 166–168
Junior's Landing, 41
Jurek, John, 237

Keechi Creek WMA, 200–202
Keith Lake, 41
Kelly's Pond camping area, 156
Kendall, George Wilkins, 87
Kerr WMA, 78–82
Kinney, Marilyn, 160
Kitchens, James, 18
Knipe, Rick, 201–202
Kraii, Kevin, 189–191
Kriegel, Kevin, 48

L'Aimable, 50
La Salle, René Robert Cavelier, Sieur de, 50, 60
Lake Conroe, 161–162
Lalla, Jerry, 76
Lange, Steve, 151, 153–154
Las Palomas WMA (Lower Rio Grande Valley Units), 244–249
Las Palomas WMA (Ocotillo Unit), 16–19
Lawyer, Tim, 89. 90
LeBeau, Larry, 151, 153–154
Ledbetter, Macy, 240–243
Leopold, Aldo, ix–x, xi, xii, 2, 26, 70,

96, 112, 149, 168, 170, 232
Lewis, Linda, 54
Lewis, Violet, 54, 55
Light family, 233
Litter, problems with, 43–44, 45, 228
Little Lake Creek Wilderness, 156
Little Sandy National Wildlife Refuge, 150
Lobpries, David, 33
Lone Star Hiking Trail, 156, 158, 159
Lower Neches WMA, 43–45
Lower Rio Grande National Wildlife Refuge, 246
Lyndon B. Johnson Historical Park, 89

M. O. Neasloney WMA, 203–205
Mad Island WMA, 46–49
Marine tours, 54
Martin Dies, Jr., State Park, 124
Mason Mountain WMA, 83–86
Matador WMA, 102–105
Matagorda Bombing and Gunnery Range, 50–51
Matagorda Island State Park, 67
Matagorda Island WMA/State Park, 50–56
Matagorda Lighthouse, 52, 56
McFaddin, William M., 39
McFaddin, William P., 39
McKinney, Bonnie, 6, 9
Merendino, Todd, 37, 46–47
Mima mounds, 209
Mittie Stephens, sinking of, 133
Moist-soil management, 214
Monahans Sandhills State Park, 105
Moore Plantation WMA, 137–141
Moran, Dan, 78
Mo-Ranch, 78
Morgan, Emily. See Emily West.
Morgan, James, 28
Mount Alamo, 88
Muleshoe National Wildlife Refuge, 109
Multiuse trails, 159–160, 182–183
Murphy, W. A., 97

National forests, boundaries of, 118, 130, 156
Native Prairies Association of Texas, 77
Nature Center WMA, 146–149
Nature tours, guided, 124

Nature trails, 12, 58, 80, 89, 97, 147, 195–196, 203–204, 223, 235, 240, 247
Neasloney, Milfred Otto, 203
Neblett's hunter camp, 157
Neches River, 113, 117, 123
Neotropical birds, 31
North Toledo Bend WMA, 142–145
Nueces Strip, 233

Oak trees, threats to, 185
Oak, Havard, 105
Obedient plant. See beautiful false dragonhead.
Old Sabine Bottom WMA, 150–154
Old San Antonio Road, 233
Old Tunnel WMA, 87–90
Ortego, Brent, 67
Overpopulation, impact of on wildlife habitat, 220

Palmer, Tom, 182
Parrie Haynes Youth Camp, 243
Partners in Flight, 31
Pat Mayse Reservoir, 206
Pat Mayse WMA, 206–209
Patten, Sam, 249
Peach Point Plantation, 57
Peach Point WMA, 57–60
Pease River, Middle, 103
Pelton family, 16
Peoria Station, 175
Perry, Emily Austin, 57
Perry, James F., 57
Picnicking, 59
Pike, Richard, 115, 120, 143
Pimple mounds. See mima mounds.
Pine Bluff, 64
Pittman, Michael, 7–8
Playa Lakes WMA, 106–109
Playa lakes, importance of, 107
Port Caddo, 133
Poteet, Micah, 116–117
Potter, Robert, 133
Prairie dogs, 98–99, 101
Prairie mounds. See mima mounds.
Pringle Lake, 54
Private Lands Enhancement Program, 77
Prochaska, Dale, 197–198
Prothonotary warbler, 124, 135, 143, 153, 195, 196, 228

Quail, Montezuma, 14
Quail, reasons for disappearance of, 226

Ramsar Convention, 133
Ray Roberts Lake, 210
Ray Roberts Lake State Park, 213
Ray Roberts Public Hunting Area, 210–214
Real, Robert, 78
Redhead Pond WMA, 61–62
Reed family, 106
Regulator–Moderator War, 133, 142
Reticulated collared lizard, 234
Rice farming, 32, 33, 38
Richland Creek WMA, 215–220
Richland-Chambers Reservoir, 215
Ringtail Cabin, 82
Rollins, Dale, 19, 226
Ruthven, Chip, 238

Sabine River Authority, 143, 151, 154, 227, 228
Saibara, Seito, 33
Salt cedar, 16, 19
Saluria, 50
Sam Houston Forest Equestrian Association, 160
Sam Houston National Forest, 155–156
Sam Houston National Forest WMA, 155–162
San Antonio, Fredericksburg, and Northern Railroad, 88
San Gabriel River, 71, 76
Santa Anna, Antonio Lopez de, 28
Schwertner, T. Wayne, 85, 86
Sciarra Wetland System, 165
Seadock Corporation, 57
Seeds of Texas Seed Exchange, 179
Shell hunter camp, 157
Sierra Diablo WMA, 20–23
Sierra, David, 229–230
Smith, Dr. Lazariah, 146
Smith, John Moses, 29
Smith, Nancy, 146
Smith's Point, 29
Smooth sumac, 148, 149
Snow geese, overpopulation of, 38
Society for Range Management, Texas Section, 77
Somerville Lake, 222
Somerville WMA, 221–226
South Llano River State Park, 91
South Sulphur River, 188
Sphagnum moss bogs, 199
Squirrel, cat. See squirrel, gray.

Squirrel, gray, 127
Stark, Henry Jacob Lutcher, 43
Stark, Nelda Childers, 43
Steed, Charlie, 213–214
Storey, Annice, 148
Stubblefield Lake Recreation Area, 156, 159
Studer, J. C., 97
Sulphur River, 163–168
Summerlin, Danny, 42
Sutherlin, Jim, 40–42
Swamp thistle, 195
Swede Johnson Lake, 143, 144
Synatzske, David, 234, 236, 237

Tamarisk. See salt cedar.
Target shooting, 160
Tarkington hunter camp, 157
Tarrant County Water Control and Improvement District Number One, 215, 216
Tawakoni WMA, 227–230
Telfair Island, 186
Telfair, Dr. Raymond C., 187
Terpe, Butch, 161–162
Texas Bighorn Society, 4, 20, 23
Texas Department of Transportation, 63, 64, 150
Texas Exotic Safari, 85
Texas gourd, 180
Texas Grand Slam, 10, 15
Texas Guides and Outfitters Association, 85
Texas horned lizard, 234, 236, 238
Texas indigo snake, 234
Texas Nature Conservancy, 62, 77
Texas tortoise, 234, 236, 247
Texas Trash-off, 53
The Forks, 123
Thomas, James, 44–45
Tidelands Controversy, 66, 67
Tobusch fishhook cactus, 91, 92, 94
Toledo Bend Reservoir, 143–145 passim
Tony Houseman State Park/WMA, 63–65
Trail Between the Lakes, 139
Trinity River, 178
Truman, Harry, 68
Tschanz, Erik, 53–55
Turkey Hill Wilderness Area, 129–131
Turney, Terry, 92, 93
Twin Lakes, 166, 167

U. S. Forest Service, 129, 130, 138, 161

Veatch, Cathleen, 54

Walker, Linda, 16
Walker, Otto, 16
Walter Buck WMA, 91–94
Water hyacinth, 144, 145
Welch, Roy, 84
Welder Flats WMA, 54, 66–67
West, Emily, 27, 28
Wetlands
    as raw water supply, 216
    degradation of, 42, 43, 44, 47, 64
    importance of, 65, 188
Wheatley, Mike, 144–145
White Oak Creek, 163–169
White Oak Creek WMA, 163–168, 188
Who breeds who study, 86
Whooping cranes, 52, 54, 67
Wildlife field days, 79
Wildlife management areas, research on, 86, 91, 109
Wildlife viewing, 6, 12, 17, 28, 30, 35–36, 40, 44, 47, 53–54, 59, 62, 64, 67, 72, 80–81, 89–90, 92, 98–99, 100, 103, 107–108, 115, 120, 124, 129–130, 134–135, 139, 143, 148, 151, 157–159, 166, 172–173, 178, 182, 187, 188–189, 196–197, 204, 206–207, 211–212, 216–218, 228–229, 236, 240–241, 245, 246–247
Williams boat ramp, Toledo Bend Reservoir, 144, 145
Winter's Bayou, 159
Wintermann, David R., 32
Wood duck, 202
Wood stork, 122, 135, 143, 217
Woodpecker, red-cockaded, 115, 129, 130, 139, 157–158, 162
World Birding Center, 245, 247
World Wide Web. See Internet.

Yellow Rose of Texas. See Emily West.